lonely pl

D0399856

Discover

Contents

Peru

Throughout this book, we use these icons to highlight special recommendations:

These icons help you quickly identify reviews in the text and on the map:

The Best...
Lists for everything from bars to wildlife – to make sure you don't miss out

Don't Miss
A must-see – don't go home until you've been there

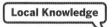 Local experts reveal their top picks and secret highlights

Detour
Special places a little off the beaten track

If you like...
Lesser-known alternatives to world-famous attractions

Sights

Eating

Drinking

Sleeping

Information

This edition written and researched by

Carolina A Miranda

Aimée Dowl, Katy Shorthouse, Luke Waterson,
Beth Williams

Iquitos &
the Amazon Basin

p279

p227 Huaraz, Trujillo &
the North

Cuzco,
Machu Picchu &
Around

Lima p51

p159

Puno & Lake Titicaca p133

Nazca, Arequipa &
the South p89

Contents

Plan Your Trip

On the Road

Contents

On the Road

In Focus

Survival Guide

This Is Peru

Luminous archaeological sites? Check. Lush rainforest? Check. An arid coast lapped by a highly surfable Pacific swell? Check. Peru, it seems, has it all.

Every cranny of the Andes offers a unique glimpse into singular cultures.

Not to mention incredible foods and enough natural wonders to keep a *National Geographic* cameraman employed for decades. On the coast, adobe pyramids and ancient temples sit quietly amid shifting desert sands and bulging seaside cities. Here, the culture is boisterous – infused with African soulfulness, indigenous know-how and the feistiness of the Spanish. The people are effusive and the music is bound to get your hips shaking.

To the east, lie the Andes.

This mountain range has served as the heart of countless empires. Its sights are staggering: mountains that seem to erupt from the earth and reach straight towards the heavens, plunging gorges, icy pinnacles and steamy cloud forest. Plus, of course, the masterful ruins of a civilization that could be put on par with ancient Rome in terms of size and infrastructure: the Incas. This is a place of chilly windswept plains and coffee-colored soil, where Catholic ritual veils indigenous belief, where the culture is stoic and the music is laced with pre-Columbian instrumentation. In comparison to the coast, it might as well be another planet.

Lastly, there is the Amazon – the earth's most fabled rainforest.

It is in this tangled jungle that Peru fuses with the lowland cultures of so many other South American countries. This sprawling lowland area is home to clutches of cackling macaws and playful pink river dolphins, as well as remote ethnicities that maintain a deep knowledge of the forest. Scattered about are old rubber boomtowns, where a previous century's entrepreneurs left behind town squares dotted with graceful tropical architecture.

All of this, combined, comes together to make up Peru.

It is a wondrous, surreal mix of peoples, cultures, geographies, languages and food. Enjoy the trip. It's going to be an adventure.

> ❝
> This mountain range has served as the heart of countless empires.
> ❞

The ruins at Machu Picchu (p214)

PHOTOGRAPHER: SEAN CAFFREY

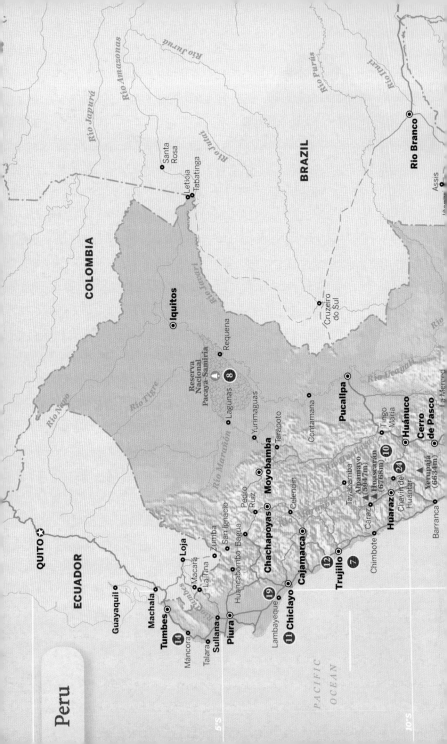

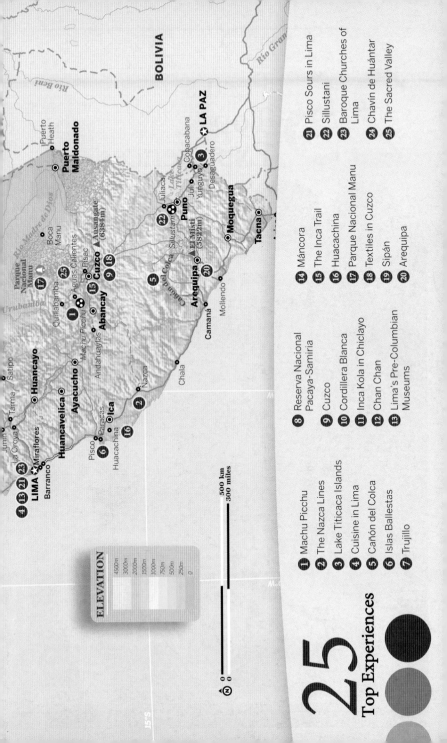

ELEVATION

4500m
3000m
2000m
1500m
1000m
750m
500m
250m
0

500 km
300 miles

25
Top Experiences

1 Machu Picchu
2 The Nazca Lines
3 Lake Titicaca Islands
4 Cuisine in Lima
5 Cañón del Colca
6 Islas Ballestas
7 Trujillo

8 Reserva Nacional Pacaya-Samiria
9 Cuzco
10 Cordillera Blanca
11 Inca Kola in Chiclayo
12 Chan Chan
13 Lima's Pre-Columbian Museums

14 Máncora
15 The Inca Trail
16 Huacachina
17 Parque Nacional Manu
18 Textiles in Cuzco
19 Sipán
20 Arequipa

21 Pisco Sours in Lima
22 Sillustani
23 Baroque Churches of Lima
24 Chavín de Huántar
25 The Sacred Valley

25 Peru's Top Experiences

Machu Picchu

There are ruins – and there are *ruins*. Machu Picchu (p214) is definitely the latter – a place so stunning it's almost difficult to believe it exists. There's the setting: soaring peaks clad in layers of steamy cloud forest. Then there are the ruins themselves: engineering marvels that have withstood half a dozen centuries worth of earthquakes and inclement weather. And, of course, there's the history: the Inca citadel that remained shrouded in forest until its rediscovery in the early 20th century. All around, an awesome sight.

1

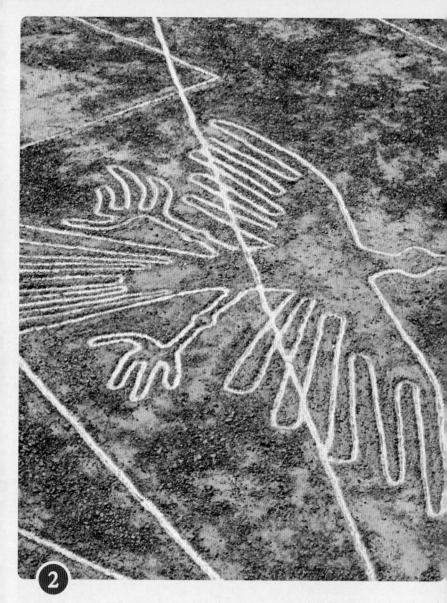

The Nazca Lines

One of the earth's greatest archaeological mysteries sits quietly on the arid southern coast. The Nazca Lines (p108) consist of more than 70 glyphs, covering 500 sq km and depicting animals and a variety of geometric shapes. What their purpose may have been, nobody knows. What we do know is that the best way to see this work of artistic prowess is by taking one of the daily overflights that allow you to admire their breathtaking size and scale.

The Floating Islands of Lake Titicaca

Peru is full of surreal sights – but probably none as fantastic as the Islas Uros (p155), a series of inhabited islands that bob around the bay just in front of Puno. Begun centuries ago, these buoyant homesteads were constructed as a way for the Uros people to escape more aggressive mainland ethnicities, such as the Incas. They are crafted out of tightly woven *totora* reeds, which are also used in the construction of boats and houses.

The Best...
Experiences for Kids

STAY WITH A FAMILY ON A LAKE TITICACA ISLAND
A unique cultural experience your children will likely never forget. (p154)

FLY OVER THE NAZCA LINES
A spectacular way of impressing your little one with some very large drawings. (p108)

VISIT THE CIRCUITO MÁGICO DEL AGUA IN LIMA
Dart about the fountains at this popular family park. (p66)

CHECK OUT THE MUMMIES AT THE MUSEO INKA IN CUZCO
The perfect gross-out activity. (p180)

The Best...
Cities for Food

LIMA
The crème de la crème of the country's singular fusion cuisine. (p75)

AREQUIPA
The locals like their dishes spicy, such as the searing stuffed peppers known as *rocoto relleno*. (p120)

CHICLAYO
A bounty of seafood, as well as stews simmered for hours in beer and cilantro. (p268)

CUZCO
Hearty soups and crackling pork dishes – not to mention plenty of guinea pig. (p189)

TRUJILLO
This coastal city is tops for all manner of seafood, including the marinated seafood dish ceviche. (p257)

CAROLINA MIRANDA

Lima's Cuisine Scene

4

There's a reason that *Bon Appétit* magazine named Lima (p75) the 'Next Great Food City.' The coastal capital is bustling with eateries that whip up some of the most delectable interpretations of Peru's unique fusion cuisine. Offering dishes that are a complex blend of Spanish, indigenous, African and Asian influences (both Chinese and Japanese), this is a city where life is often planned around the next meal. Consider it an experience worth savoring.

GRANT DIXON

Cañón del Colca

5

One of the world's deepest canyons, the Cañón del Colca (p124) can be explored on a multiday trek or on overnight visits. Expect idyllic Andean villages, mountainsides carved into spectacular shapes by ancient agricultural terraces, condors soaring on the wind currents and vistas of snowcapped peaks in the distance. Best of all, you'll get to try a local delicacy: the spicy shrimp bisque known as *chupe de camarones*.

Islas Ballestas

Off the Península de Paracas, on the country's southern coast, are a series of rocky outcrops known as the Islas Ballestas (p103). Here you'll find a geography teeming with life – honking sea lions, preening Humboldt penguins, as well as colonies of Peruvian boobies engaged in squawk-filled conversation. The islands aren't known as the 'poor man's Galápagos' for nothing.

Colonial Trujillo

Peru's environment has not been kind to its colonial buildings. Between the cataclysmic earthquakes and severe weather, few historic structures have survived unscathed. The north coast city of Trujillo (p254), however, offers an opportunity to catch a glimpse of what the country would have looked like in another era. The area around the main plaza showcases vintage structures painted in bright colors, some of them with pristine antique furnishings and baroque interiors – all of them a testament to the city's regal past.

Reserva Nacional Pacaya-Samiria

This waterlogged reserve (p298) – Peru's largest – is home to countless waterborne and amphibian species. It is here that you'll find the 3m-long native fish known as *paiche*, as well as rare river turtles, giant river otters, hundreds of bird species and several types of monkey. But the most unusual sight are the pink river dolphins, which can be spotted playfully racing along the park's principal rivers. It is a sight you will only ever see in the Amazon.

The Best...
Nightlife

LIMA
Boogie to *cumbia*, house, techno, rock or reggae until the cows (or llamas) come home. (p81)

CUZCO
The ancient capital of the Inca empire is now the capital of highland nightlife, with an array of pumping discos. (p192)

TRUJILLO
This coastal city has an array of chilled-out bars and grooving live-music spots. (p258)

IQUITOS
The liveliest bar scene in the Amazon. (p294)

Cuzco

Ancient cobblestone streets. Grandiose baroque churches. Here and there, the remnants of ancient temples and lintels, some bearing the traces of centuries-old carvings of animal figures. The ancient capital of the Inca empire may now be cluttered with the trappings of tourism, but its location and historic architecture nonetheless manage to rise above the commercial din. In Cuzco (p172) it is still possible to catch a feeling of an empire that once was – all while dining on international cuisine and enjoying the buzziest nightlife in the Andes.

The Best...
Andean Vistas

MACHU PICCHU
Soaring peaks coated by steamy cloud forest. (p214)

HUARAZ
The Cordillera Negra on one side, the Cordillera Blanca on the other – nearby lies Peru's highest peak, Huascarán. (p240)

PUNO
Rugged Andean plains surround the shimmering Lake Titicaca. (p144)

AREQUIPA
The conical volcano El Misti always looms in the distance. (p111)

THE SACRED VALLEY
An undulating mountain-scape hugs a string of local villages. (p200)

CORDILLERA HUAYHUASH
Craggy snowcapped peaks surround crystal-line highland lakes. (p250)

Cordillera Blanca

10

There are vistas that will make the most devoted couch potato want to strap on a backpack and go. The Cordillera Blanca (p249), the mountain range located east of Huaraz, is certainly toward the top of that list. This neck of Peru has craggy peaks with dollops of gleaming white snow and high-altitude lakes the color of sapphires. Packed in between are diminutive villages where life is lived by the cycle of the seasons. If the altitude doesn't take your breath away, the scenery definitely will. Scaling the white peaks of Nevado Pisco, Parque Nacional Huascarán (p249)

Inca Kola

11

It's not a grandiose ruin or a majestic church or a jaw-dropping peak, but you haven't experienced Peru until you've sampled this nuclear-colored soda. It tastes faintly of bubble gum (though it's allegedly flavored with lemon verbena). Most significantly, it's yellow, a color that is widely believed to bring good luck. You can find it anywhere, but we recommend ordering it with a hearty lunch in Chiclayo (p265). Ask for it *bien fría* (very cold) – a perfect balm for the heat of the northern desert coast.

BRUCE BI

Chan Chan

A sprawling adobe city – covering roughly 36 sq km – constitutes one of the most important archaeological sites in Peru. Time has worn down the impressive mud structures, but the majesty of Chan Chan (p260) remains. In these desert ruins, you'll find everything from a walk-in well to a room-sized chamber with pitch-perfect acoustics. Reconstructed friezes, which depict local fauna, provide a taste of what it must have all been like when ruled by the aesthetically adept Chimú culture.

Lima's Museums of Pre-Columbian Art

Sublime ceramics. Carved rock stelae. Centuries-old textiles. Lima's museums hold millennia worth of ancient treasures. Some of the most spectacular: the Museo Larco (p66), the Museo Andrés del Castillo (p66) and the Museo Nacional de Antropología, Arqueología e Historia del Perú (p67). Want to understand what Peru's ancient civilizations were all about? Begin the trip here.

Ceramic artifact, Museo Larco

CAROLINA MIRANDA

Máncora

Sometimes a vacation is just that – a break from everything real life throws your way. In Máncora (p273) expect your diet of activities to be of the leisurely sort: lounging on the beach, watching the sun set, enjoying fine seafood at breezy patio restaurants, and sipping ice-cold cocktails at one of the town's hopping drinking establishments. If it all sounds too relaxed, fear not. This trendy little beach town sits amid a series of excellent surf breaks.

14

The Best...
Adventures

EXPLORE PARQUE NACIONAL MANU
One of the Amazon's most remote corners. (p309)

SANDBOARD HUACACHINA
Fly down a sand dune as tall as a building. (p106)

TREK THROUGH THE CAÑÓN DEL COTAHUASI
One of Peru's lesser visited, but truly magnificent canyons. (p130)

SURFING IN HUANCHACO
A renowned spot for the surfing set. (p263)

The Best...
Hiking

THE INCA TRAIL
The most fabled ancient roadway in the Americas can be walked in a four-day trek you will never forget. (p220)

CORDILLERA BLANCA
A graceful mountain range offers trekking adventures that run from two days to two weeks. (p249)

CAÑÓN DEL COLCA
One of the world's deepest canyons promises pastoral sights galore. (p124)

LAKE TITICACA ISLANDS
A day hike around these islands serves up sparkling views of the lake with the mountains in the distance. (p154)

MACHU PICCHU
The famous mountaintop citadel has wondrous daylong adventures. (p214)

The Inca Trail

The continent's most famous pedestrian roadway is a tourist attraction in its own right. Snaking through the cloud forest for 43 winding kilometers, its destination is the famous Intipunku – or Sun Gate – the point at which weary trekkers can catch their first extravagant glimpse of the ruins at Machu Picchu. While there are countless ancient roads all over Peru, the Inca Trail (p220) – with its mix of majestic views, staggering mountain passes and clusters of ruins – remains the traveler favorite.

Warmiwañusca Pass on the Inca Trail

LEFT: ANTHONY PIDGEON RIGHT: RICHARD I'ANSON

Huacachina

For the adventurous set, this tiny south coast oasis offers one of Peru's more unusual adrenaline rushes: the opportunity to motor to the top of a dune the size of a small building, strap on a board and then fly down the face of a towering wall of sand. Apart from making you pick the gritty stuff out of your every nook and cranny, Huacachina (p106) is home to another highly popular activity – namely whooping it up come nightfall at one of the various local drinking establishments.

ROLF NUSSBAUMER PHOTOGRAPHY/ALAMY

Parque Nacional Manu

One of the Amazon's most remote southern corners is home to some of the planet's most intense biodiversity. With ecosystems that range in altitude from 150m to 4200m above sea level, this important park (p309) protects the watershed of the Río Manu, a tributary of the Río Madre de Dios, which is itself a tributary of the Amazon. For the visitor, this means a bounty of wildlife spotting, including jaguars, tapirs, ocelots and macaws.

Extraordinary Textiles

If there's one thing that united the myriad ancient cultures that settled the Andes over the centuries, it's a textile tradition that is beyond accomplished. Skilled weavers have long produced elaborate pieces out of wool, cotton and even feathers – some with record-setting thread counts and mind-boggling designs. Today, the practice continues all over the country, but one of the best places to acquire a singular piece is at a textile shop in Cuzco (p194), where various fair-trade organizations are keeping traditional weaving alive. We'll buy that.

The Best...
Markets

MERCADO SAN PEDRO, CUZCO
Everything from pig heads to fresh juice – along with plenty of local color. (p194)

MERCADO MODELO, CHICLAYO
Like every bustling Latin American market you ever imagined – with the bonus of an expansive witch doctors' section peddling charms and potions. (p267)

MERCADO INDIO, LIMA
For when you need to get your souvenir shopping on. (p82)

CRAFT MARKET, PISAC
Fresh vegetables, bounteous souvenirs and more photo ops than even the fastest SLR can handle. (p201)

The Treasures of Sipán

19

What we know about Peru's ancient civilizations has been pieced together over the decades by some very dedicated archaeologists. Unfortunately, history hasn't made their job easy. What the Spanish didn't ransack, generations of looters have. In the 1980s, however, a rare discovery was made outside Chiclayo: an almost-intact Moche tomb. Its treasures are now on display at the Museo Tumbas Reales de Sipán (p272), providing visitors with a rare opportunity to admire priceless objects in their historical context.

COREY WISE

The Best...
Hotels

MIRAFLORES PARK HOTEL, LIMA
This sumptuous ocean-view outpost even has a bath butler. (p74)

HOTEL LIBERTADOR, TRUJILLO
This gem of a hotel resides in a vintage colonial mansion. (p256)

HOTEL MONASTERIO, CUZCO
Housed in a 16th-century cloister, an exquisitely designed spot offers the best of everything. (p188)

LIBERTADOR CIUDAD BLANCA, AREQUIPA
Modern luxury with colonial flourishes. (p119)

RÍO SAGRADO HOTEL, URUBAMBA
A Sacred Valley resort with river views and a plush on-site spa. (p204)

BALCONES DE MÁNCORA, MÁNCORA
Thatched-roof beachfront bungalows with flair. (p275)

ANNELIES MERTENS

20 Arequipa

There is a reason why the locals like to wax poetic about this charming highland city located in the southern reaches of the Andes. Certainly, its positive attributes are many. Arequipa (p111) resides at the foot of the iconic El Misti volcano. It is home to an incredible citadel-sized monastery. It is the birthplace of Nobel Laureate Mario Vargas Llosa. And it serves up some of the country's spiciest, most exceptional cuisine in the homestyle eateries known as *picanterías*. Want an unforgettable taste of Peru? Dig in. Plaza de Armas, Arequipa

The Pisco Sour

On the continuum of cocktails, surely the pisco sour – a concoction of grape brandy with lime juice and sugar – has got to reside somewhere between 'Sublime' and 'Whoa Nelly, I'll Have Another.' In recent years, high-end lounges have begun creating exotic infusions with small-batch piscos and tropical fruits, but we recommend going old school at El Bolivarcito (p81), the legendary Lima bar known as the 'Cathedral of Pisco,' and ask for the uncomplicated classic. ¡Salud!

Sillustani

On the windswept Andean plain northwest of Puno is one of Peru's more unusual burial sites. Dotting a chain of rolling hills that comprise the Lake Umayo peninsula are a series of *chullpas* (funerary towers) that once held the remains of entire families and clans.The Sillustani *chullpas* (p152) have long since been pillaged for their artifacts, but the towers remain (some of them up to 12m tall), dotting the plain like silent sentinels from the past.

Lima's Baroque Churches

Though Lima is today a noisy, modern metropolis of almost nine million people, its colonial heart – an area of narrow streets on the southern banks of the Río Rímac – contains a veritable treasure of colonial churches. Among the finest: the Iglesia de Santo Domingo (p68), which among other things contains the skull of Santa Rosa; the Monasterio de San Francisco (p63), home to sprawling underground catacombs; and the astonishing Iglesia de la Merced (p63), which boasts a hyper-ornate facade and enough towering baroque altars to turn anyone into a believer. Iglesia de Santo Domingo

23

The Best...
Fiestas

INTI RAYMI
Cuzco's 'Festival of the Sun,' held every June 24, is a tradition with Inca roots. (p43)

LA VIRGEN DE LA CANDELARIA
In February, Puno's multiday tribute to the Virgin offers plenty of highland music and dance. (p152)

Q'OYORITI
A Christian pilgrimage with animist overtones is held on a chilly mountain in the Cuzco region every May/June. (p187)

EL SEÑOR DE LOS MILAGROS
Lima's biggest religious procession brings out the masses dressed in purple. (p44)

Chavín de Huántar

These ruins represent the earliest development of widespread culture in Peru. Dating to 1200 BC, the temple structures at Chavín de Huántar (p251) are impressive for their sophistication and scale. Not only is the exterior decorated with elaborately carved keystone blocks, a labyrinth of underground tunnels leads to a rock of white granite with a hallucinatory image of a person with snakes radiating from the head. Little is known about the site, but its location amid the craggy Andean mountainscape couldn't be more breathtaking.

The Best...
Off-the-Beaten-Path Spots

CHICLAYO
Not exactly a place of great beauty, but this bustling coastal city has excellent food and a rollicking music scene – and barely any tourists to speak of. (p265)

PUERTO MALDONADO
This humble jungle town is a gateway to some of the Amazon's least visited areas. (p300)

ANDAHUAYLILLAS
Just 45km from the tourist hotbed of Cuzco, but tranquil as can be – with a beautiful church to boot. (p224)

ICA
This southern coastal city is renowned for its vineyards, as well as its wineries and pisco plants. (p107)

25

The Sacred Valley

The Río Urubamba winds its way through the Sacred Valley (p200), alongside fetching Andean towns, crumbling Inca military outposts and agricultural terraces that have been used since time immemorial. Not only does it conveniently reside between the main attractions at Cuzco and Machu Picchu, but the Valley is also equipped with charming village inns and stylish resort complexes. It's a perfect spot to wander around if you really want to feel like you've gotten away from it all. Urubamba (p203)

Peru's
Top Itineraries

Around the Capital
Days & Nights in Lima

Five days will provide you with an opportunity to truly enjoy Lima's excellent fine dining and see a bevy of incredible pre-Columbian and fine-art museums. Better yet: you'll have time for a day trip (or two) to fabled ruins along the desert coast.

① Lima (p51)

For the Peru first-timer, Lima's chaotic, bustling downtown is a must. Begin at the **Plaza de Armas**, where you can ogle the **Palacio de Gobierno** (presidential palace), then pay a visit to the stately **Catedral de Lima**. Nearby, you'll find the **Monasterio de San Francisco**, with its bone-lined catacombs, and the **Iglesia de Santo Domingo**, which displays the skull of Santa Rosa. End up at the **Plaza San Martín** for a different type of religious experience: here, **El Bolivarcito** serves up renowned pisco sours (grape brandy cocktails).

On day two, hit the renovated **Museo de Arte de Lima**, which contains an inspiring collection of Peruvian art. For dinner, go *novoandina* (Peruvian nouvelle cuisine) at one of **Miraflores'** renowned haute cuisine restaurants.

A third day in Lima will allow you to pay a leisurely visit to the exquisite **Museo Larco**, to see fine pre-Columbian artifacts and dine at its bougainvillea-draped restaurant. Afterwards, walk off the meal in Miraflores, where you can shop for souvenirs at the sprawling **Mercado Indio**.

LIMA ● PACHACAMAC
🚗 **One hour** Taxis and tour agencies both make the trip.

② Pachacamac (p85)

A perfect half-day trip is a visit to this **archaeological complex** just 31km south of the city. Dating back to AD 100, its temple sites have been used by every culture from the Wari to the Incas. On your return to Lima, have the driver drop you off in **Barranco**, where you'll find the city's most hopping bars and lounges.

LIMA ● ISLAS BALLESTAS
🚗 **Four hours** Private taxis and tour agencies make the trip to Paracas. ⚓ **One hour** From Paracas, catch a morning tour boat to the islands.

③ Islas Ballestas (p103)

A wilder, full-day excursion is a trip to visit the rocky outcrops known as the **'poor man's Galápagos'** – islands inhabited by honking sea lions and colonies of bird life. Tours generally include a visit to the nearby Paracas reserve. Just plan on waking up early: boat tours depart around 8am.

Monasterio de San Francisco (p63), Lima
PHOTOGRAPHER: SHANIA SHEGEDYN

5 DAYS

Lima to Arequipa
Southern Highland Jaunt

This brisk itinerary allows two days to see the capital's main sights (and make a tasty gastronomic pit stop). On the third day, head south, for a visit to the charming highland city of Arequipa, known for its rich history and spicy cuisine.

LIMA

TORO MUERTO PETROGLYPHS

AREQUIPA

PACIFIC OCEAN

① Lima (p51)

Start in downtown, Lima's historic, colonial heart. At the **Plaza de Armas**, you can tour **La Catedral de Lima**. From here, numerous colonial churches radiate outwards. Among the best: the **Iglesia de Santo Domingo**, with its saints' reliquaries; the **Monasterio de San Francisco**, which contains creepy catacombs; and the hyper-ornate **Iglesia de la Merced**, full of towering baroque altars. At the **Plaza San Martín**, pop into **El Bolivarcito** for the requisite pisco sour. On the second day, see spectacular pre-Columbian artifacts at the **Museo Larco**. Afterward, do some window-shopping in the seaside neighborhood of **Miraflores**, where you can also arrange a leisurely dinner at one of the area's internationally acclaimed eateries.

LIMA ◯ AREQUIPA

✈ 90 minutes Multiple daily departures from Aeropuerto Internacional Jorge Chávez.

② Arequipa (p111)

It's a long bus ride to Arequipa, so with limited time, it's best to fly. Begin your visit by wandering around the city's handsome **Plaza de Armas**, from where you'll see the **Catedral** and the extravagant **Iglesia de la Compañía**, known for its Spanish-baroque

altar smothered in gold leaf. Just off a side street is the **Museo Santury**, which houses 'Juanita, the ice princess,' a frozen Inca maiden sacrificed on the summit of a nearby peak. Save the second day to explore the renowned **Monasterio de Santa Catalina**, a citadel-sized convent stuffed with period furnishing and religious art. The celebrated on-site restaurant is perfect for a long lunch. If you're not churched out, peek into the highly underrated **Museo de Arte Virreinal de Santa Teresa**, which contains some fantastic canvases in the style of the *escuela cuzqueña* (Cuzco School).

AREQUIPA ◯ TORO MUERTO PETROGLYPHS

🚐 Three hours Tour agencies in Arequipa can arrange private and group tours.

③ Toro Muerto Petroglyphs (p129)

On the last day, set up a day trip to these mysterious pre-Inca **glyphs**, located 170km west of Arequipa. The desert here is studded with volcanic boulders that have been carved with stylized figures, believed to date to the early Wari period (about 1200 years ago). Tours are generally a long, full-day affair and include lunch in a nearby town. Order the shrimp – this area is known for it!

Monasterio de Santa Catalina (p115), Arequipa
PHOTOGRAPHER: BRENT WINEBRENNER

10 DAYS

Lima to Cuzco & Machu Picchu
A Tour of Inca Country

Ten days allows you ample time to soak up the wonders of the ancient Inca capital and the Sacred Valley. Starting with a couple of days in Lima ensures that you won't head to the highlands without a few exquisite meals in your belly.

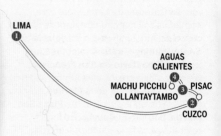

LIMA ①

AGUAS CALIENTES ④

MACHU PICCHU ○ ③ PISAC
OLLANTAYTAMBO ○ ②

CUZCO

PACIFIC OCEAN

① Lima (p51)

A couple of days in Lima is a great start to your Peruvian adventure, and will ground you in the country's pre-Columbian and colonial history. The city's **colonial churches** boast incredible religious art, while the lovely **Museo Larco** has sublime pre-Columbian pottery. Be sure to allow for some extravagant meals in the acclaimed eateries of **San Isidro**. On your second day, keep it easygoing, since the following morning you'll be flying to the high-altitude city of Cuzco. A simple plan: amble around the galleries at the **Museo de Arte de Lima** and eat a delectable dinner at a restaurant in **Miraflores**.

LIMA ➡ CUZCO

✈ One hour, 15 minutes Multiple daily departures form Aeropuerto Internacional Jorge Chávez.

② Cuzco (p172)

Fly to Cuzco – and then *chill out* (you're at 3326m above sea level). Amble about the **Plaza de Armas**, pay a visit to **La Catedral** or the ornate Jesuit church, **Iglesia de la Compañía de Jesús**, to see colonial art. Then spend the next two days grounding yourself in the area's Inca history, exploring the myriad sights. Not to be missed: the **Qorikancha**, once the Incas' most spectacular temple, and **Sacsaywamán**, a jaw-dropping fortress. Don't leave without sampling a steamy highland soup.

CUZCO ➡ OLLANTAYTAMBO

🚗 40 minutes The best option is to hire a private taxi for the day. 🚌 One hour Multiple departures daily.

③ Ollantaytambo (p206)

In the morning, drive out into the Sacred Valley. Your first stop is the charming village of **Pisac**. Here, you can explore a hilltop **Inca citadel** and visit a lively market. Then continue the journey to **Ollantaytambo** (about an hour away), a charismatic indigenous village where you will bed down for the night. Wake up early to see the **Inca ruins** above town (a historic spot where the Incas fended off the Spanish) before catching the train to Aguas Calientes.

OLLANTAYTAMBO ➡ AGUAS CALIENTES & MACHU PICCHU

🚃 Two hours

④ Aguas Calientes & Machu Picchu (p211)

A scenic train ride takes you to the town that serves as a base for exploring the fabled **Machu Picchu**. Our recommendation: arrange to spend two to three nights here. The ruins are sprawling, the scenery is spectacular and there are amazing opportunities for hikes to the peaks of **Huayna Picchu** and **Machu Picchu**.

Inca ruins at Pisac (p202)

10 DAYS

Trujillo to Máncora
Chilling on the North Coast

The remnants of adobe pyramids and walled cities, a witch doctors' market and some of Peru's best beaches: 10 days along the north coast, from Trujillo through Chiclayo and on to Máncora, will satisfy cravings for history – as well as surf and sand.

MÁNCORA **5**   ECUADOR

○ PIURA

4 CHICLAYO

HUANCHACO **3** **2** TRUJILLO

PACIFIC
OCEAN

1 LIMA

① Lima (p51)

As with all journeys in Peru, the trip begins in Lima. For something out of the ordinary, hit the **Museo Pedro de Osma** in **Barranco**, a vintage mansion stocked with a stellar collection of colonial religious art. Spend your second day taking in the treasures at the **Museo Larco**, before sampling the city's fine food.

LIMA ➡ TRUJILLO
✈ **70 minutes** Multiple daily departures from Aeropuerto Internacional Jorge Chávez.

② Trujillo (p253)

Trujillo is a chaotic coastal city that is home to some beautifully kept **colonial structures**. One not to miss: **Casa de Urquiaga**, which has been spectacularly restored. Spend the following two days exploring the area's pre-Columbian ruins. To the west is **Chan Chan**, a sprawling adobe city constructed by the Chimú (don't miss the friezes!). To the southeast are the **Huacas del Sol y de la Luna**, two mud-brick pyramids built by the artful Moche.

TRUJILLO ➡ HUANCHACO
🚗 15 minutes

③ Huanchaco (p263)

Take a beach break in this nearby **coastal village**, where local fishers still use hand crafted reed boats (*caballitos de totora*). It's a fine spot to enjoy seafood in view of a blazing Pacific sunset.

TRUJILLO ➡ CHICLAYO
🚌 **Three hours** Myriad services offer multiple departures daily.

④ Chiclayo (p265)

From Trujillo, catch a deluxe bus service north to **Chiclayo**. The city is no thing of beauty, but the food is divine and the nearby pre-Columbian museums are jaw-dropping. At the top of the list: the **Museo Tumbas Reales de Sipán**, in nearby Lambayeque, which contains the sparkling grave goods of a Moche lord. Also worthwhile is a visit to the **Mercado Modelo**, renowned for its cluttered witch doctors' market.

CHICLAYO ➡ MÁNCORA
🚌 **Six hours** 🚗 **Five hours** Using a private driver will make for a faster trip.

⑤ Máncora (p273)

A journey through various desert oases and the city of Piura (where you'll have to switch buses) will bring you to the north coast resort of **Máncora**. Plan on three to four days of serious hangout time. Activities here consist largely of reading good books, chilling on the beach and grooving at one of the local village nightspots.

Máncora (p273)
<small>PHOTOGRAPHER: PAUL KENNEDY</small>

Lake Titicaca, Cuzco & the Amazon
Highland/Jungle Combo

On this two-week trip through the Andes and then down into the Amazon, you'll see a little bit of everything Peru has to offer: Inca ruins, pastoral highland settings, steamy lowland jungle and more wildlife than you ever dreamed of.

① Lima (p51)

Ease into the journey with a relaxed day in **Lima**. The ideal plan: pay a visit to the **Museo Larco**, where you can admire artfully presented ancient treasures and dip into a tasty lunch on the patio restaurant.

LIMA ◎ PUNO

✈ **About two hours** Multiple daily departures from Aeropuerto Internacional Jorge Chávez to Juliaca.
🚌 **One hour** Airport taxis are available for the ride to Puno.

② Puno (p144)

Catch a flight to Puno and then lay low (you are now at 3830m above sea level). Some chilled-out activities include visiting the **Catedral** and strolling around the **Coca Museum**. The next day, make a day trip to one of the fabled islands of **Lake Titicaca**. If you like your islands to float, hit the **Islas Uros**, which are built out of reeds. Spend an enjoyable evening in Puno, enjoying the area's colorful nightlife.

PUNO ◎ CUZCO

✈ **55 minutes** Multiple daily departures form Aeropuerto Inca Manco Cápac in Juliaca.

③ Cuzco (p172)

Cuzco, the ancient capital of the Inca empire, is all its cracked up to be. Most flights will get you into town in the morning, leaving you plenty of time to explore the heart of the city, including **La Catedral** (where you can see a painting of Christ eating a guinea pig), as well as the over-the-top ornamentation of the **Iglesia de la Compañía de Jesús**. Then take a couple of days to explore the city's must-see Inca sights, including the **Qorikancha**, which once harbored the most important Inca temple, and **Sacsaywamán**, the photogenic fortress just above town.

CUZCO ◎ AGUAS CALIENTES & MACHU PICCHU

🚌 **Three hours** Departures from Estación Poroy, east of town.

Water lilies, Amazon Basin (p279)
PHOTOGRAPHER: LEANNE WALKER

Maldonado serves as a gateway to this storied rainforest's most remote jungle lodges. Take a day to acquaint yourself with the area – a good way to orient yourself is to clamber to the top of the **Obelisco**, a 30m tower that offers superb jungle views.

PUERTO MALDONADO ⟶ RÍO TAMBOPATA

🚤 **Two hours** There are taxi boats at the Tambopata dock, but your lodge can arrange private transfer.

⑥ Río Tambopata (p307)

A tributary of the Río Madre de Dios, the **Río Tambopata** leads into the **Reserva Nacional Tambopata**, an important protected area. Here, a string of riverside lodges offer various levels of accommodations (from jungle rustic to downright luxe) within reach of countless day hikes and one of the largest **macaw clay licks** in the country. Expect to see innumerable birds, frogs, alligators, giant river otters and the unusual spike-haired avian species known as the jungle chicken (its official name: *hoatzin*). For the best exploring, plan on spending at least three nights in the area. A lovely river-boat ride will take you back to Puerto Maldonado.

PUERTO MALDONADO ⟶ LIMA

✈ **Three hours** Several daily departures from Aeropuerto Padre José Aldámiz during high season.

④ Aguas Calientes & Machu Picchu (p211)

The picturesque train line winds through the **Sacred Valley**, depositing travelers in the teeming town of **Aguas Calientes** – base camp for Machu Picchu. Most folks come in for the day, we recommend sticking around for two to three. For one, **Machu Picchu** is massive – and exploring it takes time. Two, being there overnight means you can get in early before the crowds arrive. Be sure to book your train ride back to Cuzco, as these fill up early.

CUZCO ⟶ PUERTO MALDONADO

✈ **One hour** Multiple daily flights from Aeropuerto Internacional Alejandro Velasco Astete.

⑤ Puerto Maldonado (p300)

A quick flight plunges straight from the Andean highlands into lowland Amazon jungle. Here, the raffish town of **Puerto**

⑦ Lima (p51)

Spend your last day in the capital enjoying some excellent **shopping** and Peru's finest cuisine at the top-flight eateries of **Miraflores**.

Peru Month by Month

January

Peru's climate has two main seasons – wet and dry – though weather varies greatly from region to region. In the highlands, January is the midst of the wet season, while the coast enjoys its balmy summer.

 Año Nuevo (New Year's Day)

Partygoers wear yellow (including underwear) to ring in the New Year.

Fiesta de la Marinera

This national dance festival held during the last week of January is especially popular in Trujillo. The *marinera* (sailor dance) is a synchronized choreographed dance between a man with a straw hat and a woman with a handkerchief. They seductively step around each other without ever touching.

February

The Inca Trail to Machu Picchu is closed for its annual clean up, but no need to fret. Make like the locals and hit the beaches.

 La Virgen de la Candelaria (Candles)

This highland fiesta (February 2) is particularly colorful around Puno, where folkloric music and dance celebrations last for two weeks (p152).

Carnaval

Carnaval is held on the last few days before Lent (February/March), and is often celebrated with weeks of water fights, singing, dancing, parades and lots of rowdy mayhem. It's especially popular in the highlands.

Top Events

 Carnaval, before the start of Lent (February/March)

Inti Raymi, June 24

Fiestas Patrias, July 28 & 29

Feast of Santa Rosa de Lima, August 30

El Señor de los Milagros, October 18

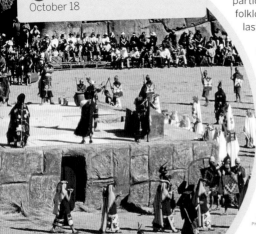

June Inti Raymi
PHOTOGRAPHER: ANTHONY PIDGEON

March

The Inca Trail is open once again, though the weather is still rainy.

Fiesta de la Vendimia (Wine Festival)

Now is the perfect time to sample local piscos and wines in Ica (p107). The festival is held in the second week of March, when you are likely to see fairs, floats, musicians, and beauty queens stomping grapes.

 # April

Holy Week is a major event, so book a hotel and transportation well in advance.

Semana Santa (Holy Week)

While Easter itself is a solemn event, the week prior to it is celebrated with spectacular religious processions almost daily all over Peru. Arequipa and Huaraz are recognized for having some particularly colorful pageants.

May

In the highlands, the rainy season begins to wind down.

Festival of the Crosses

This festival, held on May 3, is at its most intense in Lima, Ica and Cuzco. During the festivities, folks carry crosses of various sizes in a procession that leads to church.

Q'oyoriti

A Christian pilgrimage with ancient overtones is held at the chilly foot of Ausangate, a mountain outside of Cuzco in May or June (p187).

 # June

It's the beginning of the dry season in the highlands, which naturally coincides with the peak of the tourist season, lasting through to August. Reserve hotels and domestic air travel well in advance during this time.

Corpus Christi

This celebration commemorates the Holy Eucharist as the body of Christ, held on the ninth Thursday after Easter. Processions in Cuzco are especially dramatic.

Inti Raymi (Festival of the Sun)

Inti Raymi was the Inca Sun God and this festival celebrates the winter solstice in his honor on June 24. It's certainly the spectacle of the year in Cuzco, attracting thousands of visitors.

San Pedro y San Pablo (Feasts of Sts Peter & Paul)

Peter and Paul are the patron saints of fishers and farmers and are honored with a procession to the sea. An image of St Peter is taken by a decorated boat to bless the waters for the fishing season, usually near Lima and Chiclayo on June 29.

 # July

The best time to see where the wild things are as the Amazon is drier (OK, less wet) than at most other times of the year.

La Virgen del Carmen

This holiday (July 16) is mainly celebrated in the southern Andes, and is particularly important in Pisac. The Virgin is the patron of *mestizos* (people of mixed indigenous and Spanish decent).

 September

Spring begins on the Peruvian coast.

 El Festival Internacional de la Primavera (International Spring Festival)

Expect horse parades, dancing and cultural celebrations in Trujillo during the last week of September.

 Mistura

Generally held in early September, this annual weeklong foodie fest in Lima gathers Peru's top chefs, along with invited gastronomes from all over the world, for cooking demonstrations, talks and lots of sampling. Pack an appetite. For dates and locations, log on to www.mistura.pe.

 October

The bullfighting season begins this month and lasts through to November.

La Virgen del Rosario

The patron saint of slaves is honored on October 4 in Lima, Arequipa and Cuzco. Expect processions, *marinera* dance competitions and *los diablos* (devils) dancing in the streets.

El Señor de los Milagros (Lord of the Miracles)

In Lima, this is a massive religious procession honoring a local Christ. Though the main day of the celebration is October 18, there are events throughout the month, in which everyone gets decked out in purple to seek blessings and miracles. Expect processions around the country during this time.

 Fiestas Patrias (National Independence Days)

Independence from Spain is celebrated nationwide on July 28 and 29, with festivities in the southern Andes beginning with the Feast of St James (known as Santiago) on July 25. Good luck trying to find a seat on a bus or a plane during this time.

 August

This is a popular time for travel in the highlands, so plan ahead.

Feast of Santa Rosa de Lima

Major processions are held on August 30 in Lima and Arequipa to honor the patron saint of Peru and of the Americas.

November

The fog known as *garúa* lifts as summer begins along the Pacific Coast. In the Andes and the Amazon, the heavy-duty part of the wet season begins.

 Todos Santos (All Saints' Day)

The first part of a two-day holiday that begins on November 1, when families go to mass and then head to the cemetery to spend time with departed loved ones.

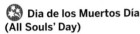 **Dia de los Muertos Día (All Souls' Day)**

The second part of the holiday is more festive – with more gifts of food, drink and flowers taken to family graves.

 Puno Week

Starting November 5, this weeklong festival involves street dancing with spectacular costumes to celebrate the legendary emergence of the first Incas, Manco Cápac, and his sister Mama Ocllo from Lake Titicaca. A perfect opportunity to imbibe lots of *chicha* (corn beer) and dance in the streets.

December

The wettest months continue through to March in the highlands, and until May in the eastern rainforest.

 Fiesta de la Purísima Concepción (Feast of the Immaculate Conception)

This national holiday (December 8) is celebrated with processions in honor of the Virgin Mary.

Christmas Day

Held on December 25, Christmas is less secular and more religious, especially in the Andean highlands. Keep an eye out for unique nativity scenes with regional holiday flourishes.

Far left: June Corpus Christi
Left: November Puno Week

What's New

For this new edition of Discover Peru, our authors have hunted down the fresh, the revamped, the hot and the happening. These are some of our favorites. For up-to-the-minute reviews and recommendations, see lonelyplanet.com/peru

1 MUSEO ANDRÉS DEL CASTILLO, LIMA
Housed in a 19th-century mansion, this sparkling new museum showcases breathtakingly displayed Nazca textiles and Chancay pottery. (p66)

2 MALABAR, SAN ISIDRO, LIMA
Celebrity chef Pedro Miguel Schiaffino's exquisite Amazon-inspired menu features deftly prepared delicacies such as crisp, seared *cuy* (guinea pig) and alpaca ham. (p77)

3 XOCOLATL, MIRAFLORES, LIMA
Lima's best chocolatier specializes in artful Peruvian sweets, stuffed with fillings such as coffee, pisco and *Ranfañote,* a traditional dessert made with coconut, molasses and nuts. (p79)

4 COLORS, PUNO
The Peruvian-Greek-Middle-East-Asian menu at this Puno fusion outpost features treats such as Andean cheese fondue and smoked-trout ravioli in vodka sauce. (p148)

5 SMOOTH JAZZ BAR, PUNO
This fresh spot has Puno's most extensive drinks menu: three pages of cocktails and five different kinds of alcoholic hot tea are just the beginning. (p150)

6 RENACIMIENTO, CUZCO
This renovated colonial mansion in the heart of the ancient Inca capital has recently been converted into 12 charming small apartments, each of which is uniquely designed. (p184)

7 RÍO SAGRADO HOTEL, URUBAMBA
A luxurious new outpost in the Sacred Valley, this river-view spot has all manner of designer amenities, including an on-site spa. Perfect for relaxing. (p204)

8 LA CASA FITZCARRALDO, IQUITOS
A paean to eccentric film director Werner Herzog, Casa Fitzcarraldo has a mahogany-floored 'Mick Jagger room' and a luxuriant 'Klaus Kinski suite.' (p292)

9 PILPINTUWASI BUTTERFLY FARM, NEAR IQUITOS
This conservation and breeding center located just outside of Iquitos has Amazonian butterflies galore – including the luminescent blue morpho (*Morpho menelaus). (p296)

10 LA CASA DE MELGAR, AREQUIPA
High ceilings, comfy beds and tucked-away inner patios help make this Arequipa inn a romantic hideaway – even though it's in the middle of the city. (p118)

11 CHICHA, AREQUIPA & CUZCO
Peru's foremost celebrity chef, Gastón Acurio, is not just in Lima anymore. Now you can find his *novoandina* sensations at Chicha, his sister restaurants in Arequipa (p120) and Cuzco (p190).

12 LATINOS HOSTAL, CHICLAYO
This new hotel in central Chiclayo is a find, offering perfect little rooms, some with floor-to-ceiling windows equipped with excellent city views. (p267)

Get Inspired

🔖 Books

Aunt Julia & the Scriptwriter (1977) Nobel Laureate Mario Vargas Llosa's classic comic novel about a radio scriptwriter in love with his much older divorced sister-in-law.

The Conquest of the Incas (1970) A historical classic by John Hemming devoted to the gripping tale of the Spanish conquest.

Cradle of Gold: the Story of Hiram Bingham, a Real-Life Indiana Jones, and the Search for Machu Picchu (2010) The wordy title sums it up for this highly readable bio by Christopher Heaney.

At Play in the Fields of the Lord (1965) Peter Matthiessen's true-to-life novel about conflicts in the Amazon.

🎞 Films

Madeinusa (2006) An Andean girl's tragic coming-of-age drama by director Claudia Llosa.

Undertow (2009) A fictional tale about a married fisherman coming to terms with his dead boyfriend's ghost.

La muralla verde (1970) Armando Robles Godoy's classic feature film about an idealistic city couple who relocate to the Amazon.

🎵 Music

Canela Fina (2005) A reissue of harmonious ballads by the celebrated trio Los Morochucos.

Chabuca Granda: Grandes Éxitos (2004) Breathy lyrics full of longing and nostalgia by the legendary singer and composer.

Eva! Leyenda Peruana (2004) Bluesy *landós* performed by a premiere Afro-Peruvian songstress, Eva Ayllón.

The Roots of Chicha (2007) Groove to Peru's Amazon-meets-the-Andes-meets-Colombian-*cumbias* dance music.

🧴 Websites

iPerú (www.peru.info) The official government tourism agency.

Peru Links (www.perulinks.com) A portal to helpful sites in Spanish and English.

Peruvian Times (www.peruviantimes.com) The latest news, in English.

The Peru Guide (www.theperuguide.com) A broad travel overview.

🕑 Short on time?

This list will give you an instant insight into the country.

Read *The Last Days of the Incas* (2007) is Kim Mac-Quarrie's page-turner about the history-making clash between two civilizations.

Watch *La teta asustada* (The Milk of Sorrow; 2009) is Claudia Llosa's film about a girl suffering from a trauma-related affliction.

Listen *Arturo 'Zambo' Cavero* (1993) is the namesake album of the crooner best known for his soulful Peruvian waltzes.

Log on *Living in Peru* (www.livinginperu.com) is an expat guide and calendar and an excellent source of news.

Still from Claudia Llosa's film *La teta asustada* (The Milk of Sorrow)
OLIVE FILMS

Need to Know

Currency
Peruvian nuevos soles (S)

Languages
Spanish, Quechua and Aymara

ATMs
In larger cities and towns.

Credit Cards
Visa and MasterCard widely accepted.

Visas
Generally not required for stays of up to 90 days.

Cell Phones
It is possible to use a tri-band GSM world phone (GSM 1900).

Wi-Fi
Common in midrange and top-end hotels.

Internet Access
Even the smallest towns have an internet cafe; access is S2 to S3 per hour.

Driving
Drive on the right; steering wheel is on the left.

Tipping
You may tip 10% for good service. Taxi drivers do not expect tips for short trips (unless they've assisted with heavy luggage), but porters and tour guides do.

When to Go

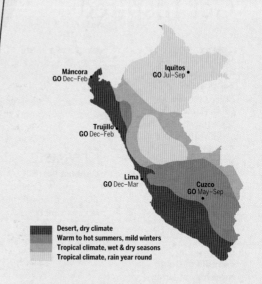

Máncora
GO Dec–Feb

Iquitos
GO Jul–Sep

Trujillo
GO Dec–Feb

Lima
GO Dec–Mar

Cuzco
GO May–Sep

Desert, dry climate
Warm to hot summers, mild winters
Tropical climate, wet & dry seasons
Tropical climate, rain year round

High Season
(Jun–Aug)
- Best time to hike the Inca Trail to Machu Picchu
- Coincides with the dry season in the Andean highlands
- Drier in the eastern rainforest and the Amazon

Shoulder
(May & Sep)
- Not as busy, but can still be wet and chilly
- Remember: the higher you climb, the colder it gets
- Can be dry in the Amazon in September

Low Season
(Dec–Mar)
- The Pacific coast warms up, making it ideal for the beach
- The wettest months in the Andes are cold and muddy
- The Inca Trail is closed in February for clean up

Advance Planning

- **Three to six months before** Make a reservation for trekking the Inca Trail (p220). Start shopping for your flight and check your passport expiration date.

- **One month before** Reserve accommodations and see your doctor for any vaccines or medications you may need (especially if you are traveling to the Amazon). Reserve in-country flights.

- **One week before** Confirm your hotel reservation. Book any tours you might wish to take.

Your Daily Budget

Although the official currency is the nuevo sol, the prices of many hotels and tours in Peru are quoted in US dollars.

Budget less than US$50

- Basic double room: US$25 a night
- Set lunch at budget eatery: US$4
- Entrance fee to many historic sights: US$4

Midrange US$50-150

- Double room at midrange B&B: US$50
- Multi-course lunch at midrange restaurant: US$12 per person
- Group city tour: from US$40 per person

Top End over US$150

- Double room at top-end hotel: from US$150 a night
- 3-course meal including wine at a top restaurant: US$60 per person
- Private city tour: from US$80 per person

Exchange Rates

Australia	A$1	S2.80
Canada	C$1	S2.76
EURO	€1	S3.70
Japan	¥100	S3.36
New Zealand	NZ$1	S2.09
UK	UK£1	S4.37
USA	US$1	S2.81

For current exchange rates see www.xe.com

What to Bring

- **Passport** You'll need one that's valid for six months beyond your entry date into the country.
- **Money belt** It can be handy in avoiding pickpockets.
- **Travel insurance** Carry a copy of your policy.
- **Spanish phrasebook** It'll make ordering food and talking to locals much easier.
- **Windbreaker** It gets cold in the Andes; pack a sturdy windbreaker or raincoat.
- **An adventurous appetite** Peru has the best gastronomic scene in South America – try something new and delicious!

Arriving in Peru

- **Aeropuerto Internacional Jorge Chávez**

Taxis S45; 30 minutes to one hour (at rush hour) for San Isidro, Miraflores and Barranco; less for downtown Lima.

Getting Around

- **Air** Numerous domestic flights; most require a change in Lima.
- **Bus** Private companies cover the whole country; go with recommended operators.
- **Car** You can rent one but it is not recommended.
- **Train** Small, privatized rail system has daily service from Cuzco to Aguas Calientes.

Accommodations

- *Hostales & hospedajes* These are generally budget accommodations; some may have shared bathrooms.
- **Homestays** In tiny villages, these may be the only option.
- **B&Bs** Popular in tourist areas.
- **Apartments** A great choice if you are staying with a group.
- **Hotels** A wide selection at every budget level.

Be Forewarned

- **Inca Trail** During the months of July and August, passes to hike the trail should be reserved up to six months in advance. (We're not kidding!)
- **Business hours** Some businesses shut down during the height of summer (December and January). In smaller towns, many shops and sights close for two hours during lunch.
- **Health** Water is unsafe to drink; boil it first or drink bottled water.
- **Crime** Robberies (pickpocketing and muggings) can be a problem at some tourist sites. Do not keep your wallet in your back pocket and make back-up photocopies of your passport.
- **Service** Meals are a leisurely affair, so relax. If you're in a rush, go to the register to ask for your bill.

Lima

Shrouded in history. Gloriously messy. Full of aesthetic delights. This is Lima.

On its surface, Lima is no thing of beauty. A sprawling desert city, it clings precariously to a set of dusty cliffs, and spends much of the year covered in a perpetual fog that turns the sky the color of Styrofoam. Travelers tend to scuttle through on their way to more pastoral destinations in the Andes. This is unfortunate.

Lima may not wear its treasures on its sleeve, but peel back the foggy layers and you'll find pre-Columbian temples sitting silently amid high-rises and extravagant colonial mansions with Moorish-style balconies. There are stately museums, baroque churches, cavernous shopping malls and a profusion of exceptional eateries, from the humble to highbrow – all part of a gastronomic revolution more than 400 years in the making.

Monasterio de San Francisco (p63)
PHOTOGRAPHER: MICAH WRIGHT

Lima

0 — 2 km
0 — 1 mile

Cerro San
Cristóbal
(409m)

Vía de Evitamiento

Av Aricash

EL AGUSTINO

Av Túpac Amaru

RÍMAC

Central Lima (p64)

Av Habich

Panamericana Norte (Av Mendiola)

5 · 1 El
Cordano

Av Abancay

Av Grau

Av 28 de Julio

LA VICTORIA

Av México

LIMA
CENTRO

Av Peru

SANTA
BEATRIZ

3 Paseo de la República (Vía Expresa)

Av Manco Cápac

Av Arica

Av Arequipa

LINCE

Av República de Argentina

Av Tingo María

BREÑA

Av M Benavides (Colonial)

Av República de Venezuela

Av Brasil

JESÚS
MARÍA

San Isidro (p70)

1
Malabar

To Aeropuerto
Internacional
Jorge Chávez
(3km)

PUEBLO
LIBRE

Museo Nacional
de Antropología,
Arqueología e
História del Perú

SAN ISIDRO

Av Universitaria

Av Bolívar

2

Av Sucre

Av S Carrión

Av Salaverry

Lima Golf
Club

Av Elmer Faucett

Parque de
las Leyendas

MAGDALENA
DEL MAR

SAN MIGUEL

Av de la Marina

PACIFIC
OCEAN

LA PERLA

Av La Paz

Circuito de Playas

LA MOLINA

Cerro El
Agustino
(482m)

Av Aylon

Vía de Evitamiento

Av N Ayllon

Av R Ferrero

Club Golf
Los Icas

Hipódromo
de Monterrico

MONTERRICO

1 Food Scene, Lima
2 Museo Larco
3 Museo de Arte de Lima
4 Barranco, Lima
5 Iglesia de Santo
   Domingo
6 Miraflores, Lima
7 Huaca Pucllana

SAN
LUIS

Av Nicolas Arriola

Av Canada

Parque
Zonal
Túpac
Amaru

Av Javier Prado Este

SAN BORJA

Av Aviación

Av Primavera

Río Surco

Av Panamericana Sur

SURQUILLO

Av Aramburu

Av República de Panamá

Av A Benavides

Av Santiago de Surco

Av Arequipa

Paseo de la República (Vía Expresa)

Av Benavides

To Pachacamac (30km);
Lurín (28km)

SANTIAGO
DE SURCO

1 Restaurant
Huaca
Pucllana

7

Av Santa Cruz

Av Jose Pardo

MIRAFLORES

6

Av Jorge Chávez

Circuito de Playas

La Rosa
Nautica

1

Miraflores (p72)

Barranco (p76)

BARRANCO

4

1

Chala

Av Aguilar Pastor

Playa
Costa Verde

Playa
Aqua
Dulce

Paseo de la República

Lima Highlights

1

Lima Food Scene

It's no secret that some of the most succulent dishes on the continent can be found in the sprawling Peruvian capital. Here, a mind-boggling number of eateries serve sophisticated renditions of the country's fusion cuisine: nutty stews, colorful potato terrines and of course, the renowned marinated seafood dish known as ceviche.

Need to Know

HOT SPOTS Miraflores is the city's busiest dining hub. **AT THE BAR** Pisco sours are the classic cocktail. **TIP** Peruvian portions are extravagant; order accordingly. **For coverage, see p75.**

Gastronomic Don't Miss List

BY ARTURO ROJAS, LIMA NATIVE, DEVOUT EATER AND FOUNDER OF THE FOODIE TOUR COMPANY LIMA TASTY TOURS

1 EL CORDANO

Located in downtown Lima, this old-world bar and cafe (p75) is in the middle of some of the city's most important historic sights. Order the *sandwich de jamón serrano* (Peruvian ham sandwich) with marinated onions and accompany it with a tall glass of *chicha morada* (a sweet, purple corn punch). Want something stronger? The bar is renowned for a cocktail known as the 'Capitán' – pisco with red vermouth and Cinzano.

2 RESTAURANT HUACA PUCLLANA

This high-end Miraflores restaurant (p77) has incredible views of the Huaca Pucllana pre-Columbian site and some award-winning dishes – including a renowned *lomo saltado* (stir-fry of beef with potatoes and onions, pictured, above left). Vegetarians will enjoy the quinoa dishes, including a salad of fava beans, corn and peppers.

3 CHALA

Situated inside a vintage home in Barranco, this modern eatery (p80) has excellent views of the Puente de los Suspiros (Bridge of Sighs) and some incredible seafood soups. I especially like the dishes made with *mero* (the whitefish known as grouper). Left: *Causa*, as served at Chala

4 LA ROSA NAUTICA

If you want ceviche and the best ocean views in Lima, I suggest this popular seafood spot (p79) on the pier just below Miraflores. It serves a long list of Peruvian dishes, but most folks come for the ceviche (pictured, far left). The menu features more than half a dozen kinds, including the Japanese-style ceviches known as *tiraditos*.

5 MALABAR

This is a distinguished restaurant (p77) run by rising celebrity chef Pedro Miguel Schiaffino and is conveniently located between the Huaca Huallamarca, a pre-Columbian adobe pyramid and the Bosque El Olivar park. The menu features a changing seasonal menu strong on ingredients from the Amazon. If you go, be sure to try the excellent pisco punch.

Museo Larco

This engaging museum of pre-Columbian art recently reopened its galleries after a five-year makeover. What should visitors expect? A scholarly and visually stunning series of exhibits detailing the triumphs of Andean civilizations over more than 5000 years. To understand Peruvian history, the journey begins here.

2

Need to Know

BEST TIME TO GO Arrive by 10am for maximum tranquility. **DINING TIP** The on-site restaurant gets busy – reserve a table when you arrive for a post-museum lunch. **For more coverage, see p66.**

MUSEO
RAFAEL
LARCO
HERRERA

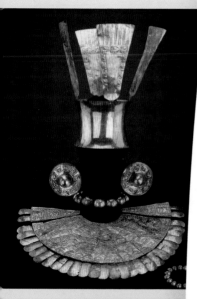

Museo Larco Don't Miss List

BY ANDRÉS ÁLVAREZ CALDERÓN,
DIRECTOR OF THE MUSEO LARCO
SINCE 2003

1 SACRIFICE VESSELS

Pre-Columbian cultures were agricultural societies that worshipped the forces of nature. Human sacrifice, therefore, was considered integral to maintaining the natural order. In the Sacrifice Ceremony Gallery you will find elaborate depictions of this ritual – the most important liturgy within the Moche culture of the north coast (see p328).

2 LORD OF CHAN CHAN

Imagine a time when the only gleaming things were the sun, the moon, the stars – and all-powerful lords dressed entirely in silver and gold. They shone like heavenly beings and were considered, by their people, divine creatures. In this context, this gold ceremonial suit from Chan Chan (p260), near Trujillo, will take your breath away.

3 THE PARACAS MANTLE

This incredible textile from the Paracas region (p102) was woven in 200 BC and is considered a treasure. It originally wrapped the body of a dead ruler – an assurance of successful passage to the afterlife. If you look closely at its borders, you'll recognize stylized representations of three animals sacred to ancient societies: the feline (representing the human world), the serpent (underworld) and birds (heaven).

4 THE EROTIC GALLERY

Indigenous cultures throughout Peru graphically depicted sexual acts in their art. While our present-day culture might look upon these as pieces of pornography, they are in fact representations of rituals associated with fertility and agriculture. This gallery showcases dozens of erotic ceramics, all in an incredible state of conservation.

5 CAFÉ DEL MUSEO

Last but not least, I like to recommend that visitors unwind on the restaurant's terrace. Not only will you sample some extraordinary local cuisine, but you can admire the museum's breathtaking grounds, which won first prize for Best Gardens in Peru in 2009. Thanks to Lima's mild climate, the colorful orchids and blooming bougainvilleas thrive all year round.

Admire the Best Peruvian Art

The glittering, recently remodeled Museo de Arte de Lima (p65) – otherwise known as MALI – is home to the country's finest collections of art through every significant Peruvian historical period. Expect to see centuries-old textiles, groundbreaking early-20th-century paintings, and cutting-edge contemporary-art installations with found object and video. Overall, a fine opportunity to investigate Peru's present as much as its past.

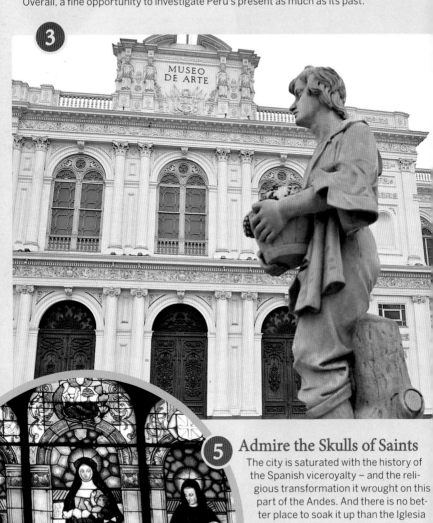

Admire the Skulls of Saints

The city is saturated with the history of the Spanish viceroyalty – and the religious transformation it wrought on this part of the Andes. And there is no better place to soak it up than the Iglesia de Santo Domingo (p68), in downtown where venerated Peruvian saints such as Santa Rosa and San Martín de Porres have their craniums on display in glass cases.

CAROLINA MIRANDA

Bar-hop Through Barranco **4**

CAROLINA MIRANDA

During the 19th century, Barranco's baronial mansions were the place to see and be seen. In many ways, they still are. This oceanside neighborhood has narrow streets that are chock full of vintage structures that house of-the-moment cocktail lounges and old bohemian watering holes. Ready for a drink? Well, you've found your place (p81). As they say in Peru – *¡Salud!* (Cheers!)

Ayahuasca (p81), Barranco.

6
Leap off the Miraflores Clifftops

If you thought Lima was all shopping and eating and drinking – well, you're right. But there are sporty activities, too. Namely: paragliding along the Miraflores clifftops (p69), past all the shoppers and diners sipping cappuccinos at the trendy LarcoMar shopping mall. A total adrenaline rush!

7
Walk the Sandy Ruins of Ancient Civilizations

Lima is a bustling, modern city – but tucked in between the condo towers are the remains of settlements that go back thousands of years. If you have only a couple of hours, pay a visit to the adobe complex at Huaca Pucllana (p69), in the heart of Miraflores. Got an afternoon? Head south, to Pachacamac (p85), a sprawling pre-Columbian temple site. Huaca Pucllana

Lima's Best...

Restaurants

○ **Astrid y Gastón** (p80) The Miraflores restaurant that helped launch Peru's gastronomic renaissance

○ **Domus** (p75) Excellent Peruvian homecooking in downtown Lima

○ **Malabar** (p77) In San Isidro, *novoandina* with Amazonian flourishes

○ **La 73** (p79) An Italian-Peruvian bistro in Barranco

○ **Xocolatl** (p79) The city's finest chocolatier, in Miraflores

Museums

○ **Museo Larco** (p66) Stunning pre-Columbian pottery in a lovely colonial mansion

○ **Museo de Arte de Lima** (p65) Pre-Hispanic to contemporary in a refurbished beaux-arts structure

○ **Casa Aliaga** (p65) One of the city's most storied colonial houses

○ **Museo Andrés del Castillo** (p66) Incredibly preserved Chancay pottery in a pristine downtown location

○ **Museo Pedro de Osma** (p69) Extravagant colonial religious art

Churches

○ **La Catedral de Lima** (p63) Contains the remains of conquistador Francisco Pizarro

○ **Iglesia de la Merced** (p63) An unbelievably ornate facade and baroque altars galore

○ **Monasterio de San Francisco** (p63) Bone-filled catacombs and a beautiful library

○ **Iglesia de Santo Domingo** (p68) The final resting place of Peru's most venerated saints

Need to Know

Shopping

o **Mercado Indio** (p82) A sprawling market for all your souvenir shopping needs

o **Dédalo** (p82) Upscale contemporary crafts – complete with cafe

o **Agua y Tierra** (p82) Finely made pieces from the Amazon in a lovingly tended shop

o **LarcoMar** (p82) For when you want to get your mall on – with eateries, alpaca boutiques and views of the ocean

ADVANCE PLANNING

o **Three Weeks Before** Make hotel reservations

o **Three Days Before** Arrange private day trips

o **One Day Before** Reserve a table at popular, high-end eateries

RESOURCES

o *El Comercio* The daily newspaper is the best place to keep up on the city's cultural events

o Living in Peru (www.livinginperu.com) Keeps a helpful up-to-date calendar of major happenings

o *Oveja Negra* (www.revistaovejanegra.com) A pocket-sized directory of nightlife goings-on distributed free at restaurants and bars

o *Lima: A Cultural History*, by James Higgins, a good read on the city's history

o *Lima la horrible*, by Sebastián Salazar Bondy, for Spanish-speakers, a renowned collection of essays from the '60s that incisively deconstructs the city's culture

GETTING AROUND

o **Air** Major airlines fly to/from Aeropuerto Internacional Jorge Chávez, 12km west of Central Lima

o **Bus** Minivans and buses ply all the major avenues, such as Avs Arequipa and Prado

o **Electric Bus** A limited line that connects Central Lima with Miraflores on the Vía Expresa

o **Taxis** Found just about everywhere, 24 hours a day

o **Walk** The best way of exploring tight neighborhoods like Central Lima, Miraflores and Barranco

BE FOREWARNED

o **Chilly City** Lima bathes in a damp fog from April to November; pack a warm sweater

o **Museums** Generally closed on Mondays

o **Noise** The city is noisy; note that street-side hotel rooms can interfere with beauty rest

o **Watch Your Pockets** Theft is an issue; dress down and carry only the cash you'll need

Left: Lima restaurant Astrid y Gastón; **Above:** LarcoMar mall, Miraflores.

PHOTOGRAPHERS: (LEFT) NEIL SETCHFIELD/ALAMY; (ABOVE) OTHER IMAGES

61

Discover Lima

LIMA

♩01 / POP 8.5 MILLION / ELEV 108M

HISTORY

In pre-Hispanic times, the area now occupied by this expansive metropolis had been an important coastal settlement to various cultures, including the Lima, the Wari and the Ichsma. When Francisco Pizarro sketched out the boundaries of his 'City of Kings' in 1535, there were roughly 200,000 indigenous people living in the area. But by the 18th century, the Spaniards had turned Lima into the capital of a continent-wide viceroyalty, where fleets of ships arrived to transport the conquest's spoils back to Europe.

In the late 19th century, the city found itself under siege when it was occupied by the Chilean military during the war of the Pacific (1879–83). A period of expansion followed, in the early 20th century, during which time a network of broad boulevards (inspired by Parisian urban design) were constructed to crisscross the city.

Since then, it has endured earthquakes, population growth, and in the '80s, bouts of guerrilla warfare due to the Internal Conflict. But the last decade has seen an unparalleled rebirth. A robust economy and a vast array of municipal improvement efforts have led to repaved streets, refurbished parks, and safer public areas – not to mention a thriving cultural and culinary life.

La Catedral de Lima
PHOTOGRAPHER: CAROLINA MIRANDA

Sights

The city's colonial heart, Lima Centro (Central Lima), lies at a bend on the Río Rímac. From here, Av Arequipa, one of the Lima's principal thoroughfares, plunges southeast, through San Isidro and into Miraflores. Immediately to the south lies Barranco.

Central Lima

PLAZA DE ARMAS   Historic Plaza

(Map p64) The 140-sq-meter **main plaza**, also called the Plaza Mayor was the heart of the 16th-century settlement established by Francisco Pizarro. To the east is the **Palacio Arzobispal** (Archbishop's Palace) boasting some of the most exquisite Moorish-style balconies in the city. To the northeast, the block-long **Palacio de Gobierno**, a grandiose baroque-style building serves as the presidential palace. Out front stands a handsomely uniformed guard that conducts a changing of the guard ceremony every day at noon – a pomp-filled affair that involves slow-motion goose-stepping and a brass band playing *El Cóndor Pasa* as a military march. (Unfortunately, you'll have to admire this all from outside the gate, because the palace is not open to visitors.)

LA CATEDRAL DE LIMA   Cathedral

(Map p64; ☎ 427-9647; admission S10; ☺9am-5pm Mon-Fri, 10am-1pm Sat) Next to the Archbishop's palace resides the cathedral, on the same plot of land that Pizarro designated for the city's first church in 1535. Though it has a baroque facade, the interior was redone in a simple neoclassical style in the 19th century. Even so, baroque pieces remain scattered throughout, such as the ornate wood **choir** from the early 17th century, a masterpiece of rococo sculpture. A worthwhile **religious museum**, in the rear, features paintings, vestments and an intricate sacristy.

By the cathedral's main door is the **mosaic-covered chapel** where the battered remains of Pizarro have long lain. The authenticity of these came into question in 1977, after workers cleaning out a crypt discovered a sealed lead box containing a skull that bore the inscription, 'Here is the head of the gentleman Marquis Don Francisco Pizarro, who found and conquered the kingdom of Peru...' After a battery of tests in the 1980s, a US forensic scientist concluded that the body previously on display was of an unknown official and that the brutally stabbed and headless body from the crypt was Pizarro's. Head and body were reunited and transferred to the chapel, where you can also view the inscribed lead box.

MONASTERIO DE SAN FRANCISCO   Church

(Map p64; ☎ 426-7377; www.museocatacumbas.com; cnr Lampa & Ancash; adult/child under 15yr S5/1; ☺9:30am-5:30pm) This bright-yellow Franciscan monastery and church is most famous for its bone-lined catacombs and remarkable library, where you can take in the sight of 25,000 antique texts, some of them predating the conquest. But this baroque structure has many other things worth seeing, including a Moorish-style cupola, over the main staircase, which was carved in 1625 (restored 1969) out of Nicaraguan cedar. Admission includes guided tours in English or Spanish.

FREE **IGLESIA DE LA MERCED**   Church

(Map p64; ☎ 427-8199; cnr Jirón de la Unión & Miró Quesada; ☺10am-noon & 5-7pm) The first Latin mass in Lima was held in 1534, on a small patch of land now marked by this incredible church. Most of today's structure dates to the 18th century, with its most striking feature being the imposing granite facade, carved in the *churrigueresque* manner (a highly ornate late baroque style). Inside, the nave is lined by more than two-dozen jaw-droppingly magnificent baroque and Renaissance-style altars, some of which are carved entirely out of mahogany.

To the right as you enter is a large silver cross that once belonged to Father Pedro Urraca (1583–1657), a priest renowned for having had a vision of the

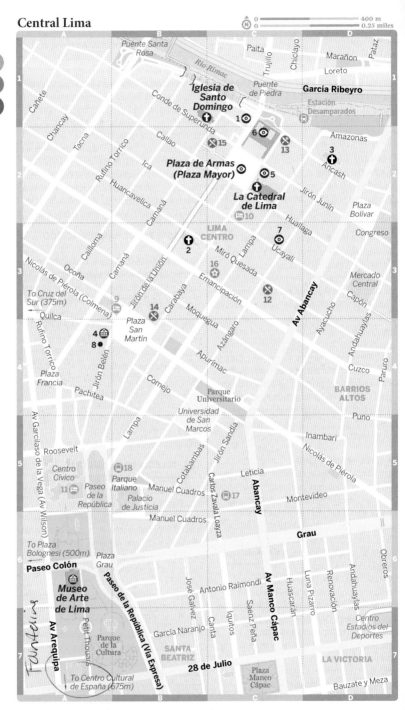

Virgin. This is a place of pilgrimage for Peruvians, who come to place a hand on the cross and pray for miracles.

Colonial Mansions

PALACIO TORRE TAGLE
Historic Building

(Map p64; Ucayali 363) There are few remaining colonial mansions in Lima since many of them have been lost to expansion and earthquakes. In addition, many now operate as private offices, which can make seeing interiors difficult. The most immaculate of these **casonas** is this famous structure, completed in 1735, with its ornate baroque portico

(the best in Lima) and striking Moorish-style balconies. Unfortunately, it is home to Peru's Foreign Ministry, so you'll only be able to see the exterior. Even so, it's worth it.

CASA ALIAGA
Historic Building

(Map p64; 427-7736; www.casadealiaga.com; Jirón de la Unión 224) Innocuously tucked on a side street by the post office stands this mansion, on land given to Jerónimo de Aliaga, one of Pizarro's followers, in 1535. Since then, it has been occupied by 16 generations of his descendants. Its interiors are lovely, with vintage furnishings and tilework. It can only be visited by making an appointment in advance or via organized excursions with Lima Tours (p70).

Other Sights

MUSEO DE ARTE DE LIMA
Museum

(Map p64; 423-6332; www.mali.pe; Paseo Colón 125; suggested donation S6-12; 10am-7pm Tue-Sun) Known locally as MALI, Lima's principal fine-arts museum is housed in a striking beaux-arts building with an excellent permanent collection – which includes pre-Columbian artifacts, colonial furniture and cutting-edge installation art by contemporary artists. Of particular interest is a strong representation of early-20th-century *indigenista* painting, which celebrated the indigenous aspects of Peruvian society. A recent top-to-bottom remodel has left the galleries sparkling. Highly recommended.

PLAZA SAN MARTÍN
Historic Plaza

(Map p64) This attractive plaza is named for the liberator of Peru, José de San Martín, who sits astride a horse at its center. At the base, don't miss the bronze rendering of Madre Patria, the symbolic mother of Peru. Commissioned in Spain under instruction to give the good lady a crown of flames, nobody thought to iron out the double meaning of the word flame in Spanish (*llama*), so the hapless craftsmen duly placed a delightful little llama on her head.

Central Lima

⊙ Top Sights
Iglesia de Santo Domingo B1
La Catedral de Lima C2
Museo de Arte de Lima A6
Plaza de Armas (Plaza Mayor) C2

⊙ Sights
1 Casa Aliaga C1
2 Iglesia de la Merced B3
3 Monasterio de San Francisco D2
4 Museo Andrés del Castillo A4
5 Palacio Arzobispal C2
6 Palacio de Gobierno C2
7 Palacio Torre Tagle C3

Activities, Courses & Tours
8 Lima Tours A4

⊜ Sleeping
9 Gran Hotel Bolívar B3
10 Hotel Maury C2
11 Lima Sheraton A5

⊗ Eating
12 Domus C3
13 El Cordano C2
14 Pastelería San Martín B3
15 Tanta C2

Drinking
El Bolivarcito .... (see 9)

⊕ Entertainment
16 Teleticket C3

Transport
17 Ormeño C5
18 Tepsa B5

65

MUSEO ANDRÉS DEL CASTILLO
Museum

(Map p64; ☎ 433-2831; www.madc.com.
pe; Jirón de la Unión 1030; admission S10;
⏰9am-6pm Wed-Mon) Housed in a pristine
19th-century mansion with Spanish-tile
floors, this worthwhile private museum
showcases a vast collection of minerals, as well as breathtakingly displayed
Nazca textiles and Chancay pottery.
Recommended.

PARQUE DE LA CULTURA
Park

(Map p64) Originally known as Parque de
la Exposición, this newly revamped park
has pleasant gardens and a small amphi-
theater for outdoor performances.

EL CIRCUITO MÁGICO DEL AGUA
Park

(Map p64; Parque de la Reserva, Av Petit
Thouars, cuadra 5; admission S4; ⏰4-10pm)
This indulgent series of **fountains** is
so over-the-top it can't help but induce
stupefaction among even the most
hardened traveling cynic. A dozen different fountains – all splendiferously

illuminated – are capped, at the end,
by a laser light show at the 120m-
long Fuente de la Fantasía (Fantasy
Fountain). The whole display is set to
a medley of Peruvian folk music. The
park is located about 500m south of
the Parque de la Cultura, on the southern edge of downtown Lima.

CENTRO CULTURAL DE ESPAÑA
Cultural Center

(CCELIMA; off Map p64; ☎ 330-0412; www.
ccelima.org; Plaza Washington, Natalio Sánchez
181, Santa Beatriz; ⏰9am-9pm) An excellent
cultural space has some of the most
intriguing, insightfully curated contemporary art and cultural exhibits in
Lima. If you want to learn about what's
happening in contemporary Peruvian
and Latin American society, consider it
a must-see.

San Isidro

MUSEO LARCO
Museum

(Map p52; ☎ 461-1825; www.museolarco.org;
Bolívar 1515, Pueblo Libre; adult/child under

Left: Palacio Arzobispal and La Catedral de Lima, Plaza de Armas;
Below: El Circuito Mágico del Agua, Parque de la Reserva
PHOTOGRAPHER: (LEFT) WES WALKER; (BELOW) PAUL KENNEDY

15yr S30/15; 9am-6pm) An 18th-century viceroy's mansion houses this museum, which has one of the best-presented displays of ceramics in Lima. Founded by Rafael Larco Hoyle in 1926, the collection showcases ceramic works from the Cupisnique, Chimú, Chancay, Nazca and Inca cultures, but the highlight is the sublime Moche portrait vessels, presented in simple, dramatically lit cases. Equally astonishing: a Wari weaving in one of the rear galleries that contains 398 threads to the linear inch – a record. What lures many visitors here, however, is a separately housed collection of pre-Columbian erotic pots that illustrate, with comical explicitness, all manner of sexual activity.

The highly recommended onsite **restaurant** (mains S28-40) faces a private garden draped in pretty bougainvillea – a perfect spot for ceviche (seafood marinated in lime juice) and a pisco sour.

MUSEO NACIONAL DE ANTROPOLOGÍA, ARQUEOLOGÍA E HISTORIA DEL PERÚ

Museum

(National Museum of Anthropology, Archaeology & History; Map p52; 463-5070; http://museo nacional.perucultural.org.pe; Plaza Bolívar, cnr San Martín & Vivanco, Pueblo Libre; adult/child S12/1; 9am-5pm Tue-Sat, 9am-4pm Sun) This rambling museum traces the history of Peru from the Preceramic Period to the early republic. Displays include the famous Raimondi Stela, a 2.1m rock carving from the Chavín culture, one of the first ancient Andean civilizations to have a widespread, recognizable artistic style. Also on view are numerous late-colonial and early republic paintings, including an 18th-century rendering of the *Last Supper* in which Christ and his disciples feast on *cuy* (guinea pig).

Notably, the building was once the home of revolutionary heroes José de San Martín (from 1821 to 1822) and Simón Bolívar (from 1823 to 1826).

RICHARD CUMMINS

Don't Miss **Iglesia de Santo Domingo**

One of Lima's most storied religious sites, the **Iglesia de Santo Domingo** and its graceful **convent** are built on land granted to the Dominican friar Vicente de Valverde, who accompanied Pizarro throughout the conquest and was instrumental in persuading him to execute Atahualpa.

The nave is lined with intricate chapels, but the church is most renowned for being the final resting place of the three most important Peruvian saints: San Juan Macías, Santa Rosa de Lima (the first saint of the Americas) and San Martín de Porres (the continent's first black saint). The convent – a sprawling courtyard-studded complex lined with baroque paintings and clad in vintage Spanish tile – contains the saints' tombs. The impressive pink church, however, has the most interesting relics: namely, the skulls of San Martín and Santa Rosa, encased in glass, in a shrine to the right of the main altar.

NEED TO KNOW

Map p64; 427-6793; cnr Camaná & Conde de Superunda; admission church free, convent S5; 9am-12:30pm & 3-6pm Mon-Sat, 9am-1pm Sun

HUACA HUALLAMARCA
Pre-Columbian Site
(Map p70; 222-4124; Nicolás de Rivera 201, San Isidro; adult/child S6/1; 9am-5pm Tue-Sun) Nestled among condominium towers and ritzy modernist homes, the simple Huaca Huallamarca is a restored adobe pyramid, produced by the Lima culture that dates back to AD 200 to 500. A small museum, complete with a mummy, details its excavation.

MUSEO DE LA NACIÓN
Museum
(Museum of the Nation; off Map p70; 476-9878; www.inc.gob.pe/expo1.shtml; Av Javier Prado Este 2466, San Borja; admission S7; 9am-5pm Tue-Sun) A brutalist concrete tower houses this catch-all museum that

provides a cursory overview of Peru's civilizations, from Chavín stone carvings and the knotted rope *quipus* of the Incas to artifacts from the colony. Large traveling exhibits are also shown here (for an extra fee), but if there is a single reason to visit, it's to view a permanent installation on the 6th floor called **Yuyanapaq** (www.pnud.org.pe/yuyanapaq/yuyanapaq.html). Named for the Quechua word meaning 'to remember,' it was created by Peru's Truth & Reconciliation Commission in 2003 and is a moving photographic tribute to those who died during the Internal Conflict (1980–2000).

BOSQUE EL OLIVAR   Park

(Map p70) This tranquil park, a veritable oasis, consists of the remnants of an old olive grove, part of which was planted by the venerated San Martín de Porres in the 17th century. Perfect for an afternoon stroll.

Miraflores

HUACA PUCLLANA

Pre-Columbian Site

(Map p72; ☎ 617-7138; cnr Borgoño & Tarapacá, Miraflores; admission S7; ☺9am-4:30pm Wed-Mon) Located near the Óvalo Gutiérrez, this *huaca* (temple) is a restored adobe ceremonial center from the Lima culture that dates back to AD 400. Though excavations continue, the site is accessible by regular guided tours in Spanish (for a tip). In addition to a tiny museum, there's a fantastic **restaurant** (p77) that offers incredible views of the illuminated ruins at night.

FREE FUNDACIÓN MUSEO AMANO

Museum

(Map p72; ☎ 441-2909; www.fundacionmuseoamano.org.pe; Retiro 160; ☺3-5pm Mon-Fri, by appointment only) A well-designed museum contains a fine private collection of ceramics, with a strong representation of wares from the Chimú and Nazca cultures. It also has a remarkable assortment of textiles produced by the coastal Chancay culture. Museum visits are allowed by a one-hour guided tour only, in Spanish or Japanese.

Barranco

An upper-class resort community during the turn of the 20th century, Barranco is lined with grand old *casonas* (mansions), many of which have been turned into eateries and bars. A block west of the main plaza, look for the **Puente de los Suspiros** (Bridge of Sighs; Map p76), a narrow, wooden bridge over an old stone stairway that leads to the beach. This is a prime spot for Peruvians on first dates.

MUSEO PEDRO DE OSMA   Museum

(Map p76; ☎ 467-0141; www.museopedrodeosma.org; Av Pedro de Osma 423; admission S10; ☺10am-6pm Tue-Sun) Housed in a lovely beaux-arts mansion surrounded by gardens, this colonial museum has an exquisite collection of art and furnishings, some of which date back to the early 16th century. Among the many fine pieces, standouts include a 2m-wide canvas that depicts a Corpus Christi procession in turn-of-the-17th-century Cuzco. Recommended.

Activities

Cycling

BIKE TOURS OF LIMA   Cycling Tours

(Map p72; ☎ 445-3172; www.biketoursoflima.com; Bolívar 150, Miraflores; ☺9am-7pm Mon-Sat) Great for day trips around Miraflores and San Isidro, as well as Sunday excursions into downtown (from S55).

Paragliding

Flights take off from the clifftop 'paraport' at the Parque Raimondi (Map p72) and start at about US$50 for 15 minutes. Agencies do not have offices on-site; reserve in advance.

Recommended companies:

Peru Fly (☎99-591-9928; www.perufly.com)

Andean Trail Peru (☎99-836-4930, 99-836-3436; andeantrailperu.com)

San Isidro

San Isidro

◎ **Top Sights**

 Tours

LIMA VISION   Lima Tours
(Map p72; 🕿 447-7710; www.limavision.com;
Chiclayo 444, Miraflores) A good agency for
half-day city tours (US$28) and day-
long trips to the pre-Columbian ruins at
Pachacamac.

LIMA TOURS   Lima Tours
(🕿 619-6901; www.limatours.com.pe; Jirón Belén
1040, Central Lima; ⏰9:30am-6pm Mon-Fri,
9:30am-1pm Sat) Another reputable, well-
known outfit that offers all manner of
tours around Lima, including gay-
friendly and gastronomic outings.

 Sleeping

Credit cards are accepted unless otherwise noted.

Central Lima
GRAN HOTEL BOLÍVAR
Historic Hotel **$$$**

(Map p64; ☎ 619-7171; Jirón de la Unión 958; s/d/tr/q US$65/75/85/95; @) This venerable 1924 hotel located on the Plaza San Martín was, in its day, one of the most luxurious accommodations in Latin America, where figures like Clark Gable, Mick Jagger and Robert Kennedy all laid their heads. Today, it is frayed at the edges, but, like any grand dame, it possesses a rare finesse.

HOTEL MAURY
Historic Hotel **$$**

(Map p64; ☎ 428-8188; hotmaury@amauta.rep. net.pe; Ucayali 201; s/d incl breakfast US$58/69, d with king-size bed US$80; ❄ @) Though the public areas at the Maury retain old-world flourishes (gilded mirrors and Victorian-style furniture), the 76 modern rooms are up-to-date: simple, clean and equipped with Jacuzzi tubs. The hotel is renowned for having been one of the first spots to cultivate the pisco sour (grape brandy cocktail) back in the '30s.

LIMA SHERATON
Hotel **$$$**

(Map p64; ☎ 619-3300; www.sheraton.com. pe; Paseo de la República 170; d US$139-360; ❄ @ 🛜 🏊) Housed in a brutalist highrise that overlooks the dour Palacio de Justicia (Supreme Court), the top hotel in downtown has more than 400 rooms and suites decorated in an array of desert tones. Units are equipped with wi-fi and cable TV and there is 24-hour room service. In addition, there are two restaurants, a bar, a gym, a swimming pool and a beauty salon – making this the best option in downtown.

San Isidro
DUO HOTEL BOUTIQUE
Boutique Hotel **$$$**

(☎ 628-3245; www.duohotelperu.com; Valle Riesta 576; s S288, d S352-384, ste S416, all incl breakfast; ❄ @ 🏊) On a serene, residential street, two blocks west of the Lima Golf Club, this intimate boutique hotel offers top-of-the-line amenities. Twenty elegant, monochromatic rooms are outfitted with marble baths, minibars, flat-screen TVs and slippers, while the public areas are chicly decorated in a contemporary-meets-pre-Columbian style. An on-site restaurant, overseen by chef Javier Paredes, produces delectable fusion specialties that marry the best of Peruvian and Italian flavors. An excellent choice all around.

South American Explorers

Now more than three decades old, the venerable **South American Explorers Club** (SAE; Map p73; ☎ 445-3306; www.saexplorers.org; Piura 135, Miraflores; 🕘 9:30am-5pm Mon-Fri, 9:30am-8pm Wed, 9:30am-1pm Sat) has long been an indispensable resource for travelers. It has an extensive library as well as a vast array of guides and maps for sale, from topographic plans to trail maps for the Inca Trail and Mt Ausangate near Cuzco and the Cordillera Blanca and Cordillera Huayhuash near Huaraz.

The club is a member-supported, nonprofit organization (it helped launch the first cleanup of the Inca Trail). Annual dues are US$60 per person (US$90 per couple) and there are additional clubhouses in Cuzco, Quito and Buenos Aires. You can sign up in person at one of the offices or via the website. Nonmembers are welcome to browse some of the information and purchase guidebooks and maps.

Miraflores

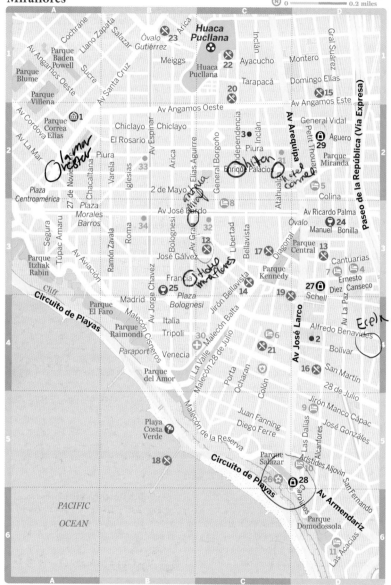

CASA BELLA PERÚ   Guesthouse **$$**
(Map p70; ☏ 421-7354; www.casabellaperu.
net; Las Flores 459; s/d/tr/q incl breakfast
US$59/65/79/89; @ 🛜) This expansive
1950s home has contemporary rooms
accented by indigenous textiles.

Fourteen varied units have comfy beds,
cable TV and remodeled bathrooms.
There is a kitchen, an ample garden and
a lounge, and services such as wi-fi are
available for an extra fee.

Miraflores

COUNTRY CLUB LIMA HOTEL
Historic Hotel **$$**

(Map p70; ☎ 611-9000; www.hotelcountry.com; Los Eucaliptos 590; d from US$200; ✳@☎) Built in 1927, this regal hotel is housed in a sprawling Spanish-style structure with wood-beam ceilings that is clad in colorful tiles and dotted with replica Cuzco School paintings. The lovely lobby cafe, where breakfast is served, is covered by a stained-glass dome. The 83 rooms – chock-full of amenities – range from the simply luxurious Master Room to the downright opulent Presidential Suite. Check the website for last-minute deals.

DELFINES HOTEL Y CASINO
Hotel **$$$**

(Map p70; ☎ 215-7000; www.losdelfineshotel.com; Los Eucaliptos 555; d incl breakfast from US$200; ✳@☎) This tall glass tower overlooking the golf course, with 206 spacious, elegant rooms and suites decorated in warm earth tones, is one of the top spots in town, having accommodated VIPs from Julio Iglesias to Kiss. There's a gym, a spa and a business center. An on-site restaurant serves seafood meals within view of a tank that houses two frolicking bottlenose dolphins.

Miraflores

CASA ANDINA
Hotel **$$-$$$**

(☎ 213-9739; www.casa-andina.com) This relatively new Peruvian chain has three hotels at various price points scattered around Miraflores. The **San Antonio** (☎ 241-4050; Av 28 de Julio 1088; d US$89-129; ✳@) and **Miraflores Centro** (Map p72; ☎ 447-0263; Av Petit Thouars 5444; d US$99-109; ✳@) branches are more affordable, each boasting 50-plus rooms decorated in contemporary Andean color schemes. **Colección Privada** (Map p72; ☎ 213-4300; Av La Paz 463, d/ste from US$300/419; ❄@☎) is the company's luxury outpost, situated in a tower that once served as the home of the now-defunct Hotel César (where Frank Sinatra once stayed). The hotel's 148 chic, earth-palette rooms are spacious, sporting stylish pre-Columbian flourishes. The best part: the nightly turn-down service. Rather than deposit chocolates on the pillow, the hotel's staff leaves a stupendous *cocada* (coconut cookie). All rates include breakfast.

MIRAFLORES PARK HOTEL
Luxury Hotel **$$$**

(Map p72; ☎ 242-3000; www.mira-park.com; Malecón de la Reserva 1035; d from US$215; ❄@☎) The best of Lima's smaller luxury hotels, the Miraflores Park has glorious ocean views and all the frills expected of a high-end inn, including a gym, a sauna and a pool overlooking the ocean. Some rooms even come with Roman-style tubs. For US$50, the bath butler will run an aphrodisiac-salt-infused, petal-strewn, candlelit bath – with sparkling wine and fresh strawberries.

HOSTAL EL PATIO
B&B **$$**

(Map p72; ☎ 444-2107; www.hostalelpatio.net; Ernesto Diez Canseco 341A; s/d/tr incl breakfast S120/180/210, ste S195-225;@) On a quiet side street near the Parque Kennedy is this little gem of a guesthouse with a cheery English- and French-speaking owner. Twenty-four small, spotless rooms with shining wood floors and colonial-style art surround a plant-filled courtyard with a trickling fountain. A few are equipped with small kitchenettes and minifridges.

HOTEL SAN ANTONIO ABAD
B&B **$$**

(Map p72; ☎ 447-6766; www.hotelsanantonio abad.com; Ramón Ribeyro 301; s/d S175/228;@) A bright-yellow 1940s mansion houses this pleasant, reader-recommended hotel with 24 comfortable rooms (some with air-con), which have carpeted floors, cable TV and soundproofed windows.

Breakfast (included) is served in a tiled dining terrace next to the garden.

CASA SAN MARTÍN
Hotel **$$**

(Map p72; ☎ 241-4434, 243-3900; www.casasanmartinperu.com; San Martín 339; s/d/tr US$60/84/105;@) A Spanish Revival building houses this comfortable inn equipped with 20 simple, terra-cotta-tiled rooms accented with Andean textiles. The staff are helpful, the water is hot and the rooms are blessedly quiet. Breakfast (included) is served in a bright cafe overlooking the terrace.

HOTEL SEÑORIAL
Hotel **$$**

(Map p72; ☎ 445-7306, 445-1870; www.senorial.com; José González 567; s/d/tr incl breakfast US$52/72/91;@ 🛜) Sixty-four rooms face the tranquil internal garden at this hospitable spot where a generation's worth of visitors have scribbled their greetings on the walls of the on-site cafe. Units are simple and airy, some with wall-to-wall carpeting; others, with polished wooden floors. All units have cable TV and access to wi-fi.

HOTEL EL DORAL
Hotel **$$**

(Map p72; ☎ 242-7799; www.eldoral.com.pe; Av José Pardo 486; s/d S225/255; ❄@☎) It may look businesslike on the outside, but inside you'll find 39 well-appointed suites facing a pleasant, plant-filled interior. All units have cable TV, minibars and sitting areas – as well as double-glazed windows to block out the noise. Breakfast (included) is served on the rooftop terrace by the pool.

JW MARRIOTT HOTEL LIMA
Chain Hotel **$$$**

(Map p72; ☎ 217-7000; www.marriotthotels.com/limdt; Malecón de la Reserva 615; d from US$250; ❄@☎) The most upscale hotel in Lima, the five-star Marriott has a superb seafront location and sparkling rooms with every amenity imaginable, including minibars and whirlpool baths. There is also an executive lounge, restaurants, a bar, a casino and an open-air tennis court and pool.

CAROLINA MIRANDA

Barranco

SECOND HOME PERÚ B&B $$
(Map p76; ☎ 247-5522; www.secondhomeperu.
com; Domeyer 366; s/d incl breakfast from
US$85/95; @ ☎) Owned by the children
of artist Victor Delfín, this charming five-
room Bavarian-style *casona* has private
gardens and breathtaking views of the
ocean from Chorrillos to Miraflores.
Public areas are dotted with Delfín's
sculptures and paintings.

AQUISITO B&B B&B $
(Map p76; ☎ 247-0712; www.aquisito.com.
pe; Centenario 114; s/d/tr incl breakfast
S50/80/110; @) Eight simple, immaculate
rooms of various sizes make up this
cozy, modern B&B run by the energetic
Malisa. There is an ample shared kitchen
and all units have cable TV and private
bathrooms. There is no sign.

Eating

The gastronomic capital of the continent, it is in Lima that you will find some
of the country's most sublime culinary
creations: from simple *cevicherías*
(informal ceviche counters) to decorous
fusion spots where the cuisine is bathed
in foam.

Central Lima

DOMUS Peruvian-Italian $
(Map p64; ☎ 427-0525; Miró Quesada 410;
3-course menús S15; ☺8:30am-5pm Mon-Fri) A
restored 19th-century mansion houses
this highly recommended, modern, yet
intimate, two-room restaurant. There is
no à la carte dining, just a rotating daily
list of well-executed Peruvian-Italian
specialties that always includes a vegetarian option. Freshly squeezed juice
accompanies this well-tended feast.

EL CORDANO Peruvian Classics $
(Map p64; ☎ 427-0181; Ancash 202; mains
S8-22; ☺8am-9pm) Since 1905, this old-
world dining hall has, at some point
or another, counted practically every
Peruvian president as a customer (the
presidential palace is right across
the street). It is known for its skillfully rendered *tacu tacu* (pan-fried rice
and beans) and sumptuous *butifarra*
sandwiches (French bread stuffed with
fresh-roasted country ham).

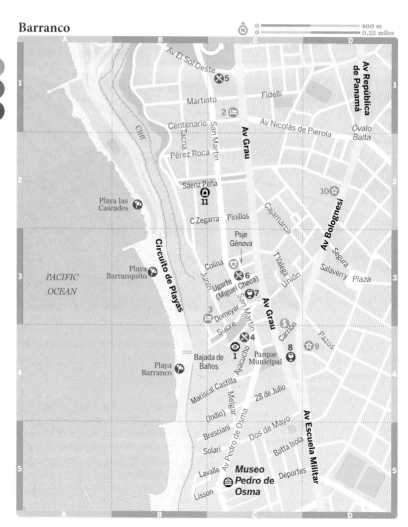

Map labels:
Av El Sol Oeste
Martinto Fidelli
Centenario Av Nicolás de Pierola Óvalo Balta
Pérez Roca Av Grau
Sáenz Peña
Playa las Caseades
Cajamarca Av Bolognesi
C Zegarra Pinillos Segura
Psje Génova Salaverry Plaza
Colina Unión
PACIFIC OCEAN Playa Barranquito Circuito de Playas Ugarte (Miguel Checa) Av Grau
Domeyer San Martín Carrión Pazos
Sucre
Playa Barranco Bajada de Baños Parque Municipal
Mariscal Castilla Ayacucho
Melgar 28 de Julio
(Indio) Dos de Mayo Av Escuela Militar
Bresciani
Solari Batta Isola
Lavalle Deportes
Lisson Museo Pedro de Osma

TANTA Fusion Bistro **$$$**
(Map p64; ☎ 428-3115; Psje de los Escribanos 142; mains S29-38; ⏱9am-10pm Mon-Sat, 9am-6pm Sun) One of several informal bistros run by celebrity super-chef Gastón Acurio, Tanta serves Peruvian dishes, fusion pastas, heaping salads, sandwiches, cocktails and a wine list strong on vintages from South America (from S46 per bottle). Don't leave without trying the heavenly passionfruit cheesecake mousse.

PASTELERÍA SAN MARTÍN Bakery **$**
(Map p64; ☎ 428-9091; Nicolás de Piérola 987; serving of turrón S4.50; ⏱9am-9pm Mon-Sat) Founded in 1930, this bakery serves what is considered Lima's finest *turrón de Doña Pepa,* a dessert associated with the religious feast of *El Señor de Los Milagros:* flaky, sticky and achingly sweet, it is best accompanied by a stiff espresso.

Barranco

diminutive sushi bar, now situated on a San Isidro side street. It's low-key, but it serves up some of the most spectacular sashimi and *maki* (sushi rolls) in Lima. A must-have: the 'acevichado,' a roll stuffed with shrimp and avocado, and then doused in a mayo infused with ceviche broth. Spectacular.

Miraflores

RESTAURANT HUACA PUCLLANA

Novoandina **$$$**

(Map p72; 📞 445-4042; www.resthuacapucllana.com; Gral Borgoño, cuadra 8; mains S28-60; 🕐 12:30pm-midnight Mon-Sat, 12:30-4pm Sun) A sophisticated establishment overlooking the illuminated ruins at Huaca Pucllana, this high-end spot has the best patio dining in Lima. The menu consists of expertly rendered contemporary Peruvian dishes (from grilled *cuy* to seafood chowders), along with a smattering of Italian-fusion specialties. It gets packed on weeknights; make a reservation.

San Isidro

MALABAR

Novoandina **$$$**

(Map p70; 📞 440-5200; www.malabar.com.pe; Cam Real 101; mains S38-55; 🕐 12:30-4pm & 7:30-11pm Mon-Sat) Pedro Miguel Schiaffino is the chef at this hot destination restaurant at the heart of San Isidro. Influenced by Amazonian produce and cooking techniques, Schiaffino's exquisite seasonal menu features deftly prepared delicacies such as crisp, seared *cuy* and alpaca ham. Don't forego the cocktails (the chef's father, a noted pisco expert, consulted on the menu).

MATSUEI

Sushi **$$$**

(Map p70; 📞 422-4323; Manuel Bañon 260; maki S30-45; 🕐 12:30-3:30pm & 7:30-11pm Mon-Sat) The venerated Japanese super-chef Nobu Matsuhisa once co-owned this

Fountain, Barranco
PHOTOGRAPHER: AARON McCOY

Gourmet chocolates at Xocolatl (p79)

CAROLINA MIRANDA

FIESTA
Peruvian **$$$**

(☎ 242-9009; www.restaurantfiestagourmet.
com; Av Reducto 1278; mains S40-45; ☽lunch
& dinner) Anyone in search of the finest
northern Peruvian cuisine in Lima,
should make a reservation at this busy
Milaflores' establishment. It cooks up
an achingly tender *arroz con pato a la
chiclayana* (duck and rice Chiclayo style)
and serves a spectacular *ceviche a la
brasa* – traditional ceviche that has been
given a quick sear before being served.
The result: a fish that is lightly smoky,
yet tender. The restaurant is located on
the southeast end of Miraflores, on Av
Reducto, which runs parallel to Paseo de
la República.

EL PUNTO AZUL
Seafood **$$**

(Map p72; ☎ 445-8078; San Martín 595; mains
S18-25; ☽noon-5pm) A family eatery that
dishes up super-fresh ceviches and *tiraditos* (Japanese-style ceviche, without
onions), as well as big-enough-to-share
rice dishes. Try the risotto with parme-
san, shrimp and *ají amarillo* (yellow chili).
It gets jam-packed, so show up before
1pm if you want a table – especially on
weekends.

RAFAEL
Novandina **$$$**

(Map p72; ☎ 242-4149; http://rafaeloster
ling.com; San Martín 300; mains S39-65;
☽1-3:30pm & 8pm-midnight) Don't let the
demure exterior fool you: this see-
and-be-seen restaurant by chef Rafael
Osterling produces a panoply of fusion
dishes, including *tiradito* bathed in
Japanese citrus or suckling goat stewed
in Madeira wine. The bar has an excel-
lent tapas menu, making it a great spot
for a cocktail and snacks, as well as solo
dining.

HAITI
Cafe **$$**

(Map p72; ☎ 445-0539; Diagonal 160; mains S12-
36) This nearly half-century-old literary
hangout is like stepping into 1960s Lima:
waiters in green jackets tend to coiffed
ladies and chattering businessmen. It's
a perfect spot to order a pressed pork
sandwich and watch the world go by.
Be forewarned: those innocent-looking
pisco sours pack a serious wallop.

LA MAR
Seafood **$$$**

(☎ 421-3365; www.lamarcebicheria.com; Av
La Mar 770; mains S39-49, ceviches S29-39;
☽noon-5pm Mon-Fri, 11:45am-5:30pm Sat &
Sun) A *cevichería* done Gastón Acurio–

style: La Mar is a polished cement patio bursting with VIPs that serves 10 types of ceviche and almost as many varieties of *tiraditos*. Can't make up your mind? Try the *degustación*, with five different kinds. Find the restaurant located about 600m northwest of the intersection of Av La Mar and Av Santa Cruz, on the northwest edge of Miraflores.

MANOLO Cafe **$$**
(Map p72; ☎ 444-2244; www.manolochurros
.com; Av José Larco 608; churros S4, mains S15-50; ⏱7am-1am Sun-Thu, 7am-2am Fri & Sat) Though this popular sidewalk cafe serves a long list of sandwiches, pasta and pizza, it is best known for its piping-hot churros, which go smashingly well with a *chocolate caliente espeso* (a thick hot chocolate) – perfect for dipping.

ALMAZEN Vegetarian **$$**
(Map p72; ☎ 243-0474; Federico Recavarren 298; mains S30; ⏱11am-11pm Mon-Fri, 5-11pm Sat) This soothing teahouse and restaurant features a rotating daily selection of organic dishes such as sweet potato and ginger soup, as well as belly-warming risottos. Wheat-free and vegan items are also available.

CAFÉ Z Cafe **$**
(Map p72; ☎ 444-5579; Diagonal 598; sandwiches S10-18; ⏱7am-midnight) A gathering spot for Lima hipsters, this buzzing cafe has live music, delicious sandwiches (the roasted mushroom one is excellent), and a mind-boggling number of coffees and herbal teas.

EL PERUANITO Peruvian **$**
(Map p72; ☎ 241-2175; Av Angamos Este 391; sandwiches S7; ⏱7am-1am) A hopping, informal sandwich spot serves fresh-roasted chicken, ham, turkey and *chicharrón* (fried pork) sandwiches on fresh French bread – each dressed with marinated onions. Delicious.

XOCOLATL Chocolates **$$**
(Map p72; ☎ 241-9554, 242-0143; www.xocolatl.
pe; Manuel Bonilla 111; chocolates from S3.50; ⏱11am-8pm Mon-Sat) This elegant chocola-

tier specializes in artful Peruvian sweets. Expect fillings such as coffee, pisco and *Ranfañote*, a traditional dessert made with coconut, molasses and nuts. Perfect if you need to take some stylish gifts home.

LA ROSA NAUTICA Seafood **$$$**
(Map p72; ☎ 445-0149; Circuito de Playas; mains S36-75, 3-course menús S60) Location, location, location. Though you can get the same seafood elsewhere for less, the views at this eatery on the historic pier are unparalleled. Go during happy hour (5pm to 7pm), when you can watch the last of the day's surfers skim along the crests of the waves.

QUATTRO D Snacks **$$**
(Map p72; ☎ 445-4228; Av Angamos Oeste 408; ice cream from S6, mains S20-31; ⏱6:30am-11:45pm Mon-Thu, 6:30am-12:30am Fri & Sat, 7-11am Sun) This bustling cafe serves hot pressed sandwiches and other dishes, but is best known for its absolutely dreamy Italian-style ice cream – some of which are crafted with exotic Peruvian fruits. (Flavors to try: *lúcuma* and *chirimoya*.)

WONG Supermarket **$**
(Map p72; ☎ 625-0000, ext 1130; www.ewong.
com; Óvalo Gutiérrez, Av Santa Cruz 771) A bright, massive supermarket for self-caterers, built around the courtyard of a vintage home; look for the baroque-style staircase.

Barranco

LA 73 Bistro **$$$**
(Map p76; ☎ 247-0780; Av El Sol Oeste 175; mains S34-39; ⏱noon-midnight) This contemporary-yet-cozy neighborhood eatery has an uncomplicated menu strong on Italian specialties, including tender yellow-potato gnocchi bathed in fresh pesto. Be sure to ask about the daily specials. Though you may want to start with dessert: the crisp, warm churros are orgasmic. Highly recommended.

CELSO

Don't Miss Astrid y Gastón

This is the restaurant that started Peru's current food revolution. Now one of the older outposts of *novoandina* (Peruvian nouvelle cuisine) cooking in Lima, Gastón Acurio's French-influenced standard-bearer nonetheless remains a culinary force to be reckoned with. His seasonal menu is equipped with traditional Peruvian fare, but it's the exquisite fusion specialties – such as the seared fillets of *cuy,* served Peking-style, with fluffy purple-corn crêpes – that make this such a sublime fine-dining experience. There is a first-rate international wine list (from S46 per bottle).

NEED TO KNOW

Map p72; 444-1496, 242-5387; www.astridygaston.com; Cantuarias 175; mains S39-69; 12:30-3:30pm & 6:30pm-midnight Mon-Sat

LA CANTA RANA   Seafood **$$**
(Map p76; 247-7274; Génova 101; mains S20-40; 8am-11pm Tue-Sat) An unpretentious place that packs in the locals for its more than 17 different types of ceviche and excellent *aguaditos* (a type of soupy risotto). If you're a fan of scallops, don't miss the *picante de conchas,* served in a mild and buttery chili sauce. There is no obvious sign: look for the green walls and the expectant-looking cats sitting outside.

CHALA   Novoandina **$$$**
(Map p76; 252-8515; www.chala.com.pe; Bajada de Baños 343; mains S26-64, 3-course lunch menú S50; 1-4pm & 8pm-midnight Mon-Sat, 1-4pm Sun) At the top of the narrow stairway that leads to the beach, a revamped *casona* serves modern dishes that blend Peruvian and Japanese flavors. Not to be missed: chicken ravioli bathed in *ají de gallina* (spicy chicken and walnut stew) and topped with seared *langostinos* (prawns).

🍷 Drinking

BRAVO RESTOBAR   Lounge
(Map p70; ☑ 221-5700; www.bravorestobar.com;
Conquistadores 1005; mains S28-54; ⏱1-11pm
Mon-Thu, 1pm-3am Fri & Sat) An inviting spot
in San Isidro has a backlit bar and a crew
of able bartenders stirring up dozens of
spectacular cocktails.

CAFÉ BAR HABANA   Bar
(Map p72; ☑ 446-3511; www.cafebarhabana.com;
Manuel Bonilla 107; ⏱6pm-close Mon-Sat) A
homey Cuban-style drinking establishment in Miraflores whips up Lima's best
mojitos.

JUANITO'S   Neighborhood Bar
(Map p76; Av Grau 274) This worn-in woody
bar – it was a leftist hangout in the
1960s – is one of the mellowest haunts
in Barranco. Decorated with a lifetime's
worth of theater posters, it's where the
writerly set arrives to swig *chilcano de
pisco* (pisco with ginger ale) and decon-
struct the state of humanity.

AYAHUASCA   Lounge
(Map p76; ☑ 247-6751; www.ayahuascabar.com;
San Martín 130; ⏱8pm-close) Barranco's of-
the-moment lounge resides in a stunning
restored *casona* full of Moorish architectural flourishes (and some intensely
surreal decor). There's a long list of
contemporary pisco cocktails, made with
infusions of purple corn and coca leaves.

HUARINGAS   Lounge
(Map p72; ☑ 447-1883; Bolognesi 460; ⏱9pm-
close Tue-Sat) A popular bar and lounge
located inside the Brujas de Cachiche
restaurant in Miraflores, Huaringas
serves a vast array of cocktails, including
a well-recommended passionfruit sour.

EL BOLIVARCITO   Bar
(Map p64; ☑ 427-2114; Jirón de la Unión 958)
Facing the Plaza San Martín from the
Gran Hotel Bolívar in downtown, this
frayed, yet bustling, spot is known as La
Catedral del Pisco for purveying some of
the first pisco sours in Peru.

⭐ Entertainment

For tickets, **Teleticket** (☑ 613-8888; www.
teleticket.com.pe) is a handy one-stop-shop
that sells admission to sporting events,
concerts, theater and some *peñas* (bars
or clubs), as well as the tourist train to
Huancayo (p86). The most convenient location can be found on the 2nd floor of the
Wong supermarket in Miraflores (p79).

Peñas

Peruvian folk music and dance is performed on weekends at *peñas*. There are
two main types of Peruvian music performed at these venues: *folklórica* and
criollo. The first is more typical of the
Andean highlands; the other, a coastal
music driven by African-influenced
beats. Admission varies; dinner is sometimes included in the price.

LAS BRISAS DEL TITICACA
    Folk Performances
(☑ 715-6960; www.brisasdeltiticaca.com;
Wakuski 168, Central Lima; admission S21-48)
The best *folklórica* show in Lima is at this
peña near Plaza Bolognesi in downtown.

LA CANDELARIA
    Folk Performances
(Map p76; ☑ 247-1314; www.lacandelariaperu.
com; Bolognesi 292, Barranco; admission S31-53)
In Barranco, a show that incorporates
both *folklórica* and *criollo* music and
dancing.

Dance Clubs

AURA   Trendy
(Map p72; ☑ 242-5516, ext 210; www.aura.com.pe;
LarcoMar, Malecón de la Reserva 610, Miraflores;
admission S40) Located in the LarcoMar
shopping mall, Lima's most exclusive
nightclub has DJs who spin a mix of
house, hip-hop, electronica and Latin.
Dress to the nines or you're not getting in.

SARGENTO PIMIENTA   Casual
(Map p76; ☑ 247-3265; www.sargentopimienta
.com; Bolognesi 755, Barranco; admission S20)
More accessible is this reliable spot
in Barranco, whose name means

'Sergeant Pepper.' The barnlike club hosts various theme nights and occasional live bands.

 **Shopping**

MERCADO INDIO — Market
(Map p72; Av Petit Thouars 5245, Miraflores) The best place to find everything from pre-Columbian-style clay pottery to alpaca rugs to reproductions of Cuzco School canvases.

AGUA Y TIERRA — Shop
(Map p72; ☎ 444-6980; Ernesto Diez Canseco 298, Miraflores; ⏰10am-2pm & 2:30-6pm Mon-Sat) Tidy shop that specializes in crafts from the Shipibo, Aguaruna and Ashánin-ka Amazon cultures. Recommended.

DÉDALO — Shop
(Map p76; ☎ 477-0562; Sáenz Peña 295, Barranco) A vintage *casona* houses this contemporary crafts store that has a lovely cafe.

ALPACA 111 — Boutique
(Map p72; ☎ 241-3484; LarcoMar, Malecón de la Reserva 610, Miraflores) A number of Miraflores boutiques sell high-quality, contemporary alpaca knits. This is one of the best.

LARCOMAR — Mall
(Map p72; Malecón de la Reserva 610, Miraflores) A well-to-do outdoor mall wedged into the clifftop beneath the Parque Salazar is full of high-end clothing shops and eateries.

ℹ️ Information

Dangers & Annoyances

While the crime situation in Lima has improved immeasurably since the 1980s, this is still a big city, where one in five people live in poverty. Naturally, some crime is to be expected. The most common offense is theft and readers have reported regular muggings. You are unlikely to be physically hurt, but it is nonetheless best to keep a streetwise attitude.

Don't wear flashy jewelry or clothes and keep your camera in your bag when you're not using it.

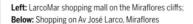
Left: LarcoMar shopping mall on the Miraflores cliffs;
Below: Shopping on Av José Larco, Miraflores
PHOTOGRAPHER: (LEFT) PAUL KENNEDY; (BELOW) CAROLINA MIRANDA

It is best to keep your cash in your pocket and take only as much as you'll need for the day. Late at night, it is preferable to take taxis, especially in downtown, or if you've been partying until late in Barranco.

Emergency

Clínica Good Hope (Map p72; ☎ 610-7300; www.goodhope.org.pe; Malecón Balta 956) Quality care and there is a dental unit.

Policía Nacional head office (☎ 460-0921; Moore 268, Magdalena del Mar; ☼24hr)

Tourism Police (Policía de Turismo, Poltur; Map p72; ☎ 460-0844; Colón 246; ☼24hr) A division of the Policía Nacional (National Police) that usually has English-speaking officers who can provide theft reports for insurance claims or traveler's check refunds.

Money

Banks are abundant, as are 24-hour ATMs, many of which dispense soles and US dollars. Use caution when making withdrawals late at night.

Tourist Information

iPerú (peru.info/iperu) Aeropuerto Internacional Jorge Chávez (☎ 574-8000; Main Hall; ☼24hr); Miraflores LarcoMar (Map p72; ☎ 445-9400; Module 14, by movie theater box office, LarcoMar, Malecón de la Reserva 610; ☼noon-8pm); San Isidro (Map p70; ☎ 421-1627; Jorge Basadre 610; ☼9am-6pm Mon-Fri) The government's reputable tourist bureau dispenses maps, offers good advice and can help handle complaints.

ⓘ Getting There & Away

Air

Lima's Aeropuerto Internacional Jorge Chávez (code LIM; ☎ 517-3100; www.lap.com.pe; Callao) is stocked with the usual facilities, including a place to store luggage and plenty of restaurants. (Tip: The ice cream shop at top of the escalators on the 2nd floor is all kinds of amazing.) For international flights, it is advisable to arrive three hours prior to check-in.

83

If You Like...
Baroque Churches

If you like Lima's magnificent baroque churches, the highland city of Ayacucho, just a one-hour flight from the capital, has 33 – one for each year of Christ's life. It makes for a perfect weekend getaway.

1 CATHEDRAL
(Plaza de Armas) Featuring a relatively simple (for the baroque) facade, this 17th-century cathedral contains an ornate golden altar, an elaborate pulpit and a religious museum. During Easter Week, the devout gather here for Ayacucho's most important religious procession.

2 TEMPLO DE SAN CRISTOBAL
(Jirón 28 de Julio, cuadra 6) The city's oldest church is crafted out of stone and dates back to 1540 – just eight years after the arrival of the Spanish in Peru.

3 IGLESIA DE SANTO DOMINGO
(Jirón 9 de Diciembre at Bellido) The embellished facade makes this one of the most photogenic churches in town – and the interiors reflect Andean baroque decorative styles.

4 IGLESIA DE LA MERCED
(Jirón 2 de Mayo at San Martín) Dating from 1550, full of colonial art and with one of Peru's oldest convents (from 1540) attached.

5 IGLESIA DE SANTA TERESA
(Jirón 28 de Julio) A gorgeous church and monastery with an altar studded (somewhat unusually) in seashells.

Note that all flights are subject to a departure tax (international/domestic US$31/6).

Bus
There is no central bus terminal; each company operates its ticketing and departure points independently. Some companies have several terminals, so always clarify from which point a bus leaves when buying tickets. In addition, companies have various classes of service. For long trips, look for buses with *bus cama* service – large reclining

seats. It is best to buy tickets in advance – especially for popular destinations such as Cuzco.

The following companies are recommended:

Cruz del Sur (☎ 311-5050; www.cruzdelsur. com.pe) Central Lima (Map p64; ☎ 431-5125; Quilca 531); La Victoria (☎ 225-5748, 903-4149; Av Javier Prado Este 1109)

Oltursa (☎ 708-5000, 225-4495; www. oltursa.com.pe; Av Aramburu 1160, Limatambo)

Ormeño (☎ 472-1710; www.grupo-ormeno. com.pe) Central Lima (Map p64; Carlos Zavala Loayza 177); La Victoria (Av Javier Prado Este 1059)

Tepsa (☎ 202-3535; www.tepsa.com.pe) Central Lima (Map p64; ☎ 427-5642, 428-4635; Paseo de la República 151-A, Central Lima); Javier Prado (☎ 202-3535; Av Javier Prado Este 1091)

Car
Lima has major intersections without stoplights, kamikaze bus drivers, spectacular traffic jams and little to no parking. If you still dare to get behind the wheel, there are several US companies that have 24-hour desks at the airport. Prices range from about US$50 to US$130 per day, not including surcharges, insurance and taxes (of about 19%). Hiring a taxi is your best option.

ℹ Getting Around

To/From the Airport
The airport is in the port of Callao, 12km west of downtown.

As you come out of customs, inside the airport to the right is the official taxi service: Taxi Green (☎ 484-4001; taxigreen.com.pe; Aeropuerto Internacional Jorge Chávez; 1-3 people to Central Lima, San Isidro, Miraflores & Barranco S45).

In a private taxi, allow at least an hour to the airport from San Isidro, Miraflores or Barranco. Traffic is lightest before 7am.

Bus
Though it is a major urban center, Lima has long functioned without a citywide public transportation system. A trans-Lima electric bus system is currently making a limited debut and will initially consist of just a single north–south route, which means that the current haphazard

network of small private buses (called *combis* and *micros*) will remain vital.

To be sure, the system is mind-boggling: caravans of minivans hurtle down the avenues with a *cobrador* (ticket taker) hanging out the door and shouting out the stops. Your best bet is to know the nearest major intersection or landmark close to your stop (eg Parque Kennedy) and tell that to the *cobrador* – he'll let you know whether you've got the right bus. *Combis* are generally slow and crowded, but startlingly cheap: fares run from S1 to S3.

The most useful routes link Central Lima with Miraflores along Av Arequipa or Paseo de la República. Minibuses along Garcilaso de la Vega (also called Av Wilson) and Av Arequipa are labeled 'Todo Arequipa.'

To get to Barranco, look for buses along Av Arequipa labeled 'Chorrillos/Huaylas/Metro' (some will also have signs that say 'Barranco'). You can also find these on the Diagonal, just west of the Parque Kennedy, in Miraflores.

Taxi

Lima's taxis don't have meters, so negotiate a price with the driver before getting in. Fares will vary depending on the length of the journey, traffic conditions and time of day. Plan for paying extra for registered taxis and any taxi you hail outside a tourist attraction. As a (very) rough guide, a trip from Central Lima to Miraflores costs around S12, while Central Lima to the airport will run about S20. Fares from Miraflores to the airport generally start at about S45. If there are two or more of you, be clear on whether the fare is per person or for the car.

The majority of taxis in Lima are unregistered (unofficial). During the day, this is generally not a problem. However, at night it is generally safer to use registered taxis. Look for green or yellow taxis with numbered dome lights and a SETAME sticker on the windshield.

Taxi Real (☎470-6263; www.taxireal.com) accepts advance reservations and is recommended.

AROUND LIMA

Pachacamac

Situated about 31km southeast of the city center, the archaeological complex of **Pachacamac** (☎430-0168; pachacamac. perucultural.org.pe; admission S6; ⏰9am-5pm Mon-Fri) is a pre-Columbian citadel made up of adobe and stone palaces and temple pyramids. If you've been to Machu Picchu, it may not look like much, but this was an important Inca site and a major city when the Spanish arrived.

It began as a ceremonial center for the Lima culture beginning at about AD 100, and was later expanded by the Waris before being taken over by the Ichsma. The Incas added numerous other structures upon their arrival to the area in 1450. The name Pachacamac, which can be variously translated as 'He who Animated the World' or 'He who Created Land and Time,' comes from the Wari god, whose

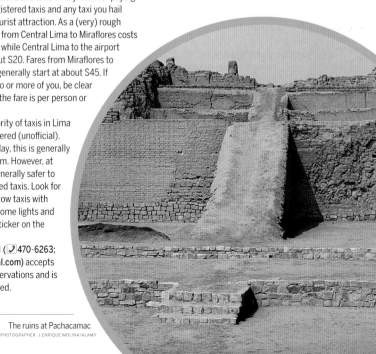

The ruins at Pachacamac
PHOTOGRAPHER: J.ENRIQUE MOLINA/ALAMY

Detour:
Huancayo

The **Ferrocarril Central Andino** (☏ 226-6363; www.ferrocarrilcentral.com.pe) railway line runs from Estación Desamparados in downtown Lima inland to Huancayo, climbing from sea level to 4829m – the second-highest point for passenger trains in the world – before descending to Huancayo at 3260m. There is no regular passenger service, but the train makes the journey a couple of times a month as a tourist attraction – a 12-hour odyssey along vertigo-inducing Andean mountainscapes.

Once you arrive in Huancayo, you'll probably be ready for a good meal. Our recommendation: **Huancahuasi** (☏ 24-4826; Mariscal Castilla 222; mains S12-20; ⊙8am-7pm Sun-Thu, to 2am Fri & Sat), a lovely, flower-filled courtyard eatery that serves tasty regional goodies such as *pachamanca* (a traditional meat and potatoes dish cooked over hot stones) and *papas a la huancaína* (a regional dish consisting of steamed potatoes topped with a spiced, creamy cheese sauce). The restaurant is located in El Tambo, about a S3 taxi ride from the town center.

The round-trip costs S125 to S300. Check the schedule in advance since the rail lines aren't always operational. Tickets can be purchased through **Teleticket** (☏ 613-8888; www.teleticket.com.pe) or at the rail company's **San Isidro office** (Av José Gálvez Barrenechea 566, 5th fl). Note that the rail company *does not* keep offices at the train station.

wooden, two-faced image can be seen in the on-site **museum**.

You can climb the switchback trail to the top of the **Templo del Sol** (Temple of the Sun), which on clear days offers excellent views of the coast. The most remarkable structure on-site, however, is the Palacio de las Mamacuna (House of the Chosen Women), commonly referred to as the **Acllahuasi**, which boasts a series of Inca-style trapezoidal doorways. Unfortunately, a major earthquake in 2007 has left the structure highly unstable and, as a result, visitors can only admire it from a distance. (Because of the extensive damage – and because there have been no funds for repair – the World Monuments Fund added Pachacamac to its 2010 Watch List of the planet's most endangered sites.)

There is a visitors center and cafe at the site entrance, which is on the road to Lurín. A simple map can be obtained from the ticket office, and a track leads

from here into the complex. Those on foot should allow several hours to explore. (In summer, take water and a hat – there is no shade to speak of.) Those with a vehicle can drive from site to site.

Various agencies in Lima (see p70) offer guided tours (about US$38) to Pachacamac that include round-trip transport and a guide. You can also hire a taxi (from S20 per hour) from Lima.

If you have a little time on your hands after visiting Pachacamac and would like to do a little crafts shopping on your way back to Lima, then have your taxi driver make a stop at **Ichimay Wari** (☏ 430-3674; www.ichimaywari.com; Jr Jorge Chávez, Manzana 22, Lote A, Lurín; ⊙8am-1pm & 2-5pm Mon-Fri), a crafts center in nearby Lurín. Featuring the works of roughly a dozen artisans from Ayacucho, here you'll find pottery, *retablos* (religious dioramas) and *arbolitos de la vida* (ceramic trees of life). The shop is small, but the prices are a bargain. If you call ahead, it's possible to meet some of the artisans and tour their studios.

To get to the craft center, take the Antigua Panamericana (old Pan-American Hwy) north from Pachacamac to Km 39 and turn inland to the Barrio Artesano. The turn-off is clearly marked with a sign.

Caral

If you enjoy exploring Lima's sprawling desert ruins, then consider a day trip to visit **Caral** (admission S11; ⊘9am-5pm), the oldest city in the Americas.

The culture that built these expansive temple platforms, roughly 200km north of Lima, rose to prominence an incredible 4500 to 5000 years ago – making it one of the largest early cities, alongside those of Egypt and China. At the site, six stone-built pyramids sit alongside amphitheaters, ceremonial rooms, altars, adobe complexes and several sunken circular plazas. Among the many artifacts you'll see are millennia-old bone flutes and Peru's oldest *quipus* (a system among Andean cultures of tying cords and knots to convey information). It's little wonder that Unesco declared the city a World Heritage Site in 2009. Lima Tours (p70) can arrange private day tours upon request.

Nazca, Arequipa & the South

A thin ribbon of highway spans Peru's southern coastal desert. The terrain is arid, punctuated by the presence of palm-fringed oases. Deep in the south, a mountain road turns east and climbs all the way to Arequipa, and beyond that, Lake Titicaca and Cuzco. Welcome to Peru's well-traveled Gringo Trail.

Despite the touristy nickname, it's an area that holds more depth and diversity than you might suspect. In Nazca, mysterious pre-Columbian glyphs cross vast expanses of desert. Off the coast of Paracas, penguins and sea lions come together on rocky outcroppings. And, in Arequipa, you'll find stately religious citadels that date back to the colony, along with some of the world's deepest canyons. It is an area that takes you through coast and mountain, through desert and gorge, along the rim of volcanoes where Incas once made human sacrifices.

What more could anybody possibly ask for?

Candelabra geoglyph, Islas Ballestas (p103)

PHOTOGRAPHER: SHANIA SHEGEDYN

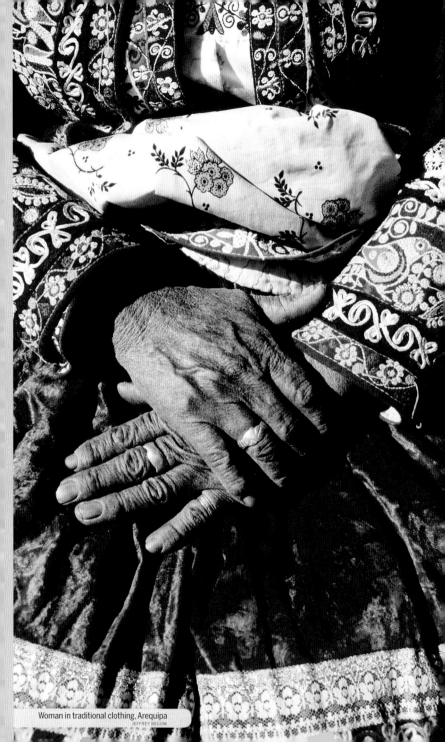

Woman in traditional clothing, Arequipa

Nazca, Arequipa & the South

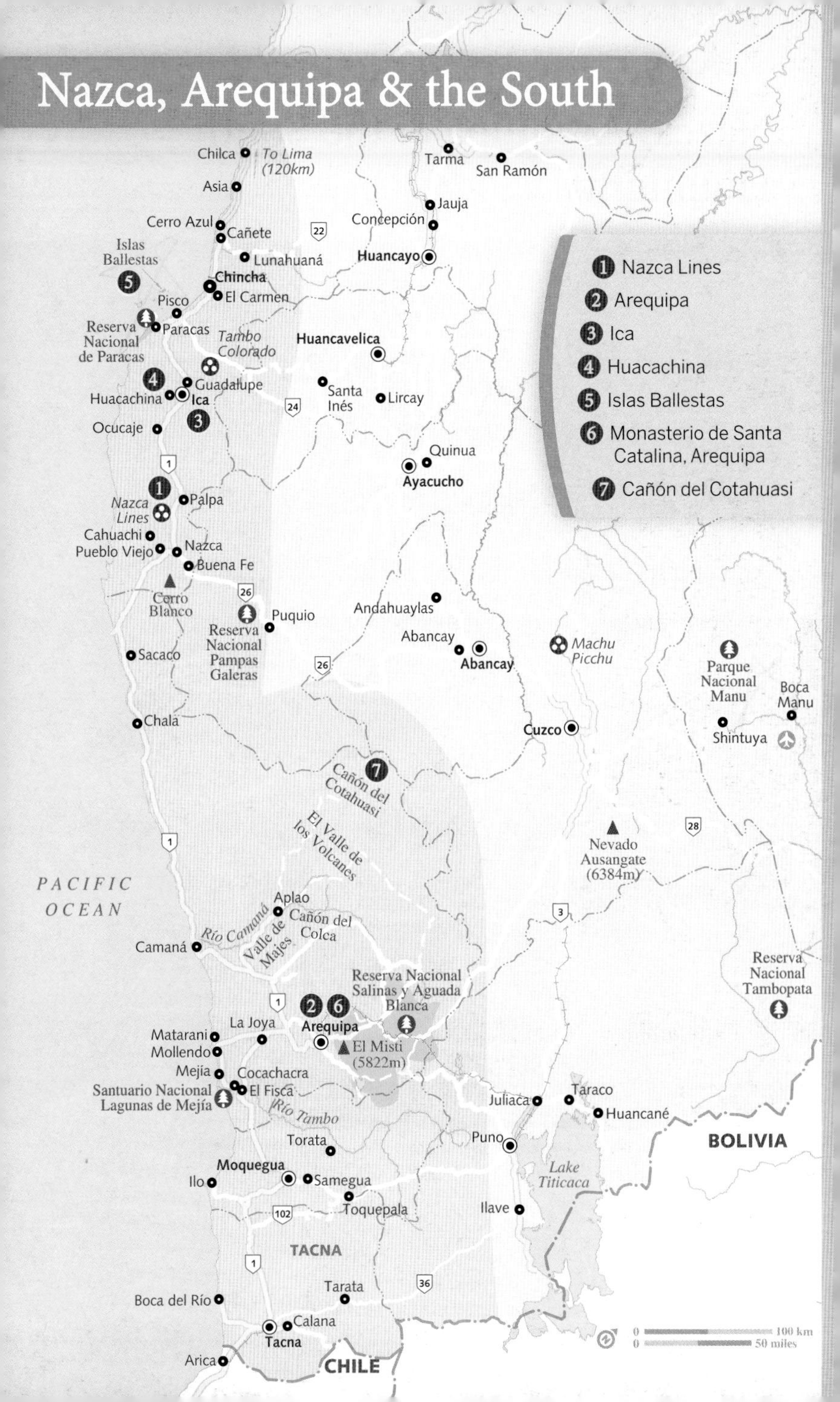

1 Nazca Lines

2 Arequipa

3 Ica

4 Huacachina

5 Islas Ballestas

6 Monasterio de Santa Catalina, Arequipa

7 Cañón del Cotahuasi

Chilca
To Lima (120km)
Tarma
San Ramón
Asia
Cerro Azul
Cañete
Jauja
Concepción
Islas Ballestas
5
Lunahuaná
Chincha
El Carmen
Huancayo
Pisco
Paracas
Reserva Nacional de Paracas
Tambo Colorado
Huancavelica
4
Guadalupe
Santa Inés
Lircay
Huacachina
Ica
3
Ocucaje
Quinua
Ayacucho
1
Palpa
Nazca Lines
Cahuachi
Pueblo Viejo
Nazca
Buena Fe
Cerro Blanco
Andahuaylas
Reserva Nacional Pampas Galeras
Puquio
Abancay
Abancay
Machu Picchu
Parque Nacional Manu
Boca Manu
Sacaco
Chala
Cuzco
Shintuya
7
Cañón del Cotahuasi
El Valle de los Volcanes
PACIFIC OCEAN
Nevado Ausangate (6384m)
Aplao
Cañón del Colca
Valle de Majes
Río Camaná
Camaná
Reserva Nacional Salinas y Aguada Blanca
Reserva Nacional Tambopata
La Joya
2 **6**
Arequipa
Matarani
Mollendo
Mejía
Cocachacra
El Misti (5822m)
Santuario Nacional Lagunas de Mejía
El Fiscal
Río Tambo
Juliaca
Taraco
Huancané
Torata
Puno
Lake Titicaca
BOLIVIA
Moquegua
Ilo
Samegua
Toquepala
Ilave
TACNA
Boca del Río
Tarata
Calana
Tacna
Arica
CHILE

0 — 100 km
0 — 50 miles

Nazca, Arequipa & the South Highlights

① Nazca Lines

The barren desert harbors mysterious ancient ruins: a set of carved glyphs so massive they can only be seen from the air. The Nazca Lines have long captured travelers' imaginations with their precision and scale. But stick around – the region is home to countless other pre-Columbian treasures, too.

Need to Know
BEST TIME TO GO December through March. **WEATHER** Temperatures are extreme. Take water, a jacket and a hat. **TIP** Book guides with a reputable agency. **For more, see p107.**

Nazca Lines
Don't Miss List

BY ALBERTO URBANO JACINTO,
ARCHAEOLOGIST OVERSEEING THE
MINISTRY OF CULTURE'S OPERATIONS
IN NAZCA

1 MUSEO MARIA REICHE

No trip to the Nazca area is complete without a visit to this wonderful little museum (p109) in honor of the archaeologist who dedicated more than 50 years of her life to excavating and documenting the Nazca lines. The region is a destination because of her.

2 MIRADOR

Right on the Pan-American Hwy at Km 424 is this 12m-tall viewing tower (p109), which offers unimpeded 360-degree views of the area. From here, you can see the glyphs known as the Tree, the Hand and the Lizard – as well as lots of trapezoidal shapes. It's great for snapping pictures.

3 MUSEO DIDÁCTICO ANTONINI

This is an excellent museum (p109) that provides a well-presented historical overview of the region. It also contains numerous finds that have turned up at the nearby tombs of Cahuachi – including lots of mummies.

4 REGIONAL COOKING

Nazca is an excellent spot to sample ceviche. We are on the coast so our seafood goes straight from ocean to plate – the freshest! To accompany that, I recommend any dish made with *pallares* (lima beans or butter beans). It's a native legume, grown in the region, and it dates back to pre-Inca times.

5 EXPLORE!

Many folks fly over the Nazca Lines and then leave. But this region has lots of amazing sites that don't always get into the guidebooks. In the nearby village of Palpa, there are ancient petroglyphs. To the west, in El Ingenio, you'll find old baroque churches. In San Fernando, about an hour south, there are wild beaches full of sea lions and penguins.

Arequipa Outdoors

Nestled into the scenic southern highlands, this region is a place known for its incredible natural wonders. Think: volcanic peaks, craggy canyons, remote valleys full of unusual geology and rivers ideal for rafting. Looking for a beckoning spot to channel your inner outdoorsman? You've come to just the right place.

Need to Know

BEST TIME TO GO The clearest weather is April through June, making this the best time for adventure activities. **AVOID** The rainy season, from December to March. **For further coverage, see p111.**

Arequipa Outdoors Don't Miss List

BY CARLOS MISTI ZÁRATE FLORES, NATIVE AREQUIPEÑO AND PROPRIETOR OF CARLOS ZÁRATE AVENTURAS, A RENOWNED TREKKING OUTFIT

1 CAÑÓN DEL COLCA
This spectacular canyon (p124) has lovely villages, charming people and incredible scenery. If you only have a couple of days, you can see parts of it by car, with an overnight stay at a hotel in one of the villages. But I recommend the three-day trek: it's a great opportunity to see condors in flight.

2 EL VALLE DE LOS VOLCANES
If you've got three days, I highly recommend a journey to this little-visited volcanic valley (p129), about an eight-hour drive from the city. It has a lunar landscape – full of strange rock formations. You'll see black volcanic geological configurations topped with bright green vegetation. The colors are just incredible. I accompanied a crew from the Discovery Channel there recently. They loved it!

3 MOUNTAINEERING
As a starter, I would recommend a visit to El Misti (p117; pictured above left), the absolutely majestic volcano overlooking Arequipa. (My father named me after it.) If you are acclimated to high altitudes and are in very good shape, it offers a relatively easy ascent. Along the way, you'll see guanacos (camelids), vizcachas (an Andean rodent) and, if you're lucky, even deer.

4 VALLE DE MAJES
This nearby valley (p117) is home to the Río Majes (which is an extension of the Río Colca), a popular spot for river running. This area is renowned for its shrimp – making this a great spot to eat after any local day trips.

5 CHUPE DE CAMARONES
Speaking of lunch, Peruvian shrimp bisque is one of the dishes that this region is known for. It's a powerful soup – and a lot of local restaurants do very good versions of it. One of my favorite places to eat it is in the village of Punta Colorada in the Valle de Majes. Don't leave without trying it!

95

Take a Tour of the Vineyards

Pisco sours. Chilcano de pisco. Pisco punch. At some point during your trip to Peru, you will likely sip the many cocktails crafted with Peru's renowned grape brandy. So why not go to the source? The pleasant coastal community of Ica (p107) is home to bodegas (wineries) from the industrial to the artisanal – a perfect place to sip! Bodega Tacama (p107)

3

5 Admire Rocking, Squawking Sea Life

Honking Humboldt penguins. Barking sea lions. Clacking Peruvian boobies. A boat tour to the Islas Ballestas (p103 – known as the 'poor man's Galapagos' – will offer you prime photo ops of the Pacific Ocean's most astonishing fauna. A plus: the journey will allow you enough distance to admire a candelabra-shaped glyph carved into a faraway mountainside.

PAL/IMAGE BROKER

Sail Down Sand Dunes

4

Surfing isn't just about catching waves. In the diminutive desert oasis (and party town) of Huacachina (p106), you can catch a ride on a dune. The area's undulating topography offers thrillseekers an opportunity to tool around in roaring dune buggies and sail down towering walls of sand on nothing but a board. Get ready to shred – and eat a lot of sand.

JAMES BRUNKER/ALAMY

6

Explore an Unusual Colonial Monastery

A city within a city is how Arequipa's rambling – and architecturally striking – Monasterio de Santa Catalina (p115) is often described. This expansive Catholic citadel, once a well-to-do nunnery, is a labyrinth of cloisters and courtyards. Among the many intriguing sights: a room that once served as a mortuary, where portraits of centuries' worth of deceased nuns cover the stone walls.

7

Trek the World's Deepest Known Canyon

Adventurers can strap on a pack and hike through idyllic Andean villages, past towering cacti and along staggering gorges in the extravagantly beautiful, less-visited Cañón del Cotahuasi (p130), outside of Arequipa. When you're all done, dip into a simmering bowl of *picante*, a local stew served with lip-smacking white cheese, typical of the area. Sipia Waterfall (p130), Cañón del Cotahuasi

Nazca, Arequipa & the South's Best...

Museums

○ **Museo Didáctico Antonini** (p109) An excellent overview of Nazca culture

○ **Museo Regional de Ica** (p107) Trepanned skulls, mummified animals and superb Paracas weavings

○ **Museo Santury** (p113) The body of a sacrificial Inca maiden...in a freezer

○ **Museo Arqueológico Chiribaya** (p116) An impressive collection devoted to a pre-Inca civilization

○ **Museo de Arte Virreinal de Santa Teresa** (p114) A Carmelite convent boasts lavish colonial religious treasures

Adventures

○ **Nazca Lines** (p108) Giant glyphs in the desert

○ **Islas Ballestas** (p103) Protected islands with wildlife galore

○ **Reserva Nacional de Paracas** (p102) A vast desert reserve

○ **Huacachina** (p106) Party by night, surf sand dunes by day

○ **Cañón del Colca** (p124) One of the world's deepest canyons

○ **El Misti** (p117) A hikeable volcano and the site of pre-Columbian human sacrifice

Restaurants in Arequipa

○ **Chicha** (p120) Regional cuisine meets global fusion

○ **La Nueva Palomino** (p121) This longtime local favorite serves homestyle classics

○ **Nina-Yaku** (p120) The perfect spot to cut into deftly prepared alpaca steaks

○ **Tradición Arequipeña** (p121) The place for tasty Sunday breakfasts

Need to Know

Wildlife Encounters

○ **Condors** (p124) Find them soaring over the Cañón del Colca

○ **Humboldt penguins** (p103) These charismatic birds like to nest on the Islas Ballestas

○ **Vizcachas** (p117) Fuzzy, super-adorable bunny-like rodents inhabit the flanks of El Misti

○ **Flamingos** (p131) Flocks of three different species descend on the Laguna de Salinas during rainy season

ADVANCE PLANNING

○ **Two Months Before** Make arrangements to trek the canyons around Arequipa

○ **One Month Before** Reserve an overflight to see the Nazca Lines

○ **One Day Before** Book a table at Chicha, celebrity chef Gastón Acurio's delectable dining outpost in Arequipa (p120)

GETTING AROUND

○ **Air** The only commercial airport is in the city of Arequipa (p122), and offers regular service to Lima and Cuzco; small-craft flights to see the Nazca lines take off from the aerodrome in Nazca (p108)

○ **Bus** Frequent and comfortable long-haul buses travel to and from Lima on the coast, as well as Cuzco and Puno in the highlands

○ **Boat** Employed only for visits of the Islas Ballestas (p103), the island nature reserve off the coast of Pisco

○ **Walk** Perfect for the tight grid of streets in Arequipa (p111) – not to mention the multiday trekking trips in nearby canyons (p116)

○ **Bike** Local mountain-biking tours are offered around Arequipa (p118)

BE FOREWARNED

○ **Museums** Most are closed on Mondays

○ **Weather** Bad weather may hamper activities such as hiking and trekking; ask about cancellation policies and keep tabs on the forecast

○ **Unlicensed Touts** There's a relentless crew of them in Nazca; stick to qualified agencies and registered guides

○ **Robberies** Be careful at isolated beaches and off-the-beaten-path urban areas; it's best to walk in a group or ask locally before setting out

Left: Entrance to Reserva Nacional de Paracas;
Above: Cañón del Colca (p124).

PHOTOGRAPHERS: (LEFT) RICHARD CUMMINS; (ABOVE) GRANT DIXON

Nazca, Arequipa & the South Itineraries

The haul down the coast is long and dusty. If you're short on time, you can do the most significant coastal sites, such as the Nazca Lines, as a day tour from Lima, allowing more time later to explore the southern Andes.

LIMA TO NAZCA
3 DAYS
Desert Caravan

This excursion takes you to the key sites of the southern Peruvian coast. The trip begins in Lima and makes its first stop at **(1) Pisco and Paracas**. The former is the port from which the liquor gets its name; the latter, a small town abutting a wilderness reserve. From here, you can ride through the **(2) Reserva Nacional de Paracas**, home to ancient cemeteries, and go for a boat tour around the **(3) Islas Ballestas**, which offers vistas of dramatic desert arches and colonies of honking birdlife. Afterwards, overnight in Paracas.

The next day, continue the journey down the coast. If you get an early start, pay a visit to the pisco-producing vineyards at **(4) Ica**. Otherwise, head to **(5) Nazca** for an overflight of the mysterious pre-Columbian glyphs etched in to the desert. While you're in town, pay a visit to the Chauchilla Cemetery, a pre-Columbian tomb site that is bursting with mummies.

You'll spend the night here (in Nazca – not the cemetery!), and the next morning, return to Lima. If you want to extend the trip, continue on to the highland city of Arequipa.

5 DAYS

AREQUIPA & THE CANYONS
A Little Bit City, A Little Bit Country

A dash of colonial splendor. A dollop of rural idyll. And a heaping dose of wilderness. That's what you'll get on this combination trip around Peru's fabled 'White City.'

Start by flying into **(1) Arequipa**, or coming overland from Nazca. (Note: you can also fly from Cuzco.) Spend a day leisurely relaxing around the city's rambling colonial center (and acclimatizing to the altitude), paying a visit to the citadel-sized Monasterio de Santa Catalina and the frozen ice princess at the Museo Santury.

From here, choose between a two- or three-day guided excursion into the

(2) Cañón del Colca. The first option is an overnight visit, done largely by car, with spurts of hiking and a stop at a lookout that allows for great views of the El Misti volcano. The second option is for the trekking set, and involves walking from **(3) Cabanaconde** to **(4) Chivay** – or vice versa – staying at simple village guesthouses along the way.

Afterwards, return to a final day (or two) of rest in Arequipa – an opportunity to enjoy spicy cuisine and a vibrant nightlife.

La Catedral, Arequipa (p114)

PHOTOGRAPHER: KARL LEHMANN

Discover Nazca, Arequipa & the South

Man playing guitar, Paracas
PHOTOGRAPHER: JEFFREY BECOM

PISCO & PARACAS

🖉056 / POP 58,200

An important port situated 235km south of Lima, Pisco and the nearby town of Paracas are generally used as bases to see the abundant wildlife of the Islas Ballestas. Pisco also shares its name with the national beverage, a brandy that is made throughout the region. The area is of historical and archaeological interest, having hosted one of the most highly developed pre-Inca civilizations – the Paracas culture from 700 BC until AD 400.

◎ Sights & Activities

Unfortunately, the 2007 earthquake left little standing of this once pretty colonial city. However, the area's natural sights are still a wonder to behold. For tour operators, see p127.

RESERVA NACIONAL DE PARACAS   Nature Reserve (admission S5; ☺7am-6pm) This vast desert reserve occupies most of the Península de Paracas. About 2km beyond the entrance is the **park visitor center** (☺7am-6pm), which has kid-friendly exhibits on ecology. The bay in front of the complex is the best spot to see Chilean flamingos, and there's a walkway down to a **mirador** (lookout; Map p104), from where these can best be spotted (June through August).

A few hundred meters behind the visitor complex are the 5000-year-old remains of the **Paracas Necropolis**, a prominent pre-Inca culture known for its lavish textiles. A stash of more than

BETH WILLIAMS

Don't Miss **Islas Ballestas**

Although grandiosely nicknamed the 'poor man's Galápagos,' the Islas Ballestas make for a memorable excursion. The only way to see them is on a boat tour – and while the tours do not disembark onto the islands (they are protected), they do get you startlingly close to the wildlife. In general, an hour is spent cruising around the islands' arches and caves and watching herds of noisy sea lions sprawl on the rocks. The most common guano-producing birds in this area are the guanay cormorant, the Peruvian booby and the Peruvian pelican, seen in boisterous colonies several thousand strong. You'll also see cormorants, Humboldt penguins and, if you're lucky, dolphins.

On the outward boat journey, which takes about 1½ hours, you can't miss the famous three-pronged **Candelabra geoglyph** (Map p104), a giant figure etched into the sandy hills in the distance, more than 150m high and 50m wide. No one knows exactly who made the glyph, or when, or what it signifies, but theories abound.

Note: boats don't come equipped with cabins, so wear a hat, and dress to protect against the wind, spray and sun.

400 funerary bundles was found here, each wrapped in many layers of colorful woven shrouds for which the Paracas culture is famous.

Beyond this, on the southern tip of the peninsula, 6km away, lies the tiny village of **Lagunillas**, a fishing outpost where a few restaurants cook up their daily catch. From the village, the road continues on for a few kilometers to a parking area near a **clifftop lookout**

(Map p104), which has grand views of the ocean and a sea-lion colony. Other seashore life around the reserve includes flotillas of jellyfish, some of which reach about 70cm in diameter with trailing stinging tentacles of 1m. Swimmers beware!

TAMBO COLORADO   Inca Ruins
(off Map p104; admission S9; ☾dawn-dusk)
This early Inca lowland **outpost**, about

Reserva Nacional de Paracas

Reserva Nacional de Paracas

45km northeast of Pisco, was named for the red paint that once completely covered its adobe walls. It's one of the best-preserved sites on the south coast and is thought to have served as an administrative base and control point for passing traffic. From Pisco, it takes about an hour to get here by car. Hire a taxi for half a day (S50) or take a tour from Pisco (S60, two-person minimum).

 Tours & Guides

Prices and services for tours of Islas Ballestas and Reserva Nacional de Paracas are usually very similar. The better tours are escorted by a qualified naturalist who speaks Spanish and English. Most island boat tours leave daily around 8am and cost around S35 per person, but do not include a S1 dock fee. Tours of the reserve can be combined with an Islas Ballestas tour to make a full-day excursion (S60).

Established tour operators:

Milsy Tours (☏ 53-5204; www.milsytours.com; San Francisco 113, Pisco)

Paracas Explorer (Map p104; ☏ 53-1487, 54-5089; www.pparacasexplorer.com; Paracas 9)

Paracas Overland (☏ 53-3855; www. paracasoverland.com.pe; San Francisco 111, Pisco)

DISCOVER NAZCA, AREQUIPA & THE SOUTH PISCO & PARACAS

Sleeping

Pisco

HOSTAL VILLA MANUELITA
Guesthouse **$$**

(☎ 53-5218; www.villamanuelitahostal.
com; San Francisco 227; s/d/tr incl breakfast
S70/95/125; @) Heavily renovated post-
earthquake, this hotel still achieves the
grandeur of its colonial foundations.
Plus, it's conveniently located half a
block from the plaza.

HOSTAL TAMBO COLORADO
Guesthouse **$**

(☎ 53-1379; www.hostaltambocolorado.com;
Bolognesi 159; s/d/tr S50/60/90; @) This
guesthouse is run by a delightful couple
who will instill in you true pride for
Pisco – both the town and the beverage!
Breakfast, from S6, is offered in a sunny
outdoor sitting area.

Paracas

HOTEL EL MIRADOR
Hotel **$$**

(Map p104; ☎ 54-5086; hotel@elmiradorhotel.
com; Km 20 Carr Paracas; s/d/tr incl breakfast
S102/138/178; @ 🏊) Hidden in the sand
dunes before the entrance to Paracas,
El Mirador is a peaceful oasis. Many
rooms afford ocean views, while others
look onto the pool and inner courtyard,
and out to the dunes beyond.

HOTEL LIBERTADOR PARACAS
Resort **$$$**

(Map p104; ☎ in Lima 01-518-6500; www
.libertador.com.pe; Av Paracas 178; r from
US$230; ❄ @ 🏊) This exclusive resort ho-
tel borders the bay and boasts beautiful
grounds, an infinity pool, and fast-boat
tours of the Islas Ballestas from its
private dock.

POSADA DEL EMANCIPADOR
Hotel **$$**

(Map p104; ☎ 95-667-2163; www.posadadel
emancipador.com; Av Paracas 25; s/d/tr/ste incl
breakfast US$50/60/70/130; @ 🏊) Perfect
for families and large groups, this
modern complex has well maintained,
charmingly decorated rooms and bungalows with kitchenettes that overlook
the pool or the ocean.

HOTEL EL CÓNDOR
Hotel **$$**

(Map p104; ☎ 53-2818; elcondor@hotelcondor.
com; Lote 4, Santo Domingo; s/d/tr incl breakfast
US$50/80/90; @ 🏊) A tranquil spot to
lounge; rooms are a bit generic and look
out to either the bay or the garden. It has
a full-service restaurant with a fireplace
and a cozy common room.

 Eating & Drinking

Pisco

EL DORADO
Peruvian **$**

(☎ 53-4367; Progreso 171; menús from S9, mains
S8-35; ⏱ 6:30am-11pm) For breakfasts as
well as tasty *menús* (set meals) this res-
taurant is a hit, and it's located smack
dab on the Plaza de Armas.

TABERNA DE DON JAIME
Tavern **$$**

(☎ 53-5023; San Martín 203; ⏱ 4pm-2am) This
smoky tavern is a favorite showcase for
artisanal wines and piscos. On weekends, the crowds show up to dance to live
Latin and rock tunes into the wee hours.

Paracas

JUAN PABLO
Peruvian **$$**

(Map p104; ☎ 79-6806, 79-7240; Blvd Turístico;
mains S15-40; ⏱ 7am-9pm) Probably the
best of the restaurants with a waterfront
view, Juan Pablo is a winner for fresh
seafood and offers breakfast for those
departing early to the Islas Ballestas.

EL CHORITO
Seafood **$$**

(Map p104; ☎ 54-5045; Paracas s/n; mains
S20-30; ⏱ noon-9pm) Located a few blocks
from the waterfront at the back of the
Hostal Santa Maria. It offers mostly
seafood specialties.

ℹ Information

There's no tourist office in Pisco, but travel
agencies (see p104), the *municipalidad* (town hall)
on the main plaza and police (☎ 53-2884; San
Francisco 132, Pisco; ⏱ 24hr) help when they can.

Everything else you'll need is found around the
Plaza de Armas, including internet cafes and a
branch of the BCP (Perez de Figueroa 162, Pisco),
which has a Visa/MasterCard ATM and changes
US dollars and traveler's checks.

Central Pisco is fairly safe, but the market and nearby beaches should be avoided after dark and visited in groups during the day. Muggings are not unheard of, even on busy pedestrian streets, so always take a taxi after sunset.

ⓘ Getting There & Around

Pisco is 6km west of the Carr Panamericana Sur, and only buses with Pisco as the final destination actually go there. Ormeño (☏ 53-2764; San Francisco, Pisco) offers multiple daily departures to Lima and points south, including Nazca and Arequipa.

A number of companies offer service between Lima and the El Chaco beach district of Paracas and stop at various points in the area. These include the following:

Cruz del Sur (☏ 53-6336) Stops at a hotel about 2km outside the center of town.

Oltursa (☏ in Lima 01-708-5000; www.oltursa.com.pe) Stops at the Hilton Doubletree Hotel.

Ormeño (☏ 53-2764) Stops at the plaza. Buy tickets through Paracas Explorer (☏ 53-1487, 54-5089; www.pparacasexplorer.com; Paracas 9).

A short taxi ride around Pisco costs S3.

HUACACHINA
☏ 056 / POP 200

This tiny oasis is surrounded by towering sand dunes that encircle a picturesque lagoon. (It is featured on the back of Peru's S50 note.) Graceful palm trees, exotic flowers and attractive antique buildings testify to the bygone glamour of this resort, which was once a playground for the Peruvian elite. These days, it's totally ruled by an international party crowd. The only way to get to Huacachina is by taxi from Ica (S5 one way).

🤸 Activities

You can rent sandboards for S5 an hour to **slide**, **surf** or **ski** your way down the irresistible dunes, getting sand lodged into all manner of bodily nooks and crannies. (Though softer, warmer and safer than snowboarding, don't be lulled into a false sense of security – people have seriously injured themselves doing this.) Many hotels offer thrill-rides in *areneros* (dune buggies). They then stop at the top of the soft slopes, from where you can slide down and be picked up at the bottom.

The going rate for tours at the time of research was S45 (plus a S4 fee that must be paid upon entering the dunes).

🛏 Sleeping & Eating

HOTEL MOSSONE
Hotel **$$$**
(☏ 21-3630; reservas@dematourshoteles.com; s/d/tr/ste from S186/235/265/292; ❄ ≋ @) Housed in an old mansion, the

Flask of local pisco, Arequipa.
PHOTOGRAPHER: BRENT WINEBRENNER

Detour:
Ica

If you're visiting Pisco, Paracas or Huacachina, a short day trip will take you to Ica, where you can visit wineries and see Peru's famous grape brandy – pisco – being made from scratch. Bodegas (wineries) can be visited year-round, but the best time is during the grape harvest from late February until early April. A few recommended spots:

Bodega El Catador (☎40-3295; off Carr Panamericana Sur Km 334; ⏱tours & tastings 9:30am-7pm) is a friendly bodega, located less than 10km north of Ica. It lets tourists join in a symbolic stomping of the grapes during February and March, and runs free tours and tastings all year. It also has a restaurant.

Bodega Vista Alegre (☎23-2919; Camino a La Tinguina, Km 2.5; ⏱8am-noon & 1:45-4:45pm Mon-Fri, 7am-1pm Sat), about 3km northeast of Ica, in the La Tinguiña district, is the easiest of the large commercial wineries to visit.

Bodega Tacama (☎22-8395; www.tacama.com; ⏱9am-4:30pm) is another place producing the right stuff. It's about 11km northeast of Ica and offers interesting tours of its industrial facilities.

While you're in town, don't miss an opportunity to visit the excellent **Museo Regional de Ica** (☎23-4383; Ayabaca, cuadra 8; admission S11.50, cameras S5; ⏱8am-7pm Mon-Fri, 9am-6pm Sat & Sun), which contains some superb examples of Paracas weavings.

Most wineries are only accessible by car. It is best to hire a taxi for the day.

Mossone has simple yet stylish rooms carefully arranged around a courtyard. All rooms have hot showers and TVs. There's also an upscale restaurant with a convivial waterfront bar.

HOSTERÍA SUIZA   Hotel $$
(☎ 23-8762; www.hostesuiza.5u.com; Balneario de Huacachina; s/d/tr/q incl breakfast S95/155/198/245;❄) At the far end of the road beside the oasis, this is a tranquil alternative: no pumping bars, just an elegant, characterful building and a restful garden.

CAROLA DEL SUR LODGE
                              Budget Hotel $
(☎ 21-5439; Perotti s/n; s/d/tr S45/60/75; ❄@) The lodge has a poolside bar, and ample green space occupied by hammocks and a roaming turtle. Rooms are simple but secure. The on-site pizzeria

serves varied plates as well as tasty cocktails, and is open late.

NAZCA & AROUND
☎056 / POP 57,500 / ELEV 590M

This sun-bleached expanse was largely ignored by the outside world until 1939, when North American scientist Paul Kosok flew across the desert and noticed a series of extensive lines and figures etched below, which he initially took to be an elaborate pre-Inca irrigation system. In fact, what he had stumbled across was one of ancient Peru's most impressive and enigmatic achievements: the world-famous Nazca Lines. Today the small town of Nazca is continually inundated by travelers who show up to marvel and scratch their heads over the purpose of these mysterious lines, which

Nazca

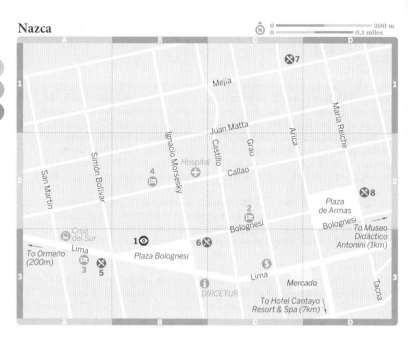

Nazca

were declared a Unesco World Heritage Site in 1994.

Sights & Activities

NAZCA LINES   Archaeological Site
The best-known lines are found in the desert 20km north of Nazca. By far the best way to appreciate them is to get a bird's-eye view from a *sobrevuelo* (overflight). For more on the lines and their possible meaning, turn to p110.

Flights are taken in light aircraft (three to nine seats) in the morning and early afternoon. Passengers are usually taken on a first-come, first-served basis, with priority given to tours or those who have made reservations in Lima. The standard 30-minute overflight costs from US$50 to US$85. Most agencies also offer combination flights that include a visit to the glyphs in the nearby community of Palpa. These take 45 minutes and cost from US$85 per person. Tour packages include transportation to the aerodrome, about 2km outside town.

Companies that fly over the lines have ticket offices near the aerodrome. Note that the aerodrome charges a departure tax of S20. Companies include the following:

Aerolca (☎ 52-2434, in Lima 01-445-0859; www.aeroica.net; Hotel La Maison Suisse, Carr Panamericana Sur Km 447)

Alas Peruanas (☎ 52-2444; www
.alasperuanas.com)

MIRADOR
Lookout

(observation tower; admission S1) This metal
lookout tower on the Pan-American
Hwy, about 20km north of Nazca, has
an oblique view of three of the figures:
the lizard, tree and hands (or frog). If you
decide to walk around the desert here,
note the signs warning of landmines.
These are a reminder that walking on the
lines is strictly forbidden: it irrepara-
bly damages them. Some tours (from
S50 per person, p127) combine a trip
to the Mirador with visits to another
natural viewpoint and the Maria Reiche
Museum.

MUSEO MARIA REICHE
Museum

(Museo de Sitio; admission S5; ⊙9am-6pm)
When Maria Reiche, the German math-
ematician and long-term researcher of
the Nazca Lines, died in 1998, her house,
which stands another 5km north along
Carr Panamericana Sur, was made into
a small museum. You can see where she
lived, amid the clutter of her tools and
sketches – and pay your respects at her
tomb.

MUSEO DIDÁCTICO ANTONINI
Museum

(☎ 52-3444; http://digilander.libero.it/
MDAntonini; Av de la Cultura 600; admission
S15, cameras S5; ⊙9am-7pm) This excellent
archaeological museum boasts an aqueduct running through the back garden,
as well as interesting reproductions of
burial tombs, a collection of ceramic pan
flutes and a scale model of the lines. You
can get an overview of both the Nazca
culture and a glimpse of most of Nazca's
outlying sites here.

PLANETARIUM MARIA REICHE
Planetarium

(☎ 52-2293; www.concytec.gob.pe/ipa/ini-
cio_ingles.htm; Nazca Lines Hotel, Bolognesi s/n;
admission S20) This small planetarium
is in the Nazca Lines Hotel and offers
scripted evening lectures on the lines
with graphical displays on a domed pro-

jection screen that last approximately
45 minutes.

CHAUCHILLA CEMETERY
Cemetery

(admission S5) The most popular excursion from Nazca, this cemetery, 30km
south of the city, will satisfy any urges
you have to see ancient bones, skulls
and mummies. Dating back to the Ica-
Chincha culture around AD 1000, the
mummies were, until recently, scattered
haphazardly across the desert, left by
ransacking tomb-robbers. Now they are
seen carefully rearranged inside a dozen
or so tombs. Organized tours last three
hours and cost US$10 to US$35 per
person.

CAHUACHI
Ruins

A dirt road travels 25km west from
Nazca to Cahuachi, the most important known Nazca center, which is still
undergoing excavation. It consists of
several pyramids, a graveyard and an
enigmatic site called Estaquería, which
may have been used as a place of mum-
mification. Tours from Nazca take three
hours and cost US$15 to US$50 per
person.

Other Activities

Beat the heat and go swimming at the
Nazca Lines Hotel (☎ 52-2993; Bolognesi
s/n; admission incl snack & drink S22).

Off-the-beaten-track expeditions
offered by several outdoor outfitters
include **sandboarding** trips down
nearby Cerro Blanco (2078m), the
highest-known sand dune in the world.
Half-day **mountain-biking** tours cost
about the same (US$25).

 ## Tours & Guides

Some established agencies:

Alegría Tours (☎52-3775; www.
alegriatoursperu.com; Hotel Alegría, Lima 168)

Nasca Trails (☎52-2858; www.nascatrails.
com.pe; Bolognesi 550)

 # Sleeping

CASA ANDINA   Hotel $$$

(☎ 52-3563; www.casa-andina.com; Bolognesi 367; r incl breakfast buffet from S272; 🌢@🖥) This reliable chain offers the best value of any of Nazca's upmarket hotels. Rooms have eminently stylish, modern furnishings with bold color schemes, air-con and cable TV.

HOTEL CANTAYO SPA & RESORT
                            Spa Hotel $$$

(☎ 52-2283; www.hotelcantayo.com; r incl breakfast from US$110; 🌢@🖥) About 7km south of town is this lovely Italian-run spot that is overrun with monkeys, alpacas and a family of peacocks – plus, there are horses for riding. The rooms are top quality and have varied decor, including four-poster beds and Japanese-style furnishings.

HOTEL ORO VIEJO   Hotel $$

(☎ 52-3332, 52-1112; www.hoteloroviejo.net; Callao 483; s/d/tr/ste incl buffet breakfast S100/140/170/315; 🌢@🖥) This charming hotel retains a familial atmosphere and has airy, well-furnished rooms, a welcoming common lounge, and an exquisitely tended garden.

HOTEL ALEGRÍA   Hotel $$

(☎ 52-2702; www.hotelalegria.com; Lima 168; s/d/tr incl breakfast US$40/50/60; 🌢@🖥) A classic travelers' haunt, this hotel has a restaurant, manicured grounds and a pool. Narrow, carpeted rooms come with TVs and fans.

 # Eating & Drinking

RESTAURANTE EL HUARANGO
                            Peruvian $

(☎ 52-2141; Arica 602; mains S7-20; ⏰8am-10pm) Serves top-rated *criollo* coastal

---

The Nazca Lines: Ancient Mysteries in the Sand

Spread across an incredible 500 sq km of arid, rock-strewn plain in the Pampa Colorada (Red Plain), the Nazca Lines (p108) remain one of the world's great archaeological mysteries. Consisting of more than 800 straight lines, 300 geometric figures (geoglyphs) and, concentrated in a relatively small area, some 70 spectacular animal and plant drawings (biomorphs), the lines are almost imperceptible at ground level. It's only when viewed from above that they form their striking network of enormous stylized figures and channels, many of which radiate from a central axis. The figures are mostly etched out in single continuous lines, while the encompassing geoglyphs form perfect triangles, rectangles or straight lines running for several kilometers across the desert.

The lines were made by the simple process of removing the dark sun-baked stones from the surface of the desert and piling them up on either side of the lines, thus exposing the lighter, powdery gypsum-laden soil below. The most elaborate designs represent animals, including a 180m-long lizard, a monkey with an extravagantly curled tail, and a condor with a 130m wingspan. There's also a hummingbird, a spider and an intriguing owl-headed person – popularly referred to as an astronaut because of its goldfish-bowl-shaped head.

Endless questions remain. Who constructed the lines and why? And how did they know what they were doing when the lines can only be properly appreciated from the air? The truth is still out there.

fare (a blend of Spanish, African and Asian influences) and has a rooftop terrace. All meals come with a complimentary pisco sour to boot!

RESTAURANT LOS ANGELES

Peruvian $$

(☑ 79-8240; Bolognesi 266; menús from S13, mains S8-24; ☺noon-11pm) This meticulously run eatery is known for delicious soups and salads, as well as tasty vegetarian options. It's owned by a local, English-speaking tour guide.

RESTAURANTE PAULITA

Snacks $

(☑ 52-3854; Tacna 450; menús S6; ☺7:30am-8:30pm) With two tiny open-air tables facing the Plaza de Armas, this place serves home-style set meals, fruit salads and cakes.

GRUMPY'S

International $$

(☑ 95-607-3295; Lima 174; mains S15-25; ☺7am-11pm) Close to the bus stations, this thatched-roof eatery gets rave reviews from homesick backpackers. In addition to traditional *criollo* fare, it also offers filling sandwiches and breakfasts.

ⓘ Information

Internet cafes abound.

BCP (Lima 495) Has a Visa/MasterCard ATM and changes US dollars and traveler's checks.

DIRCETUR (Parque Bolognesi, 3rd fl) The government tourist information office; can recommend local tour operators.

Hospital (☑ 52-2586; Callao s/n; ☺24hr) For emergency services.

ⓘ Getting There & Around

Air

People who fly into Nazca normally fly over the Nazca Lines and return the same day to Lima. Aerodiana (☑ in Lima 01-447-8540, 01-445-7188; www.aerodiana.com.pe) offers overflight tour packages departing from Lima.

Bus & Taxi

Nazca is a major destination for buses on the Carr Panamericana Sur and is easy to get to from Lima

Detour:
Reserva Nacional Pampas Galeras

This **national reserve** is a vicuña (threatened wild relatives of alpacas) sanctuary high in the mountains 90km east of Nazca on the road to Cuzco. It is the best place to see these shy animals in Peru. Every year in late May or early June is the **chaccu**, when hundreds of villagers round up the vicuñas for shearing and three festive days of traditional ceremonies. Full-day or overnight tours from Nazca cost US$30 to US$90 per person.

or Arequipa. Services to Lima and Arequipa leave in the late afternoon or evening. The following long-haul companies are recommended:

Cruz del Sur (☑ 52-3713)

Ormeño (☑ 52-2058)

A taxi from central Nazca to the aerodrome, 2km from the town, costs about S4.

AREQUIPA

☑054 / POP 864,300 / ELEV 2350M

Rocked by volcanic eruptions and earthquakes nearly every century since the Spanish arrived in 1532, Peru's second-largest city doesn't lack for drama. Locals sometimes say 'When the moon separated from the earth, it forgot to take Arequipa,' waxing lyrical about the city's grand colonial buildings, built from an off-white volcanic rock called *sillar* that dazzles in the sun. As a result, Arequipa has been baptized the *Ciudad Blanca* (White City). Its distinctive stonework graces the stately Plaza de Armas, along with countless beautiful colonial churches, monasteries and mansions scattered throughout the city.

Arequipa

0 ——————— 200 m
0 ——————— 0.1 miles

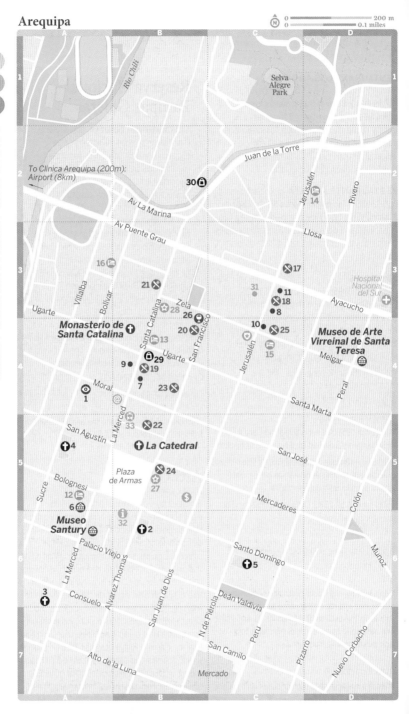

Selva Alegre Park

Río Chili

To Clínica Arequipa (200m);
Airport (8km)

Juan de la Torre

Jerusalén

Rivero

Av La Marina

Av Puente Grau

Llosa

30

Hospital Nacional del Sur

Ayacucho

16

Villalba

Bolívar

Ugarte

21

Zela

Santa Catalina

28

26

17

31

11

18

8

Monasterio de Santa Catalina

20

13

San Francisco

10

25

Museo de Arte Virreinal de Santa Teresa

Jerusalén

15

Melgar

9

29

19

Ugarte

Moral

1

7

23

Peral

Santa Marta

33

22

San Agustín

4

La Catedral

San José

Sucre

Bolognesi

12

6

24

27

Plaza de Armas

Mercaderes

Colón

Muñoz

Museo Santury

32

2

La Merced

Palacio Viejo

Álvarez Thomas

Santo Domingo

5

3

Consuelo

San Juan de Dios

Deán Valdivia

N de Piérola

Perú

Pizarro

Nuevo Corbacho

Alto de la Luna

San Camilo

Mercado

Ayacucho

14

Arequipa

Interestingly, the city boasts a fervid independence from Lima (at one point, they even designed their own passport and flag) – as well as a spicy regional cooking that has produced some of Peru's most famous dishes.

History

Evidence of pre-Inca settlement by indigenous peoples from the Lake Titicaca area leads some scholars to think the Aymara people first named the city (*ari* means 'peak' and *quipa* means 'lying behind' in Aymara; hence, Arequipa is 'the place lying behind the peak' of El Misti). However, another oft-heard legend says that the fourth *inca* (king), Mayta Cápac, was traveling through the valley and became enchanted by it. He ordered his retinue to stop, saying, *'Ari, quipay,'* which translates

as 'Yes, stay.' The Spaniards refounded the city on August 15, 1540, a date that is remembered with a weeklong fair.

 Sights

MUSEO SANTURY   Museum
(☑ 20-0345; www.ucsm.edu.pe/santury; La Merced 110; admission S15; ⊙9am-6pm Mon-Sat, 9am-3pm Sun) Officially the Museo de la Universidad Católica de Santa María, this museum exhibits 'Juanita, the ice princess' – the frozen body of an Inca maiden sacrificed on the summit of Nevado Ampato, a snow-covered volcano to the northwest of Arequipa, more than 500 years ago. Guided tours culminate in a respectful viewing of the frozen mummy, preserved in a carefully monitored glass-walled exhibition freezer.

PLAZA DE ARMAS
Plaza

Arequipa's main plaza showcases the city's *sillar* architecture and the cathedral. The colonnaded balconies overlooking the plaza are a great place to relax over a snack or a coffee.

FREE ### LA CATEDRAL
Cathedral

(☎ 23-2635; ⏰ 7-11:30am & 5-7:30pm Mon-Sat, 7am-1pm & 5-7pm Sun) To one side of the square is the cathedral, the only one in Peru that stretches the length of a plaza. The interior is simple and airy, with a luminous quality. In 1870, Belgium provided the impressive organ, said to be the largest in South America, though damage during shipping condemned the devout to wince at its distorted notes for more than a century.

FREE ### IGLESIA DE LA COMPAÑÍA
Church

(☎ 21-2141; ⏰ 9am-12:30pm & 3-6pm Mon-Fri, 11:30am-12:30pm & 3-6pm Sat, 9am-noon & 5-6pm Sun) This Jesuit church is noted for its ornate main facade and principal altar, which is carved in the *churrigueresque* style (an intricate decorative motif from the late Spanish baroque) and completely covered in gold leaf. To the left of the altar is the **San Ignacio chapel** (admission S4), with a polychrome cupola smothered in murals of tropical flowers, fruit and birds, among which mingle warriors and angels.

MONASTERIO DE LA RECOLETA
Monastery

(☎ 27-0966; La Recoleta 117; admission S5; ⏰ 9am-noon & 3-5pm Mon-Sat) This musty monastery was constructed on the west side of the Río Chili in 1648 by Franciscan friars. Bibliophiles will delight in the huge library, which contains more than 20,000 dusty books and maps. There is also a well-known museum of Amazonian artifacts collected by the missionaries, and an extensive collection of pre-Conquest artifacts and religious art of the Cuzco School.

MUSEO DE ARTE VIRREINAL DE SANTA TERESA
Convent

(☎ 28-1188; Melgar 303; admission S10; ⏰ 9am-5pm Mon-Sat, 9am-1pm Sun) This gorgeous 17th-century Carmelite convent and museum is filled with priceless votive *objets d'art*, murals, precious metalworks,

Arequipa's fine colonial architecture

OTHER IMAGES

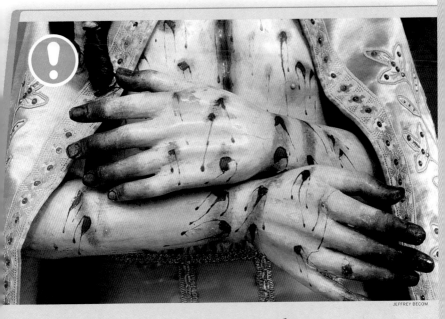
JEFFREY BECOM

Don't Miss **Monasterio de Santa Catalina**

Occupying a whole block in Arequipa is one of the most fascinating religious buildings in Peru. This **convent** – a 20,000-sq-meter citadel complex – is a disorienting place with twisting passageways, ascetic living quarters, period furnishings and religious art. In other words: a photographer's paradise.

Santa Catalina was founded in 1580 by a rich widow, Doña María de Guzmán, who chose her nuns from only the best Spanish families. Traditionally, going into a nunnery meant living a chaste life of poverty. However, in this privileged convent, nuns had servants or slaves, and would often invite musicians to have parties and live it up. After three centuries of these hedonistic goings-on, Pope Pius IX sent a strict Dominican nun to straighten things out. Sister Josefa Cadena arrived like a hurricane in 1871, sending rich dowries back to Europe and freeing the myriad servants and slaves, some of whom stayed on as nuns.

Today, visitors can examine several **cloisters** – including **the Great Cloister**, which is bordered by a chapel – as well as unusual sights, such as the **Profundis Room**, a mortuary where the dead were mourned. (Lining the walls here: portraits of deceased nuns, all painted posthumously.) Other sights include the **communal kitchen**, a small square (called **Zocodober Square**) and the **cell** of the legendary Sor Ana, a nun known for her eerily accurate predictions.

NEED TO KNOW

📞 22-9798; www.santacatalina.org.pe; Santa Catalina 301; admission S30; 🕑 9am-5pm, last entry 4pm, plus 7-9pm Tue & Thu

colonial-era paintings and other historical artifacts. A charming shop at the front of the complex sells baked goods and rose-scented soap made by the nuns.

MUSEO ARQUEOLÓGICO CHIRIBAYA
Museum

(☎ 28-6528; www.museochiribaya.org; La Merced 117; admission S15; ⏱8:30am-7pm Mon-Fri, 9am-3pm Sun) Containing an impressive collection of artifacts from the pre-Inca Chiribaya civilization, this **archaeological museum** has well-preserved textiles and the only pre-Inca gold collection in southern Peru. The museum is housed in a beautiful colonial mansion that features design details by French engineer Gustave Eiffel, of Eiffel Tower fame.

CASA DE MORAL
Colonial Mansion

(☎ 21-4907; Moral 318; admission S5; ⏱9am-5pm Mon-Sat) Built in 1730, the *casona* (mansion) is named after the 200-year-old mulberry tree in its central courtyard. Owned by the BCP

bank, the house is now one of the most accessible to visitors. Bilingual guides are available.

 **Activities**

Trekking

Most agencies can arrange an array of off-the-beaten-track routes – through canyons, gorges and charming rural villages – to suit your timeline and fitness level. Although you can trek year-round, the best (driest) time is from May to November. There is more danger of rockfalls in the canyons during the wet season (between December and April). Easier treks in the Cañón del Colca can be beautifully lush during the wet season, however, while more remote trails, especially those in the Cañón del Cotahuasi, become inaccessible.

For a list of recommended outfitters, see p127. For detailed information on the area's canyons, turn to p123.

Left: Head priest's quarters, Monasterio de la Recoleta (p114);
Below: Mummy on display at the Monasterio de la Recoleta's museum
PHOTOGRAPHER: (BOTH IMAGES) BRENT WINEBRENNER

Mountaineering

Looming 5822m above Arequipa, the city's guardian volcano **El Misti** is the most popular climb in the area. It is technically one of the easiest ascents of any mountain of this size in the world, but it's hard work nonetheless. The ascent generally takes two days (one day to reach a base camp at 4500m; another day to reach the summit). While this is not a technical climb, it does require you to be in excellent physical condition with some acclimatization to the altitude. You may also need an ice axe and crampons (supplied by area outfitters). A two-day trip will usually cost between US$50 to US$70 per person. The mountain is best climbed from July to November.

Other higher, more-difficult peaks can also be climbed. The best months for climbing are between April and December. Even in the drier months, temperatures drop to -29°C at the highest camps, necessitating very warm clothing. In addition, the Association of Mountain Guides of Peru warns that many guides offering journeys are uncertified and untrained. Climbers are advised to seek out reputable agencies with licensed guides who are trained in wilderness survival and rescue. The following companies are recommended:

Carlos Zárate Adventures (☎ 20-2461; www.zarateadventures.com; Santa Catalina 204)

Colca Trek (☎ 20-6217, 9-60-0170; www.colcatrek.com.pe; Jerusalén 401-B)

You can find gear at **Peru Camping Shop** (☎ 22-1658; www.perucampingshop.com; Jerusalén 410). For topographic maps, see Colca Trek, or the South American Explorers Club (p71) in Lima.

River Running

The **Río Chili**, which has a put-in point about 7km from Arequipa, is the most

117

If You Like…
Colonial Churches

The peaceful Arequipa suburbs of Yanahuara and Cayma offer a worthwhile afternoon excursion away from the city center – and a couple of picturesque, centuries-old churches.

1 IGLESIA SAN JUAN BAUTISTA
(Plaza, Yanahuara; admission free) Dating back to 1750, this graceful stone church has an ornate, baroque facade that features native elements among the traditional Catholic religious iconography. (Look for the feathered headdresses on the putti.) It also houses the highly venerated Virgen de Chapi, a virgin honored with her own fiesta on May 1. Nearby, at the side of the plaza, is a lookout with excellent views of Arequipa and El Misti. The church is located 1km west of central Arequipa, off of Av Puente Grau.

2 IGLESIA DE SAN MIGUEL ARCÁNGEL
(Cayma; admission free) This beautifully maintained baroque church, dating from 1730, is located in Cayma, the area dubbed 'El Balcón de Arequipa' (Arequipa's Balcony) because of its privileged views. The rectory annex is known as 'El Comedor de Bolívar' because liberator Simón Bolívar ate lunch here during Peru's independence wars. For a tip, the church's keeper may take you up to the tower, which has panoramic views.

frequently run local river, with a half-day trip suitable for beginners leaving almost daily from April to November (from US$25). Further afield, you can also do relatively easy trips on the **Río Majes**, into which the Río Colca flows. The most commonly run stretches pass Class II and III rapids.

The **Río Colca** is a dangerous, difficult trip, not to be undertaken lightly. A few outfitters will do infrequent trips to the easier sections, which can be found upriver.

Many trips are unavailable during the rainy season (between December and March), when water levels can be dangerously high. These rafting outfitters have been recommended by travelers:

Casa de Mauro (☏9-59-336-684; raftingguide@hotmail.com; Ongoro Km 5 s/n)

Cusipata (☏20-3966; www.cusipata.com; Jerusalén 408)

Majes River Lodge (☏83-0297, 9-59-797-731; www.majesriver.com)

Mountain Biking

Tailor-made mountain-biking trips at El Misti and other sites can be arranged. **Peru Camping Shop** (☏22-1658; www.perucampingshop.com; Jerusalén 410) rents bicycles for S9 per hour or S60 per day.

Tours & Guides

Some trekking agencies also offer quick two-day/one-night tours to the Cañón del Colca. These are mostly by car, but involve some hiking. A two-day jaunt runs between S65 to S225 per person, depending on the season, group size and level of the hotel you choose to stay at in Chivay.

Never accept tours from street touts. Guides usually speak some level of English. See the following agencies:

Carlos Zárate Adventures (☏20-2461; www.zarateadventures.com; Santa Catalina 204)

Colca Trek (☏20-6217, 9-60-0170; www.colcatrek.com.pe; Jerusalén 401-B)

Naturaleza Activa (☏69-5793; naturactiva@yahoo.com; Santa Catalina 211)

Pablo Tour (☏20-3737; www.pablotour.com; Jerusalén 400 AB-1)

Sleeping

LA CASA DE MELGAR Colonial Inn $$
(☏22-2459; www.lacasademelgar.com; Melgar 108; s/d/tr incl buffet breakfast US$43/53/63; @ 🛜) Housed in an 18th-century building, this hotel is

nonetheless fitted with all the expected creature comforts. High-domed ceilings and unique decor lend the entire place an old-world feel. Comfy beds and tucked-away inner patios help make this a romantic hideaway within the city limits.

CASABLANCA HOSTAL
Guesthouse **$**

(☎ 22-1327; www.casablancahostal.com; Puente Bolognesi 104; s/d/tr incl breakfast S70/120/150; @) In a beautifully renovated mansion directly off the Plaza de Armas, this guesthouse adds a touch of luxury at a great value. The stone innards lend it a gothic feel, while the terrace and eating area are inviting.

LA HOSTERÍA
Colonial Inn **$$**

(☎ 28-9269; lahosteria@terra.com.pe; Bolívar 405; s/d incl breakfast US$51/61) This picturesque colonial hotel with a flower-bedecked courtyard, offers light and quiet rooms (with minibar), carefully chosen antiques, a sunny terrace and a lounge. Apartment-style suites (US$68) on the upper floors have stellar city views.

HOTEL LA POSADA DEL MONASTERIO
Colonial Inn **$$**

(☎ 40-5728; www.hotelessanagustin. pe; Santa Catalina 300; s/d/tr incl buffet breakfast from S160/205/260; @ ☀) This hotel gracefully inhabits an architecturally mixed building combining the best of the Old and New Worlds. The comfortable modern rooms here have all the expected facilities. From the rooftop terrace there are fine views of the Santa Catalina convent across the street.

CASA AREQUIPA
B&B **$$**

(☎ 28-4219; www.arequipacasa.com; Av Lima 409, Vallecito; s/d US$55/65) Inside a cotton-candy pink colonial mansion in the gardens of suburban Vallecito, this gay-friendly B&B offers more than half a dozen guest rooms with fine design touches such as richly painted walls, pedestal sinks, antique handmade furnishings and alpaca wool blankets. A sociable cocktail bar is in the lobby.

LIBERTADOR CIUDAD BLANCA
Hotel **$$$**

(☎ 21-5110; www.libertador.com.pe; Plaza Bolívar s/n, Selva Alegre; r US$150-210, ste US$170-280; ❄ @ ☎ ☀) This is the grand dame of Arequipa's hotels, situated 1km north of the center. The stylish building is nicely set in gardens with a pool and playground. It has spacious rooms and opulent public areas with wi-fi access, plus it boasts a spa, sauna and fitness room.

Local guide, Chivay (p125).
PHOTOGRAPHER: MARK DAFFEY

Eating

CHICHA
Novoandina **$$$**

(☏ 28-7360; Santa Catalina 210; mains S25-39; ⏱noon-midnight Mon-Sat, to 9pm Sun) Gastón Acurio's well-known Arequipa outpost features noteworthy flavor fusions such as the *cuy laqueado* (a guinea-pig appetizer, with touches of corn and rocoto pepper) and *rocoto relleno* (a dessert version of the classic stuffed red pepper, with cream cheese and *manjar blanco*, a caramel sauce). The experience is rounded off with a tantalizing list of cocktails and service that leaves no detail unattended to.

NINA-YAKU
Novoandina **$$**

(☏ 28-1432; San Francisco 211; menús S35, mains S25-36; ⏱3-11pm) This nouveau-Peruvian eatery wouldn't look a bit out of place in downtown Manhattan. The modern menu includes reinventions of traditional *arequipeño* (inhabitants of Arequipa) tastes, with salads, sandwiches and tastebud-tingling desserts.

LA TRATTORIA DEL MONASTERIO
Italian **$$$**

(☏ 20-4062; Santa Catalina 309; mains S18-33; ⏱lunch from noon daily, dinner from 7pm Mon-Sat) A helping of epicurean delight has descended upon the Monasterio de Santa Catalina. The menu of Italian specialties was created with the help of superstar Peruvian chef Gastón Acurio, and is infused with the flavors of Arequipa.

CAFÉ CASA VERDE
Snacks **$**

(☏ 22-6376; Jerusalén 406; snacks S2-6; ⏱8am-6pm) This nonprofit courtyard cafe staffed by underprivileged kids is the perfect spot for a morning or afternoon break. It dishes up yummy German-style pastries and sandwiches. Attached is a local handicraft store where proceeds also go to helping kids in need.

RESTAURANT ON THE TOP
Peruvian **$$**

(☏ 28-1787; Portal de Flores 102; mains S14-32; ⏱11am-10pm) It's a hike up the stairs to this rooftop eatery, but well worth the view of the Plaza de Armas and mountains beyond. An enormous menu features everything from sandwiches to Alpaca steaks.

Las Quenas, Arequipa

BRENT WINEBRENNER

MIXTOS
Peruvian-Italian **$$**

(☎ 20-5343; Pasaje Catedral 115; mains S15-36; ⊗11:30am-9:30pm) A popular, quaint restaurant that serves mainly Italian and Peruvian seafood dishes. Try the enormous and flavorful *sudado de pescado* (fish stew) while enjoying the view from the outdoor balcony.

EL VIÑEDO
Peruvian **$$$**

(☎ 20-5053; www.vinedogrill.com; San Francisco 319; mains S20-50; ⊗noon-midnight) This intimate spot is one of the best places to knock back a steak or platters of traditional Peruvian food, all in an ornate Victorian atmosphere. The wine list is strong on South American varietals.

CREPISIMO
Creperie **$**

(☎ 20-6620; Alianza Francesa, Santa Catalina 208; mains S6-16; ⊗8am-11pm Mon-Sat, noon-11pm Sun) A cozy place to get your caffeine fix, this cafe has a crackling fireplace, balcony tables, board games and more than 100 kinds of sweet and savory crêpes filled with everything from Chilean smoked trout to exotic South American fruits.

RESTAURANTE GOPAL
Vegetarian **$**

(☎ 21-2193; Melgar 101B; menús S5, mains S4-11; ⊗8am-9pm) This basic cafe specializes in vegetarian versions of classic Peruvian dishes.

Drinking & Entertainment

DÉJÀ VU
Bar

(☎ 22-1904; San Francisco 319B; ⊗9am-late) With a rooftop terrace overlooking the church of San Francisco, this eternally popular haunt has a long list of crazy cocktails and a delicious happy hour. After dark, DJs keep the party going.

LAS QUENAS
Live Music

(☎ 28-1115; Santa Catalina 302; ⊗closed Sun) A traditional *peña* (bar or club featuring live folkloric music) that features nightly performances. The music varies, although *música folklórica* predominates.

If You Like...
Arequipeño Cooking

If you like the city's spicy regional cooking, do not miss an opportunity to visit a local *picantería* (homestyle restaurant), the best spots for sampling traditional dishes, such as the explosively spicy *rocoto relleno* (red peppers stuffed with ground meat and cheese). While you're at it, don't forget to wash it all down with *chicha*, the fermented corn beer that is typical of the Andes.

1 ARY QUEPAY
(☎20-4583; Jerusalén 502; mains S12-26; ⊗10:30am-10:30pm) This place, located in a colonial-style building, offers traditional plates including alpaca and *cuy* (guinea pig). There's enthusiastic Andean folk music most evenings.

2 LA NUEVA PALOMINO
(☎25-3500; Leoncio Prado 122; mains S14-29; ⊗lunch only) Definitely the local favorite, the atmosphere at this *picantería* is informal and can turn boisterous when groups of families and friends file in to eat and drink. The restaurant is located northwest of the Arequipa city center, about 500m east of the Río Chili off Av Puente Grau.

3 TRADICIÓN AREQUIPEÑA
(☎42-6467; www.tradicionarequipena.com; Av Dolores 111; meals S18-40; ⊗11:30am-6pm Mon-Fri, 11:30am-1am Sat, 8:30am-6pm Sun) This restaurant has mazelike gardens, live music, and offers a Sunday morning breakfast of *adobo de cerdo,* a traditional slow-cooked pork dish. It's 2km southeast of the center.

4 SOL DE MAYO
(☎25-4148; www.restaurantsoldemayo.com; Jerusalén 207, Yanahuara; menú S14, mains S18-47; ⊗11:30am-6pm) Serving good Peruvian food in nearby Yanahuara, Sol de Mayo has live *música folklórica* in the afternoons. You can combine a visit here with a stop off at the *mirador* (lookout), located in the Yanahuara district, northwest of downtown.

DADY'O DISCO PUB & KARAOKE
Dance Club
(Portal de Flores 112; admission S10; ⏰10pm-3am Thu-Sat) On the Plaza de Armas, raucous Dady'o throws open its doors for go-go dancing, live bands and karaoke, plus wickedly cheap beers.

 **Shopping**

CASONA SANTA CATALINA
Arcade
(🖉 28-1334; www.santacatalina-sa.com.pe; Santa Catalina 210; ⏰most shops 10am-6pm) A polished tourist complex features major export brands of pisco and alpaca knits.

INCALPACA FACTORY OUTLET
Outlet
(🖉 25-1025; www.incalpaca.com; Juan Bustamante s/n, Tahuayacani; ⏰9:30am-7pm Mon-Sat, 10:30am-3:30pm Sun) Located 2km west of downtown, this outlet for the Kuña brand of alpaca woolen goods also has a small petting zoo that houses the four types of American camelid.

MICHELL
Knits
(🖉 20-2525; www.michell.com.pe; Juan de la Torre 101; ⏰8am-12:30pm & 2:30-6pm) This complex functions as a tourist center for an international wool export company. It includes a well-presented commercial boutique, a museum detailing the process of wool production, and a small zoo and a cafe.

ℹ️ **Information**

Emergency

Policía de Turismo (Tourist Police; 🖉 20-1258; Jerusalén 315-317; ⏰24hr)

Internet

Access is generally cheap (S2 per hour) and easy to find.
Ciber Market (🖉 28-4306; Santa Catalina 115B; ⏰8am-10pm)

Medical Services

Clínica Arequipa (🖉 25-3424, 25-3416; Bolognesi at Puente Grau; ⏰8am-8pm Mon-Fri, 8am-12:30pm Sat) Arequipa's best.

Hospital Regional Honorio Delgado Espinoza (🖉 21-9702, 23-3812; Av Daniel Alcides Carrión s/n; ⏰24hr)

Paz Holandesa Policlinic (🖉 43-2281; www.pazholandesa.com; Av Jorge Chávez 527; ⏰8am-8pm Mon-Sat) An appointment-only travel clinic; English-speaking doctors.

Money

BCP (San Juan de Dios 125) Visa ATM; changes American dollars and traveler's checks.

Tourist Information

Indecopi (🖉 21-2054; Hipólito Unanue 100A, Urb Victoria; ⏰8:30am-4pm Mon-Fri) Deals with complaints against local tour operators and travel agencies.

iPerú airport (🖉 44-4564; 1st fl, Main Hall, Aeropuerto Rodríguez Ballón; ⏰10am-7:30pm); Plaza de Armas (🖉 22-3265; iperuarequipa@promperu.gob.pe; Portal de la Municipalidad 110; ⏰8:30am-7:30pm) Government-supported source provides helpful information.

ℹ️ **Getting There & Away**

Air

Arequipa's airport (code AQP; 🖉 44-3458) is about 8km northwest of the city center. LAN (🖉20-1224; Santa Catalina 118C) has daily flights to Lima and Cuzco.

Bus

Most bus companies have departures from the terminal terrestre or the smaller Terrapuerto bus terminal, both of which are together on Av Andrés Avelino Cáceres, less than 3km south of the city center (take a taxi for S4). Check in advance which terminal your bus leaves from and keep a close watch on your belongings while you're waiting there. There's a S1 departure tax from either terminal.

These are a few regional routes that are useful for sightseeing in the canyon country. These generally travel to Chivay (three hours), in the Cañón del Colca, with some continuing to Cabanaconde (six hours) at the end of the canyon's main road. Travel times and costs vary depending on road conditions. During the wet season (between December and April),

MARK DAFFEY

expect significant delays. Most buses are run by Andalucía (☎44-5089), while Reyna (☎43-0612) and Transportes Colca (☎42-6357) also offer services. Purchase tickets in advance.

Comfortable long-haul services are available to Puno, Cuzco, Nazca and Lima. The following operators are recommended:

Cruz del Sur (☎42-7375)
Ormeño (☎42-3855)

❶ Getting Around

To/From the Airport

An official taxi from downtown Arequipa to the airport costs around S15.

Taxi

A short ride around town costs around S3 to S4. Local taxi companies include Tourismo Arequipa (☎45-8888) and Taxitel (☎45-2020).

CANYON COUNTRY

A tour of the Cañón del Colca is the most popular excursion from Arequipa, but there are plenty of other adventurous pursuits in the area, from climbing the

city's guardian volcano El Misti to rafting the Majes canyon to visiting the petroglyphs at Toro Muerto. Most of these places can be visited by hiring a taxi or 4WD vehicle and driver.

Reserva Nacional Salinas y Aguada Blanca

The paved road from Arequipa climbs northeast past El Misti and Chachani to this **national reserve** (☎ 054-25-7461; www.inrena.gob.pe/areasprotegidas/rnsalinas/main.html; admission free; ⏱24hr), which covers 367,000 hectares at an average elevation of 4300m. Here, vicuñas are often sighted – as well as alpacas and llamas. Past the reserve, the increasingly bumpy road continues through bleak altiplano (Andean plateau) and over the highest point of 4800m, from where the snowcaps of Nevado Ampato can be seen. (Flamingos may also be seen around here between January and April.) From here, the route drops spectacularly into the Cañón del Colca before ending up at the dust-choked village of Chivay.

DISCOVER NAZCA, AREQUIPA & THE SOUTH | CANYON COUNTRY

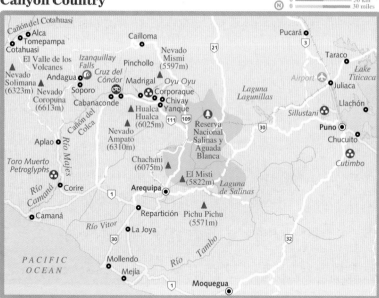

Cañón del Colca

This 100km-long **canyon** is set among high volcanoes (6613m-high Coropuna and 6310m-high Ampato are the tallest) and ranges from 1000m to more than 3000m in depth. For years there was raging controversy over whether or not this was the world's deepest canyon at 3191m, but recently it ranked a close second to neighboring Cañón del Cotahuasi, which is just more than 150m deeper. Amazingly, both canyons are more than twice as deep as the Grand Canyon in the USA.

Despite its depth, the Cañón del Colca is geologically young. The Río Colca has cut into beds of mainly volcanic rocks, which were deposited less than 100 million years ago along the line of a major fault in the earth's crust. Though cool and dry in the hills above, the deep valley and generally sunny weather produce frequent updrafts on which soaring condors often float by at close range. Vizcachas (a burrowing rodent closely related to the chinchilla) are also common around

the canyon rim, darting furtively among the rocks. In the depths of the canyon it can be almost tropical, with palm trees, ferns and even orchids in some isolated areas.

The local people are descendants of two conflicting groups that originally occupied the area, the Cabanas and the Collagua. In pre-Hispanic times, these two groups used to distinguish themselves by performing cranial deformations. Nowadays, they use distinctively shaped hats and intricately embroidered traditional clothing.

To visit most of the points of interest in the Cañón del Colca, all foreigners are required to purchase a *boleto turístico* (tourist ticket; S35). If you are taking an organized tour, this expense is generally not included. If you are traveling independently, tickets can be purchased on most public buses entering or leaving Chivay, or in the town of Cabanaconde. Half of the proceeds from this ticket go to Arequipa for general maintenance and conservation of local tourist attractions, while the other half goes to the national agency of tourism.

For more information on trekking in the area, see p116. For shorter, two-day tours, see p127.

Chivay

☎ 054 / POP 6300 / ELEV 3630M

At the head of the Cañón del Colca, this provincial capital is a small, dusty transportation hub that sees waves of tourists breeze through as part of organized tours from Arequipa. The town itself affords enchanting views of snowcapped peaks and terraced hillsides, and serves as a logical base for exploring the valley.

◉ Sights & Activities

At the Casa Andina hotel, a tiny **astronomical observatory** (☎ 53-1020; Huayna Cápac s/n; admission S18) has a nightly sky show. The price includes a 30-minute explanation and chance to peer into the telescope.

Chivay's famous **La Calera hot springs** (admission S10; ⊙4:30am-8pm) are 3.5km to the northeast of the village by road. There are large, clean pools, showers, changing rooms, a snack shop and a small ethnographic museum. The mineral-laden water leaves the ground at 85°C and is said to have curative properties. There are frequent *colectivos* (collective taxis; S1) from around the main plaza in Chivay to the springs, or you can walk by following the road downhill past the market and taking a left.

Mountain bikes in varying condition can be hired from travel agencies on the plaza or at **BiciSport** (☎ 9-58-807-652; Zaramilla 112; ⊙9am-6pm) behind the market for about S5 per day.

🛏 Sleeping

CASA ANDINA　　　　Hotel **$$$**
(☎ 53-1020, 53-1022; www.casa-andina. com; Huayna Cápac s/n; s/d incl breakfast S302/354.50) This tourist complex re-creates a rustic idyll with quaint stone-and-thatch cottages, neatly sculptured bushes and garden views of snowcapped peaks. Local artisans and a shaman who tells fortunes with coca leaves are around in the evenings. Currency exchange is available.

HOSTAL LA PASCANA　Guesthouse **$$**
(☎ 53-1001; hrlapascana@hotmail.com; Siglo XX 106; s/d/tr incl breakfast S54.50/69/86.50) It's a very good option with carpeted, well-decorated rooms and firm mattresses.

HOSTAL ESTRELLA DE DAVID
　　　　　　　　　　Guesthouse **$**
(☎ 53-1233; Siglo XX 209; s/d/tr S20/20/40) A simple, clean *hospedaje* (guesthouse) with bathrooms and there are some rooms with cable TV.

🍴 Eating & Drinking

INNKAS　　　　　　Cafe-Bar **$**
(☎ 53-1209; Plaza de Armas 705; snacks S2-8; ⊙7am-11pm) Built in the oldest house in Chivay, this spot is perfect for a decent morning cup of coffee or an evening beer and pool game.

CASA BLANCA　　　　Peruvian **$$**
(☎ 9-51-462-944; Plaza de Armas; mains S10-25; ⊙9am-10pm) Friendly service, a fireplace and there's a pick-and-choose *menú* that includes unusual local specialties.

ℹ Information

The police station is located next to the *municipalidad* (town hall). Internet access is available from various internet cafes. There's an ATM located on Calle Salaverry, one block west of the plaza.

ℹ Getting There & Around

The bus terminal is a 15-minute walk from the plaza. There are almost hourly departures to Arequipa, while buses to Cabanaconde leave four times daily.

Chivay to Cabanaconde

The road following the south bank of the upper Cañón del Colca leads past several villages that still use the Inca terracing that surrounds them.

Yanque

☏054 / POP 1900

About 7km from Chivay, this peaceful rural village has an attractive **18th-century church** on the main plaza. Also on the plaza is the excellent **Museo Yanque** (admission S5; ☻9am-5pm Mon-Sat), a university-run cultural museum with displays on traditional canyon life. From the plaza, a 30-minute walk down to the river brings you to a local hot springs called **Baños Chacapi** (admission S5; ☻3am-7pm).

In Yanque, a number of simple, family-run guesthouses were started as part of a local development project and offer lodging for S15 per night. Travelers have recommended **Sumaq Huayta Wasi** (☏83-2174; Cusco 303), just two blocks from the main plaza.

Out on the main road, you'll find the delightful **Tradición Colca Albergue** (☏42-4926, 20-5336; www.tradicioncolca.com; Av Colca 119; dm/s/d incl breakfast S35/120/140), a European-run country inn away from the bustle of the city. It offers a sauna and Jacuzzi, massage services, and a restaurant, cafe and bar with a billiards table. Rates include an afternoon guided hike to the pre-Inca ruins of Oyu Oyu.

Corporaque to Madrigal

Across the river from Yanque, in the village of Corporaque, is the excellent **La Casa de Mamayacchi** (www.lacasademamayacchi.com; d/tr incl breakfast from S224/294). Hidden away downhill from the main plaza, this inn is built with traditional materials and boasts awesome canyon views. The cozy rooms have no TVs, but there's a games library, fireplace and bar. Make reservations through the **Mamayacchi's Arequipa office** (☏24-1206; Jerusalén 606).

Between Yanque and Corporaque, you'll pass a sign marking the ruins of **Oyu Oyu**. The remnants of this pre-Incan settlement are reached by a half-hour hike up the hill, after which you can continue to a waterfall whose source is the runoff from Nevado Mismi.

Further up the northern side of the canyon is the upmarket **Colca Lodge** (☏53-1191; www.colca-lodge.com; s/d/tr/q incl

Locals celebrate a festival with *chicha* and music, Yanque

breakfast S596/660/660/724, ste from S937),
a large and attractive stone-and-thatch
hotel tucked into a bend of the river
amid Inca terracing. Activities including
horseback riding, fishing, rafting and
mountain biking can be arranged here.
There is a spa and hot springs. For
reservations, visit the **Colca's Arequipa
office** (054-20-2587, 054-20-3604;
Benavides 201).

Yanque to Pinchollo

Further along the main road on the
south side of the canyon, the spread-
ing landscape is remarkable for its Inca
and pre-Inca terracing, which goes on
for many kilometers and is some of the
most extensive in Peru.

The next big village along the main
road is **Pinchollo**, about 30km from
Chivay. From here, a trail climbs toward
Hualca Hualca (a snowcapped volcano
of 6025m) to an active geothermal area
set amid wild and interesting scenery.

Cruz del Cóndor

From Pinchollo, the road continues
past **Cruz del Cóndor** (admission with
boleto turístico), a famed viewpoint, also
known locally as Chaq'lla. A large family
of Andean condors nests by the rocky
outcrop and, with lots of luck, they can
occasionally be seen gliding effortlessly
on thermal air currents rising from
the canyon. It's a mesmerizing scene,
heightened by the spectacular 1200m
drop to the river below and the sight of
Nevado Mismi reaching over 3000m
above the canyon floor on the other side
of the ravine.

Cabanaconde

054 / POP 2700 / ELEV 3290M

The quiet rural town of Cabanaconde
makes an ideal base for some spectacular hikes into the canyon. It's a very small
place, with just a few simple spots to stay
and eat. If you plan on staying here, bring
everything you'll need to stay a couple
of days, including plenty of Peruvian
currency in small bills and any trekking
equipment, such as sleeping bags.

Activities

The most popular short trek is one that
involves a steep two-hour hike down
to **Sangalle** (also popularly known as
'the oasis') at the bottom of the canyon,
where several sets of basic bungalows
and camping grounds have sprung up
(from about S10 per person). There
are two natural pools for swimming,
the larger of which is claimed by Oasis
Bungalows, which charges S5 to swim.
The return trek to Cabanaconde is a stiff
climb and thirsty work; allow about three
to four hours.

The charming village of **Tapay** is a
destination in itself and is also a base
camp for other shorter treks, including
to **Bomboya**. Another popular trekking
route leads into the canyon via a more
gradual path (but steep nonetheless!)
and crosses the river before arriving
in **San Juan de Chuccho**. Here,
accommodation is available at the **Casa
de Rivelino** (per night S10), where there
are bungalows with warm water and a
simple restaurant. From here, trekkers
have the option of continuing on to
Sangalle to stay a second night before
returning to Cabanaconde.

Area outfitters can suggest a wealth
of other day hikes and adventures. You
can buy topographic and trekking maps
from **Colca Trek** (054-20-6217, 9-60-
0170; www.colcatrek.com.pe; Jerusalén 401B) in
Arequipa.

Tours & Guides

Local guides can be hired by consulting
with your hostel or the *municipalidad* in
Cabanaconde. The going rate for guides
is S30 to S60 per day.

Sleeping & Eating

Accommodation options are extremely
limited. There are a couple of cheap local
restaurants near the main plaza.

PACHAMAMA BACKPACKER HOSTAL
Guesthouse **$**

(9-59-316-322, 25-3879; www.pachamama home.com; San Pedro 209; dm S12, r per person with/without bathroom S30/20, all incl breakfast; @) This cozy backpackers' haunt is owned by a young Peruvian-Belgian couple who have made readers feel right at home by providing simple, yet clean, rooms. The owners are also a great source of info about guides and alternative treks, and can provide hiking gear such as maps and binoculars. Complimentary breakfasts include yummy crêpes.

HOSTAL VALLE DEL FUEGO
Guesthouse **$**

(hvalledelfuego@hotmail.com; dm S20, s/d/tr incl breakfast S35/50/70; @) This budget spot has a full bar, solar-powered showers and owners who are knowledgeable about trekking. To make a reservation, call **Pablo Tours** (054-20-3737) in Arequipa.

LA POSADA DEL CONDE
Hotel **$$**

(40-0408, 83-0033; www.posadadelconde. com; San Pedro s/n; s/d/tr incl breakfast US$25/30/40) This small modern hotel mostly has double rooms, but they are well cared for with clean bathrooms. Rates often include a welcome *mate* (herbal tea) or pisco sour in the downstairs restaurant.

HOTEL KUNTUR WASSI
Hotel **$$**

(81-2166; www.arequipacolca.com; Cruz Blanca s/n; s/d/ste incl breakfast US$45/55/70; @) This charming hotel is built into the hillside, with stone bathrooms, trapezoidal windows overlooking the gardens and a nouveau-rustic feel. Suites boast enormous bathtubs; there's a bar, restaurant, library, laundry and currency exchange.

ⓘ Getting There & Away

Buses for Chivay and Arequipa via Cruz del Cóndor leave Cabanaconde from the main plaza several times per day. Departure times change regularly; inquire locally.

Left: El Misti volcano (p117), on the outskirts of Arequipa;
Below: Toro Muerto petroglyphs
PHOTOGRAPHER: (LEFT) GRANT DIXON, (BELOW) JANE SWEENEY

Toro Muerto Petroglyphs

A fascinating, mystical site in the high desert, Toro Muerto (meaning 'Dead Bull') is named for the herds of livestock that commonly died here from dehydration as they were escorted from the mountains to the coast. A barren hillside is scattered with white volcanic boulders carved with stylized people, animals and birds. Archaeologists have documented more than 5000 such petroglyphs spread over several square kilometers of desert. Though the cultural origins of this site remain unknown, most archaeologists date the mysterious drawings to the period of Wari domination, about 1200 years ago.

From Corire, you can catch a taxi to take you to where the petroglyphs start (from S40 round-trip). Bring plenty of water, sunblock and insect repellent. The petroglyphs are visited most conveniently on full-day 4WD tours from Arequipa.

El Valle de los Volcanes

El Valle de los Volcanes is a broad valley, west of the Cañón del Colca and at the foot of Nevado Coropuna (6613m), famed for its unusual geological features. The valley floor is carpeted with lava flows from which rise many small (up to 200m high) cinder cones, some 80 in total, aligned along a major fissure, with each cone formed from a single eruption.

The lava flows have had a major influence on drainage in the valley, constraining the Río Challahuire against the east side of the valley to form the Laguna de Chachas. The outlet of the Laguna de Chachas then runs beneath lava flows for nearly 20km before emerging at Laguna Mamacocha.

The 65km-long valley surrounds the village of **Andagua**, near the snowy summit of Coropuna. Visitors seeking

129

a destination full of natural wonders and virtually untouched by travelers will rejoice in this remote setting. From Andagua, a number of sites can be visited by foot or car. Popular hikes are to a nearby *mirador* at 3800m and to the 40m-high **Izanquillay Falls**, which are formed where the Río Andahua runs through a narrow lava canyon to the northeast of town. There are some *chullpas* (funerary towers) at **Soporo**, a two-hour hike or half-hour drive to the south of Andagua. En route to Soporo are the ruins of a pre-Columbian city named **Antaymarca**.

There are several cheap and basic hostels and restaurants in Andagua. Some tour companies also visit El Valle de los Volcanes as part of multiday 4WD tours that may include visits to the Cañón del Cotahuasi and Chivay.

Cañón del Cotahuasi

While the Cañón del Colca has stolen the limelight for many years, it is actually this remote canyon, 200km northwest of Arequipa as the condor flies, that is the deepest known canyon in the world. It is around twice the depth of the Grand

Canyon, with stretches dropping below 3500m. While the depths of the ravine are only accessible to experienced river runners (p117), the rest of the fertile valley is also rich in striking scenery and trekking opportunities. The canyon also shelters several traditional rural settlements that currently see only a handful of adventurous travelers. Wild vicuña can also be spotted here on the high altiplano.

◉ Sights & Activities

The main access town is appropriately named **Cotahuasi** (population 3800) and is at 2620m above sea level on the southeast side of the canyon. Northeast of Cotahuasi and further up the canyon are the villages of **Tomepampa** (10km away; elevation 2500m) and **Alca** (20km away; 2660m), which also have basic accommodations. En route you'll pass a couple of **thermal baths** (admission S2).

From the Sipia Bridge, about an hour outside of town, you can begin a number of interesting hikes into the deepest parts of the canyon. Forty-five minutes up the trail, the **Sipia**

Cañón del Cotahuasi

waterfall is formed where the Río Cotahuasi takes an impressive 100m tumble. Another 1½ hours on a well-trodden track brings you to **Chaupo**, an oasis of towering cacti and remnants of pre-Inca dwellings.

Trekking trips of several days' duration can be arranged in Arequipa (p116); some can be combined with the Toro Muerto petroglyphs, and, if you ask, they may return via a collection of dinosaur footprints on the west edge of the canyon.

 Sleeping & Eating

HOSTAL JUSTITO   Guesthouse   **$**
(☎ 054-58-1141; off main plaza, Cotahuasi; s/d without bathroom S15/30, s/d with bathroom S20/40) Rooms at this Cotahuasi guesthouse are adequate and the owners are happy to host travelers. It's centrally located.

HOSTAL HATUNHUASI   Guesthouse   **$**
(☎ 054-58-1054, in Lima 01-531-0803; hatun huasi@gmail.com; Centanario 309, Cotahuasi; s/d S25/50) A friendly Cotahuasi guesthouse, it has plenty of rooms situated around an inner courtyard, as well as hot water. Food can be prepared upon request, and the owners are good sources of information for travelers.

HOSTAL ALCALÁ   Guesthouse   **$**
(☎ 054-83-0011; Plaza de Armas, Alca; dm/s/d without bathroom S10/15/25, s/d with bathroom S25/40) In Alca, this spot has a good mix of clean rooms and prices, including some of the most comfortable digs in the entire valley. There is 24-hour hot water here.

POSADA INTI   Guesthouse   **$**
(posada_inti@yahoo.com; near main plaza, Tomepampa; r per person S20) A clean, convenient place to crash in Tomepampa, rooms have private bathrooms with hot water and local TV.

ⓘ Getting There & Away

The 420km bus journey from Arequipa, half of which is on unpaved roads, takes 12 hours (S25). More than three-quarters of the way there, the road summits a 4500m pass between the huge glacier-capped mountains of Coropuna and Solimana (6323m) before dropping down to Cotahuasi. Reyna (☎43-0612) and Transportes Alex (☎42-4605) both offer services.

Laguna de Salinas

This lake (4300m above sea level), east of Arequipa below Pichu Pichu and El Misti, is a salt lake that becomes a white salt flat during the dry months of May to December. Its size and the amount of water in it vary from year to year depending on the rainfall. During the rainy season it is a good place to see all three flamingo species, as well as myriad other Andean water birds.

You can hike around the lake. One-day minibus tours from Arequipa cost about S150 per person; mountain-biking tours are also available (p118).

Puno & Lake Titicaca

Worlds collide around Lake Titicaca. Here, the desolate altiplano (Andean plateau) meets the storied peaks and fertile valleys of the Andes. Green, sun-dazed islands contrast with coffee-colored dirt farms. It's a place where priests bless taxis and lawyers sacrifice llamas, where you'll find crumbling colonial cathedrals, rolling hills and impossibly high mountains. A place where women in bowler hats tend llamas and entrepreneurs count their money.

In the midst of this lays the magnificent Lake Titicaca, shimmering its distinct shade of navy blue – its gemlike islands and gentle shores a centuries-old agricultural paradise. According to Andean belief, this was the lake that gave birth to the sun, as well as the father and mother of all the Incas, Manco Cápac and Mama Ocllo. It is the heartland of South America. Rug up and jump in.

The shores of Lake Titicaca
PHOTOGRAPHER: ERIC WHEATER

Puno & Lake Titicaca

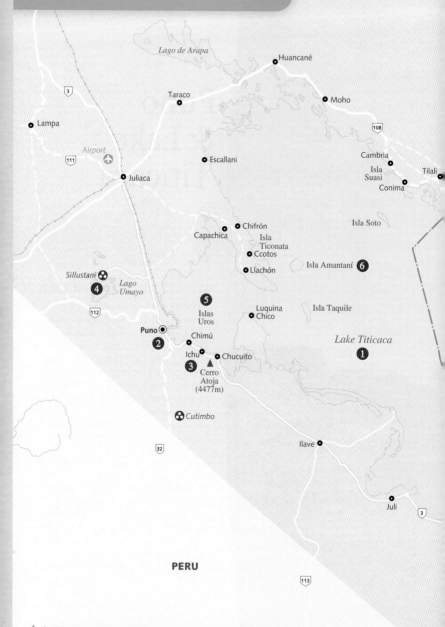

Lago de Arapa

Huancané

Taraco

Moho

Lampa

108

Airport

Cambria

Escallani

Isla
Suasi

Tilali

111

Juliaca

Conima

Isla Soto

Chifrón

Capachica

Isla
Ticonata

Sillustani

Ccotos

Isla Amantaní **6**

4

Lago
Umayo

Llachón

112

Islas
Uros

5

Luquina
Chico

Isla Taquile

Puno

2

Chimú

Lake Titicaca

Ichu

Chucuito

1

3

Cerro
Atoja
(4477m)

Cutimbo

32

Ilave

Juli

3

PERU

113

N

0   50 km
0   30 mi

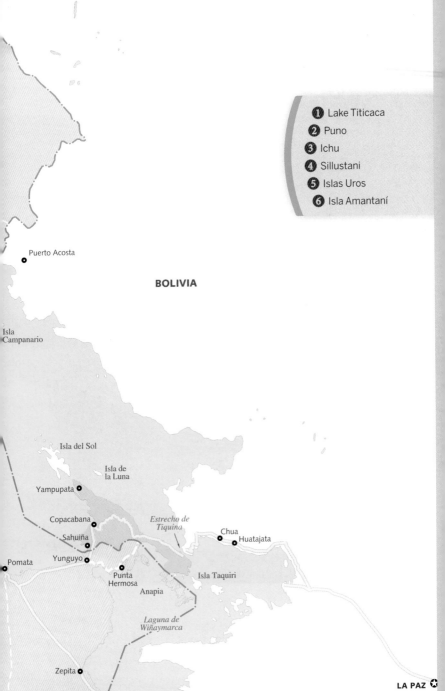

1 Lake Titicaca
2 Puno
3 Ichu
4 Sillustani
5 Islas Uros
6 Isla Amantaní

Puerto Acosta

BOLIVIA

Isla Campanario

Isla del Sol

Isla de la Luna

Yampupata

Copacabana

Estrecho de Tiquina

Chua

Huatajata

Sahuiña

Pomata

Yunguyo

Punta Hermosa

Isla Taquiri

Anapia

Laguna de Wiñaymarca

Zepita

LA PAZ

Desaguadero

Puno & Lake Titicaca Highlights

1

Around Lake Titicaca

Islands that float. A glittering lake. Ancient sites littered with towering tombs that once held entire clans. The Puno and Lake Titicaca area offer the traveler some truly wondrous, surreal sites. Who needs novels laced with magical realism, when you can see it all live?

Need to Know

HIGH SEASON June to August is when it's driest – but very cold; pack warm duds for nighttime. **ADJUST FOR ALTITUDE** This area is mind-bendingly high. Allow extra time to adjust. **For more coverage, see p155.**

Lake Titicaca Don't Miss List

BY BEN ORLOVE, ANTHROPOLOGIST RESEARCHING THE ANDES SINCE THE '70S AND AUTHOR OF *LINES IN THE WATER: NATURE AND CULTURE AT LAKE TITICACA*

1 HIT THE ISLANDS INDEPENDENTLY

If you go on a tour, you're going to be with lots of people, making it difficult to explore. If you can, hire a boat independently. In addition to seeing less-visited islands, you'll be able to poke in and out of the reeds, where you'll find incredible bird life – such as the flightless grebe, which is endemic to the area. They can hold their breath underwater for what seems like an impossible length of time. But they will surface – keep an eye out for them!

2 TAKE A MORNING WALK AROUND CHUCUITO

If you start at the main plaza in Chucuito (p154), you can hike up Cerro Atoja. It's not a hard walk and there are plenty of trails. You'll get views of the lake, but the best part is this extraordinary contrast of densely settled agricultural areas with the more isolated pastures higher up. Within hours, you can experience different worlds.

3 VISIT LAMPA

This is an extraordinary little town (p155) to the northwest of Puno, via Juliaca. It's one of those places that is preserved in amber – the center of town is lined with low, two-story buildings with balconies. It's a real flavor of how things used to be in the Andes.

4 EAT ADVENTUROUSLY

A particularly good local dish is *ají de lengua*, a spicy stew made with beef tongue. Pay close attention to the potatoes you're served – there will likely be different kinds, each with a unique flavor.

5 DON'T BE AFRAID TO GO IN THE RAINY SEASON

In the dry season, the roads are better. But in the rainy season, the entire area feels incredibly alive. If you take walks in more rural areas, you'll see these slow-flying iridescent beetles and sometimes even hummingbirds.

Gaze Upon Elaborate Costumes

Puno is Peru's *capital folklórico* (folkloric capital), where colorful processions can take over the city's streets for days – especially in early February, during the fiesta in honor of the Virgen de la Candelaria. Have a look at some of the extravagant costumes worn during these elaborate street parades at Puno's tiny, quirky Coca Museum (p145).

Locals enjoying the festivities, Isla Taquile

Visit Awe-Inspiring Funerary Towers

Massive towers of granite dot the altiplano around Sillustani (p152), where the ancient Colla people (a pre-Inca tribe) built massive cylindrical tombs in which entire family groups were interred. Known as *chullpas*, some of them reached a staggering height of 12m. In a country chock full of unusual sights, this is bound to be somewhere near the top of the list.

ERIC WHEATER

Hike to a Peaceful Ruin

ERIC WHEATER

3

Just south of Puno, the diminutive lakeside community of Ichu (p153) offers the opportunity for a short hike up to a multilayered temple complex with unimpeded 360-degree views – totally unencumbered by tour groups. (A great photo op.) The walk will take you through sleepy farmlands to an overgrown complex – a rare opportunity to have an ancient site all to yourself.

SEAN CAFFREY

5

Set Foot on a Floating Island

The Islas Uros (p155) offer an experience like no other: the opportunity to visit buoyant islands crafted entirely out of *totora* reeds. These inhabited floating settlements were begun by the Uros people centuries ago – as a way of getting away from the conquering Collas and Incas. Just remember: you're not on solid ground. Watch your step!

6

Shack Up with a Local Family

You haven't quite experienced a country until you've broken bread with its people. Isla Amantaní (p157), in the middle of Lake Titicaca, offers an opportunity to do more than that: live with them for a night or two. You'll be cooking over open fires and perhaps even joining in a traditional dance. An experience you'll likely never forget.

Puno & Lake Titicaca's Best...

Churches

○ **Catedral de Puno** (p144) Puno's majestic baroque cathedral, completed in 1757

○ **Iglesia de Santiago de Apostol** (p155) Lampa's main church contains the odd sight of St James on a taxidermied horse *and* a replica of Michelangelo's *Pietà*

○ **Templo de Santo Domingo** (p154) In Chucuito, see the altiplano's oldest church, founded in 1534

Pre-Columbian Sites

○ **Sillustani** (p152) Cylindrical funerary towers that pre-date the Incas

○ **Taquile** (p156) A small island with Inca terraces – and a small set of ruins, like a cherry on top

○ **Chucuito** (p154) More stone phalluses than you can, er, shake a stone phallus at

○ **Cutimbo** (p153) Funerary towers, some featuring ancient carvings

Vistas

○ **Cerro Huajsapata** (p145) A Puno hillside crowned with a statue of the first Inca emperor

○ **Sillustani** (p152) Funerary towers on a spit of land partially encircled by the Lago Umayo

○ **Taquile** (p156) The hillsides of this fabled island offer views of the Bolivian Andes in the distance

○ **Ichu** (p153) 360-degree views from an abandoned temple site

Puno Restaurants

○ **Keros** (p148) Lots of Peruvian classics, including excellent soups

○ **IncAbar** (p148) A stylish spot that does international dishes with a local twist

○ **Ukuku's** (p148) The place for alpaca steaks and quinoa omelets

○ **Mojsa** (p147) A thoughtful range of Andean and international dishes

Need to Know

ADVANCE PLANNING

○ **One Month Before** Make arrangements for a homestay on one of the many islands in Lake Titicaca

○ **Three Weeks Before** Reserve a hotel in Puno – especially during high season (June through August)

○ **One Day Before** Arrange day trips to Sillustani, and other pre-Columbian sites in the area

ONLINE RESOURCES

○ **Puno Information Center** www.puno.org

○ **Chucuito Travel Information** www.chucuito.org

GETTING AROUND

○ **Air** Daily flights from and to Lima arrive and depart from the airport in Juliaca, about an hour north of Puno

○ **Boat** Tour companies make jaunts to the most popular islands in private boats; there are also public ferry services

○ **Bus** Minibuses connect the disparate points around town and beyond, while long-haul operators make the journey to Cuzco, Arequipa and Lima

○ **Train** Thrice-weekly service to Cuzco from November to March – a popular tourist attraction, complete with glass-walled observation car

○ **Walk** The way to get around the narrow streets of Puno – and Lake Titicaca's many car-less islands

BE FOREWARNED

○ **Stay Warm** Weather conditions are extreme, bring warm clothes

○ **Photography** Locals don't like being photographed without permission; be respectful

○ **Operating Hours** These can be erratic – especially in tiny villages

○ **Safety** Pickpocketing and muggings have been an issue at tourist sites; stay aware and travel in groups

Left: Catedral de Puno; **Above:** The view of Lake Titicaca from Isla Taquile

Puno & Lake Titicaca Itineraries

From jaunts to see ancient ruins to boat tours of unusual islands on the world's highest commercially navigable lake – you can cover the area's top spots in three days. Opt for five if you want to do some real exploring.

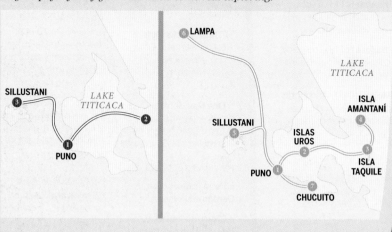

AROUND PUNO
3 DAYS
Highland Jaunts

Using the city as your base, this itinerary is perfect if you want a quick survey of the area.

On the first day, take it easy. (You're up high!) Leisurely explore the splendid sights of **(1) Puno**, such as its baroque cathedral and the charming Coca Museum, which in addition to providing all manner of information on coca, has excellent exhibits on the costumes worn during religious fiestas. If you're not winded, make a final stop at the Casa del Corregidor for a little colonial splendor and steamy cappuccino.

On day two, go on a tour of the remarkable, inhabited **(2) islands of**

Lake Titicaca. If guided tours are not your thing, you can just as easily take the ferry to one of these and wander around on your own. While you're exploring, look for intricate crafts made out of reeds. In the evening, retire to Puno for a little bit of highland nightlife.

The last day will be all about ruins – specifically *chullpas*, the massive funerary towers that look like spaceship capsules. Find them in abundance at **(3) Sillustani**, which also happens to have excellent views of the sapphire-blue Lago Umayo.

PUNO TO THE ISLANDS
Living Like a Local

Spend the first day engaged in leisurely activities in **(1) Puno**, given its literally breathtaking altitude of 3830m. Hit its cultural highlights, including the cathedral and the Coca Museum. The next day, set out for a one- to two-night homestay on one of the Lake Titicaca Islands. If you like your islands to float, then make arrangements to stay on the **(2) Islas Uros**. Otherwise, boat over to **(3) Isla Taquile** or, better yet, the less-visited **(4) Isla Amantaní**. Here, you'll cook over an open flame, watch the moon rise over the lake and generally enjoy a simple, rural existence.

Afterwards, return to Puno for some land-lubbing. Naturally, you'll want to

spend a day taking in the nearby pre-Columbian site of **(5) Sillustani**, and, if you have time, pop into the village of **(6) Lampa**, where a graceful colonial church contains a lovely baroque facade and some highly unusual decor. (Hello, taxidermy!) .

For your last full day in the area, head south to **(7) Chucuito**, where you can admire the stone phalluses at the Templo de la Fertilidad. Spend the last night back in town enjoying Puno's hospitable bars – and maybe a chilly cerveza, or two.

Totora reeds are used to make local boats and houses
PHOTOGRAPHER: ERIC WHEATER

Discover Puno & Lake Titicaca

At a Glance

○ **Puno** (p144) A bustling highland city in view of Lake Titicaca.

○ **Sillustani** (p152) A pre-Columbian site dotted with ancient funerary towers.

○ **Lake Titicaca Islands** (p154) Tiny islands protect traditional ways of life.

○ **Chuchito** (p154) A diminutive lakeside village is home to a temple with very large phalluses.

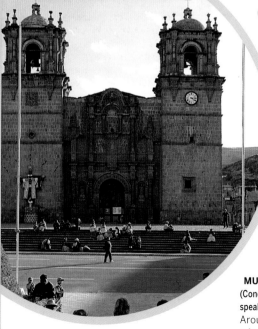

Catedral de Puno, Plaza de Armas
PHOTOGRAPHER: PAL/IMAGEBROKER

PUNO

♪ 051 / POP 120,200 / ELEV 3830M

Bustling, merrily claustrophobic Puno is known to most as a convenient jumping-off point for Lake Titicaca expeditions, but it may just capture your heart with its own rackety charm. A modern city that's a trade nexus between Peru, Bolivia and the two coasts of South America, it also serves as Peru's *capital folklórica* (folkloric capital). It's here that colorful parades in honor of the Virgen de la Candelaria (p152) are broadcast to the nation and solemn religious feasts can turn into entire days of music and dancing.

◉ Sights & Activities

On the western flank of the Plaza de Armas is Puno's baroque **cathedral** (admission free; ⊙10-11am & 3:30-6pm), which was completed in 1757.

CASA DEL CORREGIDOR
Historic Mansion
(♪ 35-1921; www.casadelcorregidor.pe; Deustua 576; admission free; ⊙10am-8pm) This 17th-century **mansion** houses a cultural center where exhibitions, workshops and concerts take place. There's also an art gallery and a bookshop. Its cafe-bar is a great place to hobnob with locals over cappuccino and pastries.

MUSEO CARLOS DREYER
Museum
(Conde de Lemos 289; admission incl English-speaking guide S15; ⊙9:30am-7pm Mon-Sat) Around the corner, this **museum** houses a fascinating collection of local archaeological artifacts and art. Upstairs there are three mummies and a full-scale fiberglass *chullpa* (funerary tower).

COCA MUSEUM
Museum

(☎ 36-5087; Deza 301; admission S5; ⏰ 9am-1pm & 3-8pm) Puno's tiny, quirky **Coca Museum** offers lots of interesting information – historical, medicinal and cultural – about the coca plant. But it's the display of traditional costumes that makes a visit here truly worthwhile – especially if you want to make sense of all the outfits worn in street parades.

CERRO HUAJSAPATA
Lookout

(400m west of the Plaza de Armas) A 10-minute walk west of the Plaza de Armas brings you to the top of this little **hill** crowned by a white, larger-than-life statue of the first Inca, Manco Cápac. The view is excellent but robberies have been reported.

MIRADOR DEL CONDOR
Lookout

(600m south of the Plaza de Armas) A stiff climb to this lookout is rewarded with fantastic views. It is helpfully signposted from the plaza. As with the Cerro Huajsapata, robberies have been an issue in the past.

 Tours

Agencies abound and competition is fierce, leading to relentless touting, undeliverable promises, and prices so low as to negate the possibility of profits for the people at the bottom of the totem pole. Some of the cheapest agencies have reputations for ripping off the natives on some of the floating islands (Amantaní and Taquile), with whom travelers stay overnight.

Island-hopping tours, even with the better agencies, can be formulaic. Seeing them independently is possible, allowing you to wander freely if you like. Otherwise, our research indicates that the following companies live up to their claims:

All Ways Travel
(☎ 35-3979; www.titicacaperu.com; Deustua 576, 2nd fl)

Edgar Adventures
(☎ 35-3444; www.edgaradventures.com; Lima 328)

Käfer Viajes y Turismo
(☎ 35-4742; www.kafer-titicaca.com; Arequipa 197)

Las Balsas Tours
(☎ 36-4362; www.balsastours.com; Tacna 240)

Nayra Travel
(☎ 36-4774, 975-1818; www.nayratravel.com; Lima 419, Office 105)

 Sleeping

COLÓN INN
Colonial Inn $$

(☎ 35-1432; www.titicaca-peru.com/colon1e. htm; Tacna 290; s/d S108/135; @) Another excellent choice: this is the only hotel in central Puno housed in an unmodernized colonial building (watch your head in the doorways). Rooms are smallish, while shared spaces are sumptuously colonial.

CASA ANDINA PUNO TIKARANI
Luxury Hotel $$$

(☎ 36-7803; www.casa-andina.com; Independencia 185; r from S307; @ 🛜) A short walk from the center, this Peruvian chain hotel is in sparkling order, with firm beds, quality furnishings and heating. There are also lofty public areas for lounging, a restaurant and free wi-fi access.

HOTEL LIBERTADOR LAGO TITICACA
Luxury Hotel $$$

(☎ 36-7780, in Lima 01-442-0166; www.liberta dor.com.pe; Isla Esteves; r/ste S967/1316; 🏊 @) This five-star local landmark fills its own private island in the western part of Lake Titicaca, connected to Puno by a causeway. All of the 108 luxurious rooms and 16 suites have fabulous views out over the lake, but furniture in the suites feels more board meeting than vacation getaway. There are beautiful gardens on the island's slopes and a collection of pet llamas.

INTIQA HOTEL
Hotel $$

(☎ 36-6900; www.intiqahotel.com; Tarapacá 272; s/d/tr S180/210/240; @) Jazzy and bright, Intiqa's refreshingly modern reception area will bring a smile to your face. The superb rooms do not

Puno

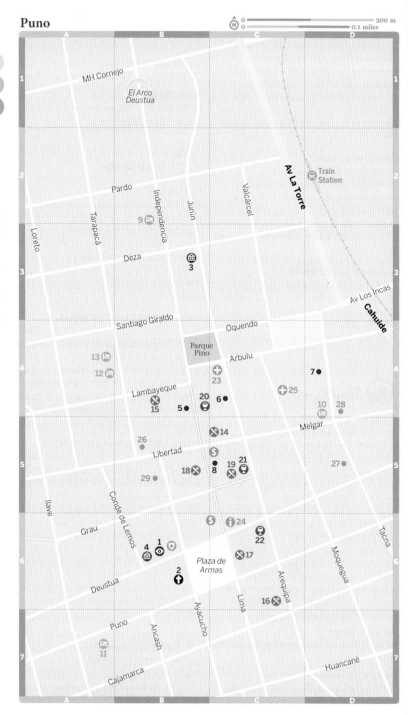

0 — 200 m
0 — 0.1 miles

MH Cornejo

El Arco
Deustua

Train
Station

Av La Torre

Pardo

Independencia

Junín

Valcárcel

Tarapacá

Loreto

9

Deza

3

Santiago Giraldo

Oquendo

Av Los Incas

Cahuide

Parque
Pino

Arbulu

13

12

23

7

25

Lambayeque

15

20

6

10   28

5

Melgar

14

26

Libertad

27

8

18   19   21

29

Ilave

Grau

Conde de Lemos

24

Tacna

22

4   1

17

Plaza de
Armas

2

Moquegua

Deustua

Ayacucho

Lima

Arequipa

16

Puno

Ancash

11

Huancané

Cajamarca

Puno

disappoint, with fabulously comfy beds, goose-down quilts, cable TV, indigenous art, and a bathtub in every room.

CONDE DE LEMOS INN   Hotel **$$**
(☎ 36-9898; www.condelemosinn.com; Puno 675-681; s/d S145/190) Housed in a startlingly jagged, glass-fronted ziggurat, bang on the Plaza de Armas, this small hotel has been recommended by many travelers for its personable staff and high standards.

DUQUE INN   Guesthouse **$**
(☎ 20-5014; Ayaviri 152; r per person with/without bathroom S20/15) Highly recommended for budget travelers, this spot has rooms with shared bathrooms that enjoy the best view in Puno at a ridiculously low price. Better yet: archaeologist owner Ricardo Conde takes guests on free tours, and at the time of research was in the process of constructing a scale model of an Egyptian pyramid on the hotel's roof. Eccentric gold! To find it, continue south along Ilave for three blocks beyond Huancané and turn right into Ayaviri.

POSADA DON GIORGIO
      Guesthouse **$$**
(☎ 36-3648; dongiorgio@titicacalake.com; Tarapacá 238; s/d S79/110; @) Don Giorgio offers very good value for money. It's small enough to provide personal service, and rooms have phones, cable TV and deep armchairs.

 Eating

MOJSA   Peruvian Classics **$**
(☎ 36-3182; Lima 635, 2nd fl; sandwiches from S10, mains from S18; ⊙ 8am-10pm) Mojsa lives up to its name, which is Aymara for 'delicious.' It has a thoughtful range of Peruvian and international food, a design-your-own salad option and a menu full of random and interesting facts. Did you know that astronauts eat *quinua* (quinoa)?

TULIPAN'S   Snacks **$**
(☎ 35-1796; Lima 394; sandwiches from S10, mains from S20) Highly recommended for its yummy sandwiches, big plates of meat and steaming piles of vegetables,

147

cozy Tulipan's is warmed by the pizza oven in the corner and the hordes of people swarming through the door.

LA BARCA
Seafood **$$**

(📞 36-4210; Arequipa 754; mains from S20; ⏱9am-4pm) Puno's best *cevichería* (ceviche restaurant). The world holds little greater pleasure than swigging down beer in its sunny green courtyard while scoffing piles of delicious marinated fish. The *tiradito* (Japanese-style ceviche without onions) is the house specialty, and is highly recommended if you like your food *picante* (hot).

INCABAR
International Fusion **$$**

(📞 36-8031; Lima 348; mains from S20; ⏱8:30am-10pm) This stylishly low-slung, cheerily chic restaurant does creative international food with a local twist. The massive Andean platter – bread, chips, to-die-for olives, cheese, ham, avocado and more – is a favorite.

COLORS
International Fusion **$$**

(📞 36-9254; Lima 342; mains from S20; ⏱7am-11pm; @) Colors is Puno's best kick-back couch cafe – with free wireless, naturally. The Andean-Greek-Middle East-Asian menu features fusion treats such as Andean cheese fondue and smoked trout ravioli in vodka sauce. There are reasonably priced breakfasts and great coffee, too. Hmm, you could lose a whole day here.

BALCONES DE PUNO
Peruvian Classics **$$**

(📞 36-5300; Libertad 354; mains from S20) Offers traditional local food with an emphasis on desserts, but what really sets it apart is its nightly show (7:30pm to 9pm), which stands out for the quality and enthusiasm of its performers, and the lack of cheesiness – no panpipe butchering of *El Cóndor Pasa* here.

UKUKU'S
Peruvian Classics **$$**

(Grau 172, 2nd fl; mains from S20) Crowds of travelers and locals thaw out in this toasty restaurant, which dishes up good local and Andean food (try alpaca steak with baked apples, or the quinoa omelet), as well as pizza, pasta, Asian-style vegetarian fare and espresso drinks.

KEROS
Peruvian Classics **$$**

(📞 36-4602; Lambayeque 131; mains from S20) Low-key Keros has a full bar and is

A plentiful supply of potatoes, Puno

BRENT WINEBRENNER

Don't Miss **The Yavari Project**

The **Yavari** is the oldest steamship on Lake Titicaca. In 1862 the *Yavari* and its sister ship, the *Yapura*, were built in Birmingham, England, of iron parts – a total of 2766 for the two vessels. These were shipped around Cape Horn to Arica, from where they were moved by train to Tacna, before being hauled by mule over the Andes to Puno – an incredible undertaking that took six years to complete.

The ships were assembled in Puno and the *Yavari* was launched on Christmas Day 1870. The *Yapura* later became a Peruvian Navy medical ship named the *BAP Puno*. Both had coal-powered steam engines, but due to a shortage of coal, the engines were fueled with dried llama dung!

After long years of service, the *Yavari* was decommissioned and the hull left to rust on the lakeshore. In 1982, Englishwoman Meriel Larken visited the forgotten boat and established the Yavari Project to buy and restore the vessel. Now open as a museum, the *Yavari* is moored behind the Sonesta Posada Hotel del Inca, about 5km from the center of town. A devoted crew gives regular guided tours.

NEED TO KNOW

☎ 36-9329; www.yavari.org; admission by donation; ☺ 8am-5pm

heated by a sometimes-stifling open fire. It's a great place to try *sopa a la criolla* (a creamy noodle soup with beef and peppers) and *tiradito,* both of which it prepares to perfection. Its motto is 'Eat like an Inca, pay like a peasant.'

Drinking & Entertainment

KAMIZARAKY ROCK PUB　　　Pub
(Grau 158) With our vote for southern Peru's best watering hole, this place feels like your best friend's living room. It

has a classic-rock soundtrack, unbelievably cool bartenders and liquor-infused coffee drinks essential for staying warm during Puno's bone-chilling nights.

SMOOTH JAZZ BAR   Bar
(☏ 36-4099; Arequipa 454) This hole-in-the-wall wins hearts for its phone-book-like list of drinks: three pages of cocktails and five different kinds of alcoholic hot tea are just the beginning. Videos blasting from the TV are more likely to be Rod Stewart than Miles Davis, but 34 different piscos later, who cares?

EKEKO'S   Dance Club
(Lima 355, 2nd fl) Travelers and locals alike gravitate to this loud, ultraviolet dance floor splashed with psychedelic murals.

 **Shopping**

Artesanías (handicrafts) are sold in every second shop in the town center. You'll find musical instruments, scale models of reed islands, wool and alpaca sweaters, jewelry and other trinkets.

🛈 Information

Dangers & Annoyances

Puno's high altitude gives it extreme weather conditions. Nights get especially cold, particularly during the winter months of June through to August (high season), when temperatures can drop well below freezing. Meanwhile, days are very hot and sunburn is a common problem.

The elevation also means that travelers arriving directly from the coast run a real risk of getting *soroche* (altitude sickness; see p349). Plan on spending some time in Arequipa (2350m) or Cuzco (3326m) first to acclimatize, or take it very easy after arriving in Puno.

Robberies have been reported at the Mirador del Condor and Cerro Huajsapata. Go in the morning and preferably not alone. In addition, attacks on travelers have been reported on the city's outskirts. It is best to travel in groups.

Left: Calle Lima, Puno; **Below:** Crafting traditional embroidery, Islas Uros
PHOTOGRAPHER: (LEFT) RYAN FOX; (BELOW) EMILY RIDDELL

Emergency

Policía de Turismo (Tourist Police;
☎ 35-3988; Deustua 558; ⏱24hr) There
is also a policeman on duty in the *terminal
terrestre* bus station (24 hours) – ask around if
you need them.

Medical Services

Botica Fasa (☎ 36-6862; Arequipa 314; ⏱24hr)
A well-stocked pharmacy that's attended 24
hours – pound on the door late at night.

Medicentro Tourist's Health Clinic (☎ 36-
5909, 951-62-0937; Moquegua 191; ⏱24hr)
English spoken; will also come to your hotel.

Money

Various banks have 24-hour ATMs that dispense
soles and US dollars.
BCP (Jirón Lima 444)
Interbank (Lima at Libertad)

Tourist Information

iPerú (☎ 36-5088; Plaza de Armas, cnr Lima
& Deustua; ⏱8:30am-7:30pm) Helpful and
well-informed; also runs Indecopi, the
tourist-protection agency, which registers
complaints about travel agencies and
hotels.

ⓘ Getting There & Away

Air

The nearest airport is in Juliaca, about an hour
away. Hotels can book shuttle buses for around
S15. **LAN** (☎36-7227; Tacna 299), which has
daily flights to Lima, has an office in Puno.

Boat

There are no passenger ferries across the lake
from Puno to Bolivia, but you can take one- and
two-day tours on the lake with outfits such as
Transturin (☎35-2771; www.transturin.com;
Ayacucho 148) and **Crillon Tours** (☎35-1052,
35-1884; www.titicaca.com; Libertad 355).

Regular ferries to the Lake Titicaca Islands
depart from the port on the east side of town.

151

If You Like...
Fiestas & Folklore

If you like festivals, you've come to the right place. Puno is said to be the folkloric capital of Peru, boasting as many as 300 traditional dances and celebrating numerous fiestas throughout the year. The dazzlingly ornate costumes can range from strikingly grotesque masks and animal costumes to glittering sequined uniforms. Accompanying music uses a host of instrumentation, from Spanish-influenced brass and string instruments to percussion to wind instruments that have changed little since Inca times.

1 **LA VIRGEN DE LA CANDELARIA**
(Feb 2) The festival in honor of Puno's patron virgin is one of the most spectacular fiestas held in a city that is renowned for them. Celebrated over several days with masses and processions, it culminates with a thunderous street party on February 2, where thousands of splendidly attired dancers perform.

2 **PUNO WEEK**
(1st week Nov) Centered on Puno Day (November 5), this festival is celebrated in style, and marks the birth of the Inca Empire, when Manco Cápac and Mama Occlo first emerged from Lake Titicaca.

3 **EPIPHANY**
(Jan 6) Masked paraders take to the streets for the festival better known as Día de los Reyes (Three Kings Day), when celebrants honor the magi who bestowed gifts on the baby Jesus.

4 **FIESTA SAN JUAN DE DIOS**
(Feast of St John of God; Mar 8) This more demure religious procession honors the patron saint of the sick and hospitals, during which time his image is carried on a litter through the streets.

7 **FIESTA DE SAN DIEGO**
(Feast of St James; Jul 25) A big feast day on Isla Taquile, when dancing, music and general carousing last several days, and islanders make traditional offerings to Pachamama (Mother Earth).

Bus

The terminal terrestre (📞36-4737; Primero de Mayo 703), located about 300m east of downtown, houses Puno's long-distance bus companies, which offer services to Cuzco, Arequipa and beyond. Note that there's a departure tax of S1. Recommended companies include the following:

Ormeño (📞36-8176; www.grupo-ormeno.com.pe)

Tour Peru (www.tourperu.com.pe)

If you are looking for something more unique, Inka Express (📞36-5654; www.inkaexpress.com; Tacna 346) has luxury buses to Cuzco with panoramic windows, buffet lunch, English-speaking guide and pit stops at pre-Columbian and colonial sites en route. The whole deal will set you back S135 and take eight hours.

Train

The fancy Andean Explorer train to Cuzco, which includes a glass-walled observation car and lunch, costs S704. Trains depart from Puno's train station (📞36-9179; www.perurail.com; Av La Torre 224; ⏰7am-noon & 3pm-6pm Mon-Fri, 7am-3pm Sat) at 8am, arriving at Cuzco around 6pm. Services run on Monday, Wednesday and Saturday from November to March.

ℹ Getting Around

A short taxi ride anywhere in town costs S3. *Mototaxis* (rickshaw taxis) are cheaper at S2.

AROUND PUNO
Sillustani

Sitting on rolling hills on the Lago Umayo peninsula, the funerary towers of **Sillustani** (admission S6.50; ⏰8am-5pm) stand out for miles against the desolate altiplano landscape.

The ancient Colla people who once dominated the area were a fearsome, Aymara-speaking tribe, who later became the southeastern part of the Inca empire. They buried their nobility in *chullpas* (funerary towers), which can be seen scattered widely around the hilltops of the region.

The most impressive of these are at Sillustani, where the tallest reach a height of 12m. The cylindrical structures housed the remains of complete family groups, along with plenty of food and belongings for their journey into the next world. Nowadays, nothing remains of the burials, but the *chullpas* are well preserved. The area is partially encircled by the sparkling Lago Umayo (3890m), which is home to a wide variety of plants and Andean waterbirds, plus a small island with vicuñas (threatened, wild relatives of llamas).

Tours leave Puno at around 2:30pm daily and cost from S25. The round-trip takes about 3½ hours and allows you about 1½ hours at the ruins. If you'd prefer more time at the site, hire a private taxi for S60.

For longer stays, **Atun Colla** (☎ 951-90-5006, 951-50-2390; www.turismovivencialatuncolla.com) offers *turismo vivencia* (homestays). You can help your host family with farming, hike to lookouts and lesser-known archaeological sites, visit the tiny museum and eat dirt – this area is known for its edible *arcilla* (clay). Served up as a sauce on boiled potato, it goes down surprisingly well.

Cutimbo

A little more than 20km from Puno, the dramatic site of **Cutimbo** (admission S3; ⊙ 8am-5pm) has an extraordinary position atop a table-topped volcanic hill surrounded by a fertile plain. Its modest number of well-preserved *chullpas*, built by the Colla, Lupaca and Inca cultures, come in both square and cylindrical shapes. Look closely and you'll find several monkeys, pumas and snakes carved into the structures.

This place receives few visitors, which can make it problematic for solo travelers, who have been assaulted here. Go in a group and be aware. A taxi here will cost approximately S70.

Ichu

The rural community of Ichu, 10km south of Puno and spread across a gorgeous green valley, is home to an incredible multilayered temple complex with breathtaking 360-degree views. This is one ancient site where you won't have to battle crowds of fellow sightseers, which is great if you prefer a little solitude with your pre-Columbian architecture. To get there, leave the Carr Panamericana at Ichu's second exit (after the service station) and head inland past the house marked 'Villa Lago 1960,' bearing left at a junction. (Aim for the two small, terraced hills you see to the left of the valley.) After bearing left at a second junction, turn left again, straight up the first hill.

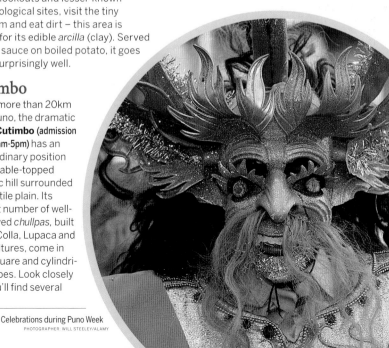

Celebrations during Puno Week
PHOTOGRAPHER: WILL STEELEY/ALAMY

A 15-minute walk will bring you the top. This can be done as an easy half-day trip from Puno. A taxi to take you to the foot of the hill and wait for your return will cost around S25. Take plenty of water and food as there's no store.

Chucuito

About 19km south of Puno, this little village (pop 1100) on Lake Titicaca's south shore, offers one outlandish attraction: the **Templo de la Fertilidad** (Inca Uyu; admission S5; ⏱8am-5pm). Its dusty grounds are scattered with large stone phalluses, some up to 1.2m in length – that make for an, um, interesting photo op.

Further uphill from the main road is the main plaza, which has two attractive colonial churches, **Santo Domingo** and **Nuestra Señora de la Asunción**. (Ask around for the caretakers if you want to get a glimpse inside.)

If you fancy spending the night, try the unmissable new age-y **Taypikala Hotel** (☎79-2252; www.taypikala.com; Km18 Panamericana Sur; s/d/tr S167/220/287), buried under a confusion of model condors and artificial rocks. Rooms have lake and garden views. Across the highway, their swanky new sister hotel **Taypikala Lago** (☎79-2266; www.taypikala.com; Calle Sandia s/n; s/d/tr S200/250/320) offers better views, with understated luxury and less-startling architecture.

Otherwise, agencies in Puno offer day trips here upon request.

LAKE TITICACA ISLANDS

Lake Titicaca's islands are world famous for their peaceful beauty and well-preserved traditional agrarian cultures, which you can see up close by staying with families on the islands – a privileged glimpse at a way of life that you're unlikely to forget.

That said, negative impacts from tourism have been felt in many communities. Taquile, which has attracted the lion's share of travelers since the 1970s, is an example. Tourism income goes mostly to the few families who own restaurants and guesthouses, and resentment towards tourists is evident in some parts of the community.

Templo de la Fertilidad, Chucuito

Detour:
Lampa

The charming little town of Lampa is known as La Ciudad Rosada (the Pink City) for its dusty, pink-colored buildings. A significant commercial center in colonial days, it still shows a strong Spanish influence. Located northwest of Puno, via Juliaca, it's an excellent place for a day trip from Puno (or to kill a few hours before flying out of Juliaca).

On the main plaza, the lovely baroque **Iglesia de Santiago de Apostol (Plaza de Armas)** is well worth seeing for its life-size sculpture of St James on a real stuffed horse, returning from the dead to trample the Moors. Oh, and did we mention the huge domed tomb topped by a copy of Michelangelo's *Pietà*? Sublime.

Also worth a look in is the **Municipalidad de Lampa (Lampa Town Hall; admission S2; ⏱8am-12:45pm & 1:30-4pm Mon-Fri; 9am-1pm Sat & Sun)**, a historic spot that has a little museum honoring Peruvian expressionist painter Victor Humareda (1920–86) – as well as yet another copy of Michelangelo's *Pietá*. Forget the Vatican – Lampa has a *twofer*!

Lampa isn't all that geared up for overnight stays. There are a few basic accommodations, including cozy, quirky, recommended **Casa Romero** (📞952-65-1511, 952-71-9073; casaromerolampa@hotmail.com; Aguirre 327; s/d/tr incl breakfast S40/60/80), where full board is available with advance booking. There are a couple of restaurants around the Plaza de Armas.

A taxi from Juliaca will cost about S5. Likewise, you can hire a taxi for the day to drive you over from Puno and wait around while you see the sights.

Nearby Amantaní has tried to avoid this predicament by introducing *turismo vivencial* (homestay tourism), where food and lodging are offered at a set price in family homes, following a strict rotation system enforced by the community. Unfortunately, tour operators sometimes undercut this system. Despite decades of tourism, many islanders live in poverty.

Our advice: go with a recommended agency (see p145), and, if possible, visit the islands independently so that your expenditures end up benefitting the villages you are visiting. All ferry tickets are valid for 15 days, so you can island hop at will.

Islas Uros

Just 5km east of Puno, the unique floating **Islas Uros (admission S5)** are Lake Titicaca's top tourist attraction. They're built using the buoyant *totora* reeds that grow abundantly in the shallows of the lake. The lives of the Uros people are interwoven with these reeds, which are used to make their homes, their boats and the crafts they create for tourists. (They're even partially edible.) The islands are constructed from many layers of the *totora*, which are constantly replenished from the top as they rot from the bottom, so the ground is always soft and springy. Some islands also have elaborately designed versions of traditional tightly bundled reed boats on hand. Be prepared to pay for a ride or to take photographs.

Always a small tribe, the Uros began their unusual floating existence centuries ago in an effort to isolate themselves from the aggressive Collas and Incas.

Getting here independently is easy. Ferries leave from the port in Puno (S10) at least once an hour from 6am to 4pm.

Stone archway, Isla Taquile

SEAN CAFFREY

The community-owned ferry service visits two islands, on a rotation basis. Ferries to Taquile and Amantaní can also drop you off in the Uros.

Nearly the only, and certainly the best, accommodation provider on Uros is **Cristina Suaña** (📞 951-69-5121, 951-47-2355; uroskhantati@hotmail.com; r per person S120), on Isla Khantati. Highly recommended by readers, she offers top-notch accommodations, three meals, fishing, lots of cultural activity, and the pleasure of her effervescent company. Book in advance so that she can pick you up from Puno in a private boat.

Isla Taquile

Inhabited for thousands of years, **Isla Taquile** (admission S5), 35km east of Puno, is a tiny 7-sq-km island with a population of about 2000 people. The Quechua-speaking islanders are distinct from most of the surrounding Aymara-speaking island communities and maintain a strong sense of group identity.

The island has a fascinating tradition of handicrafts, and the creations are made according to a system of deeply ingrained social customs. Men wear tightly woven woolen hats that resemble floppy nightcaps, which they knit themselves. They wear red hats if they are married and red and white hats if they are single; different colors can denote a man's current or past social position.

Taquile women weave thick, colorful waistbands for their husbands, which are worn with roughly spun white shirts and thick, calf-length black pants. Women wear eye-catching outfits comprising multilayered skirts and delicately embroidered blouses. These fine garments are considered some of the most well-made traditional clothes in Peru, and can be bought in the cooperative store on the island's main plaza.

◎ Sights & Activities

Taquile's scenery is beautiful. In the strong island sunlight, the deep, red-colored soil contrasts with the intense blue of the lake and the glistening backdrop of Bolivia's snowy Cordillera Real on the far side of the lake. Several hills boast Inca terracing on their sides and small ruins on top. Visitors are free to wander around, explore the ruins and enjoy the tranquility. The island is a wonderful place to catch a sunset and gaze at the moon, which looks twice as bright in the crystalline air, rising over the breathtaking peaks.

A stairway of more than 500 steps leads from the dock to the center of the island. The climb takes a breathless 20 minutes if you're acclimatized – more if you're not.

Take in the lay of the land while it's still light – with no roads or streetlights to use as landmarks, travelers have been known to get so lost in the dark that they end up roughing it for the night. (A limited electricity supply on the island is not always available – bring a flashlight.)

 Sleeping & Eating

There are many *hospedajes* (small, family-owned inns) on Taquile, offering basic accommodation for around S15 a night. Options range from a room in a family house to small guesthouses. Most offer indoor toilets and showers with electric hot water.

There are plenty of restaurants too, all offering the same fare of *sopa de quinua* (quinoa soup – absolutely delicious everywhere) and lake trout for S18. Consider eating in the **Restaurante Comunál**, Taquile's only community-run food outlet.

 Information

Make sure you already have lots of small bills in local currency, because change is limited and there's nowhere to exchange dollars. Bring extra money to buy some of the exquisite crafts sold in the cooperative store.

 Getting There & Away

Ferries (round-trip S30) leave from the port in Puno for Amantaní at 8am every day. There are departures from Amantaní to Taquile and Puno around 4pm every. Check ahead, as times vary.

Isla Amantaní

A few kilometers north of the smaller Isla Taquile is **Isla Amantaní** (admission S5), population 4000. Almost all trips here involve an overnight homestay, where you can help your hosts cook on open fires in dirt-floored kitchens and meet their small children, many of whom walk an hour each way to school every day. It is a humbling and sometimes life-changing experience.

The villagers sometimes organize rousing traditional dances, letting travelers dress in their traditional party gear to dance the night away. Don't forget to look up at the incredibly starry night sky as you stagger home.

The island is very quiet (no dogs allowed!), boasts great views and has no roads or vehicles. Several hills are topped by ruins, among the highest and best known of which are **Pachamama** (Mother Earth) and **Pachatata** (Father Earth). These date to the Tiwanaku culture, a pre-Columbian culture that appeared around Lake Titicaca and expanded rapidly between 200 BC and AD 1000.

When you arrive, island families will allocate you to your accommodation according to a rotating system. Please respect this system and, if you're with a guide, insist that they do. There's no problem with asking for families or friends to be together. A bed and full board costs from S30 per person per night.

Cuzco, Machu Picchu & Around

The former heart of the Inca Empire effortlessly enchants.
Ladies with llamas walk cobblestone streets. Coca-chewing honchos parade to church in ornate regalia for Catholic mass in Quechua. Exquisitely engineered ancient citadels draw explorers from all over the world. Climb any hill in this part of the Andes and chances are you'll stumble upon a piece of history, be it the globally famous Machu Picchu or baroque Spanish churches standing majestically over sleepy town squares.

For the traveler, it's an idyllic setting in which to experience Peru's dynamic highland culture. The views are stunning (think: stately mountains and picturesque villages) and the pageantry is rich. And it's all here for you to walk, eat, ride, drink, dance and shop your way through.

The welcoming party at Machu Picchu
PHOTOGRAPHER: RALPH HOPKINS

Cuzco, Machu Picchu & Around

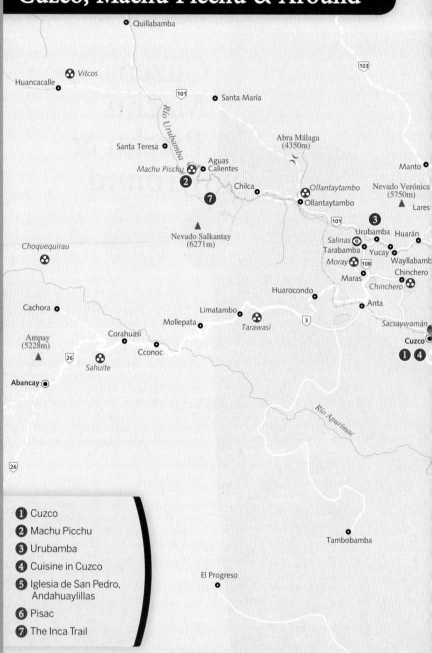

Quillabamba

Vitcos
Huancacalle

Río Urubamba

[101]
Santa María

Santa Teresa

Machu Picchu

Aguas
Calientes

Abra Málaga
(4350m)

Manto

Ollantaytambo
Ollantaytambo

Nevado Verónica
(5750m)

Lares

Chilca

[101]

Urubamba
Salinas
Tarabamba
Moray
Maras

Huarán
Yucay
[108]

Wayllabamba
Chinchero
Chinchero

Choquequirau

Nevado Salkantay
(6271m)

Huarocondo

Anta

Sacsaywamán

Cachora

Limatambo
Mollepata
Tarawasi

[3]

Cuzco

Ampay
(5228m)

[26]

Corahuasi
Cconoc

Sahuite

Abancay

Río Apurímac

[26]

Tambobamba

El Progreso

Colquemarca

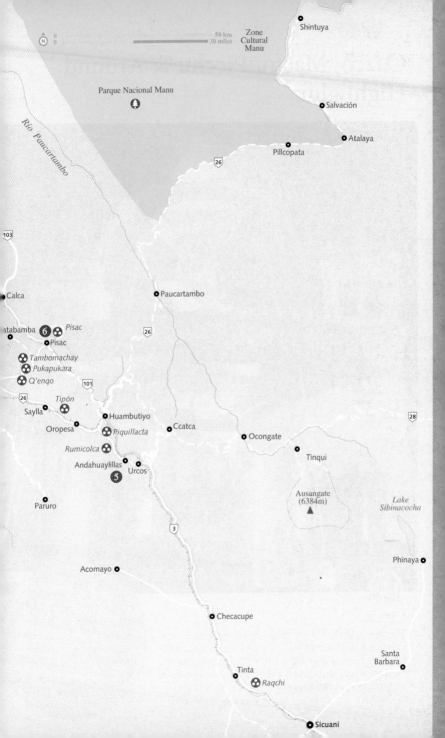

Cuzco, Machu Picchu & Around Highlights

① Cuzco

The former capital of the sprawling Inca empire remains a capital of sorts – a global village attracting travelers from all over with its mix of outstanding architecture, ornate baroque churches, a lively cuisine scene and some great nightlife. Above: Plaza de Armas; Top Right: Mercado San Pedro; Bottom Right: Inca stone walls along Hatunrumiyoc

Need to Know

NAME GAME The city is often referred to by its Quechua spelling, Q'osqo. **TAKE IT EASY** Cuzco sits at a dizzying 3362m. Rest, stay hydrated and eat light if arriving from sea level. **For more coverage, see p172.**

Cuzco Don't Miss List

BY ANDREA CONFALONIERI,
FORTUNATA HUAMAN AND ADA
LUZ CARDENAS, THE TRAVEL TEAM AT
TURISMO CAITH, A LOCAL NONPROFIT THAT ALSO
ORGANIZES COMMUNITY TOURS

1 MERCADO SAN PEDRO

In Cuzco, a market isn't just for shopping – it's a place where people come to socialize. A great time to visit the mercado (p194) is on a weekend, when wholesalers from the surrounding agricultural communities gather to buy and sell goods. It's an event – a place where the modern and the traditional, the rural and the urban, all mix.

2 SAN JERÓNIMO

Explore neighborhoods beyond the city center. At the eastern end of Cuzco, the area of San Jerónimo has a beautiful plaza and narrow streets. Life here is lived in a more traditional Andean way. We recommend going with a well-informed guide who can fill you in on the town's history and traditions.

3 EAT LOCAL FOODS

Cuzco offers incredible international dining, but we suggest finding a *picantería* (informal homestyle restaurant) and sampling local foods (p191). Some of the best: *cuy* (guinea pig), tamales (corn cakes) or *chiriuchu* (a sampler of meats and other items) – served with a glass of *chicha amarilla* (yellow corn beer).

4 WANDER THE STREETS

For a couple of hours, scrap the itinerary and just let yourself amble around Cuzco. Check out the community centers, see the local libraries, admire the murals at the Almudena cemetery (on the southern edge of town). Above all, be sure to fully explore the area around San Blas (p178), both during the day and at night, when it's illuminated and provides incredible views of the city.

5 EXPLORE THE AREA'S LIVING HISTORY

Archaeological sites such as Sacsaywamán are impressive, but we also recommend getting to know the city's living culture. Visit the markets, interact with the locals – and if you're in town during a religious holiday, join a procession. One of the most remarkable is held every June, for Corpus Christi.

Machu Picchu

A sublime stone citadel. A staggering cloud-forest perch. And a back-story that's out of a movie. This extraordinary Inca settlement (and Unesco World Heritage Site) came to light in the early 1900s, when an American explorer by the name of Hiram Bingham extolled its presence to the world.

Need to Know

WHEN TO GO June to August are the sunniest months. **AVOID** February, when it's soggy and the Inca Trail is closed. **TIP** Pack the insect repellent – it gets buggy. **For further coverage, see p214.**

2

Machu Picchu Don't Miss List

BY CHRISTOPHER HEANEY, AUTHOR OF *CRADLE OF GOLD, THE STORY OF HIRAM BINGHAM, A REAL-LIFE INDIANA JONES, AND THE SEARCH FOR MACHU PICCHU*

1 WATCH THE SUN RISE OVER MACHU PICCHU

The best time to visit Machu Picchu is very early in the morning or late in the day, when the trains have come and gone. This means spending the night in Aguas Calientes. It's worth it: at dawn, the light is especially beautiful and you'll have the possibility of exploring the ruins in some solitude.

2 EXPLORE THE EAST SIDE

The tours will take you to key sights like the Intihuatana (an astronomical point), but be sure to go east, where the terraces meet the jungle. You'll get a feel for what it was like to live at Machu Picchu, either as an *inca* (king) or one of their servants.

3 VISIT THE MUSEO DE SITIO MANUEL CHÁVEZ BALLÓN

This museum (p211) might seem small, but it's worthwhile. It has the only gold found at Machu Picchu, as well as excellent displays that chronicle the history of the site and how it fit into a larger entire network of Inca settlements.

4 HIKE UP TO THE RUINS FROM AGUAS CALIENTES

There's a little footpath that leads up the side of the mountain to the ruins. It's a little steep, but in terms of experience, you'll put yourself right in the mindset of the explorers. Hiram Bingham used to see if he could beat his personal best every time he climbed.

5 READ A GOOD BOOK BEFOREHAND

John Hemmings' *Conquest of the Incas* is a classic. But for fun, I recommend *Plunder of the Sun*, by David Dodge. It's a noir novel about bruisers fighting for an Inca treasure and will give you a good sense of what Cuzco was like in the 1950s. Machu Picchu is rich with history – these will make it come alive.

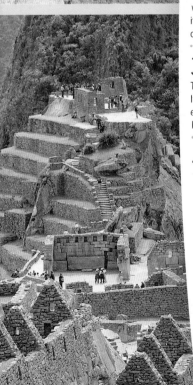

Enjoy Tranquility in Urubamba

If Cuzco's staggering heights and noisy streets make you feel light-headed, the laid-back country town of Urubamba (p203), surrounded by beautiful countryside, offers a delightful alternative base for exploring the Sacred Valley. Expect chilled-out lodges, excellent horse ranches, tasty restaurants and one of the area's most magnificent spas. Are you ready to relax? You've found your spot.

3

5 See the 'Sistine Chapel of Latin America'

A sleepy village east of Cuzco contains one of the most surprisingly extravagant churches in the region. The Iglesia de San Pedro (p224) in Andahuaylillas doesn't look like much from the outside, but on the inside, it's layered with some of the finest examples of Andean baroque design. Be sure to look up: the ceiling is laced in an array of intricate, indigenous-influenced patterns. Divine.

JEFFREY BECOM

Dig into the Rich Cuisine

Crackling *chicharrones* (deep-fried chunks of pork). Starchy Andean corn with squeaking hunks of cheese. Brothy soups that warm the bones on chilly highland nights. Oh, and did we mention the roasted guinea pigs? Every region in Peru offers a bounty of regional cooking and the Cuzco area is no exception (p191). Get ready to be enriched – not just your mind, but also the belly.

Shop 'til You Drop in Pisac

Who knew a single highland town could have so much to offer? Magnificent ruins, tasty local restaurants and one of the most bustling outdoor markets in the entire region. In Pisac (p201), dedicated shoppers can find bright, hand-woven textiles, finely painted ceramics, alpaca knits, and a mind-boggling assortment of fresh local produce. You've never seen so many potatoes!

Trek the Inca Trail

The world's most famous ancient roadway (p220) offers adventurous travelers a four-day bonanza of sumptuous cloud forest, remote Inca ruins, mind-bending passes with extravagant views, and crystalline waterfalls – not to mention the bragging rights of saying that you made it to the lost city of Machu Picchu the old-fashioned way: you walked there.

Cuzco, Machu Picchu & Around's Best...

Inca Ruins

◦ **Qorikancha** (p179) The remains of a graceful Inca sun temple

◦ **Sacsaywamán** (p199) A hillside fortress that is also a feat of masonry and engineering

◦ **Pisac** (p202) A hilltop citadel sits astride two gorges in the Sacred Valley

◦ **Moray** (p204) Amphitheatre terracing with its own microclimates

◦ **Machu Picchu** (p214) The fabled mountaintop citadel

Churches

◦ **Iglesia de La Compañía de Jesús** (p177) Cuzco's splendorous baroque Jesuit church

◦ **Iglesia de San Blas** (p178) A simple adobe house of worship contains a pulpit that is allegedly encrusted with the skull of its carver

◦ **Cuzco's Cathedral** (p176) An incredible repository of colonial art contains a *Last Supper* in which Christ feasts on *cuy* (guinea pig)

◦ **Iglesia de San Pedro** (p224) In Andahuaylillas, this church is lavishly decorated in an earthy Andean baroque style

Adventures

◦ **River Running** (p182) The waterways around Cuzco contain heart-pounding whitewater runs

◦ **Trekking the Inca Trail** (p220) The continent's most famous stone road

◦ **Zip Lining** (p222) About 2500m of vertigo-inducing lines in Santa Teresa

◦ **Horseback Riding** (p204) Trotting around Urubamba in the Sacred Valley on a Peruvian *paso* horse

Need to Know

Surreal Sights

○ **Salinas** (p203) Ancient saltpans cascade down a mountain outside of Urubamba

○ **Guinea Pig Castles** (p201) Pisac shops feature architecturally extravagant homes for Peru's favorite protein treat

○ **Q'oyoriti** (p187) A sacred pilgrimage on a mountain of ice

○ **Mercado San Pedro** (p194) A sensory overload, in every imaginable way

ADVANCE PLANNING

○ **Six Months Before** Make a reservation for trekking the Inca Trail

○ **Three Months** Buy domestic airplane tickets within Peru

○ **One Month** Make hotel reservations for Cuzco and Aguas Calientes

○ **One Day** Book day tours around Cuzco

RESOURCES

○ **Exploring Cuzco, by Peter Frost** The best source of historical and archaeological information on the area

○ **Municipalidad del Cusco** (www.municusco. com.pe) The city's official website

○ **Diario del Cusco** (www. diariodelcusco.com) Online edition of the local daily newspaper, in Spanish

○ **El Caminerito** (www. elcaminerito.com) Exhaustive coverage of all the latest cultural and fine-arts happenings around Cuzco, in Spanish

GETTING AROUND

○ **Walk** The best way to explore the compact (often Inca-designed) settlements that dot the Sacred Valley

○ **Bus** Local service connects disparate points in Cuzco as well as outside towns; long-haul services are available to Puno, Arequipa and Lima, among other points

○ **Train** Tourist services to Aguas Calientes, at the base of Machu Picchu, as well as Puno

○ **Taxi** Plentiful in Cuzco, and other larger towns

BE FOREWARNED

○ **Inca Trail** Closes for maintenance for the entire month of February

○ **Solo Women** Watch out for 'Cuzco Casanovas' on the hunt for ladies who will pay their way

○ **Robberies** Crowded locales bring out pickpockets; late-night muggings are not unheard of

Left: Detail of Cuzco's Cathedral;
Above: Inti Raymi, Sacsaywamán

Cuzco, Machu Picchu & Around Itineraries

Cuzco, Machu Picchu and the Sacred Valley can keep you occupied for weeks with extravagant mountainscapes, rural villages and more Inca ruins than you can shake a stick at.

CUZCO TO MACHU PICCHU
Heart of the Inca Empire

Start with a leisurely couple of days acclimatizing in **(1) Cuzco**, strolling around the Plaza de Armas and visiting the area's churches and ruins. Highlights include the ruins of Qorikancha and Sacsaywamán, as well as a visit to the incredible Iglesia de San Francisco, which contains a trove of colonial art. While you're in the city, be sure to enjoy the delicious highland cooking at one of its many restaurants.

Head out of town to somewhat less gasping altitudes in **(2) Pisac**, a charming Sacred Valley town with a colorful market, before exploring the incredible ruins of **(3) Ollantaytambo**. Spend the night there, then continue on by train to **(4) Aguas Calientes**, the bustling cloud-forest village that serves as the base for exploring the fabled **(5) Machu Picchu**. To get the most out of your visit, spend at least two nights in the area – allowing you ample time to explore the ruins.

Top Left: Plaza de Armas, Cuzco; **Top Right:** Inca ruins in Ollantaytambo

PHOTOGRAPHER: (TOP LEFT) EMILY RIDDELL; (TOP RIGHT) SEAN CAFFREY

CUZCO TO MACHU PICCHU ON FOOT

To Machu Picchu along the Inca Trail

Arrive in **(1) Cuzco** and allow for a leisurely first day of strolling (and acclimatization). Afterwards, transfer to the Sacred Valley village of **(2) Ollantaytambo**, to visit the lovely local ruins and prepare for the big trek. From here, you'll spend the next four days walking along one of Peru's most dramatic ancient trails – the **(3) Inca Trail**. The hike will take you over high passes, along steamy cloud forest and will offer views of majestic Andean peaks in the distance. Along the way, you'll see plenty of lesser Inca ruins as well.

On the last day of the trek, you will emerge at a mountain pass, where you will get your first glimpse of the majestic **(4) Machu Picchu**. Spend a day exploring the site, before taking a train from **(5) Aguas Calientes** at the foot of the ruins back to **(6) Cuzco** for a day of urban exploring before you have to depart. You might like to treat yourself to an extravagant, well-deserved meal at Gastón Acurio's Cuzco outpost, Chicha, and get a little crafts shopping done in the artisan quarter of San Blas.

Discover Cuzco, Machu Picchu & Around

Family time, Ollantaytambo
PHOTOGRAPHER: RALPH HOPKINS

CUZCO

♪084 / POP 350,000 / ELEV 3326M

As legend has it, the Inca civilization was born in the 12th century when Manco Cápac and his sister Mama Ocllo, children of the sun, emerged from Lake Titicaca to establish a civilization in the Cuzco Valley. Whether Manco Cápac was a historical figure is up for debate, but what is certain is that the location he chose is inspired. Cuzco (*qosq'o* in the Quechua language), as the Incas saw it, was the navel of the world, the source of all life.

In that regard, it remains that way still – a lively ancient city that unselfconsciously bursts with vigor. Walk through the main plaza and you'll find entrepreneurs hawking everything from finger puppets to massages. There are flamboyant discotheques, bustling markets and singing shoeshine boys, but take a moment to explore Cuzco's labyrinthine streets and you'll also find hushed churches, stately museums and delectable haute cuisine. It is a diverse and irresistibly vital madhouse. However long you plan to spend here, it won't be enough.

History

For almost 200 years beginning in the 12th century, the Incas were a relatively small ethnicity confined to the Cuzco Valley. This changed in the 14th century, under the ninth *inca* (king) Pachacutec, a fervent expansionist who extended the limits of Inca territory to include much of the central Andes as well as the area around Lake

Titicaca. Cuzco was the shining capital of his sprawling empire and the city owes much of its physical glory to him: Pachacutec was the one who allegedly gave the city its layout in the shape of a puma and built some of the area's most magnificent stone monuments, such as Sacsaywamán (p199) and quite possibly, Machu Picchu (p214).

The Inca expansion would come to an abrupt end with the arrival of the Spanish. Francisco Pizarro entered the city on November 8, 1533, after dispatching emperor Atahualpa in the northern highland city of Cajamarca. By that point, the Spanish had already gotten to work demolishing indigenous monuments and stripping Cuzco's temples of their silver and gold. All of this was followed, in 1536, by a fierce indigenous rebellion led by Manco Inca, Atahualpa's half brother, who had originally served as the Spaniard's puppet leader. Manco would lay siege to the city for almost a year, but was ultimately unsuccessful in wresting control from the Spanish.

After the Spanish moved the nation's capital to Lima, Cuzco's importance as an urban center would decline. Even so, it remained the site of significant events. During the 16th century, the city produced one of Peru's most renowned chroniclers: El Inca Garcilaso de la Vega (1539–1616), the son of an Inca princess and a Spanish military captain, and author of the vital historical document *The Royal Commentaries of the Incas*.

Cuzco was the birthplace of a remarkable 16th-century art movement known as the *escuela cuzqueña* (Cuzco School), in which indigenous painters created Catholic religious imagery that drew inspiration from Andean life. (You can find paintings of this nature in museums around Peru.) The city was also at the heart of the last major indigenous uprising, in 1780. Led by the grandson of an Inca noble, José Gabriel Condorcanqui (known as Túpac Amaru II), it didn't last long. Condorcanqui was captured by colonial authorities and violently executed in the city's main square.

Apart from devastating earthquakes in 1650 and 1950, the city remained a quiet provincial capital, until the early 20th century, when an American explorer by the name of Hiram Bingham broadcast the existence of Machu Picchu to the world.

 Sights

A resurgence of indigenous pride means that many streets have been signposted with Quechua names, though they are still commonly referred to by their Spanish titles. The most prominent example is Calle Triunfo, which is labeled Sunturwasi.

To visit many of Cuzco's principal historic sights, foreign travelers have to purchase a **boleto turístico** (adult/student with ISIC card S130/70), a ticket that covers your entry fee into around a dozen spots. There is also a **boleto religioso** (religious tourist ticket; adult/student S50/25), valid for entry at a number of Cuzco's religious sites. These are sold on-site at the city's various historic and religious attractions and are valid for 10 days.

Note that opening hours can be erratic.

Central Cuzco

PLAZA DE ARMAS   Plaza
In Inca times, the plaza, called Huacaypata or Aucaypata, was the heart of the Inca capital. Today it's the nerve center of the modern city. Two flags usually fly here – the red and white Peruvian flag and the rainbow-checkered flag of Tahuantinsuyo, representing the four quarters of the Inca empire. (Foreigners often mistake the latter for an international gay-pride banner. Bringing this up is an excellent way to make normally easygoing *cuzqueños* lose their cool.)

Colonial arcades surround the plaza, which in ancient times was twice as large as it is today. On the square's northeastern side is the imposing cathedral, fronted by a large flight of

Cuzco

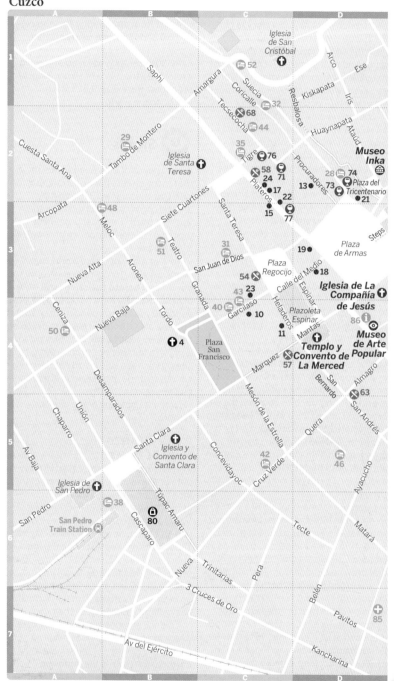

DISCOVER CUZCO, MACHU PICCHU & AROUND CUZCO

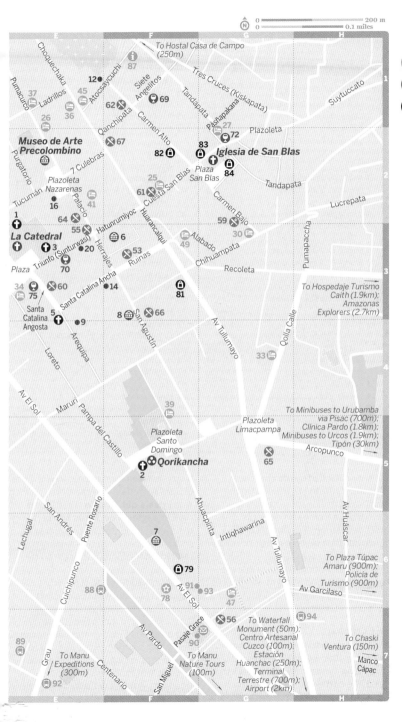

0   200 m
0   0.1 miles

To Hostal Casa de Campo
(250m)

Choquechaka

Pumacurco
Ladrillos
37
45
Atocsaycuchi
12
Siete
Angelitos
69

Suytuccato

Tres Cruces (Kiskapata)

Qanchipata

Carmen Alto

62

26
36

Tandapata

Pashapakana

Museo de Arte
Precolombino

67

7 Culebras

27

72

Plazoleta

82
83
84
Iglesia de San Blas

Plaza
San Blas

Tandapata

Lucrepata

Tucumán

Purgatorio

Plazoleta
Nazarenas
16

Palacio
41

25

61

Cuesta San Blas

Carmen Bajo

1

La Catedral

64
55
Hatunrumiyoc
6

Huarancalqui

59

30

49

Alabado

Pumapaccha

3
Triunfo (Sunturwasi)
70

20

53

Ruinas

Chihuampata

Recoleta

To Hospedaje Turismo
Caith (1.9km);
Amazonas
Explorers (2.7km)

Plaza

34
75
60

Santa Catalina Ancha

14

81

Santa
Catalina
Angosta

5

9

8

66

San Agustín

Qolla Calle

Loreto

Arequipa

Maruri

Av El Sol

Pampa del Castillo

33

Av Tullumayo

39

Plazoleta
Santo
Domingo

Qorikancha

2

Plazoleta
Limacpampa

To Minibuses to Urubamba
via Pisac (700m);
Clínica Pardo (1.8km);
Minibuses to Urcos (1.9km);
Tipón (30km)

Arcopunco

65

San Andrés

Puente Rosario

7

Ahuacpinta

Intiqhawarina

Av Tullumayo

Av Huáscar

To Plaza Túpac
Amaru (900m);
Policia de
Turismo (900m)

Lechugal

Cuichipunco

88

79

78

91
93

Av El Sol

47

94

Av Garcilaso

To Chaski
Ventura (150m)

Manco
Cápac

89

Grau

Centenario

To Manu
Expeditions
(300m)

92

Av Pardo

Pasaje Grace

90

San Miguel

To Manu
Nature Tours
(100m)

56

To Waterfall
Monument (50m);
Centro Artesanal
Cuzco (100m);
Estación
Huanchac (250m);
Terminal
Terrestre (700m);
Airport (2km)

Cuzco

stairs and flanked by the churches of Jesús María and El Triunfo. On the southeastern side is the strikingly ornate church of La Compañía de Jesús. The quiet pedestrian alleyway of Loreto, which has Inca walls, is a historic means of access to the area.

It's worth visiting the plaza at least twice – by day and by night – as it takes on a strikingly different look after dark, all lit up and even prettier.

LA CATEDRAL   Church
(Plaza de Armas; admission S25 or with boleto religioso; ⏲10am-5:45pm) Started in 1559 and taking almost a hundred years to build, the **cathedral** squats on the site of an old Inca palace and was built using

blocks pilfered from the nearby Inca site of Sacsaywamán. The cathedral is joined with **Iglesia del Triunfo** (1536) to its right and **Iglesia de Jesús María** (1733) to its left. El Triunfo, Cuzco's oldest church, houses a vault containing the remains of the famous Inca chronicler Garcilaso de la Vega.

The cathedral is one of the city's greatest repositories of colonial art, especially for works from the *escuela cuzqueña*, noted for its decorative combination of 17th-century European devotional painting styles with the color palette and iconography of indigenous Andean artists. A classic example is the frequent portrayal of the Virgin Mary wearing a mountain-shaped skirt with a river running around its hem, identifying her with Pachamama (Mother Earth). One of the most famous paintings here is *The Last Supper* by Quechua artist Marcos Zapata, which depicts Christ and his disciples feasting on Andean ceremonial food. (Look for the juicy roast *cuy* – guinea pig – stealing the show.)

Also look for the **oldest surviving painting** in Cuzco, showing the entire city during the great earthquake of 1650. The inhabitants can be seen parading around the plaza with a crucifix, praying for the tremors to stop. This precious crucifix, called **El Señor de los Temblores** (The Lord of the Earthquakes), can still be seen in the alcove to the right of the door leading into El Triunfo. Particularly worthwhile is the magnificently carved **choir**, dating from the 17th century.

The doors are open to worshippers between 6am and 10am. If you decide to visit during this time, remain seated and do not take pictures.

IGLESIA DE LA COMPAÑÍA DE JESÚS
Church

(Plaza de Armas; admission S10 or with boleto religioso; ☺9-11:30am & 1-5:30pm) This elaborate baroque **church** is built upon the palace of Huayna Cápac, the last Inca to rule an undivided, unconquered empire. Constructed by the Jesuits in 1571, it was reconstructed after the 1650 earthquake. The Jesuits planned to make it the most magnificent of Cuzco's churches, but the archbishop of Cuzco complained that its splendor should not rival that of the cathedral. The squabble grew to a point where Pope Paul III was called upon to arbitrate. His decision was in favor of the cathedral, but by the time word had reached Cuzco, La Compañía was just about finished, complete with a baroque facade and Peru's biggest altar, all crowned by a soaring dome.

The church also contains two large canvases near the main door that depict scenes of early marriages in Cuzco. These are well worth examining for their wealth of period detail. Local students are available to show you the church, including the grand view from the second-floor choir, reached via rickety steps. Tips are gratefully accepted.

IGLESIA Y MONASTERIO DE SANTA CATALINA
Church

(Arequipa s/n; admission S8; ⊙8:30am-5:30pm Mon-Sat) This **convent** houses many colonial paintings from the *escuela cuzqueña,* as well as an impressive collection of vestments and other religious embroidery. It also contains a baroque side chapel with dramatic friezes, and many life-sized (and sometimes startling) models of nuns praying, sewing and going about their lives.

TEMPLO Y CONVENTO DE LA MERCED
Church

(✆ 23-1821; Mantas 121; admission S6; ⊙8am-noon & 2-5pm Mon-Sat) Cuzco's third most important colonial **church**, La Merced has a beautiful colonial **cloister** (⊙8-11am) hung with paintings that chronicle the life of San Pedro Nolasco, who founded the order in 1218 in Barcelona. The church to the far side contains the tombs of conquistadors Diego de Almagro and Gonzalo Pizarro (brother of Francisco). Here, you'll also find a small religious museum that houses vestments rumored to have belonged to conquistador and friar Vicente de Valverde. The exhibit's most famous piece is a priceless solid-gold monstrance, 1.2m

high and covered with rubies, emeralds and no fewer than 1500 diamonds and 600 pearls. (Ask to see it if the display room is locked.)

The entrance to the monastery and museum is located to the left of the church, at the back of a small courtyard.

IGLESIA SAN FRANCISCO
Church

(Plaza San Francisco; admission free; ⊙6:30-8am & 5:30-8pm Mon-Sat, 6:30am-noon & 6:30-8pm Sun) More austere than many of Cuzco's other churches, **Iglesia San Francisco** dates back to the 16th century, and is one of the few that didn't need to be completely reconstructed after the 1650 earthquake. It has a large collection of colonial religious paintings and a well-carved cedar choir. The attached **museum** (admission S5; ⊙9am-noon & 3-5pm Mon-Fri, 9am-noon Sat) houses what is alleged to be one of the largest paintings in South America: a 9m by 12m canvas that shows the family tree of St Francis of Assisi, founder of the order. Also of macabre interest are the two crypts, which contain plenty of carefully arranged human bones.

San Blas

IGLESIA DE SAN BLAS
Church

(Plaza San Blas; admission S15 or with boleto religioso; ⊙10am-6pm Mon-Sat, 2-6pm Sun) This simple **adobe church** is comparatively small, but the baroque, gold-leaf altar is awe-inspiring. The exquisitely carved pulpit – made from a single tree trunk – has been called one of the finest examples of colonial wood carving in the Americas. Legend has it that its creator was an indigenous man who miraculously recovered from a deadly disease and subsequently dedicated his life to carving this pulpit. According to the lore, his skull is nestled into the topmost part of the carving.

MUSEO DE ARTE PRECOLOMBINO
Museum

(✆ 23-3210; http://map.perucultural.org. pe; Plazoleta Nazarenas 231; admission S20; ⊙9am-10pm) Inside a Spanish colonial mansion with an Inca ceremonial courtyard, this dramatically curated

RALPH HOPKINS

Don't Miss Qorikancha

If you visit only one site in Cuzco, make it these **Inca ruins** that form the base of the colonial church and convent of Santo Domingo. Once the richest temple in the Inca empire, the Qorikancha (Quechua for 'Golden Courtyard') was literally covered in gold. Temple walls were lined with solid-gold sheets and the building housed life-sized gold and silver replicas of corn, which were ceremonially 'planted' in agricultural rituals. The building also allegedly held solid-gold llamas and babies, as well as a replica of the sun. Moreover, it has been reported that the mummified bodies of deceased *incas* (kings) were kept here, brought out into the sunlight each day and offered food and drink.

Unfortunately, the only thing that remains of the Inca temple is its masterful stonework. Within months of the Spanish arrival, the precious metals had all been looted. What remains, however, is some of the finest Inca architecture in Peru: a curved, perfectly fitted 6m-high wall that encircles the site.

The temple was built in the mid-15th century during the reign of the 10th *inca* (king), Túpac Yupanqui. After the conquest, Francisco Pizarro gave it to his brother Juan, but he was not able to enjoy it for long – Juan died in battle in 1536, leaving it to the Dominicans in his will.

Today's site is a bizarre combination of Inca and colonial architecture, topped with a roof of glass and metal. Colonial paintings around the outside of the courtyard depict the life of St Dominic, which contain several representations of dogs holding torches in their jaws. These are God's guard dogs (*dominicanus* in Latin), hence the name of the order.

NEED TO KNOW

Plazoleta Santo Domingo; admission S10; ⊘8:30am-5:30pm Mon-Sat, 2-5pm Sun

pre-Columbian art museum showcases a stunningly varied, if small, collection of archaeological artifacts. Dating from between 1250 BC to AD 1532, these demonstrate the artistic and cultural achievements of many of Peru's ancient cultures. Highlights include the Nazca and Moche galleries of multicolored ceramics, *queros* (ceremonial Inca wooden drinking vessels) and dazzling displays of gold and silver jewelry.

MUSEO INKA   Museum
(23-7380; Tucumán at Ataúd; admission S10; 8am-6pm Mon-Fri, 9am-4pm Sat) This charmingly modest **museum** is the best spot in town for those interested in the Incas. The restored interior is jam-packed with a fine collection of metalwork, jewelry, pottery, textiles, mummies, models and the world's largest collection of *queros*. The museum building, which rests on Inca foundations, is known as the Admiral's House, after the first owner, Admiral Francisco

Aldrete Maldonado. Look for the massive stairway guarded by sculptures of mythical creatures, and the corner window column that from the inside looks like a statue of a bearded man but from the outside appears to be a naked woman.

MUSEO DE ARTE RELIGIOSO   Museum
(cnr Hatunrumiyoc & Herrajes; admission S15 or with boleto religioso; 8-11am & 3-6pm Mon-Sat) Originally the palace of Inca Roca, the foundations of this **museum** were converted into a grand colonial residence and later became the archbishop's palace. The beautiful mansion is now home to a notable religious art collection, rich in period detail. The building contains some impressive ceilings and colonial-style tile work.

Avenida El Sol & Downhill

MUSEO DE ARTE POPULAR   Museum
(Av El Sol 103, basement; admission with boleto turístico; 9am-6pm Mon-Sat, 8am-1pm Sun). Winning entries in Cuzco's annual Popular

Left: Iglesia y Monasterio de Santa Catalina; **Below:** Paintings in the *escuela cuzqueña* (Cuzco school) style on show at the Monasterio de Santa Catalina
PHOTOGRAPHER: (BOTH IMAGES) GAIL MOONEY-KELLY/ALAMY

Art competition are displayed in this engaging **museum,** where the artisans and artists of San Blas strut their creative stuff in styles ranging from high art to cheeky cute. Focused on depicting aspects of everyday life, the small-scale ceramic models show drunken debauchery in the *picantería* (local restaurant), torture in the dentist's chair, carnage in the butcher shop, and even a caesarean section.

There's also a display of photographs of Cuzco, many by renowned local photographer Martín Chambi (1891–1973).

MUSEO DE SITIO DE QORIKANCHA
Museum

(admission with boleto turístico; ⊙9am-6pm Mon-Sat, 8am-1pm Sun) There are sundry moth-bitten archaeological displays interpreting Inca and pre-Inca cultures at this small underground **archaeological museum** that is entered via Av El Sol.

IGLESIA DE SANTO DOMINGO
Church

The **church** of Santo Domingo is adjacent to Qorikancha. Less baroque and ornate than many of Cuzco's churches, it is notable for its charming paintings of archangels depicted as Andean children in jeans and T-shirts. Opening hours are erratic.

MUSEO QUIJOTE
Museum

(San Agustín 275; admission S10 or with boleto religioso; ⊙9am-7:30pm) This privately owned **museum of contemporary art** houses a diverse, thoughtful collection of painting and sculpture ranging from the folksy to the macabre. The displays are accompanied by some good interpretive information about 20th-century Peruvian art history, some of it translated into English.

# Activities

Trekking

The Cuzco area is a hiker's paradise, with imposing mountain ranges, winding rivers, steamy cloud forest, isolated villages and ruins, and a huge range of altitudes and ecosystems. The most famous trek is the stunning Inca Trail, but it can get crowded and permits are required. If for some reason you can't secure a permit, there are other paths that lead to Machu Picchu – so there are alternatives. Likewise, treks to other, little-trafficked locations, such as Choquequirau, Ausangate and Vilcabamba, are also available.

There are regular departures from May to September, and private departures can be organized at any time of year. The best trekking months are June to August. In the wettest months (from December to April), trails can be slippery and campsites muddy. If renting equipment, always check it before setting out. In addition, be sure to pack rain gear, insect repellent, sunblock, a flashlight, basic first-aid supplies and water-purification tablets. For the Inca Trail, trekking poles are highly recommended, since you'll be descending a number of cartilage-crunching stone steps. If you're on a guided trek, take a stash of cash for tipping the guide and porters. (About US$10 per day per trekker is the minimum decent tip for a guide; a similar amount to divide among your porters is appropriate.)

For information on hiking the Inca Trail, turn to p220. For a detailed guide to other treks in the area, we recommend picking up a copy of *Alternative Inca Trails Information Packet* from the South American Explorers Club (p196).

For tips on booking a good trek, turn to p183. Some recommended outfitters and guides:

Amazonas Explorer (☎25-2846; www.amazonas-explorer.com; Av Callasuyo 910, Miravalle)

Andina Travel (☎25-1892; www.andinatravel.com; Plazoleta Santa Catalina 219)

Aracari (☎in Lima 01-651-2424; www.aracari.com)

Apus Peru (☎978-2720; www.apus-peru.com)

Eco Inka (☎22-4050; www.ecoinka.com)

Eco Trek Peru (☎24-7286; www.ecotrekperu.com; Atocsaycuchi 599)

Explorandes (☎in Lima 01-715-2323; www.explorandes.com)

GAP (☎in North America 1-416-260-0999; www.gapadventures.com)

Intrepid Adventures (☎in Australia 61-3-9473-2626; www.intrepidtravel.com)

Lorenzo Expeditions (☎984-85-1385; www.lorenzoexpeditions.com; Plateros 348B)

Miguel Jove (☎984-79-2227; miguelj24@hotmail.com; contact via South American Explorers Club)

Naty's Travel (☎26-1811; www.natystravelcusco.com; Triunfo 342)

Peruvian Odyssey (☎22-2105; www.peruvianodyssey.com; Pasaje Pumaqchupan 196)

Reserv Cusco (☎26-1548; www.reserv-cusco-peru.com; Plateros 326)

Tambo Trek (☎23-7718; www.tambotreks.net)

Peru Treks (☎22-2722; www.perutreks.com; Av Pardo 540)

Peruvian Highland Trek (☎24-2480; www.peruvianhighlandtrek.com; Calle del Medio 139)

X-treme Tourbulencia (☎22-4362; www.x-tremetourbulencia.com; Plateros 358)

River Running

Cuzco is becoming increasingly popular for river running, with nearby waterways that range in difficulty from Class I to Class V. The most popular of these is one of the many day runs on the Río Urubamba, through the Sacred Valley, which offers Class II and Class III runs on the stretch between **Cusipata** and **Quiquihana**. Closer to Cuzco, the section from **Pampa** to **Huambutio** (Class I to II) is beautiful and ideal for small

Booking a Great Trek

Trekking in the area around Cuzco has become increasingly popular, especially the journey on the Inca Trail. Unfortunately, this has brought out some less than stellar operators. Common complaints include minimal food, missing train tickets, leaking tents and overloaded porters. Here's what you need to know to book a great trek:

INCA TRAIL: REGULATIONS & FEES

Only 500 people each day are allowed on the trail and they must be in the company of a licensed guide. Tour prices generally include a tent, food, a cook, porters to carry group gear (you are expected to carry your own pack), one-day admission to the ruins and train fare back to Cuzco. Average price: US$350 to US$500 per person.

Book six months in advance between May and August.

ALTERNATIVES TO THE INCA TRAIL

If you can't get a permit for the Inca Trail, there are other equally stellar treks that go to Machu Picchu, via the village of Santa Teresa, through the Lares Valley, or along the snowy peak of Salkantay. **Mountain Lodges of Peru** (☎ 23-6069; mountainlodgesofperu.com) has pioneered a luxury approach to the latter.

PORTER WELFARE

Poor treatment of porters has been an issue. Any Inca Trail trip priced at less than US$250 means that cost cutting is occurring – and porter welfare is likely affected. If you don't like what you see, register an official complaint with **iPerú** (www.peru.info).

For a comprehensive list of reputable agencies and guides, turn to the Activities section on p182.

children (ages three and over). There are many more difficult stretches as well. Likewise, tougher runs on more inaccessible waterways – such as the Río Santa Teresa and the Río Apurimac – are also available, but generally as part of multiday trips. The area around Ollantaytambo is polluted and is not recommended for rafting.

Note that river running isn't regulated in Peru and fly-by-night operators abound. Go with reputable companies. The following have the best reputations for safety:

Amazonas Explorer (☎ 25-2846; www.amazonas-explorer.com)

Apumayo (☎ 24-6018; www.apumayo.com; Calle Garcilaso 265, Interior 3)

Mayuc (☎ 24-2824; www.mayuc.com; Portal Confiturías 211)

River Explorers (☎ 77-9619; www.riverexplorers.com; Calle Garcilaso 210, Interior 128)

Mountain Biking

Mountain-biking tours are also a growing industry, and the local terrain is superb. However, rental bikes tend to be of poor quality and at time of research only *rígida* (single suspension) models were available for hire. Outfitters can organize day trips in the neighboring hillsides, though most folks come for multiday excursions. The following bike operators are recommended:

Amazonas Explorer (📞 25-2846; www.amazonas-explorer.com)

Andean Xtreme Adventure (📞 23-4599/974-79-0386; www.axaperu.com)

Cusco Aventuras (📞 984-13-7403; cuscoaventura@hotmail.com)

Gravity Peru (📞 22-8032; www.gravityperu.com; Santa Catalina Ancha 398)

Loreto Tours (📞 23-6331; www.loretotours.com; Calle del Medio 111)

 Tours

Tour agencies are plentiful in Cuzco. Classic options include half-day tours of the city and/or nearby ruins, half-day trips to visit Sunday markets at nearby villages and full-day tours of the Sacred Valley. Agents also offer Machu Picchu day trips that include transportation, admission tickets to the archaeological site, an English-speaking guide and lunch. Note that these only allow you a few hours at the ruins before it's time to return to the train station.

The following agencies are recommended:

Andean Xtreme Adventure (📞 23-4599/974-79-0386; www.axaperu.com)

Chaski Ventura (📞 23-3952; www.chaskiventura.com; Manco Cápac 517)

Fertur (📞 22-1304; www.fertur-travel.com; Procuradores 341)

Hospedaje Turismo Caith (📞 23-3595; www.caith.org; Centro Yanapanakusun, Urb Ucchullo Alto, N4, Pasaje Santo Toribio) A nonprofit (the organization helps teenagers working as domestic help) that offers personalized itineraries.

Chances are you will be solicited for tours on the street. If you would like to book a trip directly with a guide, it is preferable to find a licensed guide via the local professional association:

Asociación de Guías Oficiales de Turismo (Agotur; 📞 24-9758; www.agoturcusco.org.pe; Heladeros 157)

 **Sleeping**

Cuzco fills to bursting between June and August, especially during the 10 days before Inti Raymi on June 24 and during Fiestas Patrias (Independence Days) on July 28 and 29. Book well in advance during this time.

Central Cuzco

WALKON INN   Guesthouse **$**
(📞 23-5065; www.walkoninn.com; Suecia 504; dm S25, s & d S60; @) Perched on a sunny green corner, this tranquil little place is only a five-minute puff up from the Plaza de Armas but feels almost like the country. Gorgeous views of red-tiled roofs and green hills add to the serenity. Recently refurbished, cozy and family-friendly. Excellent value.

RENACIMIENTO   Apartotel **$$**
(📞 22-1596; www.cuscoapart.com, rapart@gmail.com; Ceniza 331; r per person S60-95; @) An unsigned treasure, this colonial mansion has been converted into 12 stylish one- and two-bedroom apartments sleeping one to six people, each of which is uniquely designed. Cool and classy but cozy and comfortable, it's fabulous for families. Recommended.

HOTEL LOS MARQUESES   Colonial Inn **$$**
(📞 26-4249; www.hotelmarqueses.com; Calle Garcilaso 256; s/d/tr incl breakfast from S180/240/300) An air of romance perfumes this fabulously refurbished colonial villa, built in the 16th century by Spanish conquistadors. Traditional *escuela cuzqueña* paintings, courtyard fountains and balconies with views of the cathedral on the Plaza de Armas will all seduce you. The wood-floored rooms are large and airy; some have split-level sleeping areas and skylights.

HOSTAL LORETO
B&B $$

(☎ 22-6352; www.loretohostal.com; Loreto 115; s/d/tr/q S90/135/165/195) This amiable place has four rooms with Inca walls, which make them rather dark and musty – but then how often do you get to sleep next to an Inca wall? Other rooms are bright, and the location is unbeatable, just steps from the Plaza de Armas. The mirrors and the staircase spiraling like a slide in the center create a bit of a funhouse vibe. Singles and doubles include breakfast.

HOTEL WIRACOCHA
Colonial Inn $$

(☎ 22-1014; www.hotelwiracochacusco.com; Cruz Verde 364; s/d/tr/q S75/120/180/255) Hotel Wiracocha's inviting patio is a haven of colonial charm in a frenetic commercial area. Rooms are varied; many have low ceilings and some are a bit poky, but all have phone and cable TV. Three rooms boast mezzanines and can comfortably accommodate up to five. The eccentrically decorated patios and balconies are a good place to be.

LOS ATICOS
Apartotel $$

(☎ 23-1710; www.losaticos.com; Quera 253, Pasaje Hurtado Álvarez; s/d/apt S90/105/120; @) Hidden in an alley, this sleepy, homely place stays under the radar. Rates include a self-service laundry room and a full guest kitchen. The three mini-apartments sleep up to four and are good value for self-catering groups or families. A smaller sister hotel is located on Av Pardo.

🖉 HOTEL EL ROSAL
Guesthouse $$

(☎ 23-1118; www.residenciaelrosal.com; Cascaparo 116; s/d/tr/q S160/192/224/304) You'll be greeted with smiling faces at this delightful guesthouse over the road from the Mercado San Pedro. The hostel is run by nuns who use the proceeds to fund the neighboring San Pedro home for girls. It feels like a charming hidden world, with manicured rose gardens, long, dreamy hallways, and a soundtrack of children playing. The building has several courtyard gardens, each more inviting than the last, and 29 guestrooms in a spacious modern annex. Highly recommended.

The train from Cuzco to Aguas Calientes passes 5750m-high Nevado Verónica

MARK DAFFEY

DEL PRADO INN   Boutique Hotel $$$
(☎ 22-4442; www.delpradoinn.com;
Suecia 310; s/d/tr incl buffet breakfast
S263/385/507; @ 📶) Located almost
on the Plaza de Armas, this welcome
addition to the Cuzco accommoda-
tion scene has very professional staff
who give highly personalized service.
The hotel contains just over a dozen
snug rooms reached by elevator, all of
which come with lots of extras, includ-
ing wooden floors, central heating,
bathtubs and wi-fi access. Some rooms
have tiny balconies with corner views
of the plaza, though these can be noisy,
especially on weekends. Best of all, the
dining room has original Inca walls.

NIÑOS HOTEL   B&B $$
(☎ 23-1424; www.ninoshotel.com; Meloc
442; s/d without bathroom S60/120, d/tr/q
incl breakfast S132/192/240; @) Run by
a Dutch-founded nonprofit foundation, this hotel helps underprivileged
children in Cuzco by providing food,
medical aid and after-school activities. It inhabits a fetching colonial-era
house with a sunny courtyard, and has
chic yet cozy rooms. Long beloved and
highly recommended. There's another
branch at Fierro 476.

EL BALCÓN HOSTAL   Colonial Inn $$
(☎ 23-6738; www.balconcusco.com;
Tambo de Montero 222; s/d/tr incl break-
fast S120/210/255; @) This attractively
renovated building dating from 1630 has
just 16 guest rooms, all with balconies.
It has a beautiful little garden filled with
curiosities and some great views over
Cuzco. There's also a sauna on the
premises.

HOSTAL CORIHUASI   Colonial Inn $$
(☎ 23-2233; www.corihuasi.com; Suecia 561;
s/d/tr incl breakfast S126/165/198) A brisk
walk uphill from the main plaza, this
cozy guesthouse inhabits a mazelike
colonial building with postcard views
of the Andes. Amply sized rooms are
outfitted in a warm, rustic style with
alpaca-wool blankets, hand-woven rugs
and solid wooden furnishings. Room 1 is
the most in demand for its wraparound
windows, which are ideal for soaking up
panoramic sunsets.

TEATRO INKA B&B   B&B $$
(☎ 24-7372, in Lima 01-976-0523; www.
teatroinka.com; Teatro 391; s/d/tr & ste incl
breakfast S97.50/130/180; @) Classy,
colorful and a bit cosmic, Teatro
Inka is a well-located gem, of-
fering simple, tasteful rooms
with tribal and colonial
touches. All rooms are
good value, and the pent-
house suite is well worth
splurging on. Recom-
mended.

LOS ANGELES B&B
B&B $$
(☎ 26-1101; www.losangeles
cusco.com; Tecsecocha 474;
s/d S120/150; @) While the
public patio is nothing

The sacred peak of Ausangate
PHOTOGRAPHER: GRANT DIXON

Q'oyoriti

Life in Peru often comes to a halt during one of the country's myriad religious rituals. One of the most unusual is the celebration of Q'oyoriti.

Held in late May or early June, between the feasts of the Ascension and Corpus Christi, this procession takes worshippers up one of the area's most sacred mountains: Ausangate (6384m), the *pakarina* (sacred place of origin) of llamas and alpacas. Though it's officially about the icy image of Christ that appeared here in 1783, the festival remains an indigenous appeasement of an *apu* (a sacred deity found in the geographical landscape).

The traditional way to go about this is to buy an *alacita* (miniature scale model) of your desire. Sold en route, these included houses, cars and money. You then line up at the church on the mountain to have it blessed by a priest. It's a three-hour trek up the mountain, traditionally in the wee small hours to arrive around dawn. It's a fervent belief among many inhabitants of the region that if you attend Q'oyoriti three times, you'll get your heart's desire

Note that discomfort will be an aspect of the pilgrimage: Q'oyoriti takes place at an altitude of 4750m. It's brutally cold, there's no infrastructure and the temporary toilets are an ordeal. But the whole thing is other-worldly and monumentally striking. Welcome to Peru – this is the pointy end.

to write home about, rooms are white and bright, with a light colonial touch to make them interesting. The front corner room, furnished with baronial splendor yet spacious and spare, far outshines other rooms.

LOS ANDES DE AMERICA
Chain Hotel $$$

(60-6060; www.cuscoandes.com; Calle Garcilaso 150; s/d/tr/q incl breakfast S330/390/420/480) A Best Western hotel noted for its buffet breakfast, which includes regional specialties such as *mote con queso* (cheese and corn) and *papa helada* (frozen potato). Rooms are warm and comfortable, bathrooms are big and relatively luxurious, and the atrium boasts an impressive scale model of Machu Picchu.

HOSPEDAJE MONTE HOREB
Hotel $$

(23-6775; montehorebcusco@yahoo.com; San Juan de Dios 260, 2nd fl; s/d/tr incl breakfast S66/102/144) Serene and mint fresh with nice big rooms, an inviting balcony, a be-doilied dining room and a curious mix of furnishings. (Check out the wood-look couch cover.)

HOSTAL RESIDENCIAL ROJAS
Guesthouse $$

(22-8184; Tigre 129; s/d/tr/q incl breakfast S60/90/120/150; @) The vine-covered tree you see as you walk in sets the tone for the rest of this dreamy, undersea-feeling family inn – fresh green and white is the order of the day. Rooms are nothing special, and some (namely 205 and 206) are much bigger than others. Still, it's good value for its killer location, just a three-minute walk from the Plaza de Armas.

San Blas

HOSTAL CASA DE CAMPO
B&B $$

(24-4404; www.hotelcasadecampo. com; Tandapata 298; s/d/tr incl breakfast S135/165/195; @) After climbing steeply to reach this irresistibly charming hillside inn, you may have to persevere for many more flights of stone steps before reaching your room. But the reward is

187

The central cloister garden at the Hotel Monasterio

JOHN BORTHWICK

huge: condor's-eye views over the city and incredibly romantic rooms, some with wood fireplaces. Highly recommended.

LOS APUS HOTEL & MIRADOR

Hotel **$$$**

(26-4243; www.losapushotel.com; Atocsaycuchi 515; d S387; ❄ @) Los Apus is a neat, classy little hotel under Swiss management, with an airy courtyard and quality rooms with wooden furnishings. It's so eye-catching that Peruvian feature films have been shot here. It's overpriced, but comes with luxuries such as central heating and direct-dial telephones as well as its own emergency water supply. The rooftop terrace is ideal for meeting other travelers. Note that it can get noisy.

HOTEL MONASTERIO

Luxury Hotel **$$$**

(60-4000; www.monasterio.orient-express. com; Palacio 136; basic r/luxury r S1690/1901, ste S2150-5952; @) Elegantly arranged around graceful 16th-century cloisters, the Monasterio has long been Cuzco's top hotel, with majestic public areas and more than 100 exquisitely designed rooms and suites surrounding its genteel courtyards. Although it has been wholly renovated over the years, the accommodations still show their Jesuit roots, with irregular floor plans and varying room sizes. There are two on-site restaurants.

AMARU HOSTAL

Guesthouse **$$**

(22-5933; www.cusco.net/amaru; Cuesta San Blas 541; s/d/tr incl breakfast S99/129/165; @) In a characterful old building in a prime location, Amaru can't be beat. Flowerpots sit outside relatively peaceful rooms, which have windows to let the sunshine in. Some have rocking chairs from which to admire the rooftop view. Those in the outer courtyard are noisier, and those at the back are newer.

HOTEL ARQUEÓLOGO

Boutique Hotel **$$$**

(23-2569; www.hotelarqueologo.com; Pumacurco 408; s & d/tr/ste incl breakfast S404/502/585; @) This antique Frenchowned guesthouse is renowned for its lovely design. Tastefully done rooms overlook a vast interior courtyard. You can relax in the garden deck chairs, or sip a complimentary pisco sour (grape brandy cocktail) in the fireplace lounge. French, English and German are spoken.

CASA CARTAGENA   Luxury Hotel   **$$$**
(☏ in Lima 01-242-3147; www.casacartagena.com; Pumacurco 336; basic r/luxury r/ste S1845/1901/5400; @ ☒) Ultramodern and uberhip, Casa Cartagena spares no expense. This colonial mansion has been restored and furnished by Italian designers with stunning results. Tinkling water features and oversized installation art, a lap pool, a spa, a sauna and the funkiest multicolored plastic bar furniture this side of Milan – it all adds up to a breathtakingly bold venture. The royal suite, complete with imported Jacuzzi from Italy, sets the benchmark for luxury in Cuzco.

HOSTAL RUMI PUNKU
Boutique Hotel   **$$$**
(☏ 22-1102; www.rumipunku.com; Choquechaca 339; s/d/tr incl breakfast S210/270/345; @) A gem of a place, recognizable by the monumental Inca stonework around the entrance, Rumi Punku (Stone Door) sprawls up and down through a stylish complex of old colonial houses, gardens and terraces. The rooftop terraces and other outdoor areas are utterly charming. Rooms ooze comfort, with central heating, wooden floors and European bedding. Sauna and Jacuzzi are available for a minimal charge.

EUREKA HOSTAL   Boutique Hotel   **$$**
(☏ 23-3505; www.peru-eureka.com; Chihuampata 591; s/d/tr S150/180/250; @) A funky blend of old and new, Eureka's stylish lobby and sun-soaked cafeteria invite further acquaintance. Rooms don't disappoint, with jolly decor strong on traditional motifs. Orthopedic mattresses and down quilts make them as comfortable as they are cool. Flexible tariffs can make it an even better deal.

CASONA LOS PLEIADES   B&B   **$$**
(☏ 22-4713; www.casona-pleiades.com; Tandapata 116; s & d/tr incl breakfast S150/200) A sun-drenched B&B with tidy rooms

overlooking the city, plus a TV and video lounge.

ORQUÍDEA REAL HOSTAL
Guesthouse   **$$**
(☏ in Lima 01-444-3031; www.orquidea.net; Alabado 520; s/d/tr incl breakfast S99/132/165) Owned by a package-tour company, this efficiently run small guesthouse has rustic rooms with working fireplaces, exposed wooden beams and skyline views over the city. All rooms have cable TV, phones and safes; some have king-sized beds.

Avenida El Sol & Downhill
HOTEL LIBERTADOR PALACIO DEL INKA
Luxury Hotel   **$$$**
(☏ 23-1961; www.libertador.com.pe; Plazoleta Santo Domingo 259; s & d/ste S1300/1640; ❄ @) Set in a huge, opulently furnished colonial mansion with a fine interior courtyard, the Libertador boasts Inca foundations. Other parts of the building date back to the 16th century, when Francisco Pizarro was an occupant. It's luxurious and beautiful, even if its rooms have less personality than those of the competing Hotel Monasterio.

HOSTAL INKARRI   B&B   **$$**
(☏ 24-2692; www.inkarrihostal.com; Qolla Calle 204; s/d/tr incl breakfast S99/120/165; @) An airy, roomy place with a sunny garden, well-kept colonial terraces and whimsical collections of old sewing machines, phones and typewriters. Staff is friendly and welcoming. Recommended.

MIRADOR HOSTAL   Guesthouse   **$**
(☏ 24-8986; soldelimperiocusco@yahoo.es; Ahuacpinta s/n; s/d/tr/q incl breakfast S48/66/84/102, q without bathroom S80) A cheery, rambling, yellow concrete jungle overlooking a main road. Friendly, helpful staff make it a favorite. Rates include breakfast.

 Eating

Cuzco's location, nearly dropping off the eastern edge of the Andes, gives it access to an unbelievable range of produce. The local food scene has taken off over the last decade as global influences have seen local products – many of them not available outside Peru – combined in ever more innovative ways.

Central Cuzco

CHICHA
Novoandina $$$

(24-0520; Regocijo 261, 2nd fl; mains S24-40) Celebrity chef Gastón Acurio's first venture in Cuzco serves up a strangely wide-ranging menu in a too-cool-for-school setting. Burgers, pasta and pizza share space with haute versions of meaty classics such as *chicharrones* (deep-fried pork) and *estofado de res* (hearty beef melting off the bone). Expect an experience that is eye-rollingly, plate-lickingly positive.

EL AYLLU
Cafe $

(Marquez 263; snacks from S3.50; 6:30am-10pm) Beloved by Peruvians for its pastries, especially *lengua de suegra* ('mother-in-law's tongue'; a sweet confection) and *sandwich de cerdo* (pork sandwich), El Ayllu is a slow-paced, old-fashioned, high-ceilinged taste of another time. Most of the solemn, suit-clad staff has worked here for decades.

MAKAYLA
Peruvian Classics $$$

(23-4806; cnr Loreto & Plaza de Armas, 2nd fl; mains S30-38) A smart and snappy breath of fresh air in the tourist-trap heavy Plaza, Makayla offers a Peruvian-focused menu with fusion touches, evenly weighted between red meat, white meat and vegetarian dishes. Its *alitas picantes* (spicy chicken wings) and *yuquitas a la huancaína* (fried yucca sticks with creamy cheese sauce) are particularly fabulous for sharing.

JACK'S CAFÉ
International $$

(25-4606; Choquechaca 509; breakfast from S12.50, mains from S14; 7:30am-11:30pm) The only food outlet in the world this reviewer considers worth standing in line for, and she's clearly not alone in her appreciation – the ever-present crowd of hungry travelers waiting outside Australian-run Jack's tells you how popular it is. One breakfast here and you're hooked.

CICCIOLINA
Italian $$$

(23-9510; Triunfo 393, 2nd fl; snacks from S16, mains from S36; 8am-late) Inhabiting a lofty colonial courtyard mansion, Cicciolina has long held its position as Cuzco's best restaurant. The eclectic, sophisticated food is divine, all the way from home-marinated olives through squid-ink pasta to melt-in-the-mouth desserts and biscotti. The service is impeccable, and the ambience will make any laid-back globetrotter feel at home. Highly recommended.

GREEN'S ORGANIC
Healthy $$$

(24-3399; Santa Catalina Angosta 235, 2nd fl; mains S30-38; 11am-10pm; @) With all-organic food and a bright farmhouse feel, Green's Organic oozes health. The salads and wraps are fabulously tasty, telling their own story of pesticide-free, free-range ingredients. The atmosphere is calm and uncluttered, with attentive professional staff.

LOS TOLDOS
Peruvian Classics $

(cnr Almagro & San Andrés; mains from S10; lunch & dinner Mon-Sat) A local favorite contains what has to be Cuzco's best salad bar (try the purpley black olive sauce), and an extensive menu of well-rendered pre-prepared foods. Most people don't get past the Peruvian classic *cuarto de pollo* (spit-roasted quarter chicken), done here to perfection.

ALDEA YANAPAY
International $$

(25-5134; Ruinas 415, 2nd fl; menú S15, mains from S22; 9am-11:30pm) With stuffed animals, board games and decor that evokes the circus you dreamed of running away with as a child, Aldea Yanapay is pitched at families but will appeal to anyone with a taste for the quixotic. Food includes burritos, falafel and tasty little fried things to pick at. Plus, there's a whole separate menu for vegetarians. Profits go to projects helping abandoned children. Highly recommended.

EL REY DE FALAFEL
Street Stand **$**

(Plateros s/n; burgers from S4, falafel from S6; ⏰midnight-5am) Many stalls serve late-night revelers along Plateros and Saphi, but this is by far the best spot to go to at 4am. Not only are the sandwiches tasty, the falafel is the best in Cuzco.

VICTOR VICTORIA
Peruvian Classics **$**

(☎ 25-2854; Tecsecocha 466; mains from S14; ⏰7am-10pm) Around the corner from the Plaza is this budget restaurant, providing princely portions of primarily Peruvian food. Backpackers can't recommend it enough, especially for its filling portions.

San Blas

JUANITO'S
Peruvian Classics **$**

(Qanchipata 596; from S8; ⏰8am-8pm) Good sandwiches were hard to find in Cuzco until Juanito's came along. All the traditional favorites are here, plus some treats such as *lechón* (suckling pig) and *lomo saltado* (a stir-fry of beef with onion, tomato, potato and chili). The inner room could be San Blas' most inviting lounge hangout.

MARCELO BATATA
Peruvian Classics **$$**

(Palacio 121; mains from S28; ⏰2-11pm) As if the stunning view from the rooftop terrace, Cuzco's longest coffee list and a daring array of cocktails weren't enough, Marcelo Batata's food is dangerously delicious. Try pasta with *ají de gallina* (spicy chicken and walnut stew) for an exquisite fusion moment.

GRANJA HEIDI
Cafe Restaurant **$$**

(☎ 23-8383; Cuesta San Blas 525, 2nd fl; mains from S18) Follow the pictures of cows upstairs to this light Alpine cafe with terrific fresh produce, yogurts, cakes and other snacks on offer. The hot breakfasts are gigantic, and can satisfy any carnivorous cravings you may have.

Cuzco Cuisine

Steaming soups, fresh-grilled meats, and an ice-cold *chela* (that's Peruvian slang for beer). Here are some local dishes not to miss when you're in Cuzco.

○ **Anticucho** The Peruvian answer to the lollipop is beef heart on a stick, with a potato on the end for punctuation. Much more delicious than it sounds – many who try it without realizing it's heart end up addicted.

○ **Caldo de gallina** It's impossible to find bad soup in Cuzco, but simple, healthy, hearty *caldo de gallina* (chicken soup) is a standout, and a local favorite for hangovers. It also goes down well if the altitude has you dizzy.

○ **Chicharrones** Deep-fried chunks of pork, served with corn, mint leaves and onion. This one is definitely more than the sum of its parts: get a bit of each ingredient on your fork and you'll experience coronary-inducing heaven.

○ **Choclo con queso** *Choclo* are the huge, pale cobs of corn that are typical of the area. Served with a teeth-squeaking chunk of cheese, it's a great, cheap snack. Look for it in the Sacred Valley.

○ **Cuy** Yes, they really do eat guinea pig. Nothing to be afraid of (it tastes like chicken – honestly!), though it's often served complete with head, which can be, er, disconcerting.

○ **Lechón** Suckling pig with plenty of crackling, generally served with tamales (corn cakes). Another shortcut to a heart attack, but what a way to go.

GOVINDA LILA'S
Vegetarian $

(Carmen Bajo 225B; menú S5; ⏰breakfast, lunch & dinner) Cuzco's best deal and best-kept secret, Lila's unassuming vegetarian restaurant offers cheap, clean, fresh fare to a devoted following of office workers and San Blas hippies. Her sporadically available chocolate and banana cake is worth flying to South America for. Highly recommended.

PICANTERÍA MARÍA ANGOLA
Peruvian Classics $

(Choquechaca 292; mains S10-15; ⏰11am-7pm) A good place to try local foods such as *ubre* (udder), *tripa* (tripe) or *panza apanada* (breaded stomach lining), or less confronting *chicharrones* (pork) and *costillares* (ribs). Turn right and head up the stairs when you walk in.

Avenida El Sol & Downhill
DON ESTÉBAN & DON PANCHO
Bakery $

(☎25-2526; Av El Sol 765A; items from S4.50; ⏰8am-10pm) First it was Cuzco's coolest coffee bar. Then it started baking its own bread and created a generation of ciabatta addicts. Now it has specialty empanadas (turnovers) – you must try *empanada de ají de gallina* before you die. Service is slow, giving you plenty of time to check out the mesmerizing wall display telling the story of the founders.

MELI MELO
Bakery $

(☎23-8383; Limacpampa s/n; items from S2.50) A big bakery with meal-sized slabs of *pastel de acelga* (a savory tart made with Swiss chard) also serves some of Cuzco's best empanadas. Cakes here are fabulous, too. The trick is to ignore the colorful ones – they're all the same bland sponge. Go for the *tres leches*, a cake made with three types of milk.

MONI
Vegetarian $$

(☎23-1029; San Agustín 311; mains S9-14; ⏰8am-9pm) Tiny Moni is much loved for its good-value vegetarian fare, including a mean veg-and-quinoa curry and other adapted Peruvian dishes. The ambience is fresh and airy. Recommended.

🍷 Drinking & Entertainment

Clubs open early, but crank up a few notches after about 11pm. Happy hour is ubiquitous and generally consists of two-for-one offers on beer or certain mixed drinks.

Central Cuzco
INDIGO
Bar Lounge

(Tecsecocha 2, 2nd fl; ⏰noon-late) Indigo is the perfect bar to warm up for a big night out, with fresh Thai and Peruvian food (mains from S15), good coffee, games, hookah pipes and locally famous mojitos. Genuinely friendly

British pub Cross Keys, Cuzco
PHOTOGRAPHER: BRUCE BI

Is That A Toad In Your Beer?

The next time you're in a *picantería* (local restaurant) or *quinta* (house serving typical Andean food), look out for a strange metal *sapo* (frog or toad) mounted on a large box and surrounded by various holes and slots. Men will often spend the whole afternoon drinking *chicha* (fermented corn beer) while competing at this old test of skill in which players toss metal disks as close to the toad as possible. Top points are scored for landing one smack in the mouth. Legend has it that the game originated with Inca royals, who used to toss gold coins into Lake Titicaca in the hopes of attracting a *sapo,* believed to possess magical healing powers and the ability to grant wishes.

staff, comfy couches, an open fire and a seriously cool circus vibe (there are swings!) make it hard to move on. Highly recommended.

CROSS KEYS Pub

(Triunfo 350; ☺10am-late; @) Cross Keys is the most established expat and traveler watering hole in town. It's smothered in the trappings of a typical British pub, with leather barstools and plenty of dark wood. As well as a huge list of British beer, it offers good-value comfort food. Some say the S15 steak is the best-value meal in town.

NORTON RATS Bar

(cnr Santa Catalina Angosta & Plaza de Armas, 2nd fl; ☺7am-late) Run by a motorcycle enthusiast, this down-to-earth bar overlooking the Plaza de Armas has the best damn burgers in town. It also has TVs, darts and billiards to help you work up a thirst.

PEPE ZETA Bar

(Tecsecocha s/n; ☺7pm-late Tue-Sat) The place for *cuzqueños* to see and be seen, Pepe Zeta is cool and breezy, with bamboo decor and a bewildering array of unusual, uncomfortable yet fascinating seating.

MYTHOLOGY Bar & Disco

(Portal de Carnes 300; ☺8pm-late) The iconic nightspot in an iconic party town, Mythology advertises itself as 'only for gods' – though whether you will feel god-like the morning after is debatable. Early in the night it's dominated by rafting groups watching videos of their exploits on the big screen. After midnight the dance floor goes wild to the sounds of 1980s classics, Latino dance favorites and the guy next to the DJ whose job it is to shout encouragement to the sweating hordes.

UKUKU'S Bar & Disco

(☎ 24-2951; Plateros 316; ☺8pm-late) The most consistently popular nightspot in town, Ukuku's plays a winning combination of crowd pleasers – Latin and Western rock, reggae and *reggaetón* (a blend of Puerto Rican *bomba,* dancehall and hip-hop), salsa, hip-hop et al – and often hosts live bands. Usually full to bursting after midnight with as many Peruvians as foreign tourists, it's good, sweaty, dance-a-thon fun.

MAMA AFRICA Bar

(Portal Harinas 191, 2nd fl; ☺7pm-late) A favorite with Israelis, Mama Africa is the classic backpackers' hangout, usually packed with people sprawled across cushions or swaying to rock and reggae rhythms.

San Blas

KM 0 Bar

(☎ 23-6009; Tandapata 100; ☺11am-late Tue-Sat, 5pm-late Sun & Mon) This convivial bar just off Plaza San Blas has a bit of everything. It serves good Thai food in the evening, and there's live music late every night – local musicians come here to jam after their regular gigs.

7 ANGELITOS Lounge
(Siete Angelitos 638; ☺6pm-late Mon-Sat) This tiny hillside haunt is the city's unofficial hipster lounge and late-night backup: when everything else has closed and the sun has come up, knock on the door.

Avenida El Sol & Downhill

CENTRO QOSQO DE ARTE NATIVO
Live Dance
(☎ 22-7901; Av El Sol 604; admission with boleto turístico) For live, nightly performances of traditional Andean music and dance, this is the place to go. The shows get started daily at 6:45pm.

 Shopping

CENTRO ARTESANAL CUZCO
Souvenirs
(cnr Avs El Sol & Tullumayo; ☺9am-10pm) A centralized market southeast of town offers one-stop shopping for jewelry, ponchos, textile, teapots, ceramics – and much, much more.

MERCADO SAN PEDRO Central Market
(Túpac Amaru & Cascaparo, south of Santa Clara)
For the prototypical South American market experience, this sprawling Cuzco market is a must-see. Pig heads for *caldo* (soup), frogs (to enhance sexual performance), vats of fruit juice, roast *lechón* (suckling pig) and tamales are just a few of the foods on offer. Around the edges are stalls stocking clothes, spells, incense and other random products to keep you entertained for hours. Note: professional pickpockets work the area.

Artisan Workshops

The artisan quarter of San Blas – packed with the workshops and showrooms of local craftspeople – offers Cuzco's best shopping. Prices and quality vary greatly, so take time to explore and shop around. Some of the best-known include **Taller Olave** (☎ 23-1835; Plaza San Blas 651), which sells reproductions of colonial sculptures and pre-colonial ceramics. **Taller Mendivil** (☎ 23-3247; Cuesta San Blas, Plaza San Blas) is nationally famous for its giraffe-necked religious figures and sun-shaped mirrors, and **Taller & Museo Mérida** (☎ 22-1714; Carmen Alto 133) offers striking earthenware statues that straddle the border between craft and art.

Textile Workshops

CENTRO DE TEXTILES TRADICIONALES DEL CUZCO
Textiles
(☎ 22-8117; www.textiles cusco.org; Av El Sol 603A; ☺7:30am-8:30pm Mon-Sat, 8:30am-8:30pm Sun) This nonprofit organization, founded in 1996,

Local weaver with her wares
PHOTOGRAPHER: RICHARD I'ANSON

Traditional tapestry, Ollantaytambo

RALPH HOPKINS

promotes the survival of traditional weaving. You may be able to catch a shop-floor demonstration illustrating different weaving techniques in all their finger-twisting complexity.

SHOP OF THE WEAVERS OF THE SOUTHERN ANDES Textiles
(☎ 26-0942; inside CBC, Tullumayo 274; ⏱9am-noon & 3-6pm Mon-Sat) A good cooperative run by 12 mountain communities from Cuzco and Apurimac.

CASA ECOLÓGICA Textiles
(☎ 25-5646; Triunfo 393; ⏱9am-9pm Mon-Sun) Handmade textiles from 29 communities as far away as Ausangate, plus homemade jams and essential oils – a little slice of hippie heaven.

ℹ️ Information

Dangers & Annoyances

Like any big city, Cuzco has crime. Pickpocketing can be a problem in crowded areas. It is advisable to avoid walking around by yourself late at night. Lastly, there are occasional reports of spiked drinks. Solo women travelers should only accept drinks from people they trust.

That said, your biggest concern during your visit will likely be the altitude. Take it easy the first few days. (For advice on dealing with altitude sickness, see p349.)

Emergency

Policía de Turismo (Tourist Police; ☎ 23-5123; Plaza Túpac Amaru s/n; ⏱24hr) Can issue police reports for stolen items.

Medical Services

Clínica Pardo (☎ 24-0997; Av de la Cultura 710; ⏱24hr) Well equipped and expensive – perfect if you're covered by travel insurance. The clinic is located about 2km east of the town center.

Clínica Paredes (☎ 22-5265; Lechugal 405; ⏱24hr) Consultations S60.

Money

ATMs abound in and around the Plaza de Armas, and are also available at the airport, Huanchac train station and the bus terminal. *Casas de cambio* (foreign-exchange bureaus) give better exchange rates than banks, and are scattered around the main plazas and especially along Av El Sol.

Post

Main post office (☎ 22-4212; Av El Sol 800; ⏰8am-8pm Mon-Sat)

Tourist Information

iPerú (☎ 25-2974; www.peru.info; Galerías Turísticas, Av El Sol 103, Office 102; ⏰8:30am-7:30pm) Apart from providing tourist information about Peru in general, iPerú runs Indecopi (☎ 25-2974), the tourist-protection and complaints agency, from its efficient, helpful and knowledgeable city-center office.

South American Explorers Club (SAE; ☎ 24-5484; www.saexplorers.org; Atocsaycuchi 670; ⏰9:30am-5pm Mon-Fri, to 1pm Sat) This indispensable traveler-support organization has good-quality maps, books and brochures for sale, wi-fi access and a book exchange. It can also provide up-to-date information on hiking the Inca Trail, as well as other area treks. The Club's *Alternative Inca Trails Information Packet* is a great resource. An annual membership fee is required to use the facilities. (See p71 for additional information.)

🛈 Getting There & Away

Air

Aeropuerto Internacional Alejandro Velasco Astete (CUZ; ☎ 22-2611) is Cuzco's main airport and offers daily flight to and from Lima, Puerto Maldonado (in the Amazon) and Arequipa. There are international flights to Bolivia three days a week. Check in at least two hours before your flight. During the rainy season (December to April), flights to Puerto Maldonado may be seriously delayed. There is a departure tax of S13 for domestic flights, S36 for international.

Helicusco (☎ in Lima 01-993-52-6251; www.helicusco.com) is located inside Cuzco's airport, and offers scenic helicopter flights between Cuzco, Machu Picchu, Choquequirau and the Sacred Valley.

Bus & Taxi

Buses to major cities leave from the terminal terrestre (☎ 22-4471, Vía de Evitamiento 429), about 700m out of town towards the airport. Buses for more unusual destinations leave from elsewhere. Check carefully in advance.

Left: Youngs boys with lamb, Cuzco; **Below:** The well worn stone streets of Central Cuzco

PHOTOGRAPHER: (BOTH IMAGES) RALPH HOPKINS

Ormeño (📞26-1704; www.grupo-ormeno.com.pe) offers services to most South American capitals. Littoral (📞24-8989), Real Turismo (📞24-3540), San Luis (📞22-3647) and CIAL (📞in Lima 01-330-4225) all travel to the Bolivian capital of La Paz. Tour Peru (📞24-9977, www.tourperu.com.pe) has daily service to Copacabana, on the border.

For long-distance services to major cities within Peru, Ormeño and Cruz del Sur (📞22-1909; www.cruzdelsur.com.pe) have the safest and most comfortable buses across the board. Inka Express (📞24-7887; www.inkaexpress.com; Av La Paz C32, El Óvalo) and Turismo Mer (📞24-5171; www.turismomer.com; Av La Paz A3, El Óvalo) both have daily departures to Puno.

A network of minibuses connects the city to nearby towns. These depart from stops around the city. Minibuses to Pisac leave frequently from the terminal at Tullumayo 207 and the terminal in Puputi, just north of Av de la Cultura. Buses to Urubamba can also be found near Puputi, as well as near the Puente Grau. This latter location also has buses that travel on to Ollantaytambo.

Colectivos (collective taxis) to Andahuaylillas, Tipón and Piquillacta leave from the middle of the street outside Tullumayo 207.

It is easy to hire private taxis for day trips to nearby villages and the Sacred Valley. Be sure to negotiate rates in advance.

Car

Given all the hazards of driving yourself around, it is *highly* recommended to consider hiring a taxi for the day – it's cheaper and safer than renting a car. Otherwise, you'll find a couple of car-rental agencies at the bottom of Av El Sol.

Train

Cuzco has two train stations. Estación Poroy (📞58-1414, Av Pachacutec s/n) is on the outskirts of the city and serves travelers headed to Ollantaytambo and Machu Picchu. A tourist bus (S6) to the station departs every day at 6:15am from Av Pardo. The bus also meets returning trains, dropping passengers off in Plaza Regocijo. You can buy tickets at Estación

197

If You Like...
Pre-Columbian
Ruins

If you enjoy clambering around ruins – and would like to do it in relative solitude – a number of less trafficked sites around Cuzco offer just that:

1 TIPÓN
(admission with boleto turístico; ⊙7am-6pm) About 30km east of Cuzco, you'll find this impressive site, which contains some exceptional terracing and an ingenious irrigation system. The steep dirt road at the turnoff has some excellent spots for eating *cuy* (guinea pig). Taxis from Cuzco can bring you here.

2 PIQUILLACTA & RUMICOLCA
(admission with boleto turístico; ⊙7am-6pm) Literally translated as 'the Place of the Flea,' Piquillacta is the only major pre-Inca ruin in the area. Built around AD 1100 by the Wari (another empire-building culture), it consists of a large ceremonial center surrounded by a defensive wall. On the opposite side of the road about 1km further east is the huge Inca gate of Rumicolca, built on Wari foundations. These sites are located east of Tipón.

3 RAQCHI
(admission S10) About 125km southeast of Cuzco is this ruin that looks from the road like a strange alien aqueduct. These are the remains of the Temple of Viracocha, one of the holiest shrines in the Inca empire. Twenty-two columns made of stone blocks helped support the largest-known Inca roof. Unfortunately, most were destroyed by the Spanish – though there is a reconstruction process underway. The surrounding village is known for its ceramics.

Huanchac, but the easiest way is directly through **PERURAIL** (www.perurail.com). Estación Huanchac (☎58-1414; ⊙7am-5pm Mon-Fri, to midnight Sat & Sun) is near the end of Av El Sol, and serves passengers headed to Puno and Lake Titicaca. (Downtown Estación San Pedro is used only for local trains, which foreigners cannot board.)

ⓘ Getting Around

To/From the Airport
The airport is about 2km south of the city center. A taxi to or from the city center to the airport costs about S5. An official radio taxi from within the airport costs S10. Many hotels offer free pickup with advance reservations.

Bus
A network of *combis* (minibuses) connects different points in the city for less than S1, but it's usually easier to walk or take a taxi than to figure out where any given *combi* is headed.

Taxi
There are no meters in taxis, so be sure to establish a rate when you get in. At time of research, trips within the city center cost about S3. Official taxis, identified by a lit company telephone number on the roof, are more expensive than taxis flagged down on the street, but they are safer. **AloCusco** (☎22-2222) is a reliable company. Unofficial 'pirate' taxis, which only have a taxi sticker in the window, have been complicit in crimes.

Tram
The Tranvía is a free-rolling tourist tram that conducts a 1½ hour hop-on, hop-off city tour (S15). It leaves at 8:30am, 10am, 11:30am, 2pm, 3:30pm, 5pm and 6:30pm from the Plaza de Armas.

AROUND CUZCO

The four ruins closest to Cuzco are Sacsaywamán, Q'enqo, Pukapukara and Tambomachay. They can all be visited in a day – far less if you're whisked through on a guided tour. If you wish to visit these independently, a taxi will charge roughly S40 to take you to all four sites. If you only have time to visit one, Sacsaywamán is the most important (and spectacular), and less than a 2km trek uphill from the Plaza de Armas in central Cuzco.

Each site can only be entered with the *boleto turístico* and is open daily from 7am to 6pm. Local guides hang around offering their services. Agree on a price before beginning any tour.

Robberies at these places are uncommon but not unheard of. It is best to visit in daylight hours, between 9am and 5pm.

Sacsaywamán

This **immense ruin** of both religious and military significance is the most impressive in the immediate area around Cuzco. The long Quechua name means 'Satisfied Falcon,' though tourists will inevitably remember it by the mnemonic 'sexy woman.'

The site is composed of three different areas, the most striking being the magnificent three-tiered zigzag fortifications. One stone, incredibly, weighs more than 300 tons. It was the ninth *inca*, Pachacutec, who envisioned Cuzco in the shape of a puma, with Sacsaywamán as the head and these 22 zigzagged walls as its teeth.

In 1536 the fort was the site of one of the most bitter indigenous rebellions of the conquest. More than two years after Pizarro's entry into Cuzco, Manco Inca recaptured the lightly guarded Sacsaywamán and used it as a base to lay siege to the conquistadors in Cuzco. Manco was on the brink of defeating the Spaniards when a desperate last-ditch attack by 50 Spanish cavalry succeeded in retaking Sacsaywamán and putting an end to the uprising. Manco Inca survived, and retreated to Ollantaytambo, but most of his forces were killed. Thousands of dead littered the

site after the Incas' defeat, attracting swarms of carrion-eating Andean condors. The tragedy was memorialized by the inclusion of eight condors in Cuzco's coat of arms.

Opposite is the hill called **Rodadero**, with retaining walls, polished rocks and a finely carved series of stone benches known as the Inca's Throne. Three towers once stood above these walls. Only the foundations remain, but the 22m diameter of the largest, Muyuc Marca, gives an indication of how big they must have been. With its perfectly fitted stone conduits, this tower was probably used as a huge water tank for the garrison. Other buildings within the ramparts provided food and shelter for an estimated 5000 warriors.

Between the zigzag ramparts and the hill lies a large, flat parade ground that is used for the colorful tourist spectacle of **Inti Raymi**, held every June 24.

Festivities of Inti Raymi, Sacsaywamán
PHOTOGRAPHER: RICHARD I'ANSON

BRENT WINEBRENNER

Q'enqo

The name of this small but fascinating **ruin** means 'zigzag.' It's a large limestone rock riddled with niches, steps and extraordinary symbolic carvings, including the zigzagging channels that probably gave the site its name. These channels were likely used for the ritual sacrifice of *chicha* or, perhaps, blood. Scrambling up to the top you'll find a flat surface used for ceremonies and, if you look carefully, some laboriously etched representations of a puma, a condor and a llama. Back below you can explore a mysterious subterranean cave with altars hewn into the rock.

Q'enqo is about 4km northeast of Cuzco, on the left of the road as you descend from Tambomachay.

Pukapukara

Just across the main road from Tambomachay is this commanding structure looking down on the Cuzco valley. In some lights the rock looks pink, and the name literally means 'Red Fort,' though it is more likely to have been a hunting lodge, a guard post or a stopping point

for travelers. It is composed of several lower residential chambers, storerooms and an upper esplanade with panoramic views.

Tambomachay

In a sheltered spot about 300m from the main road, this site consists of a beautifully wrought ceremonial stone bath channeling crystalline spring water through fountains that still function today. It is thus popularly known as *El Baño del Inca* (The Bath of the Inca), and theories connect the site to an Inca water cult. Pukapukara can be seen from the small signaling post opposite.

THE SACRED VALLEY

The beautiful Río Urubamba valley, popularly known as El Valle Sagrado (The Sacred Valley), is about 15km north of Cuzco as the condor flies. The star attractions are the lofty Inca citadels of Pisac and Ollantaytambo, which preside over its undulating twists and turns. But the valley is also packed with other Inca sites, as well as hectic markets and fetching Andean villages. It's famous for some high-adrenaline activities, from river running to trekking to rock climbing. Most activities can be organized in Cuzco or at some hotels in Urubamba.

Pisac

☎084 / POP 900 / ELEV 2715M

Lying 33km northeast of Cuzco by paved road, Pisac is the most convenient starting point for a visit to the Sacred Valley. There are two distinct parts to Pisac (also spelled Pisaq): the colonial village lying beside the river and the Inca fortress perched dramatically on a mountain spur above.

◎ Sights & Activities

CRAFTS MARKET   Souvenirs

(Plaza de Armas) Pisac is known far and wide for its **outdoor market**, by far the biggest and most touristy in the region. Official market days are Tuesday, Thursday and Sunday, when group tours descend on the town in droves. However, the market has taken over Pisac to such an extent that it fills the Plaza de Armas and surrounding streets every day. Visit on Monday, Wednesday, Friday or Saturday if you want to avoid the crowds.

HORNO TÍPICO DE SANTA LUCÍA
     Bakery & Souvenirs

(Manuel Prado s/n) Huge clay ovens for baking empanadas and *castillos de cuyes* (miniature castles inhabited by guinea pigs) are found in many nooks and crannies, particularly on Mariscál Castilla. This **bakery and store** also incorporates an *artesanía* (crafts) shop. If, for some strange reason, you only have five minutes in Pisac, spend it here – you'll get a pretty good feel for the place.

CHURCH   Religious Site

(Plaza de Armas) At time of research, the INC (Instituto Nacional de Cultura) had demolished the **church** in the

main square in order to reconstruct it in colonial style. Though masses have moved to a nearby chapel, they are nonetheless worth tracking down. On Sundays at 11am, services are celebrated in Quechua, attracting traditionally dressed locals, including men in highland dress blowing horns and *varayocs* (local authorities) with silver staffs of office.

SEAN CAFFREY

Don't Miss Pisac Ruins

This hilltop **Inca citadel** lies high above the village on a triangular plateau with a plunging gorge on either side. It's a truly awesome sight – one that, on most days, is relatively uncrowded. This dominating structure guards not only the Urubamba Valley below, but also a pass leading into the jungle to the northeast.

The most impressive element of the ruins is the agricultural **terracing**, which sweeps around the south and east flanks of the mountain in huge and graceful curves, almost entirely unbroken by steps. Instead, the terracing is joined by diagonal flights of stairs made of flagstones set into the terrace walls. Above the terraces are cliff-hugging footpaths, watched over by caracara falcons and well defended by massive stone doorways, steep stairs and a short tunnel carved out of the rock. Vendors meet you at the top with drinks.

Topping the terraces is the site's **ceremonial center**, with an *intihuatana* (literally 'hitching post of the sun'; an Inca astronomical tool), several working water channels, and some painstakingly neat masonry in the well-preserved **temples**. A path leads up the hillside to a series of ceremonial baths. Looking across the Kitamayo gorge from the back of the site, you'll also see hundreds of holes honeycombing the cliff wall. These are **Inca tombs** that were plundered by *huaqueros* (grave robbers) and are now off-limits.

Many travelers arrive on group tours from Cuzco, but it is easy enough to get here on your own. You can walk the steep – but spectacular – 4km trail from town. (The walk begins on the west side of the church and takes about two hours up and 1½ hours back.) Likewise, you can take a taxi.

NEED TO KNOW

admission with boleto turístico; ☺dawn-dusk

Sleeping

PISAC INN Hotel **$$**
(20-3062; www.pisacinn.com; Plaza de Armas; d with/without bathroom S150/120) Recognizable by its funky geometric designs, this plaza hotel has a pretty courtyard and rustic rooms with hand-painted, indigenous-inspired murals. German, English and French are spoken. Rates include breakfast.

ROYAL INKA HOTEL PISAC Resort **$$**
(20-3064, 20-3066; www.royalinkahotel.com; s/d incl breakfast S187/270;) About 1.5km from the plaza, this large converted hacienda is impressive but endearingly un-splendid – more comfy than commanding. Rooms are generous, many with views of the ruins, and it's all surrounded by lovingly kept flowerbeds and conservatories. Guests have access to an on-site spa and Jacuzzi, as well as the facilities of the Club Royal Inka across the road (which has an Olympic swimming pool, a restaurant, a duck pond and grassy areas for lounging). Highly worthwhile.

Eating

BLUE LLAMA International Fusion **$$**
(Plaza de Armas; www.bluellamacafe.com; menú S19, mains from S10; 9am-9pm) Blue Llama's surreal, dreamlike interior with a children's-story theme is inviting enough. Happy staff, unusually Western-minded vegetarian dishes (steamed vegetables!), desserts to die for, and some funky jewelry and clothes on sale make it irresistible.

ULRIKE'S CAFÉ
International Fusion **$$**
(20-3195; Plaza de Armas; veg/meat menú S17/20, mains from S11; 9am-9pm) This sunny cafe serves up a great vegetarian menú, plus homemade pasta dishes and melt-in-the-mouth cheesecake and brownies. There's a book exchange,

DVDs and special events such as yoga classes. English, French and German are spoken.

RESTAURANTE CUCHARA DE PALO
Novoandina **$$$**
(20-3062; Plaza Constitución; mains S25; 7am-9pm) This cozy, classy place inside the Pisac Inn offers the finest dining available in downtown Pisac, and very fine it is too. It offers the sorts of interesting combinations – such as quinoa in the style of Chinese fried rice – that give *cocina novoandina* (New Andean cuisine) a good name.

ⓘ Information

There's an ATM on the Plaza de Armas. There are slow cybercafes around the plaza and a mini-supermarket on Bolognesi.

ⓘ Getting There & Away

Buses to Urubamba and Cuzco leave frequently from the downtown bridge. Many travel agencies in Cuzco also operate tour buses to Pisac, especially on market days.

Urubamba & Around
084 / POP 2700 / ELEV 2870M
Though the town of Urubamba has little of historical interest, it is surrounded by beautiful countryside and enjoys great weather – making it a convenient base from which to explore some of the surrounding sites in the Sacred Valley. (This attribute has made it a popular pit stop for tour groups.) Located at a significantly lower altitude than Cuzco, it's also an idyllic place to acclimatize prior to visiting Machu Picchu.

◉ Sights & Activities

SALINAS Salt Pans
(4km southwest of Urubamba; admission S5; 9am-4:30pm) This is one of the most spectacular sights in the whole Cuzco area. The thousands of **salt pans** here have been used for salt extraction since Inca times. A hot spring at the top of the valley discharges a small stream

Detour: Moray

South of Salinas, via the village of Maras, you'll find the impressively deep amphitheater-like terracing of this **ancient Inca site** (admission S10; ☉dawn to dusk). If you have the time, it is a fascinating spectacle: different levels of concentric terraces are carved into a huge earthen bowl, each layer of which has its own microclimate. For this reason, some theorize that the Incas used them as a kind of laboratory to determine the optimal conditions for growing crops of each species. There are three bowls, one of which has been planted with various crops as a kind of living museum.

Taxis from Urubamba to visit Moray (with a stop at the salt pans at Salinas) will cost around S80.

of heavily salt-laden water, which is diverted into the mountainside pans and then evaporated to produce a salt used for cattle licks. It may sound pedestrian, but the visuals are beautiful and surreal.

Most folks arrive on tours, but it's just as easy to get here by taxi.

PEROL CHICO   Horse Ranch
(☏ 984-62-4475; www.perolchico.com) Run by Dutch-Peruvian Eduard van Brunschot Vega, this excellent **ranch** outside Urubamba has Peruvian *paso* horses. Eduard organizes horseback-riding tours that last up to two weeks. One-day trips start at US$150. Advance bookings are required.

CUSCO FOR YOU   Horse Ranch
(☏ 79-5301; www.cuscoforyou.com) Another **ranch** offering horseback-riding and trekking trips lasting from one to eight days. A one-day horse trip to Salinas and the nearby Inca terraces at Moray costs about US$89.

Sleeping

LAS CHULLPAS   Cabins $$
(☏ 984-68-5713; www.chullpas.uhupi.com; Pumahuanca Valley; s/d/tr/q S80/130/280/200; @) Hidden 3km above town, these woodland cottages with fireplaces and private bathrooms make

for the perfect getaway. The site is nestled beneath a mountain and thick eucalyptus trees. There are hammocks, an open kitchen where vegetarian food is available, and a sweat lodge (available on request). Much of the food served is grown organically at the hotel's own minifarm, and efforts are made towards composting and recycling. The affable Chilean owner also guides treks. Highly recommended.

RÍO SAGRADO HOTEL   Resort $$$
(☏ 20-1631; www.riosagradohotel.com; s/d US$600/800, 3-bedroom villa US$3500; @) Brand-new and dripping with designer features, Río Sagrado is nestled into the riverside – its modest, jasmine-smelling, water-tinkling exterior coyly downplaying the opulence within. Elegant rooms boast showers with picture windows and artisanal furnishings. The facilities include two Jacuzzis, an electric sauna, a bar crafted from woven marble, sculptures by well-known artists, and – wait for it – breakfast in a hot-air balloon suspended above the lawn. Headshakingly fabulous.

QUINTA PATAWASI   Hotel $$
(☏ 20-1386; www.quintapatawasi.com; s/d/tr/q S115/255/330/405; @) Quinta is a characterful spot recommended for its extremely cheerful, attentive service. English is spoken.

QUINTA LOS GERANIOS
Hotel $

(☎ 20-1093; geraniosurubamba@yahoo.com; Conchatupa s/n; s/d/tr/q S45/60/70/105) Los Geranios has airy, spotless rooms and a breathtaking river view from its open-air staircase. Both the hotel and on-site restaurant (mains from S13; lunch only) are popular and good value.

HOSTAL LOS PERALES
Guesthouse $

(☎ 20-1151; Pasaje Arenales 102; s/d/tr S20/35/60) Tucked away up a dusty country lane near the bus terminal, family-run Los Perales is a hidden treasure. Behind its high wall lies a romantic overgrown orchard, where you could lose yourself for days. Rooms are basic but sunny and spotless, the owners are kind and English is spoken.

K'UYCHI RUMI
Cabins $$$

(☎ 20-1169; www.urubamba.com; d/q S470/810; @) Between Km 74 and Km 75 on the main highway, more than 2km west of town, you'll find half a dozen rustic two-story private cottages built of colorful clay. Each comes with its own kitchenette, fireplace, terrace balcony and two bedrooms. Buffet breakfast costs US$5. The name means 'rainbow stone' in Quechua.

Eating & Drinking

TRES KEROS RESTAURANT GRILL & BAR
Novoandina $$$

(☎ 20-1701; cnr hwy & Señor de Torrechayoc; mains from S26; ☀lunch & dinner) Garrulous chef Ricardo Behar dishes up rich, flavorful *novoandina* fare to pique any gourmet's interest. He also smokes his own trout and imports steak from Argentina – he's serious about his food, and you will be too after you try it. It's 500m west of town.

LA ALHAMBRA
Novoandina $$$

(☎ 20-1200; buffet US$18; ☀11:30am-3:30pm) This *novoandina* buffet place 2km west of town is the spot to be if you're hungry. Set amid charming gardens, where pet alpacas roam, it serves up a dazzling array of *cuzqueño* dishes. Save room for dessert – the *sauco* (Andean blackberry) cheesecake deserves your stomach space.

The salt pans of the Sacred Valley have been in use since Inca times

🛍 Shopping

Internationally known local potter Pablo Seminario creates bright ceramic works with folk and indigenous influences. His workshop, **Seminario Cerámicas** (☎20-1002; www.ceramicaseminario.com; Berriozabal 405; ⏱8am-7pm) – actually a small factory – is open to the public and offers a well-organized tour.

ℹ Getting There & Away

Urubamba is quite spread out, so expect to do a lot of walking or pay for *mototaxis* (three-wheeled motorcycle rickshaw taxis).

Buses leave the terminal on the main highway about 1km west of town for Cuzco every 15 minutes. Here, you'll also find regular buses and *colectivos* to Ollantaytambo as well.

Ollantaytambo

☎084 / POP 700 / ELEV 2800M

Dominated by two massive Inca ruins, the quaint village of Ollantaytambo (known to locals and visitors alike as Ollanta) is the best surviving example of Inca city planning, with narrow cobblestone streets that have been

Inca stone work at the ruins in Ollantaytambo

continuously inhabited since the 13th century. After the hordes passing through on their way to Machu Picchu die down around late morning, Ollanta is a lovely place to be. It's perfect for wandering mazy byways, past stone buildings and babbling irrigation channels, pretending you've stepped back in time. It also offers access to excellent hiking and biking.

👁 Sights & Activities

OLLANTAYTAMBO RUINS   Inca Site
(admission with boleto turístico; ⏱7am-5pm)
The huge, steep terraces that guard Ollantaytambo's spectacular **Inca ruins** mark one of the few places where the Spanish conquistadors lost a major battle. It was to this fortress that the rebellious Manco Inca retreated after his defeat at Sacsaywamán. Then in 1536, Hernando Pizarro (Francisco Pizarro's younger half-brother) led a force of 70 cavalrymen here, supported by large numbers of indigenous and Spanish foot soldiers, in an attempt to capture Manco Inca.

JEFFREY BECOM

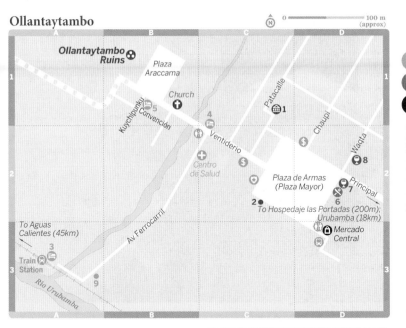

Ollantaytambo

Ollantaytambo map legend reproduced below.

Ollantaytambo

Pizarro's men were showered with arrows, spears and boulders from atop the steep terracing and were unable to climb to the fortress. They were further hampered when Manco Inca, in a brilliant move, flooded the plain below the fortress through previously prepared channels. The Spaniards' horses were bogged down in the water and Pizarro ordered a hasty retreat, which almost became a rout when the conquistadors were followed down the valley by thousands of Manco Inca's victorious soldiers.

The Inca victory was short lived, however. The Spanish forces soon returned with reinforcements and Manco was forced to flee to the jungle stronghold at Vilcabamba.

Though Ollantaytambo was a highly effective fortress, it was also a temple. A finely worked **ceremonial center** is at the top of the terracing. In addition, you'll find some extremely well-engineered walls – which were under construction at the time of the conquest and were never completed. The stone for these was quarried

Ollantaytambo

⊙ **Top Sights**

Ollantaytambo Ruins...........................B1

⊙ **Sights**
1 Museo CATCCO.................................C1

Activities, Courses & Tours
2 Sota Adventures................................C2

🛏 **Sleeping**
3 El Albergue Ollantaytambo Bed & Breakfast...............................A3
4 KB Tambo Hostal C1
5 Kuychipunku Hostal B1

🍴 **Eating**
Café Mayu ....(see 3)
6 Hearts Café.....................................D2
Puka Rumi ....(see 4)

🍷 **Drinking**
7 Bar Cactus D2
8 Ganso D2

Transport
9 PeruRail Ticket Office.........................A3

from the mountainside 6km away, high above the opposite bank of the Río Urubamba. Transporting the

DISCOVER CUZCO, MACHU PICCHU & AROUND OLLANTAYTAMBO

A colorful purchase from the local market in Ollantaytambo

RALPH HOPKINS

huge stone blocks to the site was a stupendous feat: rather than move the massive blocks through the river, the Incas diverted the entire river channel around them.

MUSEO CATCCO   Museum

(🕿 20-4024; www.ollanta.org; Patacalle s/n; suggested donation S5; ⏱9am-6pm) Local community history and ethnography are the main focus at this lovingly tended **museum**. Its displays hold a wealth of fascinating information, all in Spanish, about archaeology, agriculture and religious belief.

SOTA ADVENTURE   Adventure Outfitter
(🕿 45-5030; alanelamigo20@hotmail.com; Plaza de Armas s/n) This **outdoor adventure company** comes highly recommended by readers, particularly for horseback riding. The family-run business also offers mountain biking and multiday hikes. (Though river running is offered, the Ollantaytambo area is not recommended for river running due to problems with pollution.)

 **Sleeping**

**EL ALBERGUE OLLANTAYTAMBO
BED & BREAKFAST**   B&B $$

(🕿 20-4014; www.elalbergue.com; s/d/tr incl breakfast S174/222/284) By the train platform, 800m from the center of the village, El Albergue is a romantic B&B in a characterful early-20th-century building with a lovely garden and a tiny sauna. It's captivating – think colonial hacienda meets the age of steam.

KUYCHIPUNKU HOSTAL

Family Inn $$

(🕿 20-4175; http://kuychipunku.hotels. officelive.com; s/d/tr/q incl breakfast S75/105/135/180) Run by the outstandingly friendly and helpful Bejar-Mejía family, Kuychipunku has it all: Inca walls, colonial archways, modern plumbing and Ollanta's most photographed dining room. Half of the hotel is housed in an Inca building with 2m-thick walls. Rooms in the modern section have less personality, though the huge, light-filled, top-floor units are exceptional value. Recommended.

HOSPEDAJE LAS PORTADAS
Guesthouse **$**

(📞 20-4008; Principal s/n; dm/s/d/tr S15/30/50/60) Although all of the tourist and local buses pass by outside, this family-run place still manages to achieve tranquility. It has a flowery courtyard, a grassy lawn and a rooftop terrace that's excellent for star-gazing.

KB TAMBO HOSTAL
Guesthouse **$$**

(📞 20-4091; www.kbperu.com; Ventiderio s/n; per person S45-75; @ 🛜) Affable North American KB has nailed the 'flashpacker' market with this homey, colorful *hostal* (guesthouse). Travelers who like their home comforts (including, unusually, wi-fi) but enjoy a laid-back, hostel vibe suck this place up like a pisco sour after a dusty day.

Eating

HEARTS CAFÉ
Cafe Restaurant **$$**

(📞 20-4078; www.livingheartperu.org; Plaza de Armas s/n; menú S15, mains from S22 🕗 7:30am-10pm) Hearts Café dishes out delicious, healthy and hearty food and fabulous coffee. The cafe was set up to raise money for the Living Heart Association, an NGO founded by English nutritionist Sonia Newhouse, which has helped improve school lunch programs, among other wellness-related projects. It gratefully accepts donations of warm clothing for people living at 4200m above the Sacred Valley.

PUKA RUMI
Fusion **$$**

(📞 20-4091; Ventiderio s/n; mains from S17; 🕗 7:30am-10pm) Locals rave about the steaks, travelers melt over the breakfasts, and everyone goes into ecstasy over the burritos. In name and appearance it

is no different from thousands of touristy restaurants across Peru, but Puka Rumi is set apart by its simply superb food.

CAFÉ MAYU
Cafe Restaurant **$$**

(mains from S22; 🕗 5am-late) Part of El Albergue, Café Mayu serves excellent espresso to eager train travelers from first departure to last. Inside, its open kitchen quietly turns out a well-balanced menu that includes homemade pasta, lots of vegetarian options and brownies to die for. It's hard to resist the delicious aromas of homemade desserts and pastries wafting through the station.

Drinking

GANSO
Bar

(📞 984-30-8499; Waqta s/n; 🕗 2pm-late) Treehouse meets circus meets *Batman*! The hallucinatory decor in tiny, friendly Ganso is enough to drive anyone to drink. The firemen's pole and swing seats are the icing on the cake.

Doorstep food prep, Ollantaytambo
PHOTOGRAPHER: RICHARD I'ANSON

BAR CACTUS Bar Restaurant
(☎ 79-7162; Principal s/n; ⏰6pm-late) As well as cheap drinks and plenty of chat, Bar Cactus offers a S10 *menú* till 9pm.

 Information

There are a couple of internet cafes and ATMs in and around Plaza de Armas. There are no banks, but several places change money.

Getting There & Away

Bus & Taxi

Frequent minibuses and *colectivos* shuttle between Urubamba and Ollantaytambo. To get to Cuzco, it's easiest to change in Urubamba, though there are occasional departures direct from Ollantaytambo to Cuzco's Puente Grau.

Train

The local station offers service to Aguas Calientes (for Machu Picchu), as well as to Cuzco. PeruRail (www.perurail.com; ⏰5am-8pm) has more than a dozen departures each way per day. Check the website for exact times and costs. It is best to buy tickets at least one day in advance. During high season, make reservations as far in advance as possible. If heading to Aguas Calientes, buy a return ticket since returning trains are frequently booked to capacity.

MACHU PICCHU & AROUND

Aguas Calientes

☎084 / POP 1000 / ELEV 2410M

Also known as Machu Picchu Pueblo, this town lies in a deep gorge below the ruins, enclosed by towering walls of stone cliff and cloud forest, and divided by two rushing rivers. The location is eye-poppingly gorgeous – that's the good news. The bad news is that every traveler to and from Machu Picchu must pass through here, so Aguas Calientes is about as touristy a town as you'll ever come across. Come prepared for high prices and a sea of touts. What keeps it worthwhile is the gorgeous setting and easy access to the ruins: only those who sleep here or walk the Inca Trail get to catch Machu Picchu at sunrise.

◉ Sights & Activities

MUSEO DE SITIO MANUEL CHÁVEZ BALLÓN

Museum

(admission S21; ⏰9am-5pm) Located by the Puente Ruinas, at the base of the footpath to Machu Picchu, this **museum** has superb information (in Spanish and English) on the archaeological excavations of Machu Picchu and Inca building methods. Stop here before or after the ruins

The train from Aguas Calientes to Cuzco
PHOTOGRAPHER: BRENT WINEBRENNER

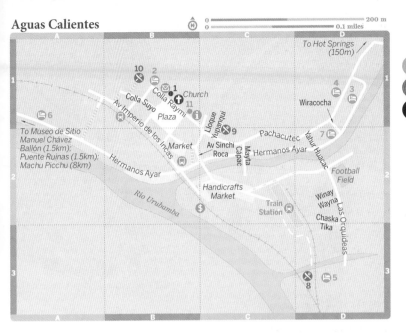

to get a sense of context (and to enjoy the air-conditioning and soothing music if you're walking back from the ruins after hours in the sun!). There's a small botanical garden outside, down a set of Inca stairs.

HOT SPRINGS   Hot Springs
(admission S10; ☺5am-8:30pm) Weary trekkers soak away their aches in the town's **hot springs** (from which the town derives its name), about a 10-minute walk up Pachacutec from the train tracks. Note that the springs are tiny and can get a little scungy by late morning. Towels can be rented by the entrance.

ANDEAN SPA   Spa
(☎ 21-1355; Plaza Manco Capac s/n) Traveler-recommended **spa** offering massages.

 Sleeping

MACHU PICCHU PUEBLO HOTEL
                                      Hotel $$$
(☎ in Lima 01-610-0400; www.inkaterra.com; d US$463-960; ❄ @) For nature lovers who crave creature comforts, this

Aguas Calientes

Activities, Courses & Tours

trendy eco-themed hotel is a 100m walk southeast of the train station. Set amid tropical gardens featuring a bamboo-and-eucalyptus sauna, the hotel's hand-hewn cottages are done up in nouveau-Andean style and are connected by stone pathways. The whole complex is comfortable and inviting. Recommended.

SUMAQ MACHU PICCHU HOTEL
Luxury Hotel **$$$**

(☎ 21-1059; www.sumaqhotelperu.com; Hermanos Ayar s/n; s/d incl some meals from S1312/1593; ❄ @) From the outside, Sumac bears an unfortunate resemblance to Fred Flintstone's house, but the inside is a wonderland of hushed, pampering luxury. Light-filled spaces with playful splashes of bold color give this new hotel a modern, stylish look. Rooms boast views of the river or the mountains. There are multiple eating and drinking areas, as well as a full spa (treatments from S176). Room rates include breakfast, afternoon tea and either lunch or dinner.

LA CABAÑA HOSTAL Guesthouse **$$**
(☎ 21-1048; Pachacutec s/n; s & d/tr incl breakfast S225/285; @) Further uphill than most of the hotels, this popular, airy spot has woody, rustic-feel rooms with phones, heating and free internet access. Buffet breakfast in the colorful, cushioned restaurant is included.

GRINGO BILL'S Hotel **$$**
(☎ 21-1046; www.gringobills.com; Colla Raymi 104; s & d/junior ste/ste/f ste S225/315/405/450) One of the original places for tourists to stay in Aguas Calientes, multilayered Gringo Bill's continues to charm with its white-walled, flower-bedecked open spaces and comfortable, uniquely decorated rooms. At time of research it was undergoing a remodel. The two-bedroom family suite sleeps up to five.

WIRACOCHA INN Hotel **$$**
(☎ 21-1088; wiracocha-inn@peru.com; Wiracocha s/n; s & d/tr/q S195/240/285) On a side street crowded with midrange hotels, this newer option has well-kept and polished rooms, amiable service and a sheltered patio area near the river. In some rooms you'll be lulled to sleep by the Andean mountain waters rushing by.

HOSTAL MAYURINA Guesthouse **$$**
(☎ 77-7247; www.hostalmayurina.com; Hermanos Ayar s/n; s/d/tr incl breakfast

Left: Hot springs, Aguas Calientes; **Below:** Wooden handicrafts for sale in Aguas Calientes

PHOTOGRAPHER: (LEFT) MARK DAFFEY. (BELOW) JUDY BELLAH

S90/120/180) Sparkling new and keen to please, Mayurina is nothing if not airy, with an open-air reception area and spiral staircase. Rooms have phones and televisions.

 Eating

CAFÉ INKATERRA　　Novoandina　**$$**
(📞 21-1122; Machu Picchu Pueblo Hotel; mains from S25; 🕙 11am-9pm) A stylish spot for a filling Peruvian-fusion spread, this restaurant is hidden behind the train station. With flickering votive candles and a chilled-out soundtrack to match the tantalizing *novoandina* menu, the atmosphere here is truly an escape from the masses.

TREE HOUSE　　Novoandina　**$$**
(📞 21-1101; Huanacaure s/n; mains from S27; 🕙 lunch & dinner) The aptly named Tree House's woody ambience provides just the right laid-back setting for its food.

Lovingly prepared and locally focused, this is what *novoandina* cuisine is all about – recipes that combine international influences with fresh, distinctive local produce. Alpaca loin with bacon and *chimichurri* (a savory sauce of local herbs), quinoa risotto, and *lúcuma* (an earthy Andean fruit) caramel are some lip-smacking examples.

INDIO FELIZ
　　　　　　International Fusion　**$$$**
(📞 21-1090; Lloque Yupanqui 4; menú S50, mains from S38; 🕙 11am-10pm) Indio Feliz's award-winning French chef whips up fantastic meals, which have made this place deservedly popular – and 'world famous' in Aguas Calientes. The S50 *menú* is extremely good value for a decadent dinner.

213

ℹ Information

There's a helpful branch of iPerú (📞21-1104; Edificio del Instituto Nacional de Cultura, Pachacutec, cuadra 1; ⏱9am-1pm & 2-8pm) near the Machu Picchu ticket office (⏱5am-10pm). There's currently one ATM, at BCP (Av Imperio de los Incas s/n), but it often runs out of money, particularly on weekends. Currency and traveler's checks can be exchanged in various places at unfavorable rates, so it's best to bring plenty of cash. There's a small post office (Colla Raymi s/n).

ℹ Getting There & Away

There are only three options to get to Aguas Calientes, and hence to Machu Picchu: trek it, catch the train via the Sacred Valley, or travel by road and train via Santa Teresa.

Train

PeruRail (www.perurail.com) offers two classes of service to Aguas Calientes directly from Cuzco. The Vistadome (S228 each way) is the more standard option, while the fancier Hiram Bingham (S1882 each way) includes brunch, afternoon tea, entrance to Machu Picchu and a guided tour. Buy a round-trip ticket to avoid getting stranded in Aguas Calientes – outbound tickets sell out much quicker than tickets in.

Check PeruRail's website for up-to-date schedules and prices.

Machu Picchu

For many visitors to Peru and even South America, a visit to the Inca city of Machu Picchu is the sweet cherry on the top of their trip. One of the best-known archaeological sites on the continent, this awe-inspiring ancient city was never revealed to the conquering Spaniards and was virtually forgotten until the early part of the 20th century. In the high season (late May until early September), an estimated 2500 people arrive daily. Despite this influx, Machu Picchu nonetheless retains an air of grandeur and mystery.

For any visitor to Peru, this is a must.

History

Machu Picchu is not mentioned in any of the chronicles of the Spanish conquistadors. Apart from a couple of German adventurers in the 1860s, who apparently looted the site with the Peruvian government's permission, nobody apart from local Quechua people knew of its existence until American historian Hiram Bingham was guided to it by locals in 1911.

The Machu Picchu site was initially overgrown with thick vegetation, forcing Bingham's team to be content with roughly mapping the site. He returned in 1912 and 1915 to carry out the difficult task of clearing the thick forest. It was at this point that he also mapped some of the ruins on the so-called Inca Trail. (You can read Bingham's own account in *Inca Land: Explorations in the Highlands of Peru,* first published in 1922.) Peruvian archaeologist Luis E Valcárcel undertook further studies in 1934, as did a Peruvian-American expedition under Paul Fejos in 1940–41.

Bingham's search was originally for the lost city of Vilcabamba, the last stronghold of the Incas, and he thought he had found it at Machu Picchu. (In fact, he died believing he had.) But we now know that the remote ruins at Espíritu Pampa, much deeper in the jungle, are actually the remains of Vilcabamba. Despite scores of more recent studies, knowledge of Machu Picchu remains sketchy. Even today archaeologists are forced to rely heavily on speculation as to its function. Some believe that it was founded in the waning years of the Inca Empire, while others think it was a royal retreat or country palace abandoned at the time of the Spanish invasion. The site's director believes that it was a city, a political, religious and administrative center. Its location, and the fact that at least eight access routes have been discovered, suggests that it was a trade

Machu Picchu

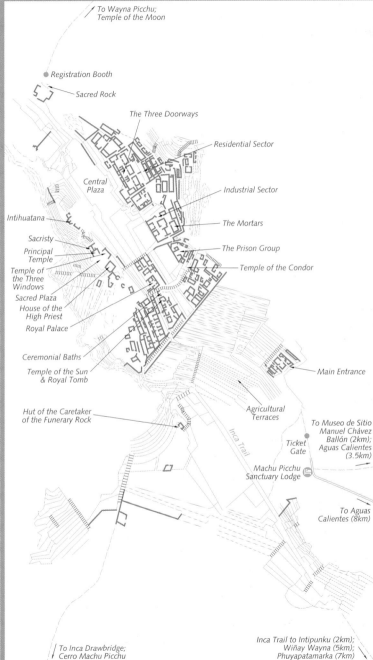

0   200 m
0   0.1 miles

To Wayna Picchu;
Temple of the Moon

Registration Booth

Sacred Rock

The Three Doorways

Residential Sector

Central
Plaza

Industrial Sector

Intihuatana

The Mortars

Sacristy

Principal
Temple

The Prison Group

Temple of
the Three
Windows

Temple of the Condor

Sacred Plaza

House of the
High Priest

Royal Palace

Ceremonial Baths

Temple of the Sun
& Royal Tomb

Main Entrance

Hut of the Caretaker
of the Funerary Rock

Agricultural
Terraces

To Museo de Sitio
Manuel Chávez
Ballón (2km);
Aguas Calientes
(3.5km)

Ticket
Gate

Machu Picchu
Sanctuary Lodge

Inca Trail

To Aguas
Calientes (8km)

To Inca Drawbridge;
Cerro Machu Picchu

Inca Trail to Intipunku (2km);
Wiñay Wayna (5km);
Phuyapatamarka (7km)

nexus between the Amazon and the highlands.

It seems clear from the exceptionally high quality of the stonework and the abundance of ornamental work that Machu Picchu was once vitally important as a ceremonial center. Indeed, to some extent, it still is: Alejandro Toledo, the country's first full-blooded indigenous president, staged his inauguration here in 2001.

 ## Sights & Activities

Inside the Ruins

Unless you arrive via the Inca Trail, you'll officially enter the ruins through a ticket gate on the south side of Machu Picchu. About 100m of footpath brings you to the mazelike main entrance of Machu Picchu proper, where the ruins lie stretched out before you, roughly divided into two areas, and separated by a series of plazas.

To get a visual fix of the whole site and snap the classic postcard photograph, climb the zigzagging staircase on the left immediately after entering the complex, which leads to a hut. Known as the **Hut of the Caretaker of the Funerary Rock**, it is one of a few buildings that have been restored with a thatched roof, making it a good shelter in the case of rain. The Inca Trail enters the city just below this hut. The carved rock behind the hut may have been used to mummify the nobility, hence its name.

If you continue straight into the ruins instead of climbing to the hut, you pass through extensive terracing to a series of 16 connected **ceremonial baths** that cascade across the ruins.

Just above and to the left of the baths is Machu Picchu's only round building, the **Temple of the Sun**, a curved and tapering tower that contains some of the site's finest stonework. It appears to have been used for astronomical purposes. Inside are an altar and a curiously drilled trapezoidal window that looks onto the site. The Temple of the Sun is cordoned off to visitors, but you can see into it from above, which is likely to be how you will approach it.

Machu Picchu's Temple of the Sun and the view down into the Urubamba Valley

Don't Miss Cerro Machu Picchu

A roughly two-hour climb brings you to the top of Machu Picchu hill, to be rewarded with the site's most extensive view – all the way to the Inca trail to Wiñay Wayna and Phuyupatamarka, down to the valley floor and the impressive terracing near Km 104 and across the site of Machu Picchu itself. This walk is more spectacular than Wayna Picchu, and less crowded. Allow yourself plenty of time to enjoy the scenery (and catch your breath!). Recommended.

Below the temple is an almost hidden, natural rock cave that was carefully carved, with a steplike altar and sacred niches, by the Inca stonemasons. It is known as the **Royal Tomb**, though no mummies were actually ever found here.

Climbing the stairs above the ceremonial baths, you reach a flat area of jumbled rocks, once used as a quarry. Turn right at the top of the stairs and walk across the quarry on a short path leading to the four-sided **Sacred Plaza**. The far side contains a small viewing platform with a curved wall, which offers a view of the snowy Cordillera Vilcabamba in the far distance and the Río Urubamba below.

Important buildings flank the remaining three sides of the Sacred Plaza. The **Temple of the Three Windows** commands an impressive view of the plaza below through the huge trapezoidal windows that give the building its name. With this temple behind you, the **Principal Temple** is to your right. Its name derives from the massive solidity and perfection of its construction. The damage to the rear right corner of the temple is the result of the ground settling below this corner rather than any inherent weakness in the masonry itself. Opposite the Principal Temple is what is known as the **House of the High Priest**.

KARL LEHMANN

Behind the Principal Temple lies a famous small building called the **Sacristy**. It has many well-carved niches, perhaps used for the storage of ceremonial objects. The Sacristy is especially known for the two rocks flanking its entrance; each is said to contain 32 angles.

A staircase behind the Sacristy climbs a small hill to the major shrine in Machu Picchu, the **Intihuatana**. This Quechua word loosely translates as the 'Hitching Post of the Sun' and refers to the carved rock pillar, often mistakenly called a sundial, which stands at the top of the Intihuatana hill. The Inca astronomers were able to predict the solstices using the angles of this pillar, but exactly how it was used for these astronomical purposes remains unclear. Nonetheless, its elegant simplicity and high craftsmanship make it a highlight.

At the back of the Intihuatana is another staircase. It descends to the **Central Plaza**, which separates the ceremonial sector of Machu Picchu from the more mundane residential and industrial sectors, which were not as well constructed. At the lower end of this latter area is **The Prison Group**, a labyrinthine complex of cells, niches and passageways, positioned both under and above the ground. The centerpiece of the group is the **Temple of the Condor**, which contains a carving of the head of a condor, with the natural rocks behind it resembling the Andean bird's outstretched wings. Behind the condor is a well-like hole and, at the bottom of this, the door to a tiny underground cell that can only be entered by bending double.

Intipunku

The Inca Trail ends after its final descent from the notch in the horizon called Intipunku (Sun Gate). Looking at the hill behind you as you enter the ruins, you can see both the trail and Intipunku. This hill, called Machu Picchu (Old Peak) gives the site its name. It takes about an hour to reach Intipunku, and if you can spare at least half a day for the round trip, it may be possible to continue as far as Wiñay Wayna, on the Inca Trail. Expect to pay S15 or more as an unofficial reduced-charge admission fee to the trail, and be sure to return before 3pm, which is when the checkpoint typically closes.

Inca Drawbridge

A scenic but level walk from the Hut of the Caretaker of the Funerary Rock takes you right past the top of the terraces and out along a narrow, cliff-clinging trail to the Inca Drawbridge. The walk takes 30 minutes and the trail gives you a good look at cloud-forest vegetation and an entirely different view of Machu Picchu. This walk is recommended, though you'll have to be content with photographing the bridge from behind a barrier meters above it. Someone crossed the bridge some years ago and, tragically, fell to their death.

Wayna Picchu

Wayna Picchu is the small, steep mountain at the back of the ruins. At first glance, it would appear that Wayna Picchu is a difficult climb but it is not. Although the ascent is steep, it's not technically difficult. The path zigzags up the side of the mountain and lands at a small set of Inca constructions at the top.

Part of the way up Wayna Picchu, a marked path plunges down to your left, continuing down the rear of Wayna Picchu to the small **Temple of the Moon**. The trail is easy to follow, but involves steep sections, a ladder and an overhanging cave, which is a bit tricky to get past. The descent takes about an hour, and the ascent back to the main Wayna Picchu trail longer. But it's spectacular: the trail drops and climbs steeply as it hugs the sides of Wayna Picchu before plunging into the cloud forest. Suddenly, you reach a cleared area where the small, very well-made ruins are found. From here, another cleared path leads up behind the ruin and steeply onward up the back side of Wayna Picchu.

Note that access to Wayna Picchu is limited to 400 people per day – the first 200 in line are let in at 7am, and another 200 at 10am. Lines are long and competition for places is fierce – get here early if you're serious about doing this climb. Cerro Machu Picchu is a very good alternative to this climb.

 Sleeping & Eating

MACHU PICCHU SANCTUARY LODGE
Hotel $$$
(☎ 984-81-6953; www.sanctuarylodge hotel.com; r standard/mountain view/ste US$852/1009/1440) This is the only place to stay at Machu Picchu itself and is criminally overpriced. There is no earthly reason to stay here – you can catch the bus up from Aguas Calientes in time to be here when the site opens. Even so, it's often full. Book ahead.

 Information

The ruins are most heavily visited between 10am and 2pm, and June to August are the busiest months. Plan your visit early or late in the day to avoid the crowds. A visit early in the morning midweek during the rainy season guarantees you room to breathe, especially during February, when the Inca Trail is closed.

It's well worth buying entrance tickets for **Machu Picchu** (adult/student S124/62; ⏰6am-5pm) in advance, at the **ticket office** (Edificio del Instituto Nacional de Cultura, Pachacutec s/n; ⏰5am-10pm) in Aguas Calientes, to avoid long line-up times and possible hassles getting change at the overstretched ticket office on site.

You are not allowed to bring walking sticks or backpacks of more than 20L capacity into the ruins – they have to be checked in at one of the two luggage-storage offices.

Local guides are readily available for hire at the entrance. Make sure to agree upon a price in advance and clarify whether it's per person or covers the whole group, and how long the tour will be.

Food at the cafe just outside the gate is overpriced, but eating inside the site is forbidden. If you bring your own food, eat it outside the gate. Disposable plastic bottles are also forbidden – the only way to get water in is in camping-type drink bottles. Water is sold at the cafe just outside the entrance, but only in glass bottles.

Tiny sandfly-like bugs abound. Use insect repellent.

Lastly, the weather at Machu Picchu seems to have only two settings: heavy rain or bright, burning sunlight. Don't forget rain gear and, more importantly, sunblock.

For a truly in-depth exploration of the site, take along a copy of *Exploring Cuzco* by Peter Frost.

ⓘ Getting There & Around

From Aguas Calientes, buses for Machu Picchu leave from a ticket office along the main road for the winding 8km trip up the mountain. Departures are frequent, starting at 5:30am and finishing at 2:30pm. Buses return from the ruins when full, with the last departure at 5:45pm.

Otherwise, it's a 20-minute walk from Aguas Calientes to Puente Ruinas, where the road to the ruins crosses the Río Urubamba, near the museum. A breathtakingly steep but well-marked trail climbs another 2km up to Machu Picchu, taking about an hour to hike (less coming down!).

The Inca Trail

This 43km, four-day trek – the most famous in South America – snakes over high Andean passes, through lush cloud forest and past cliff-hugging Inca ruins from the Sacred Valley to Machu Picchu. It is an unforgettable experience.

Most treks begin at Km 82 on the railway that leads to Aguas Calientes. After crossing the Río Urubamba (2200m), you'll climb to the first archaeological site, **Llactapata** (Town on Hillside), before heading down a side valley of the Río Cusichaca. The path then leads south, to the hamlet of **Wayllabamba** (Grassy Plain; 3100m), where many groups camp the first night – and where you can take in views of the **Nevado Verónica** (5750m).

From here, the route crosses the Río Llullucha, then climbs steeply through the area known as **Tres Piedras** (Three White Stones). It's a steep 3km climb through humid woodlands, before emerging on the bare mountainside of **Llulluchupampa**.

The trail then ascends to **Warmiwañusca Pass**. At 4198m above sea level, this is the highest point of the trek – leaving many a seasoned hiker gasping. It's followed by a steep decline to the river, where you'll find **Paq'aymayo**, at an altitude of about

The Inca Trail offers stunning vistas of the rainforests of the Andes

KARL LEHMANN

Inca Trail

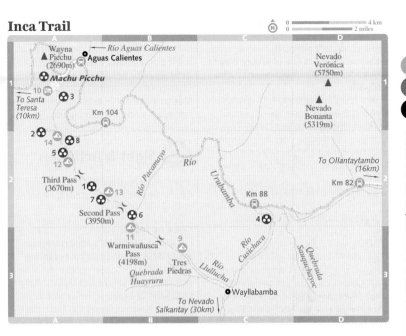

3500m, where there are campsites. The trail crosses the river over a small footbridge and climbs toward **Runkurakay** (Basket-Shaped Building), a round ruin with superb views.

Above Runkurakay the trip continues, past two small lakes, to the top of the Second Pass at 3950m, which has views of the snowcapped Cordillera Vilcabamba. You're now on the Amazon slope of the Andes and the ecology immediately gets lush. The path then descends to the ruin of **Sayaqmarka** (Dominant Town), a complex on a mountain spur with incredible views, and continues downward, crossing a tributary of the Río Aobamba (Wavy Plain).

From here, the trail climbs through cloud forest and an old Inca tunnel, up to the third pass, at almost 3700m. This spot has grand views of the Río Urubamba valley, as well as campsites where some groups spend their final night. Just below is the well-restored ruin of **Phuyupatamarka** (Town Above the Clouds), which contains a series of ceremonial baths.

Inca Trail

Afterwards, the trail dives down a masterfully engineered flight of Inca steps. (These can be nerve-racking in the early hours – pack a flashlight.)

221

Eventually, you will zigzag down to a red-roofed building that marks the final night's campsite. Here, trails lead to the exquisite little Inca site of **Wiñay Wayna** and a spectacular terraced spot called **Intipata**.

The last day begins before dawn, winding through cloud forest before reaching **Intipunku** (Sun Gate). This is where you'll enjoy your first glimpse of of the majestic Machu Picchu. The final triumphant descent takes about an hour.

For details on finding a reputable operator for the trip – or alternate routes to Machu Picchu – turn to p183.

Santa Teresa

📞 084 / POP 460 / ELEV 1900M

Located northwest of Machu Picchu, Santa Teresa is an unprepossessing town. Most buildings in its tiny center are emergency-relief prefabricated shells donated after the flood of 1998, which leveled the town. Once you've familiarized yourself with the center, listened to the chickens clucking in the Plaza de Armas, and marveled at

the statue of the strangely ferocious man threatening some flowers, you've pretty much exhausted the entertainment possibilities. The real attractions here are outside of town: namely, the Cocalmayo hot springs, the Cola de Mono zipline and – most intriguingly – backdoor access to Machu Picchu.

👁 Sight & Activities

Treks in the area are organized out of Cuzco. See Activities (p182) for a list of outfitters.

COLA DE MONO   Zipline
(📞 79-2413, 984-70-9878; info@canopyperu. com; US$40) This is Peru's only **zipline** and South America's highest – in other words, a must for thrill seekers. A total of 2500m of zipline in six separate sections whizzes you back and forth high above the Sacsara Valley. The owners also do **river running** on the spectacular, and so far little-exploited, Santa Teresa river.

Walking the stone paths of the Inca Trail (p220)

MARGIE POLITZER

Detour: Cocalmayo

About 4km from Santa Teresa, the stunningly landscaped, council-owned **Baños Termales Cocalmayo** (admission S10; 🕙24 hr) are truly a world-class attraction. As if huge, thermal hot springs and a natural shower straight out of a jungle fantasy weren't enough, you can buy beer and snacks and even camp in the gorgeous grassy grounds. The astonishing fact that the baths are open 24 hours has caused many delirious travelers to think they have in fact died and gone to heaven.

You can reliably catch a *colectivo* from Santa Teresa to Cocalmayo at around 3pm, when vehicles head down to collect Inca Jungle Trail walkers arriving from Santa María. Otherwise, you can take a taxi for about S10.

The site is located east out of town. Allow about 2½ hours for the zipline tour. Taxis can take you for S10.

Sleeping

HUGO'S LODGE Hotel $
(☎ 77-9956; www.hugoslodge.com; r per person S20) This spot is a bargain – and the Santa Teresa area's finest option. Airy bungalows and an expansive bar-restaurant overlook Cocalmayo, a 10-minute hike away.

ALBERGUE MUNICIPAL Hostel $
(☎ 79-2376; alberguemunicipal _st@hotmail. com; dm/s/d/tr S25/50/80/90) Next to the football field, this is the best option in town. It has a manicured lawn and cool, spacious rooms. The one dorm holds up to 11 people. Book ahead.

Eating & Drinking

The best food options are **Crudo's Club**, which offers standard fast food and decent *menús,* and **Mama Coca**, which serves (at glacial speeds) some yummy regional classics.

Crudo's Club is Santa Teresa's most happening nightspot, with a big bar and

a small dance floor. **Sentidos**, behind the plaza, is the best choice for a quiet beer.

 Information

There are no banks or ATMs in Santa Teresa – you must bring all the cash you need. Don't count on being able to change dollars or find internet access, either.

 Getting There & Away

Most travelers arrive in Santa Teresa as part of an organized trek.

You can take the train to Aguas Calientes for visits to Machu Picchu from here. The Peru Rail ticket office (🕙6-8am & 10am-3pm daily, 6-8pm Wed & Sun) is in the Santa Teresa bus terminal. Train tickets on this route are sold only at this ticket office, and only on the day of departure. To get to the station, you can take a minibus from the bus terminal (departing at 3:45pm) or take a taxi.

EAST OF CUZCO

The rickety railway and the paved road to Lake Titicaca shadow each other as they both head southeast from Cuzco. En route you can investigate ancient ruins and pastoral Andean towns that are great detours for travelers who want to leave the Gringo Trail behind.

Iglesia de San Pedro, Andahuaylillas

BRENT WINEBRENNER

For points of interest closer to Puno, see p133.

Andahuaylillas

📞 084 / POP 840 / ELEV 3123M

Andahuaylillas is more than 45km southeast of Cuzco, about 7km before the road splits at Urcos. (Not to be confused with Andahuaylas, another highland settlement west of Cuzco.) It's a pretty Andean village that is most famous for its lavishly decorated Jesuit church.

 **Sights & Activities**

IGLESIA DE SAN PEDRO

Church

(admission S5; ⏰ 7am-5:30pm) Dating back to the 17th century this **picturesque church** may have a simple exterior, but its interior is an extravaganza of unusual rococo embellishments – including woodcarvings draped in gold leaf

and an unusual Andean baroque ceiling that is painted in the earthy colors generally used in *escuela cuzqueña* art. The church also contains countless religious canvases, including a painting of the Immaculate Conception that is attributed to legendary Spanish baroque painter Esteban Murillo (1617–82). It is for this reason that San Pedro is frequently referred to as the 'Sistine Chapel of Latin America.' There are reportedly many gold and silver treasures locked in the church, and the villagers are all involved in taking turns guarding it 24 hours a day. Is the rumor true or not? All we can tell you is that the guards take their job *very* seriously.

MUSEO DE RITOS ANDINOS

Museum

(admission by donation; ⏰ 7am-6pm) An eclectic little **museum** whose somewhat random displays include a mummified child and an impressive number of deformed craniums.

Shopping

Q'EWAR PROJECT Crafts
(www.qewar.com) Across from the
church you'll find this **shop** for a local
women's cooperative that makes distinctive dolls clad in traditional costumes.

Getting There & Around

To reach Andahuaylillas, take any Urcos-bound
bus from the terminal just off Av de la Cultura
in Cuzco. Taxis from Cuzco will bring you to the
church and will wait for you while you visit the
town. Negotiate the fare in advance.

Huaraz, Trujillo & the North

In the north, expect the unexpected. Majestic mountains – the highest outside the Himalayas – are bordered by desert coast studded with the remnants of artful pre-Columbian civilizations.

To the interior, you'll find the Cordillera Blanca, a mecca for hiking, trekking and mountain climbing – all located within convenient reach of the 3000-year-old ruins at Chavín de Huántar. Along the coast you'll find long-forgotten adobe pyramids and splendid museums tucked between the bottle-green oases of Trujillo and Chiclayo. Oh, and did we mention that the area has a pumping surf scene?

The north offers dramatic mountain landscapes, hospitable rural villages, hip-shaking *cumbias* and delectable regional cuisine.

Child-friendly travel Andes-style
PHOTOGRAPHER: RICHARD I'ANSON

227

Llamas grazing in the Andes

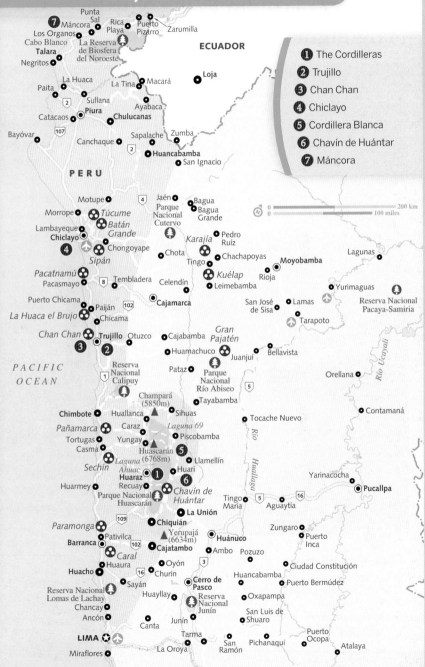

Punta Sal
Máncora
Rica Playa
Puerto Pizarro
Zarumilla
Los Organos
Cabo Blanco
Talara
La Reserva de Biosfera del Noroeste
Negritos

ECUADOR

La Huaca
La Tina
Macará
Loja
Paita
Sullana
Ayabaca
Piura
Catacaos
Chulucanas
Bayóvar
Canchaque
Sapalache
Zumba
PERU
Huancabamba
San Ignacio

1. The Cordilleras
2. Trujillo
3. Chan Chan
4. Chiclayo
5. Cordillera Blanca
6. Chavín de Huántar
7. Máncora

0 ——— 200 km
0 ——— 100 miles

Motupe
Jaén
Bagua
Morrope
Parque Nacional Cutervo
Bagua Grande
Túcume
Batán Grande
Karajía
Pedro Ruíz
Lambayeque
Chiclayo
Chongoyape
Chota
Tingo
Chachapoyas
Moyobamba
Sipán
Kuélap
Rioja
Pacatnamú
Tembladera
Celendín
Leimebamba
Yurimaguas
Pacasmayo
Cajamarca
San José de Sisa
Lamas
Reserva Nacional Pacaya-Samiria
Puerto Chicama
Paiján
Tarapoto
La Huaca el Brujo
Chicama
Gran Pajatén
Chan Chan
Trujillo
Otuzco
Cajabamba
Bellavista
Huamachuco
Juanjuí
PACIFIC OCEAN
Reserva Nacional Calipuy
Pataz
Orellana
Parque Nacional Río Abiseo
Champará (5850m)
Tayabamba
Chimbote
Huallanca
Sihuas
Tocache Nuevo
Contamaná
Pañamarca
Caraz
Laguna 69
Tortugas
Yungay
Piscobamba
Casma
Huascarán (6768m)
Llamellín
Sechín
Laguna Ahuac
Huari
Yarinacocha
Huaraz
Recuay
Chavín de Huántar
Pucallpa
Huarmey
Parque Nacional Huascarán
Tingo María
Aguaytía
La Unión
Paramonga
Chiquián
Zungaro
Pativilca
Yerupajá (6634m)
Huánuco
Puerto Inca
Barranca
Cajatambo
Ambo
Pozuzo
Caral
Huaura
Oyón
Churín
Ciudad Constitución
Huacho
Huancabamba
Sayán
Cerro de Pasco
Puerto Bermúdez
Reserva Nacional Lomas de Lachay
Huayllay
Reserva Nacional Junín
Oxapampa
Chancay
Ancón
Junín
San Luis de Shuaro
Canta
Tarma
Pichanaqui
Puerto Ocopa
LIMA
La Oroya
San Ramón
Atalaya
Miraflores

Huaraz, Trujillo & the North Highlights

① The Cordilleras

Icy mountaintops. Rugged valleys. Crystalline, high-altitude lakes. Hikers and climbers the world over arrive in the area around Huaraz to lay eyes on some of Peru's most majestic vistas – not to mention the Andes' highest, most dramatic peaks. Above: Cordillera Blanca; Top Right: Cordillera Huayhuash; Bottom Right: Mountaineering on Nevado Pisco

Need to Know

Before You Book Ask your outfitter about quality of tents, what type of food is served, how they plan for emergencies and if national park fees are included. **For more information on trekking, see p249.**

The Cordilleras Don't Miss List

BY BRAD JOHNSON, AUTHOR OF *CLASSIC CLIMBS OF THE CORDILLERA BLANCA, PERU* AND THE MAN BEHIND THE TREKKING AND CLIMBING SITE, *PEAKSANDPLACES.COM*

1 MOUNTAIN BIKE AROUND HUARAZ

I highly recommend a ride with Julio Olaza of Mountain Bike Adventures (p241), the first guy to do this in the area. He speaks English, has a good sense of humor and he does a great day trip that takes you to the Cordillera Negra. You'll ride a single-track trail that has views of the Cordillera Blanca in the distance.

2 SANTA CRUZ TREK

If you only have five days available for trekking, this is the best trip to do (see p248). To start with, the drive to the drop-off point is beautiful: you'll get marvelous views of Huascarán (6768m), the highest peak in Peru. Once on the trek you'll see incredible valleys, local hamlets and seven peaks over 6000m – including Alpamayo, one of the country's most famous.

3 CORDILLERA HUAYHUASH

If you've got 10 days for trekking, then I recommend the complete Cordillera Huayhuash Circuit (p250). I've been in Nepal, Kilimanjaro and China, and this rivals any other trek in the world. Every day you're beneath peaks that are 6000m. It's got a wild feeling and there are lakes where you camp. Plus, you often see condors.

4 PISCO

If you're a novice mountain climber, I recommend Pisco (p248), which stands at 5750m. It's a short, relatively easy glaciated climb, though previous experience using crampons and an ice ax is recommended. You can do a round-trip from Huaraz in about three to four days (if you're acclimatized). The views from the top are spectacular.

5 CAFÉ ANDINO

In Huaraz, I recommend this cafe (p245), which has fresh-brewed coffee, good breakfast, lunch and dinner, as well as incredible views of the mountains. There's even wi-fi and a little library – a good spot to rest.

Trujillo

The bustling city founded in 1534 by conquistador Francisco Pizarro has a little bit of everything: pre-Columbian ceremonial centers, picturesque colonial architecture, exquisite regional cooking and a tradition of music and dance. Situated off the main tourist trail, it offers an experience that is refreshingly, authentically Peruvian.

Need to Know

WHEN TO GO If you want to combine your trip with a visit to region's beaches, go in summer (December to February). **WHAT TO PACK** It's hot! Take a hat and sunscreen. **For further coverage, see p253.**

Trujillo Don't Miss List

BY CAROLINA ZÁRATE MELY,
TRUJILLO NATIVE AND MANAGER AT
TRUJILLO TOURS, AN AGENCY THAT'S
BEEN AROUND FOR MORE THAN FOUR DECADES

1 HUACAS DEL SOL Y DE LA LUNA

If there's one place that people should absolutely visit during their trip to Trujillo its this Moche ceremonial center (p262), which now has an impressive new on-site museum. The displays include ceramics, gold and textiles – all found at the site. Top Left: Moche artifact, Huaca de la Luna

2 COMPLEJO ARQUEOLÓGICO LA HUACA EL BRUJO

This archaeological complex (p263, pictured far left) is less visited by travelers, but it's fascinating. Recent discoveries show that the Moche that built this temple may have been a matriarchal society. Score one for the matriarchy!

3 HUANCHACO

A great day trip is a visit to this beach community (p263, pictured left), just outside of Trujillo. My recommendation: go for a late lunch (the seafood is out of this world), stroll along the boardwalk and visit the souvenir stands. Then, watch the sun set over the Pacific. It'll make for a very relaxing day.

4 NORTHERN PERUVIAN COOKING

Northern Peru and the Trujillo area are renowned spots for their cuisine. Some of my favorite dishes include *ají de gallina* (a walnut and chicken stew), *shambar* (bean soup with pork) and *seco de cabrito* (goat stewed in cilantro and beer). *Cabrito* is a must: it doesn't get more northern than that.

5 TRUJILLO ARTS SCENE

What a lot of visitors don't know is that Trujillo is a really dynamic place for all things arts related. We have excellent museums and galleries. There's even a symphony orchestra. Every two years we host a visual-arts biennial (the next is in 2012); in November, there is a singing competition, and in January, people from all over Peru come to see our festival devoted to the *marinera* – Peru's national dance.

Get Lost in an Ancient City near Trujillo

The ancient city of Chan Chan (p260) was, in its heyday, a staggeringly large adobe urban center, covering more than 36 sq km of coastal desert. Today, its remains boast reconstructed decorative friezes bearing stylized images that were highly important to the Chimú culture that built it: fish, waves and seabirds.

3

5 Hike to the Sacred Ruins in Chavín

The two- to three-day trek from Olleros to Chavín de Huántar (p248) takes you past pretty villages along remnants of pre-Inca roads — providing some breathtaking views of snowcapped mountain peaks in the process. The best part: you'll beat the crowds to the ruins, who usually don't arrive until the afternoon.

EMIL VON MALTITZ/ALAMY

Gaze Upon the Vast Wealth of a Moche Burial Site ④

Outside the northern oasis of Chiclayo, a powerful Moche lord was entombed in an adobe pyramid amid ornaments, ceramics and a headless llama. In a rare stroke of luck, his tomb was discovered – largely untouched – 17 centuries later. Now its incredible treasure can be seen in its entirety at the Museo Tumbas Reales de Sipán (p272). Do not miss!

PAUL KENNEDY

⑥ Visit a Mountain Temple That is Two Millennia Old

Dating back to 800 BC, the temple structure at Chavín de Huántar (p251) is evidence of one of the oldest cultures in the Andes, but there's more to it than that. The locale is breathtaking and the temple boasts a maze of alleys that deliver the unwary viewer to a terrifying carving of a creature with snakes radiating from its head. A perfect spot to channel your inner Indiana Jones.

⑦ Hang Ten in Máncora

Peru's beachside hot spot (p273) is the perfect place to indulge in some serious sun, surf and sand – along with plenty of divine seafood eateries and pumping nightspots. On offer is surfing and kite surfing and every other water activity in between. When you're ready for a break from the scene, just hop over to one of the solitary beaches nearby.

Huaraz, Trujillo & the North's Best…

Museums

○ **Museo Nacional de Chavín** (p251) Stone objects from one of Peru's most ancient ruins sites

○ **Museo Tumbas Reales de Sipán** (p272) A Moche pyramid's treasure, beautifully showcased

○ **Museo Nacional Sicán** (p272) An exhibit devoted to one of Peru's most unusual pre-Columbian burials

○ **Museo de Sitio Chan Chan** (p261) Detailed displays explain the Chimú culture and a sprawling ruins site

North Coast Restaurants

○ **Mar Picante, Trujillo** (p257) Hyperfresh seafood and delectable ceviche

○ **Club Colonial, Huanchaco** (p265) Classic Peruvian meets classic French in a lovely colonial mansion

○ **Restaurant Típico La Fiesta, Chiclayo** (p268) Sink your teeth into the best *arroz con pato a la chiclayana* (duck stewed in beer and cilantro) in the north

○ **Chan Chan, Máncora** (p276) This breezy spot dishes up well-rendered Italian specialties, including thin-crust pizza

Adventures

○ **Surfing the longest left-hand wave** (p264) In Puerto Chicama, just a 90-minute drive north of Trujillo

○ **Trekking to Laguna 69** (p250) Take in the beauty of an impressive array of glistening high-altitude lakes over the course of 48 hours

○ **Kite surfing** (p273) Catch the breeze in Máncora

○ **Mountain biking** (p241) Race down the coffee-colored hillsides of the Cordillera Negra

Sunsets

○ **Huanchaco** (p263) Gazing at the Pacific from the boardwalk

○ **Santa Cruz Trek** (p248) The view at the foot of Nevado Taulliraju while camping on this famous trek through the Cordillera Blanca

○ **Máncora** (p273) A Pacific sunset from the convenience of your very own beachfront bungalow

○ **Huaraz** (p240) Watching the light change color on the Andean peaks surrounding Huaraz

ADVANCE PLANNING

○ **Three Months Before** Book your Cordillera Blanca trek

○ **One Month Before** Arrange a guided side trip to Chachapoyas from Chiclayo

○ **Three Weeks Before** Reserve a hotel in Huaraz

○ **One Day Before** Make reservations at the renowned Restaurant Típico La Fiesta in Chiclayo

GETTING AROUND

○ **Air** Huaraz, Trujillo and Chiclayo are all serviced by nearby airports with multiple daily flights to Lima; Máncora is reached by the airport at Talara, 40 minutes away

○ **Bus** Minibuses connect points within cities, while comfortable long-haul vehicles offer service all over the region

○ **Walk** The best way of exploring the narrow town centers of cities such Huaraz, Trujillo and Chiclayo

○ **Taxis** Found just about everywhere in bigger cities and towns; some smaller areas may be serviced by *mototaxis* – motorcycle taxis

BE FOREWARNED

○ **Museum Closings** Many city museums are closed on Mondays

○ **Altitude** The areas around Huaraz get staggeringly high – allow plenty of time to acclimatize

○ **Unlicensed Operators** Be especially cautious when booking treks or climbs; recommended agencies are generally best

○ **Robberies** As in all places in Peru, they happen – especially in crowded markets and archaeological sites, and even along some remote, but popular, trekking trails

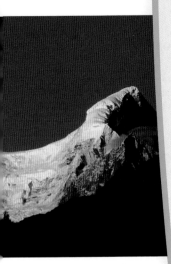

Left: Gold ceremonial knife from the Sicán era;
Above: Cordillera Blanca (p249)

PHOTOGRAPHERS: (LEFT) PETER HORREE/ALAMY; (ABOVE) KARL LEHMANN

Huaraz, Trujillo & the North Itineraries

Desert oases that harbor pre-Columbian ruins, majestic mountains that offer some of the continent's most superlative trekking, and sunny beaches. You can do the beaches in three days, but for serious trekking, allot at least five.

3 DAYS

TRUJILLO TO HUANCHACO
Surf & Turf on the Desert Coast

Begin in the coastal city of **(1) Trujillo**, where you can spend a day admiring the fine colonial mansions and churches in the city's picturesque center. Of particular interest: the pristinely preserved and extraordinarily graceful Casa de Urquiaga, which will give you an idea of what the city looked like in the early 17th century. Finish off the day with a delicious dinner at one of Trujillo's many bustling restaurants. If you're wondering what to eat, try *seco de cabrito* – stewed goat in cilantro, with beans – a real northern treat!

The second day, pay a visit to the monumental adobe city of **(2) Chan Chan**, to the west – the largest pre-Columbian adobe city in the world – and capital of the famously urban Chimú culture. Be sure to check out the myriad friezes and a fascinating room with perfect acoustics.

Spend your third day further west over in **(3) Huanchaco**, indulging in a little beachside R&R. Our recommended activities: walking the boardwalk, surfing the beach break and eating plenty of hyperfresh seafood.

HUARAZ TO THE CORDILLERAS

Mountain Majesty in the Andes

5 DAYS

Begin with a day of gentle acclimatization in **(1) Huaraz**. Stroll around the town center and pay a visit to the Museo Regional de Ancash, where you'll see mummies with trepanned skulls. You can use your second day in town to do a gentle hike in the area – as a way of conditioning your body to the altitude. A short two-hour walk will take you to the Wari ruins at **(2) Wilkahuaín**, but if you'd like to get a full day of walking in, a longer hike (six hours) will take you all the way to **(3) Laguna Ahuac**, a lovely lake. On the third day, organize a day trip to the ancient temple site of **(4) Chavín de Huántar**, one of Peru's earliest ruins.

For your last couple of days, head out to explore the majestic peaks of the **(5) Cordillera Blanca**. This is best done with an overnight stay so you can wake up surrounded by snowcapped peaks. One particularly scenic trip includes the overnighter to Laguna Rajucolta. Expect dizzying mountain passes, beautiful lakes and towering walls of granite – an Andean landscape you will never forget.

Laguna Chinancocha, Parque Nacional Huascarán (p249)

PHOTOGRAPHER: KARL LEHMANN

Discover Huaraz, Trujillo & The North

Plaza de Armas, Trujillo (p253)
PHOTOGRAPHER: JANE SWEENEY

HUARAZ

☎043 / POP 48,500 / ELEV 3091M

Huaraz lies sandwiched in a valley carved out by the Río Santa, flanked to the west by the brown Cordillera Negra and to the east by the frosted Cordillera Blanca. The city may not be a thing of beauty, but it commands staggering views, and has plenty of personality – and that personality goes a long way. First and foremost, this is a trekking metropolis. During the high season the streets buzz with adventurers planning expeditions and returning from arduous hikes, but it's also a good base to visit one of Peru's oldest, most mysterious archaeological sites: Chavín de Huántar.

◉ Sights

MUSEO REGIONAL DE ANCASH Museum
(☎ 42-1551; Plaza de Armas; admission incl guided tour S6; ⏱8am-6:30pm) This **museum** houses the largest collection of ancient stone sculptures in South America. Small but interesting, it has a few mummies, some trepanned skulls and a garden of stone monoliths from the Recuay and Wari cultures.

MIRADOR DE RATAQUENUA Lookout
(7km southeast of the town center) About a 45-minute walk southeast of the center, this **viewpoint** has expansive views of the city and its mountainous backdrop. Muggings have been known to be an issue en route. It's advisable to walk in a group or take a taxi.

MONUMENTO NACIONAL WILKAHUAÍN
Archaeological Site

(adult/student S4/2; ☺8am-5pm) This is a small **Wari archaeological site** about 8km north of Huaraz that is remarkably well preserved. Dating from about AD 600 to 900, it's an imitation of the temple at Chavín done in the Tiwanaku style. The three-story temple has seven rooms on each floor, each originally filled with bundles of mummies.

The two-hour walk up to Wilkahuaín (sometimes spelled Wilcawain) is relatively easy and can be a good first acclimatization jaunt. It also provides a rewarding glimpse into Andean country life. Ask locally if it is safe before you set off. Taxis to the ruins cost about S15.

MONTERREY HOT SPRINGS
Hot Springs

(9km north of Huaraz; admission S3; ☺6am-6pm) If you've gone trekking and are ready to relax, then these **hot springs**, in Monterrey, 9km north of Huaraz, are a good option. Divided into two sections, the upper pools are nicer and have private rooms (S2.50 per person for 20 minutes). Before you wrinkle your nose at the brown color of the water, know that it's due to high iron content rather than questionable hygiene practices. The pools get crowded on weekends and holidays; mornings are best.

Activities

Trekking & Mountaineering

Whether you're arranging a mountain expedition or going for a day hike, Huaraz is the place to start. Numerous outfits can prearrange entire trips so that all you need to do is show up. See p242 for a list of recommended outfits and the section on the Cordilleras (p249) for a list of some popular routes in the area.

Rock Climbing

Rock climbing is one of the Cordillera Blanca's most popular pastimes. Avid climbers will find some gnarly bolted sport climbs in nearby villages, such as Chancos, Recuay and Hatun Machay, among many others. Many trekking tour agencies (see p242) offer excursions. In addition, Galaxia Expeditions (p242) and Monttrek (p242) have indoor *rócodromos* (climbing or bouldering walls).

Mountain Biking

Mountain Bike Adventures   Biking
(✆ 42-4259; www.chakinaniperu.com; Lúcar y Torre 530, 2nd fl; ☺9am-1pm & 4-8pm Mon-Sat) Owned by Julio Olaza, a lifelong resident of Huaraz who has spent time mountain biking in the US, this company comes well recommended. Olaza knows the region's single-track possibilities better than anyone. He offers bike rentals or guided tours, ranging from an easy five-hour cruise to 12-day circuits around the Cordillera Blanca. Rates start at S60 per day for equipment rentals and S90 for one-day tours.

Tours & Guides

Day Tours

Dozens of agencies along Luzuriaga can organize outings. One popular tour visits the ruins at Chavín de Huántar (see p251); another passes through the village of Yungay to the beautiful Lagunas Llanganuco, where there are superb vistas of Huascarán; a third takes you through Caraz to Laguna Parón, which is ravishingly surrounded by glaciated peaks; and a fourth travels through Caraz to see *Puya raimondii* (a massive plant that looks straight out of Dr Seuss) and then includes a visit to the Nevado Pastoruri, to see ice caves and glaciers

Any of these trips cost between S25 and S35 each; prices may vary depending on the number of people going, but typically include transport (usually in minibuses) and a guide (who may or may not speak English). Admission fees and lunch are extra. Trips generally take a full day; bring warm clothes, water, sunblock and snacks.

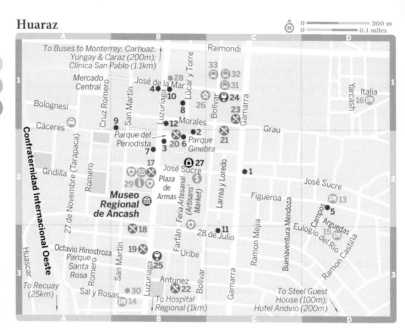

Huaraz

These agencies have the best reputations:

Huaraz Chavín Tours (☎42-1578; hct@chavintours.com.pe; Luzuriaga 502)

Pablo Tours (☎42-1145; pablotours@terra.com.pe; Luzuriaga 501)

Sechín Tours (☎42-1419; www.sechintours.com; Morales 602)

Trekking & Mountaineering

Mountaineers and trekkers should check out **Casa de Guías** (☎42-1811; www.casadeguias.com.pe; Parque Ginebra s/n 28G; ⏱7-11am & 5-11pm), the headquarters of the **Mountain Guide Association of Peru**, for a list of certified guides.

All of the agencies below arrange full expeditions that include guides, equipment, food, cooks, porters and transportation. Depending on the number of people, the length of your trip and what's included, expect to pay from under S50 to S150 per person per day. Try not to base your selection solely on price, as is often the case: you get what you pay for. The list below

is by no means exhaustive; things change, good places go bad and bad places get good. In this regard, the South American Explorers Club in Lima (p71) can be an excellent source of information and maps.

Active Peru (☎42-3339; www.activeperu.com; Gamarra 699)

Galaxia Expeditions (☎42-5335; www.galaxia-expeditions.com; Parque del Periodista)

Huascarán (☎42-2523; Campos 711)

Montañero (☎42-6386; Parque Ginebra)

Monttrek (☎42-1124; www.monttrek.com; Luzuriaga 646, 2nd fl)

Peaks & Places (☎in USA 970-626-5251; www.peaksandplaces.com) Though not based in Huaraz, this reputable outfitter has been doing custom treks since 1982. Reserve well in advance.

Community Tourism

It is possible to arrange trips in the area to learn about traditional aspects of local life. These agencies are recommended:

Huaraz

Incaroca Travel (☎77-0843; www.incaroca
.it, in Italian)

Mountain Institute (☎42-3446; mtorres@
mountain.org; Ricardo Palma 100)

Respons Sustainable Tourism Center
(☎42-7949; www.respons.org; Calle 28 de Julio
821)

Sleeping

Hotel prices can double during holiday
periods and rooms become scarce.
Reserve in advance. For a recommended selection of mountain lodges,
see p245.

HOTEL COLOMBA   Hotel $$
(☎42-7106, 42-1501; www.huarazhotel.com;
Francisco de Zela 278; s/d S150/200) One of
the best picks in town, the bungalows
here are speckled around a dense and
compulsively trimmed hedge forest.

Each unit comes with a veranda, TV and
telephone and the sprawling gardens
conceal a kids' playground, huge bird
enclosures and a dainty restaurant.
It's located about 1km north of town,
beyond the Río Quilcay.

HOTEL ANDINO   Hotel $$$
(☎ 42-1662; www.hotelandino.com; Pedro
Cochachín 357; s/d S281/339, with balcony
S314/388; @) All the immaculate, carpeted rooms at this Swiss-run hotel
have great views and mod cons such as
cable TV and a hair dryer. Splurge on a
room with a balcony if you can. It's very
popular with international trekking and
climbing groups, and reservations can
be hard to come by in high season.

ALBERGUE CHURUP   Guesthouse $
(☎ 42-2584; www.churup.com; Figueroa 1257;
dm S25, s/d incl breakfast S65/90) This im-
mensely popular family-run hostel has
immaculate rooms, colorful chill-out

areas on every floor and a massive, top-floor lounge space with magnificent 180-degree views of the Cordillera. The affable Quirós family also have a sauna, a cafe, bar and communal kitchen, as well as a book exchange and laundry facilities. Reservations recommended.

HOTEL SIERRA NEVADA   Hotel **$$**
(☎ 44-9613; Monterrey Km 3.5; s/d S65/90) Laid out in a large V shape, this hotel sits perched on a hilltop 3.5km north of town and has sensational views of the valley below. The rooms are just comfortable enough and you can take your breakfast in the dainty garden gazebo while the pet alpaca roams the grounds.

OLAZA'S BED & BREAKFAST   Hotel **$$**
(☎ 42-2529; www.olazas.com; Arguedas 1242; s/d/tr S80/90/120; @) A smart little hotel with a boutique feel, spacious bathrooms and comfortable beds. The best part: the big lounge area upstairs and great breakfasts (not included), served on the terrace. Julio, the owner, is an established figure in the Huaraz outdoors scene and is a great source of advice.

HOTEL EL TUMI   Hotel **$$**
(☎ 42-1784, 42-1852; www.hoteleltumi.com; San Martín 1121; s/d S85/150; @ 🛜) With an all-round cozy retreat feel, rooms here are handsomely finished with dark wood and come with cable TV; many have great mountain views. Downstairs there's a lounge with wi-fi, and a posh restaurant with room service.

STEEL GUEST HOUSE   Guesthouse **$$**
(☎ 42-9709; www.steelguest.com; Pasaje Maguina 1467; s/d S108/141; @) Staying here is a little like landing at your grandma's house: the rooms are frilly and white-glove clean and the owner tends to dote on her guests. Loads of facilities round out the offerings: cable TV, outdoor hammocks, billiards, sauna and a roof terrace.

SAN SEBASTIÁN   Hotel **$$**
(☎ 42-6960; Italia 1124; s/d incl breakfast S150/170) This four-story hotel is a neo-colonial architectural find: expect a fetching white-walled, red-roofed compound with balconies overlooking an inner courtyard with a fountain. All rooms have a writing desk, good beds and TV on request; a few have balconies.

Nevado Quitaraju, Cordillera Blanca (p249)

GRANT DIXON

Eating

SEEDS OF HOPE CAFÉ
Cafe $

(39-6305; www.peruseeds.org; Antunez 782; breakfast from S4; 7am-2pm) Who thought filling up on delicious coffee and homemade granola and cakes would help a good cause? Run by the aid organization Seeds of Hope, profits at this cafe go to helping needy children in Huaraz.

PASTELERÍA CAFÉ TURMANYÉ
Bakery Restaurant $

(Morales 828; sandwiches S5-8, pastries S3-5; 8am-6pm) Serving paella, sandwiches and rich Spanish-style pastries, this little eatery also has the distinction of benefiting the local Arco Iris Foundation, which helps children and young mothers.

EL FOGÓN
Grill $

(42-1267; Luzuriaga 928, 2nd fl; mains S6-15; noon-11pm) A bright and slightly upscale twist on the traditional Peruvian grill house, this place will grill anything that moves – including the usual chicken, trout and rabbit, in addition to terrific *anticuchos* (beef heart skewers).

CAFÉ ANDINO
Cafe Restaurant $$

(42-1203; www.cafeandino.com; Lúcar y Torre 530, 3rd fl; breakfast S6-20; 8am-8pm Tue-Sun; @) This modern, top-floor cafe has space and light in spades, as well as comfy lounges, photos, books and groovy tunes – making it the ultimate all-day hangout. The best part: you can get breakfast anytime (Belgian waffles!), as well as house-roasted coffee.

EL HORNO
Grill $$

(42-4617; www.elhornopizzeria.com; Parque del Periodista; pizzas S12-18; mains S12-26; 10am-11pm Mon-Sat) If you can cook it on a grill or in a wood oven, El Horno can make it sing. The meat skewers and pizzas are the best picks here. This place fills up; arrive early or make a reservation.

If You Like…
Mountain Retreats

If you like to enjoy your mountains minus the trappings of the city, these cozy lodges will let you explore the stunning hills by day – and return to a comfortable bed every night. Hiking and trekking excursions, as well as additional meals, are available. Reserve in advance.

1 LAZY DOG INN
(978-9330; www.thelazydoginn.com; s/d without bathroom S120/180, d inside main house S240, 2-person cabins S260, all incl breakfast & dinner) Run by Canadians Diana and Wayne, this hand-built adobe inn sits at the mouth of the Quebrada Llaca, 8km east of Huaraz. There are comfortable double rooms in the main lodge, while fancier private cabins come with fireplaces. Horse rentals are available. Top choice.

2 WAY INN LODGE
(42-8714; www.thewayinn.com/lodge.htm; bungalows incl breakfast S120-180) A 40-minute drive out of Huaraz, this very popular spot has private, well-appointed bungalows with fireplaces. There is also a sauna and hot tub. Check the website for directions on how to get there.

3 LLANGANUCO MOUNTAIN LODGE
(94-366-9580; www.llanganucolodge.com; dm S38, s/d from S140/180) To the north, outside of Yungay, this recommended lodge run by Brit Charlie Good is in a prime position for exploring the Llanganuco Lakes area. Lodge rooms have down-feather beds and balconies. Mountain biking is available.

4 HUMACCHUCO COMMUNITY-TOURISM PROJECTS
(42-7949; www.respons.org; per person incl meals from S108) This community-tourism program operates a comfy guesthouse in Humacchuco (outside of Yungay). Here, visitors can learn about local culture and savor a *pachamanca* (a stew cooked in the ground with rocks). Bookings are handled by Respons, in Huaraz.

CALIFORNIA CAFÉ

Cafe Restaurant $$

(☎ 42-8354; www.huaylas.com; Calle 28 de Julio 562; breakfast S12-18; ⏱7:30am-7pm; @ 🛜) Run by Tim (from California), this hip pad does breakfasts all day, plus light lunches and salads. It's also a good spot to while away a few hours: there's a good book exchange and wi-fi for the laptop junkies, as well as rich espressos and herbal teas.

SIAM DE LOS ANDES

Thai $$

(☎ 40-9173; Gamarra 560; mains S12-38; ⏱6-10pm) The authentic fare here – from aromatic veggie soups to Pad Thai noodles – is prepared by an infectiously cheery Thai chef and well worth the extra soles.

BISTRO DE LOS ANDES

International Fusion $$

(☎ 42-6249; Plaza de Armas; mains from S18; ⏱7:30am-11pm) A European-influenced spot serves an international and Peruvian menu that includes pancakes, pasta, fabulous fish dishes, delectable desserts and good coffee. Service is excellent, as are the views of the plaza.

 **Drinking & Entertainment**

LOS 13 BUHOS

Bar Lounge

(José de la Mar 812, 2nd fl; ⏱5pm-late) The most popular place in town to kick back on a couch and chat while listening to funk-filled sounds. Warm lighting flickers over graffiti-covered walls and climbing paraphernalia clings to the rafters.

X-TREME BAR

Bar

(☎ 42-3150; Luzuriaga 1044, 2nd fl; ⏱7pm-late) This classic watering hole hasn't changed in years. Bizarre art, drunken graffiti, strong cocktails and good rock keep things rambunctious well into the night.

EL TAMBO BAR

Dance Club

(☎ 42-3417; José de la Mar 776; ⏱9pm-4am) If you're hankerin' to shake your groove-

Left: Churches and plazas grace the center of most towns in Peru; **Below:** The distinctive Queen of the Andes *(Puya raimondii)* is endemic to the area

PHOTOGRAPHER: (LEFT) ANDREW HALIBURTON/ALAMY : (BELOW) PAL/IMAGE BROKER

thang, this is the most popular dance club in town and is fashionable with *extranjeros* (foreigners) and Peruvians. Expect everything from techno-*cumbia* to Top 20, to salsa to reggae to everything in between.

 **Shopping**

Inexpensive woolen knits of all kinds are available at the many **craft stalls** on the pedestrian alleys off Luzuriaga or at the **feria artesanal** (artisans' market) off the Plaza de Armas. Respons Sustainable Tourism Center (p242) also hawks some pretty hip knits made by Huaraz-area artisans. Quality climbing gear is sold by several trekking agencies (p242).

Some recommended Huaraz gift shops:

Last Minute Gift Store (Lúcar y Torre 530; ☺10am-1pm & 4-8pm Mon-Sat)

Perú Magico (José Sucre btwn Farfán & Bolívar; ☺9am-2pm & 3-9pm Mon-Sat)

✆ **Tejidos Turmanyé** (Morales 828; ☺8am-5pm)

ⓘ **Information**

Dangers & Annoyances

Trying to race into the mountains without acclimatizing will likely result in altitude sickness, which can get pretty serious. (See p349 for details.)

Overall, the city is safe, though there have been robberies, especially in the area of the Mirador de Rataquenua and the Wilkahuaín ruins. It is best to go with a group or hire a taxi to avoid problems.

Emergency

Local Police (☎ 42-1221, 42-1331; José Sucre near San Martín)

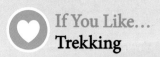

If You Like…
Trekking

If trekking is your thing, you might like to spend some time tackling the longer hikes around the Cordilleras.

1 SANTA CRUZ TREK
The most popular trek in the area is a five-day walk that ascends the spectacular Quebrada Santa Cruz valley and crosses the Punta Union pass (4760m) before tumbling into Quebrada Huarípampa on the other side.

2 PISCO
Pisco (5750m) is one of the most sought-after summits in the Cordillera Blanca, with hundreds of mountain climbers bagging it every summer. This approximately 5km trek takes two to three days and brings you into stone-throwing distance of this thrilling peak (at least it looks that way). Short but very challenging.

3 OLLEROS TO CHAVÍN DE HUÁNTAR
If you're short on time but still want to soak in some icy-peak time, this relatively easy two- to three-day trek comes to the rescue. It starts in the village of Olleros (population 1390), south of Huaraz, and travels along pretty villages and pre-Inca roads – some with great views of the Uruashraju (5722m), Rurec (5700m) and Cashan (5716m) Mountains.

4 VINTAGE INCA ROADWAY
Part of a new tourism initiative, this three- to six-day hike along an old Inca trail, between Huari and the city of Huánuco, is just starting to be developed. Hikers cross well-preserved parts of the old Inca trail and end up in Huánuco Viejo.

Policía de Turismo (☏ 42-1341; Plaza de Armas, above iPerú; ☺8am-1pm Mon-Sat & 5-8pm Mon-Fri) Some officers speak limited English.

Internet Access
Dozens of places on Plaza Ginebra and the corresponding block of Luzuriaga.

Laundry
Laundries on José de la Mar, between San Martín and Lúcar y Torre, will wash your duds for roughly S3 per kg.

Medical Services
Clínica San Pablo (☏ 42-8811; Huaylas 172; ☺24hr) The best medical care in Huaraz. Some doctors speak English.

Farmacia Recuay (☏ 42-1391; Luzuriaga 497) Will restock expedition medical kits.

Hospital Regional (☏ 42-4146; Luzuriaga, cuadra 13) Rudimentary care at the southern end of town.

Money
Numerous banks have ATMs and can exchange US dollars and Euros.
Scotiabank (☏ 42-1500; José Sucre 760)

Post
Post office (☏ 42-1031; Luzuriaga 702)

Tourist Information
Casa de Guías (☏ 42-1811; www.casadeguias.com.pe; Parque Ginebra 28G; ☺7-11am & 2-11pm) This group keeps a list of licensed guides and will arrange rescues if you're trekking or climbing with a guide certified by the Mountain Guide Association (AGM). Register here before heading out on a trek or climb.

iPerú (☏ 42-8812; Plaza de Armas, Pasaje Atusparia, Oficina 1; ☺9am-6pm Mon-Sat, to 2pm Sun) Good for general tourist information, but little in the way on trekking.

Parque Nacional Huascarán Office (☏ 42-2086; www.areasprotegidasperu.com/pnh; Sal y Rosas 555) Limited information about visiting the park.

ⓘ Getting There & Away

Air
The Huaraz airport (ATA; ☏ 44 3095) is 23km north of town, in Anta. A taxi will cost about S12. LC Busre operates daily flights to and from Lima.

Bus

Minibuses go to surrounding villages (such as Monterrey, Taricá Yungay, Carhuaz and Caraz) from near the petrol station on Calle 13 de Diciembre, north of the town center.

For long-haul trips to other major cities, the following companies are recommended:

Cruz del Sur (☎ 42-8726; Bolívar 491)

Línea (☎ 42-6666; Bolívar 450)

Movil Tours (☎ 42-2555; Bolívar 452)

🛈 Getting Around

A taxi ride around central Huaraz costs about S3.

THE CORDILLERAS

A pair of dramatic *cordilleras* (mountain chains) runs parallel to each other on either side of Huaraz. To the west is the Cordillera Negra, with its coffee-colored soil. To the east is the snow-covered crown of the Cordillera Blanca. Between them, in the valley, runs a paved road known as the Callejón de Huaylas, which furnishes visitors with perfect views of the lofty elevations.

The star of the show here is the Cordillera Blanca. About 20km wide and 180km long, it is an elaborate collection of toothed summits, razor-sharp ridges, emerald-colored lakes and grassy valleys draped with crawling glaciers. More than 50 peaks of 5700m or higher grace this fairly small area. North America, in contrast, has only three mountains in excess of 5700m; Europe has none. Huascarán, at 6768m, is Peru's highest mountain and the highest pinnacle in the tropics anywhere in the world.

South of the Cordillera Blanca is the smaller, more remote, but no less spectacular Cordillera Huayhuash – which contains Peru's second-highest mountain, the 6634m Yerupajá.

🛈 Information

To get the lowdown on conditions, your first stop should be Casa de Guías (see opposite), which has information on weather, trail conditions and guides. Some topographic maps are sold here.

Trekking and equipment-rental agencies are also good sources of local knowledge and can also advise on day hikes. For more impartial advice, visit popular Huaraz haunts such as California Café (p246) and Café Andino (p245), whose foreign owners keep abreast of local developments.

The following agencies are recommended for renting gear:

Skyline Adventures (☎ 64-9480; www.skyline -adventures.com; Pasaje Industrial 137, Huaraz) Highly recommended; located 2km north of the town center.

MountClimb (☎ 42-6060; www.mountclimb. com; Cáceres 421, Huaraz) Good for top-end climbing gear.

Cordillera Blanca

The world's highest tropical mountain range encompasses some of South America's most breathtaking peaks. Andean leviathans include the majestic Nevado Alpamayo (5947m), once termed 'the most beautiful mountain in the world' by the German Alpine Club. Others include the Nevado Huascarán (at 6768m, Peru's highest), Pucajirca Oeste (6039m), Nevado Quitaraju (6036m) and Nevado Santa Cruz (Nevado Pucaraju; 6241m).

Sights & Activities

PARQUE NACIONAL HUASCARÁN
National Park

(admission per day/month S5/60) Established in 1975, this 3400-sq-km park encompasses practically the entire area of the Cordillera Blanca above 4000m, including more than 600 glaciers and nearly 300 lakes, and protects extraordinary and endangered species such as the giant *Puya raimondii* plant, the spectacled bear and the Andean condor.

Visitors should bring their passports to register at the park office in Huaraz (see opposite page) and pay the park fee. You can also do this at one of the control stations.

HUARAZ–WILKAHUAÍN–LAGUNA AHUAC
1-Day Hike

This is a relatively easy, well-marked day hike to **Laguna Ahuac** (4560m) starting from Huaraz or the Wilkahuaín ruins (p241). From Huaraz, the walk will take six hours; from Wilkahuaín, four. It makes an excellent early acclimatization trip. Look for furry, rabbit-like vizcachas sniffing around and the big mountain views of the Cordillera Blanca.

LAGUNA CHURUP
1-Day Hike

If overnight trekking isn't your bag, but you'd like to experience the sight of some of the area's extravagant high-altitude lakes, this one-day hike is for you. It begins at the hamlet of Pitec (3850m), just above Huaraz, and takes you to the emerald green **Laguna Churup** (4450m), at the base of Nevado Churup. Note the altitudes and the ascent (it's a steep 600m straight up). The walk takes roughly six hours and is a good acclimatization hike. A taxi from Huaraz to Pitec will cost about S30.

LAGUNA RAJUCOLTA
2-Day Hike

Having been compared to Zion National Park in Utah, this trek is best known for its unparalleled views of Huantsán (6395m). It begins in the village of Macashca. From there, a well-defined path works its way up the Quebrada Rajucolta toward **Laguna Rajucolta** (4250m), passing through meadows overshadowed by skyscraper-tall granite walls, some marshy stretches and a massive boulder field.

LAGUNA 69
2-Day Hike

A beautiful, overnight trek offers backdrops dripping with marvelous views. The campsite is a true highlight: you'll wake up to a morning vision of Chopicalqui (6354m), Huascarán Sur (6768m) and Norte (6655m) all around you. From here, you'll then scramble up to **Laguna 69**, which sits right at the base of Chacraraju (6112m). From there, the journey takes you past the famous Llanganuco lakes – a lot of impressive lakes crammed into just two days.

Cordillera Huayhuash

The more remote Cordillera Huayhuash hosts an equally impressive medley of glaciers, summits, lakes and high altitude passes (over 4500m), all packed into a hardy area only 30km across. The feeling of utter wilderness, particularly along the unspoiled eastern edge, is the big draw and you are more likely to spot the graceful Andean condor here than in other parts of the Cordilleras.

It's popular with visitors wishing to hike the **Cordillera Huayhuash Circuit**, a stunning 10- to 12-day trek through multiple high-alpine passes with spine-tingling views. The dramatic lakes along the eastern flank provide

Vizcachas can be spotted in the Cordilleras
PHOTOGRAPHER: PAUL KENNEDY

Chavín Culture

Named after the site at Chavín de Huántar, the Chavín culture is considered one of the oldest major cultures in Peru, strutting its stuff from 1000 BC to 300 BC. The principal Chavín deity was feline (jaguar or puma), although condor, eagle and snake deities were also worshipped.

Representations of these animal figures are highly stylized and cover many Chavín sites, as well as a number of extraordinary objects, including the Tello Obelisk at the Museo Nacional de Chavín (p252), the *Lanzón*, which stands in mystical glory in the tunnels underneath the Chavín site, and the Raimondi Stone, at the Museo Nacional de Antropología, Arqueología e Historia del Perú in Lima (p67).

The latter has carvings of a human figure, sometimes called the Staff God, with a jaguar face and large staffs in each hand – an image that is believed to indicate a belief in a tripartite universe consisting of heavens, earth and underworld. It has shown up at archaeological sites along the northern and southern coasts of Peru and suggests the long reach of Chavín influence.

great campsites (and are good for trout fishing) and give hikers a wide choice of routes to make this trek as difficult or as easy as they care to make it.

Though this trek doesn't feature technical climbing, it requires good acclimatization and physical fitness. Daily ascents range from 500m to 1200m and the average day involves about 12km on the trail, or anywhere from four to eight hours of hiking. (Though you may experience at least one 10- to 12-hour day.) Most trekkers take extra rest days along the way because of the length and altitude. For more information on this trek, contact one of the outfitters listed on p242.

Chavín de Huántar

☑ 043 / POP 2000 / ELEV 3250M

The Conchucos Valley (called the Callejón de Conchucos) runs parallel to the Callejón de Huaylas on the eastern side of the Cordillera. Chavín de Huántar, at the south end of the valley, is the most accessible area of the lot and lays claim to one of the most important and mysterious pre-Inca ruins in the Andes. While many folks whiz through on day trips from Huaraz, consider spending the night: if you can see this impressive archaeological site in the morning, chances are you'll have it all to yourself.

 Sights & Activities

CHAVÍN DE HUÁNTAR RUINS
Archaeological Site
(adult/student S11/5; ⊙8am-5pm) This **archaeological site** is thought to be the only large structure left behind by the Chavín culture (see p251) and consists of a series of temple arrangements built between 1200 BC and 800 BC. In the middle is a massive sunken square, with an intricate and well-engineered system of channels for drainage.

From the square, a broad staircase leads up to the most important building, the **Castillo**. Built on three different levels, the walls here were at one time embellished with *tenons* (keystones of large projecting blocks carved to resemble human heads with animal or perhaps hallucinogen-induced characteristics). A series of tunnels underneath this structure comprise a maze of complex alleys and chambers. At the heart of this is an exquisitely carved (somewhat terrifying), 4.5m rock

ANNELIES MERTENS

of white granite known as the **Lanzón de Chavín**, which represents a person with snakes radiating from the head.

Several construction quirks, such as the strange positioning of water channels and the use of highly polished minerals to reflect light led Stanford archaeologists to believe that the complex was used as an instrument of shock and awe. Here, priests could manipulate light and sound, blowing on Strombus trumpets and amplifying the rush of running water in the channels. The disoriented were probably given hallucinogens before entering the darkened maze. These tactics endowed religious leaders with an awe-inspiring power.

To get the most from your visit, it's worth hiring a guide to show you around (S25) or go on a guided day trip from Huaraz.

FREE **MUSEO NACIONAL DE CHAVÍN**
Museum
(☑ 45-4011; ⊙9am-5pm Tue-Sun) Funded jointly by the Peruvian and Japanese governments, this excellent new **museum** adjacent to the archaeological site houses most of the intricate *tenons*, as well as the magnificent Tello Obelisk,

a stone object with relief carvings of a caiman and other fierce animals.

THERMAL BATHS   Hot Springs
(30min walk south of town; admission S2) If your muscles need a break, take a soak in one of the four private baths or the larger pool.

 Sleeping & Eating

Restaurants tend to close after sunset, so dig in early.

GRAN HOTEL RICKAY   Hotel **$$**
(☑ 45-4011; Calle 17 de Enero 600; s/d S45/85) A grandiose, newly renovated neo-colonial option has top rooms with hot showers and TV. There is also a patio restaurant (serving pizzas and pasta dishes).

CAFETERÍA RENATO   Cafe **$**
(☑ 50-4279; Plaza de Armas; breakfast & snacks S7-14; ⊙7am-4pm) This cozy place serves yummy breakfasts alongside homemade yogurt, cheese and *manjar blanco* (caramel spread). There's a lovely garden you can laze in and the own-

252

ers organize well-recommended horse tours.

BUONGIORNO Peruvian Classics **$**
(☎ 45-4112; Calle 17 de Enero 439; meals S10-15; ⏰ 10am-9pm) The best place in town serves well-executed local dishes in a garden setting. The *lomo a la pimienta* (grilled steak in wine, cream and cracked-pepper) is excellent.

 Shopping

A few hundred meters along the road to Huari, **Centro Artesanal CEO Chavín** (Tello Sur 350; ⏰ dawn-dusk) sells locally made textiles, alpaca weavings and stone carvings.

ℹ️ Information

Banco de la Nación (Plaza de Armas; ⏰ 7am-5:30pm Mon-Fri, 9am-1pm Sat) Doesn't have an ATM but will change US dollars.

ℹ️ Getting There & Away

Tour buses make day trips from Huaraz. See p241 for details.

TRUJILLO
☎ 044 / POP 291,400

Stand in the right spot and the glamorously colonial streets of this coastal settlement look like they've barely changed in hundreds of years (except for the honking taxis). Founded by Francisco Pizarro, the city has a reputation for being independent-minded. In 1536 the town was besieged during the Inca rebellion. Three hundred years later, in 1820, it was the first Peruvian city to declare independence from Spain. And, in the 20th century, it was here that the populist workers' party APRA (Alianza Popular Revolucionaria Americana) was founded – a political party that spent of much of the 20th century banned.

Today, Trujillo remains a vibrant center of art and culture. (It's the home of Peru's national dance – the *marinera*.) It is also conveniently situated alongside some of the country's most incredible pre-Columbian sites, including the behemoth Chimú capital of Chan Chan and the Moche ceremonial sites of Huacas del Sol y de la Luna (Temples of the Sun and Moon), which date back 1500 years.

When you get yourself ancient-cultured out, the village of Huanchaco, to the north, beckons with its sandy beach, respectable surf and contemporary interpretations of sun worship.

Buildings on the Plaza de Armas, Trujillo
PHOTOGRAPHER: TOM COCKREM

Trujillo

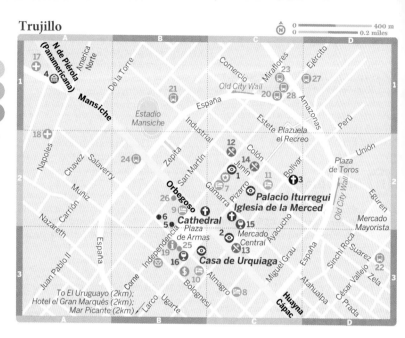

Sights

The downtown area is chock full of colonial buildings and churches that make for excellent photo ops – only a few of which are listed here. Note that hours can be erratic.

PLAZA DE ARMAS   Town Square
Trujillo's fetching **main square** has an impressive statue dedicated to work, the arts and liberty. Every Sunday at 8am, there is a flag-raising ceremony here, complete with parade. To the northeast, the plaza is fronted by the **cathedral**, which dates back to 1647 and contains a museum of religious and colonial art.

FREE **CASA DE URQUIAGA**
                    Colonial Mansion
(Pizarro 446; ⏰9:30am-3:15pm Mon-Fri, 10am-1:30pm Sat) A pristinely maintained **colonial house** (which now belongs to the Banco Central de la Reserva del Perú) offers a glimpse of gilded-age Trujillo.

FREE **IGLESIA DE LA MERCED**   Church
(Pizarro & Gamarra) This lovely baroque-style **church**, built in the 17th century, has a striking organ and cupola, but it is most noteworthy for its altar, which is painted onto the wall – an economical shortcut when construction funds ran out.

FREE **PALACIO ITURREGUI**
                    Colonial Mansion
(Pizarro 688; ⏰8am-10:30pm) This canary yellow 19th-century **mansion** is impossible to ignore unless you're color-blind. Built in neoclassical style, it has beautiful window gratings, slender interior columns and gold moldings on the ceilings. General Juan Manuel Iturregui lived here after he famously proclaimed independence.

IGLESIA DEL CARMEN   Church
(cnr Colón & Bolívar; museum admission S2.50; ⏰9am-1pm Mon-Sat) The small religious museum located inside this **Carmelite church** has an excellent collection of colonial art.

Trujillo

FREE **CASONA ORBEGOSO**
Colonial Mansion
(Orbegoso 553; ⊙9:30am-1pm & 4:30-7pm Tue-Sun) Named after a former president of Peru, this beautiful 18th-century **manor** has a collection of well-worn art and period furnishings.

FREE **CASONA GANOZA CHOPITEA**
Colonial Mansion
(Independencia 630; ⊙hours vary) This *casona* is considered to be the best **mansion** of the colonial period in Trujillo. The tourist police are housed here and sometimes it puts on good displays of contemporary Peruvian art.

MUSEO CASSINELLI   Museum
(N de Piérola 601; admission S8; ⊙9am-1pm & 4-7pm Mon-Fri, 9am-1pm Sat) One of the most unusual archaeological museums in Peru, this private collection is housed in the basement of a gas station and contains hundreds of fascinating pieces – including bird-shaped whistling pots.

Tours & Guides

Dozens of agencies offer day tours of the city (about S20 per person), as well as group excursions to nearby pre-Columbian sites (S40 to S50). Note that admission to archaeological sites is generally not included in the tour price. The following agencies are recommended:

Trujillo Tours (✆23-3091; Almagro 301; ⊙7:30am-1pm & 4-8pm)

Chan Chan Tours (✆24-3016; Independencia 431; ⊙7am-1:30pm & 4-8pm)

Sleeping

Hotels can get noisy if you get streetside rooms. Book well in advance in late September, when places fill up for the International Spring Festival.

HOTEL LIBERTADOR

Luxury Hotel $$$

(☎ 23-2741; www.libertador.com.pe; Independencia 485; d S270, ste S375-600, both incl breakfast; ☒) The grand dame of the city's hotels, the Libertador is in a stunning colonial building that's the Audrey Hepburn of Trujillo – it wears its age with refined grace. The hotel earns its four stars with a sauna, good restaurant, amiable bar, airport pick-up and very comfortable rooms. As with everywhere else, however, avoid noisy street-side rooms.

LOS CONQUISTADORES HOTEL

Hotel $$

(☎ 24-4505; www.losconquistadoreshotel. com; Almagro 586; s/d S150/180, ste from S330, all incl breakfast; ✳ @ 🛜) Courteous doormen greet you at the entrance of this contemporary venture, a few steps away from the Plaza de Armas. Carpeted rooms come with cable TV, wi-fi, phone, minibar and 24-hour room service. Suites have Jacuzzi tubs. The swanky restaurant-bar is a good place to unwind over a pisco sour. Rates include airport transfers.

HOSTAL COLONIAL

Colonial Inn $$

(☎ 25-8261; hostcolonialtruji@hotmail.com; Independencia 618; s/d/tr S55/85/110) This tastefully renovated, rose-colored colonial mansion has a great location just a block from the Plaza de Armas. It also has cozy rooms (some with balconies with views), as well as helpful staff, a tour desk and a pleasant courtyard. A real winner.

HOSTAL SOLARI

Hotel $$

(☎ 24-3909; Almagro 715; s/d incl breakfast S60/92) A contemporary spot, this place has massive, sensibly decorated 'executive' rooms, which feature polished floorboards, sitting areas, excellent mattresses, cable TV, minifridge and phone. A cafe provides room service, and the helpful front-desk staff can arrange tours.

SAINT GERMAIN HOTEL

Hotel $$

(☎ 25-0574; www.saintgermainhotel.net; Junín 585; s/d S90/159) Good rooms come with a slew of modern conveniences, as well as immaculate bathrooms. The rooms facing inward are quieter and have windows onto a bright light well. There's a bar and cafe.

Los Baños del Inca, Cajamarca

Detour:
Cajamarca

A day's driving from Trujillo takes you to Cajamarca, the charming highland settlement where the Spanish first encountered Inca emperor Atahualpa. If you've got an extra three days in your itinerary, it's a good spot to enjoy a chilled-out family-friendly vibe and some attractive historic sites.

Attractions radiate from the lovely Plaza de Armas, which is surrounded by two ornate churches. Don't miss the **Cuarto del Rescate** (Puga, just east of the Plaza; ☺9am-1pm & 3-6pm), where the Spanish held Atahualpa ransom.

The surrounding areas have some interesting sights, too. Twenty kilometers southwest of Cajamarca, **Cumbe Mayo** is an incredible rock forest that boasts a network of pre-Columbian aqueducts that channel water around the area. It makes for a pleasant hike and some absolutely wild pictures. Guided tours from Cajamarca are about S20.

Located six kilometers to the southeast of Cajamarca, **Los Baños del Inca** (☺4:30am-8pm; admission S3-6) were the hot springs where Atahualpa was relaxing when the Spanish arrived. Today, it may not look like much – a sprawling complex of low-slung concrete buildings – but the steaming mineral-rich water will tenderize you in minutes.

In Cajamarca, **Salas** (☎36-2867; Puga 637; mains S10-20; ☺7am-10pm), a cavernous restaurant on the Plaza, has white-clad servers who will guide you through an extensive menu strong on regional specialties, including stewed goat and tamales (steamed corn cakes).

El Portal del Márques (☎36-8464; www.portaldelmarques.com; Jirón del Comercio 644; s/d/ste incl breakfast S150/183/300; @) is housed in a restored colonial mansion with an immaculately groomed garden and features tidy, modern rooms.

HOTEL EL GRAN MARQUÉS
Hotel **$$$**

(☎24-9161, 24-9366; www.elgranmarques.com; Díaz de Cienfuegos 145; s/d S250/330, ste from S330; ❋ ☜) A couple of kilometers southwest of the city center, this modern hotel offers spacious, contemporary rooms equipped with the usual amenities. There is also a sauna, gym, restaurant and bar.

Eating

JUGUERÍA SAN AGUSTÍN
Juice Bar **$**

(Bolívar 526; juice S2; ☺8am-10pm) Look for the near-constant lines of locals waiting for drool-inducing juices.

OVIEDO
Peruvian Classics **$$**

(☎22-3305; Pizarro 737; breakfast & sandwiches S4-12; ☺7am-midnight) This local favorite has a long list of breakfasts – from a simple continental to a hearty *criollo* (spicy Peruvian fare), which comes with a steak.

MAR PICANTE
Seafood **$$**

(☎22-1544; América Sur 2199; meals S8-25; ☺11am-10pm) This large, packed-to-the-gills seafood palace specializes in some of Trujillo's freshest ceviche (seafood marinated in lime juice). Try the heaping *ceviche mixto*, which has various kinds of fish and crustaceans. It is a S3 taxi ride south of town.

CAFÉ BAR MUSEO
Cafe **$$**

(☎29-7200; cnr Junín & Independencia; mains S10-21; ☺7:30am-midnight) Wood-paneled walls covered in artsy posters and a classic, marble-top bar make this spot feel like a cross between an English pub and a Left Bank cafe. A long drinks and dessert menu make it a great spot to hang out.

RESTAURANT ROMANO
Peruvian Classics **$$**

(☎ 25-2251; Pizarro 747; mains S10-25; ☺7am-midnight) Romano has been around since 1951, so you know these guys have been doing something right. Whipping up a decent espresso, as well as breakfast, sandwiches (including vegetarian options) and Peruvian classics, it is one of the most popular eateries in town.

RESTAURANT DEMARCO
Italian **$$$**

(☎ 23-4251; Pizarro 725; mains S10-25; ☺7:30am-11pm) This small bistro specializes in Italian food and crisp pizzas, as well as mouthwatering *chupe de camarones* (traditional spicy shrimp bisque). The desserts are excellent, from classic tiramisu to mile-high *tres leches* (a spongy cake made with three types of milk).

EL URUGUAYO
Grill **$$$**

(☎ 28-3369; América Sur 2219; meals S15-30; ☺6:30pm-1am) Located a S3 taxi ride south of town, little El Uruguayo serves up delicious barbecued meat to a nightly crowd of salivating in-the-know patrons. If you're hungry, try the massive sizzling plate of mixed meats (Argentinean steak, chicken, chorizo, beef heart, plus a few surprises).

 Drinking

MECANO BAR
Dance Club

(☎ 20-1652; www.mecanobarperu.com; Gamarra 574; admission S20; ☺9pm-late) This is the current top spot to see and be seen in Trujillo. Sway your hips to salsa, reggae and techno alongside a mix of well-to-do Peruvians and expats.

TRIBUTO BAR
Bar Lounge

(☎ 29-4546; cnr Pizarro & Almagro; ☺9pm-late) This pleasant bar on the plaza is great for a quiet tipple and a chat with your friends. It gets livelier on weekends, when there is live music.

Left: Plaza de Armas, Trujillo; **Below:** Chan Chan (p260)
PHOTOGRAPHER: (LEFT) NEIL JULIAN PHOTOGRAPHY/ALAMY ; (BELOW) OTHER IMAGES

ℹ️ Information

Internet cafes are plentiful around town. Most midrange hotels will supply laundry services at reasonable rates.

Emergency

Policía de Turismo (Tourist Police, Poltur; ☎ 29-1705, 20-4025; Independencia 630)

Medical Services

Clínica Americano-Peruano (☎ 23-1261; Mansiche 702) High-end care.

Hospital Regional (☎ 23-1581; Napoles 795) More rudimentary services.

Money

Numerous banks change foreign currency and come equipped with 24-hour ATMs. Scotiabank (Pizarro 314) has an ATM.

Post

Post office (Independencia 286; ⏰9am-7pm Mon-Fri, to 1pm Sat)

Tourist Information

iPerú (☎ 29-4561; cnr Almagro & Independencia, Municipalidad de Trujillo; ⏰8am-7pm Mon-Sat, to 2pm Sun) Provides tourist information and a list of certified guides and travel agencies.

ℹ️ Getting There & Away

Air

The airport (code TRU; ☎46-4013) is 10km northwest of town. LAN (☎80-11-1234; Almagro 490) has daily flights to and from Lima. There's a departure tax of S11. Taxis to downtown from the airport generally cost around S15.

Bus

Buses fill up, so buy tickets in advance. Several companies that go to southern destinations have terminals on the Panamericana Sur, separate from the ticket office; check where your bus departs from when buying a ticket.

259

The following companies travel to points south: Línea (📞 24-5181; cnr San Martín & Orgoboso; ⏰ 8am-8pm Mon-Fri) The ticket sales office in the historical center is listed here. Buses depart from south of the city center, at the terminal (📞 24-3271; Panamericana Sur 2857), a S3 taxi ride away.

Other companies depart from the stations located on the north end of town, at España and Amazonas:

Cruz del Sur (📞 26-1801; Amazonas 237)

Ormeño (📞 25-9782; Ejército 233)

Oltursa (📞 26-3055; Ejército 342)

For trips to the north, including Chiclayo and Máncora, the following carriers are recommended:

Ittsa (📞 25-1415; Mansiche 145)

Movil Tours (📞 28-6538; Panamericana Sur 3959)

❶ Getting Around

A short taxi ride around town costs about S2. For sightseeing, taxis charge from S25 per hour, depending on distance.

Minibuses to Huaca Esmeralda, Chan Chan and Huanchaco pass the corners of España and Ejército, and España and Industrial every few minutes. Buses for La Esperanza go northwest along the Panamericana and can drop you off at La Huaca Arco Iris. *Combis* (minibuses) leave every half hour from Suarez for the Huacas del Sol y de la Luna. Fares are generally S2. Watch for pickpockets on these routes.

A taxi to most of these archaeological sites will cost around S15.

La Huaca el Brujo, about 60km northwest of Trujillo, is generally reached as part of a group tour.

AROUND TRUJILLO

Five major archaeological sites are easily reached from Trujillo. For the most part, these are best reached via a group tour.

All sites are open from 9am to 4:30pm and tickets are sold at every site, except La Huaca Esmeralda. The entrance ticket for Chan Chan is also valid for La Huaca Esmeralda and La Huaca Arco Iris, as well as the Chan Chan museum – provided it is used within two days.

 Sights

CHAN CHAN Pre-Columbian Ruins (admission S11; ⏰ 9am-4:30pm) Built around AD 1300 and covering 36 sq km, **Chan Chan** is the largest pre-Columbian city in the Americas, and the largest adobe city in the world. At the height of the Chimú empire, it housed an estimated 60,000 inhabitants and contained a vast wealth of gold, silver and ceramics (which the Spanish quickly looted). Over time, devastating El Niño floods and heavy rainfall have severely eroded the mud walls of the city. Today the most impressive aspect of the site is its sheer size.

The area known as the **Tschudi Complex** – also called the Palacio Nik-An – is the only area within the site that is open to visitors. The complex's centerpiece is a massive restored **Ceremonial Courtyard**, whose 4m-thick interior walls are decorated with re-created geometric designs. Ground-level designs closest to the door, representing three or four sea otters, are the only originals left and are slightly rougher looking than the modern work. Nearby, an **outside wall** – one of the best restored in the complex – displays friezes of fish and seabirds.

Other elements to the complex include a set of labyrinthine rooms filled with friezes of birds, fish and waves, as well as a walk-in well that once supplied the daily water needs of the royal compound. Also on view is a **Mausoleum**, where a king was buried with human sacrifices, as well as the fascinating **Assembly Room**, a large rectangular room with 24 seats set into niches in the walls. Its acoustic properties are such that speakers sitting in any one of the niches can be clearly heard all over the room.

Though there are signs that direct visitors around the site, a guide is a great help in order to gain the best

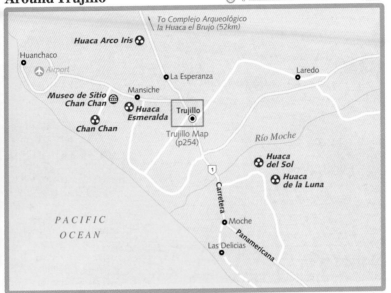

understanding of what remains of the structures.

On the main road, 500m before the Chan Chan turnoff, you'll find the **Museo de Sitio Chan Chan** (admission free with Chan Chan ticket), which contains exhibits explaining the Chimú culture. The aerial photos and maps showing the huge extension of Chan Chan are fascinating. There are a few signs explaining the displays, but a guide is nonetheless useful.

Here, you will also find bathrooms, as well as souvenir and snack vendors.

HUACA ESMERALDA   Chimú Ruins
(admission free with Chan Chan ticket) Halfway between Trujillo and Chan Chan, this **temple** was discovered, buried in the sand, by an unsuspecting landowner in 1923. Although little restoration work has been done to its adobe friezes, it is still possible to make out the characteristic Chimú designs of fish, seabirds, waves and fishing nets.

Note: thieves reportedly prey on unwary tourists wandering around. It is best to go with a group or guide.

HUACA ARCO IRIS   Chimú Ruins
(Rainbow Temple; admission free with Chan Chan ticket) Also known locally as Huaca del Dragón, this temple is in the suburb of La Esperanza, about 4km northwest of Trujillo. Dating from the 12th century, it is one of the best preserved of the Chimú temples – simply because it was buried under sand until the 1960s and excavation did not begin until 1963.

The *huaca* (tomb) used to be painted, but these days only faint traces of its yellow hues remain. It consists of a defensive wall more than 2m thick enclosing an area of about 3000 sq meters, which houses the temple itself. The walls are slightly pyramidal and covered with repeating rainbow designs, most of which have been restored. A ramp leads to the very top of the temple, from where a series of large bins, found to contain the bones of infants – possibly human sacrifices – can be seen.

There is a tiny on-site **museum**, and local guides are available to show you around.

NATHAN BENN

Don't Miss Huacas del Sol y de la Luna

The **Temples of the Sun and the Moon** are a pair of adobe pyramids that reside on the south side of the Río Moche. Built by the Moche culture, 700 years prior to the construction of Chan Chan, the **Huaca del Sol** is the largest single pre-Columbian structure in Peru (though a third of it has been washed away). It was built with an estimated 140 million adobe bricks, many of them marked with symbols representing the workers who made them. At one time the pyramid consisted of several different levels connected by steep flights of stairs (the views from the top are excellent), huge ramps and walls sloping at 77 degrees. Unfortunately, the last 1500 years have wrought their inevitable damage.

The smaller, but more interesting, **Huaca de la Luna** is about 500m away across the open desert. This structure is riddled with rooms that contain ceramics, precious metals and some of the beautiful polychrome friezes for which the Moche were famous. The *huaca* (tomb or grave) was built over six centuries to AD 600, with six succeeding generations expanding on it and completely covering the previous structure. Archaeologists are currently onion-skinning selected parts of the *huaca* and have discovered that there are friezes of stylized figures on every level. It's well worth a visit; you'll see newly excavated friezes every year.

As you leave, check out the souvenir stands, some of which sell pots made using the original molds found at the site. Also look around for a *perro biringo,* the native Peruvian hairless dogs that hang out here.

The site is about 10km southeast of Trujillo via a rough road. The entrance price includes a guide.

NEED TO KNOW

admission S11; ⏲9am-4pm

COMPLEJO ARQUEOLÓGICO LA HUACA EL BRUJO
Moche Ruins

(admission negotiable; ⏰9am-5pm) This **archaeological complex** consists of various sites: Huaca Prieta, the recently excavated Moche site of Huaca Cao Viejo and Huaca el Brujo, which is only starting to be excavated. The best site for visitors is the Huaca Cao Viejo, a 27m truncated pyramid with some of the best friezes in the area. They show magnificently multicolored reliefs with stylized life-sized warriors, prisoners, priests and human sacrifices.

The complex is 60km from Trujillo on the coast and is hard to find without a guide. It's technically not open to the public, but tour agencies in Trujillo can arrange a visit.

HUANCHACO
☎044 / POP 41,900

This once-tranquil fishing hamlet, 12km outside Trujillo, woke up one morning to find itself an international beach destination. Even so, it nonetheless manages to retain a certain village-y appeal. In fact, things change slowly here –

so slowly that local fishers are still using the very same narrow reed boats depicted on 2000-year-old Moche pottery. Fishers ride these neatly crafted boats like seafaring cowboys, with their legs dangling on either side – which explains their nickname: *caballitos de totora* (little reed horses). The inhabitants of Huanchaco are among the few remaining people on the coast who known how to construct and use them.

 Sights & Activities

The curving, gray-sand beach here is fine for swimming during the December to April summer, but expect serious teeth chatter during the rest of the year. The surf is good for beginners and has its regular followers. You can rent surfing gear (S15 to S30 per day for a wet suit and surfboard) from several places along the main drag, including **Wave** (☎58-7005; Victor Larco 525). For surfing lessons, visit **Un Lugar** (☎957-7170; www .otracosa.info; cnr Bolognesi & Atahualpa), two blocks back from the main beach road.

Locals with their distinctive *totora* reed boats, Huanchaco

AARON MCCOY

Detour:
Puerto Chicama

About a 90-minute drive to the north, the small fishing outpost of Puerto Chicama doesn't look like much, but it lays claim to one of the longest left-hand point breaks in the world. Originally a busy port for the sugar and cotton industries, the port now draws adrenaline-seeking surfers trying to catch a ride. (Peru's National Surfing Championship is usually held here in March.) Good waves can be found year-round, but the marathon breaks only come about when the conditions are just so, usually between March and June.

Some surf shops in Huanchaco, including Un Lugar (p263), arrange surfing safaris in season.

SANTUARIO DE LA VIRGEN DEL SOCORRO
Historic Church

(⊙dawn-dusk) It's worth pulling yourself off the beach for a visit to this church, said to be the second oldest in Peru. (It was built between 1535 and 1540.) Find sweeping views of the area from the restored belfry.

Sleeping

LAS PALMERAS
Resort $$

(🕿 46-1199; www.laspalmerasdehuanchaco. com; Larco 1150; s S100, d S130-170; ❄@🏊) Probably the nicest place to stay in town, this well-trimmed, mellow-yellow resort hotel has spotless rooms (some with sea views), a secluded green lawn, a lovely pool, spots of shade and a restaurant to boot. Great for families with kids.

HOTEL BRACAMONTE
Hotel $$

(🕿 46-1162; www.hotelbracamonte.com.pe; Los Olivos 503; s/d S110/132, bungalows per person from S40; @🏊) Popular, friendly, welcoming and secure, this long-time spot has nice gardens, a games room, barbecue, restaurant, bar, and toddlers' playground. The rooms include cable TV, fan and phone. A top choice.

NAYLAMP
Guesthouse $

(🕿 46-1022; www.hostalnaylamp.com; Larco 1420; campsites/dm S10/15, s S30-40, d S50-60) Top of the pops in the budget stakes, Naylamp has one building on the waterfront and a second, larger building up a hill behind the hotel. There is a spacious sea-view patio stocked with plenty of hammocks. Kitchen and laundry facilities, hot showers and a cafe are part of the deal.

LA CASA SUIZA
Guesthouse $

(🕿 46-1285; www.casasuiza.com; Los Pinos 451/310; r per person from S20; @) Spacious rooms have Peru-themed murals and good mattresses, while the cafe downstairs dishes out pizza. Good-quality bikes are also available for rent (per half-day S15).

HUANKARUTE RESTAURANT & HOSPEDAJE
Hotel $$

(🕿 46-1705; www.hostalhuankarute.com; La Rivera 233; s/d S120/140; 🏊) This small place has simple, bright rooms with fan and cable TV. The top-floor doubles afford great vistas as well as a real treat: bathtubs!

Eating

Huanchaco has oodles of seafood restaurants, especially near the *caballitos de totora* stacked at the north end of the beach.

OTRA COSA
Vegetarian $

(🕿 46-1346; www.otracosa.info; Larco 921; dishes S3-9; ⊙9am-8pm Wed-Sun) Decorated with a Middle Eastern flair, this cozy, hammock-filled beachside pad serves up yummy hummus and falafel.

Bootmaker at the local market, Chiclayo

CAROLINA MIRANDA

MAMMA MÍA   Italian **$**

(997-3635; Larco at Independencia; pasta
S15, pizza S25; 6-11pm) Come here for
delicious pasta dishes and concoct-your-
own pizzas prepared with the freshest
ingredients. For a real treat, however,
check to see if the owner, Fernando, is
making his famous, secret-recipe crab
lasagna.

CLUB COLONIAL

International Fusion **$$**

(46-1015; Grau 142; meals S15-28; noon-
11pm) On the plaza, this Belgian-run
place is in a striking, candle-lit colonial
mansion (perfect for a date) and serves
up finely prepared Peruvian and French
dishes. Hours can be erratic.

RESTAURANTE MOCOCHO

Seafood **$$$**

(46-1350; Bolognesi 535; 3-course meals
about S45; 1-3pm) This tiny eatery sits in
a walled garden where patrons wait to
see what amazing seafood concoctions
the skilled don Victor will serve up that
day. Seafood does not get any better
than this.

ⓘ Information

See www.huanchacovivo.com for useful tourist
information.

Banco Continental Has an ATM that accepts
Visa cards. Located next to the *municipalidad*
(town hall).

Post office (Manco Cápac 220; 9am-7pm
Mon-Fri, to 1pm Sat) It's a block back from the
pier.

ⓘ Getting There & Away

Combis between Huanchaco and Trujillo are
frequent and cost about S2. A taxi costs S9 to S14.

CHICLAYO

074 / POP 256,900

Spanish missionaries founded a small
rural community on this site in the 16th
century. Either by chance, or through
help from above, Chiclayo has pros-
pered ever since. In one of the first
sharp moves in Peruvian real estate, the
missionaries chose a spot that sits at
the hub of vital trade routes connecting
the coast, the highlands and the deep

Chiclayo

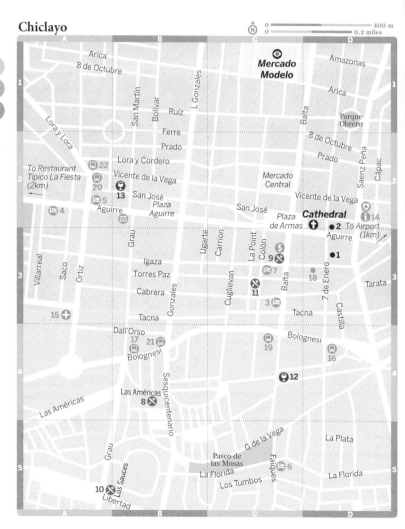

jungle. The result: a bustling coastal city that shows no signs of slowing down.

The town is light on tourist attractions, but its unique combination of fine regional cooking and surrounding pre-Columbian sites may inspire you to hang around for a while.

◉ Sights & Activities

PLAZA DE ARMAS AREA   Plaza
The **central plaza** is a great place to amble as it fills nightly with sauntering

couples, evangelical preachers and an army of underemployed shoe shiners. To the east, find the **cathedral**, which was built in the late 19th century.

PASEO DE LAS MUSAS   Park
One of the odder sights you'll see in northern Peru: a park chock full of statues that pay homage to Greek mythology. A favorite photo-op spot for local newlyweds.

Chiclayo

MERCADO MODELO   Market
(cnr Arica & Balta; ⏰9am-5pm) This fascinating market sprawls for several blocks and is a thick maze of fresh produce, woven goods, live animals, fish, meats and, most interestingly, the *mercado de brujos* (witch doctors' market) in the southwest corner – a one-stop shop for whale bones, amulets, snake skins and vials of indeterminate tonics. This is a good spot to buy *huayruros* (red and black seeds that bring good fortune) as well as *seguros* (religious charms meant to ward off evil). As in any crowded market: watch your pockets.

Tours & Guides

Agencies offer group tours to nearby pre-Columbian sites, as well as to the museums in Lambayeque. Tours cost between S30 and S50, depending on whether entrance fees are included.

Moche Tours (📞22-4637; mochetourschiclayo.blogspot.com; Calle 7 de Enero 638; ⏰8am-2pm & 5-8pm)

Sipán Tours (📞22-9053; www.sipantours. com; Calle 7 de Enero 772; ⏰8am-1pm & 4-8pm)

Sleeping

LATINOS HOSTAL   Hotel $$
(📞 23-5437; Igaza 600; s/d S70/100) An excellent choice, this new hotel is thoroughly well maintained with perfect little rooms; some of the corner rooms have giant curving floor-to-ceiling windows for great street views and plenty of light. The staff is helpful.

GRAN HOTEL CHICLAYO   Hotel $$$
(📞 23-4911; www.granhotelchiclayo.com.pe; Villarreal 115; s/d S252/296; ✳@☈) The top end of Chiclayo living, it's all superswanky here – with room service, laundry, travel agency, car rental, cappuccino bar, karaoke and casino. Serious-looking businessmen flock here in droves.

COSTA DEL SOL   Luxury Hotel $$$
(📞 22-7272; www.costadelsolperu.com; Balta 399; s/d/ste S268/329/503; ✳@☈) Part of a northern Peruvian chain, this establishment has all the creature comforts, including pool, gym, sauna, Jacuzzi and impeccable service. The tastefully and simply designed rooms have cable TV, minibar, safe, and direct-dial phone.

HOTEL EL SOL   Hotel $
(📞 23-2120; www.hotelelsoltresestrellas.com; Aguirre 119; s/d S45/63; ☈) This fastidiously maintained hotel has tip-top rooms with all the mod cons – TV, fan and phone. (Though we wouldn't want to be responsible for cleaning the spotless white leather couches downstairs.)

HOTEL LAS MUSAS
Hotel **$$**

(☎ 23-9884; nazih@viabpc.com; Faiques 101; s/d incl breakfast S105/140; ❄ @) Overlooking the peaceful Paseo de las Musas, this hotel has modern, spacious rooms with cable TV, phone and minifridge. There's a cascading 'waterfall' backed by a mossy green wall in the foyer and the bathrooms all have bathtubs as well as showers. Some rooms have good views of the park. There is a restaurant, and room service is available 24 hours.

Eating

Chiclayo is a top dining destination on the north coast. *Arroz con pato a la chiclayana* (duck and rice cooked in cilantro and beer) and *tortilla de manta raya* (Spanish omelet made from stingray) are favorites.

RESTAURANT TÍPICO LA FIESTA
Upscale Peruvian **$$$**

(☎ 20-1970; Salaverry 1820; mains S28-38; ⏱ noon-11pm) If you want to experience the absolute best of this region's world-famous cuisine, Fiesta is the place to splurge. You'll get pisco sours constructed tableside and elegant meat dishes, such as rack of lamb with risotto and sirloin with poached quail egg. Or try the farm-raised duck, which must be a black-feathered quacker not a day over three months old. It is located in the Residencial 3 de Octubre suburb, about 2km west of central Chiclayo.

SE SALIÓ EL MAR
Seafood **$**

(cnr Colón & Torres Paz; mains S6-12; ⏱ 8am-8pm) The warm-hearted owner here whips up fresh-from-the-sea grills and ceviche in a tiny family-owned shop with plastic tablecloths. A gem.

EL FERROCOL
Seafood **$**

(Las Américas 168; meals S9-21; ⏱ 11am-7pm) This hole-in-the-wall, a little out of the center, is well worth the trip, as chef Lucho prepares some of the best ceviche in all of Chiclayo.

HEBRON
Rotisserie Chicken **$**

(☎ 22-2709; Balta 605; mains from S12; ⏱ 24hr) A flashy, contemporary and bright two-story *pollería* (rotisserie chicken restaurant) on steroids has impeccable

Churros vendor, Chachapoyas

PAUL KENNEDY

Detour:
Chachapoyas

From Chiclayo, a winding day's drive inland through the Andes brings you to the charming settlement of Chachapoyas, a low-key town that is an excellent base for exploring the area's ruins. Your best bet: sign on with the highly reputable **Chachapoyas Tours** (☎ 47-8078; www.kuelapperu.com; Santo Domingo 432, Chachapoyas), which organizes private multiday excursions from Chiclayo.

Capping a dramatic mountaintop, the fabulous, ruined citadel of **Kuélap** (admission S12), southeast of Chachapoyas, is one of the most dynamic archaeological sites in Peru. Built by a pre-Inca culture, the site features a fortified entryway, temple structures and the remains of more than 400 circular dwellings. Best of all: the dramatic cloud-forest views.

The extraordinary funerary site of **Karajía** (Cruz Pata; admission S3) holds painted sarcophagi high up a sheer cliff face, where they stand guard over a valley. An astonishing sight.

South of Chachapoyas and nestled into the hills above Leimebamba, the worthwhile **Museo Leimebamba** (www.museoleymebamba.org; admission S10; ⏰9:30am-4:30pm Tue-Sun) contains artifacts and mummy bundles discovered at the nearby Laguna de Cóndores grave site.

If you're spending the night in Chachapoyas, a good option is **La Casona Monsante** (☎ 47-7702; www.lacasonamonsante.com; Amazonas 746; s/d/tr S60/90/130), located in a lovely colonial mansion. It has inviting, well-equipped rooms decorated with photos of the region. Two blocks east of the plaza, **El Tejado** (Santo Domingo 426; mains S15-19; ⏰noon-4pm & 7-9pm) serves delectable Peruvian classics such as *tacu tacu* (pan-fried rice and beans) and a soul-warming *sustancia de pollo* (chicken soup with fresh oregano).

service and a giant children's playground that would put some chain restaurants to shame.

RESTAURANT EL HUARALINO
Peruvian Classics $$
(☎ 27-0330; Libertad 155; mains S15-30; ⏰noon-11pm Mon-Sat, to 5pm Sun) One of Chiclayo's most upscale restaurants, this place serves good Chiclayan specialties, *criollo* dishes and international cuisine. Bonus brownie points for some of the cleanest bathrooms in Peru.

 **Drinking**

PREMIUM
Bar
(☎ 22-6689; Balta 100; ⏰9pm-late) Turns into a popular place for a tipple and a dance after hours, with loud international music, a mixed crowd, free entry and a boisterous vibe.

SABOR Y SON CUBANO
Bar & Dance Club
(☎ 27-2555; San José 155; ⏰9pm-late Fri-Sun) This spot gives the over-35 crowd somewhere to shake their rumps on the weekends, with jazz, classic salsa and Cuban music setting the pace.

ℹ Information

Emergency
Policía de Turismo (☎ 23-6700; Saenz Peña 830)

Internet Access
Internet cafes abound.

COREY WISE

Medical Services

Clínica del Pacífico (☎ 23-6378; Ortiz 420) The best medical assistance in town.

Money

There are several banks on *cuadra* (block) 6 of Balta.

Scotiabank (☎ 22-4724; Balta 609)

Post

Post office (Aguirre 140; ⏰ 9am-7pm Mon-Fri, to 1pm Sat)

Tourist information

Centro de Información Turístico (☎ 23-3132; Sáenz Peña 838) Has lots of information on the area.

❶ Getting There & Away

Air

The **airport** (code CIX; ☎ 23-3192) is 1.5km east of town; a taxi ride there is a S3 and departure tax is S11. **LAN** (☎ 27-4875; Izaga 770) and **StarPeru** (☎ 22-5204; 7 de Enero 632) both have daily flights to and from Lima.

Bus

The minibus terminal at the corner of San José and Lora y Lora has regular buses to Lambayeque. The following companies are recommended for long-distance travel:

Cruz del Sur (☎ 22-5508; Bolognesi 888)

Ittsa (☎ 23-3612; Bolognesi 155)

Línea (☎ 23-3497; Bolognesi 638)

Movil Tours (☎ 27-1940; Bolognesi 199)

Oltursa (☎ 23-7789; Vicente de la Vega 101)

AROUND CHICLAYO

There are numerous sites in towns in the vicinity of Chiclayo; tour companies can arrange visits or you can just as easily get around on your own by taxi.

 Sights

SIPÁN Archaeological Site
(Huaca Rajada; ☎ 80-0048; www.huacarajada sipan.cb.pe; admission S8; ⏰ 9am-5pm) Located about an hour east of Chiclayo, **Sipán** was initially discovered by grave robbers, but in 1987, sharp-eyed

Around Chiclayo

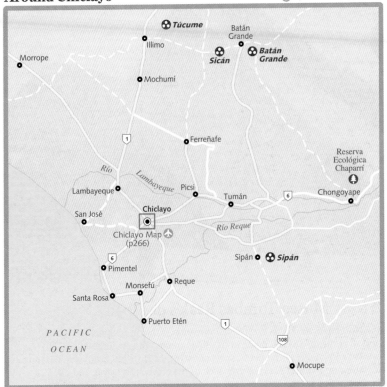

archaeologist Walter Alva noticed an influx of pre-Columbian artifacts on the black market and realized that a burial site in the area was being ransacked. Careful questioning led him to this series of earthen mounds, which were actually disintegrating adobe pyramids that date back to AD 300. This discovery led to the untouched tomb of a major Moche leader known as El Señor de Sipán (Lord of Sipán), who was buried with hundreds of precious objects and numerous sacrificial beings.

Though little remains of the pyramids beyond a mound of earth, some of the tombs have been restored with replicas to show what they looked more than 1500 years ago. Opposite the entrance is the **Museo de Sitio Sipán** (admission S8, or free with site ticket; 9am-5pm Mon-Fri), opened in January 2009, which is worth a visit, but note that the most impressive artifacts were placed in the Museo Tumbas Reales de Sipán in Lambayeque.

Spanish- and English-speaking guides can be hired (S15).

BRUNING MUSEUM Museum
(28-2110, 28-3440; Av Huamachuco s/n, Lambayeque; www.museobruning.com; admission S8; 9am-5pm) Situated in Lambayeque, this **museum**, now greatly overshadowed by the Museo Tumbas Reales de Sipán, houses a good collection of Chimú, Moche, Chavín and Vicus artifacts. Architecture and sculpture lovers may find some interest in the Corbusier-inspired building, bronze statues and tile murals adorning the property. Models of several important sites are genuinely valuable for putting the archaeology of the region

271

PHOTOGRAPH: CAROLINA MIRANDA (ARCHITECT CELSO PRADO)

Don't Miss Museo Tumbas Reales de Sipán

Opened in November 2002, this exceptional **museum** is the pride of northern Peru, containing all of the discoveries made in the Sipán tombs. This includes impossibly fine turquoise-and-gold ear ornaments, spectacularly reconstructed beadwork, dazzling pectoral plates representing sea creatures such as the octopus and crab, and mass amounts of ceramics – some of them displayed as they were found. Also on show: *narigueras* (nose shields). Since emperors were considered animal-gods, these served the purpose of concealing their all-too-human teeth.

The signage is all in Spanish, but English-speaking guides are available for S20. The museum lies in the town of Lambayeque, about 10km northwest of Chiclayo. A taxi here will cost about S12.

NEED TO KNOW

☎ 28-3977, 28-3988; www.tumbasreales.org; Vizcardo y Guzmán s/n, Lambayeque; adult/child S10/3; ⏰ 9am-5pm Tue-Sun, last admission 4pm

into perspective. English-speaking guides charge S15.

MUSEO NACIONAL SICÁN   Museum
(☎ 28-6469; sican.perucultural.org.pe; Av Batán Grande Cuadra 9 s/n, Ferreñafe; admission S8; ⏰ 9am-5pm Tue-Sun) Situated in Ferreñafe, about 18km north of Chiclayo, this splendid **museum** displays replicas of the 12m-deep tombs found in the area. These were among the largest ever found in South America, and the most enigmatic: the Lord of Sicán was buried upside down, in a fetal position, with his head separated from his body. Produced by the Sicán culture, which had its apogee in the Lambayeque area from AD 750 to 1375, these unusual exhibits are definitely worth the trip.

Guided tours from Chiclayo travel here as part of a package deal that includes a visit to the nearby archaeological site of Túcume (which contains remnants of adobe pyramids) for about S50 per person.

MÁNCORA

☎073 / POP 9700

In the summer months, Máncora is *the* place to see and be seen along the Peruvian coast. It's not hard to see why – Peru's best sandy beach stretches for several kilometers in the sunniest region of the country, while dozens of plush resorts offer up rooms within meters of the lapping waves. On shore, a plethora of restaurants provide seafood straight off the boat and the raucous nightlife keeps visitors busy well after the sun dips into the sea.

Máncora has the Pan-American Hwy passing right through its middle, within 100m of the surf. Addresses are not used much here – just look for signs in the center.

 **Activities**

Surfing & Kitesurfing

Surf here is best from November to February, although good waves are found year-round. In addition to Máncora, the nearby breaks at Los Organos, Lobitos, Talara and Cabo Blanco are popular. You can rent surfboards from several places at the southern end of the beach in Máncora (per day S15 to S20).

Soledad (☎ 929-1356; Piura 316) sells boards, surf clothing and organizes lessons for about S60 per hour (including board rental). The friendly Pilar, at **Laguna Camp** (☎ 9-401-5628; www.vivamancora.com/lagunacamp), also does surf lessons for S60 for 90 minutes of instruction (including board rental). For something a little more extreme, you can get lessons in kitesurfing (per hour S120); ask about it at **Del Wawa** (☎ 25-8427; www.delwawa.com).

Other Activities

About 11km east of town, up the wooded Fernández valley, a natural **hot spring** (admission S2) has bubbling water and powder-fine mud – perfect for a face pack. It's slightly sulfurous, but is said to have curative properties. It can be reached by *mototaxi* (S35, including waiting time).

Máncora Rent (Hospedaje Las Terrazas; ☎ 25-8351; Piura 496) rents off-road motorbikes (per hour/24 hours S18/95), small quad bikes for teens (per hour S60), and jet skis (per 30 minutes S100). For transportation with a mind of its own, horses are available for hire along the beach for S18 per hour.

Máncora
PHOTOGRAPHER: OTHER IMAGES

There are remote, deserted beaches around Máncora; ask your hotel to arrange a taxi. Just be prepared to walk – not all beaches lie right off the road.

Tours & Guides

Ursula Behr from **Iguana's** (📞 9-853-5099; www.vivamancora.com/iguanastrips; Piura 245) organizes full-day trips (per person S90) to the Los Pilares dry forest, which include wading through sparkling waterfalls, swimming, horseback riding and a soak in the mud baths. She also organizes sea-kayaking trips (S110), ideal for bird-spotting.

Sleeping

During the December to March summer period, accommodation prices tend to double, but year-round sun means that this is one of the few resort towns on the coast that doesn't turn into a ghost town at less popular times. High-season rates are given here.

DEL WAWA Hotel **$**
(📞 25-8427; www.delwawa.com; s/d S45/75) This surfers' mecca has a great set-up right on the beach with warm-colored adobe rooms all facing the ocean. There are lots of hammocks, a chill space with great views of the best breaks on the beach, and surfboard rental. Del Wawa also organizes kitesurfing lessons for S120 per hour.

HOSTAL LAS OLAS Guesthouse **$**
(📞 25-8099; lasolasmancora@yahoo.com; r per person incl breakfast S70) Rooms here are minimalist white and some come with ocean views, though they're all the same price. The small, cozy restaurant looks onto the beach's best breaks and is a surf-spotter's dream. Boards are available for rental.

South of Máncora

More upscale resorts tend to be located south of Máncora, along the Antigua Panamericana. All have restaurants and can be reached by *mototaxi* (S5 to S10) from the town center. The following places are listed in the order you will reach them when traveling from Máncora.

Mototaxi in the main street of Máncora

PAUL KENNEDY

PUNTA BALLENAS INN
Hotel **$$**

(☎ 25-8136; www.puntaballenas.com;
Panamericana Km 1164; d S150; ✈) At the
southern end of town where the Antigua
Panamericana branches off, this white
brick hotel is far enough away from
town to be silent but still close enough
to allow frequent visits. It has a laid-
back vibe, with a great restaurant, an
inviting pool, a colorful bar and foosball
tables.

CASA DE PLAYA
Boutique Hotel **$$**

(☎ 25-8005; www.casadeplayamancora.net;
s/d S110/175; ✈) About a kilometer to the
south, this large place offers up modern,
slick dwellings colored in warm orange
and yellow tones and constructed with
lots of gently curving lines. All the large
rooms have arty bits and a balcony with
hammock and sea views. The restaurant here is good and a lovely two-story
lounge hangs out over the sea.

SUNSET HOTEL
Boutique Hotel **$$**

(☎ 25-8111; www.hotelsunset.com.pe; d
S186-234, q S297-475; ✈) The ultra-hip,
boutique-styled Sunset wouldn't be
out of place on the cover of a glossy
travel mag. It has beautifully furnished
interiors and great aqua-themed rock
sculptures, plus good-sized rooms with
solid mattresses, balconies and views of
the seascape. The pool is tiny and ocean
access is rocky, though a short walk
brings you to a sandy beach. The hotel's
Italian restaurant is excellent.

BALCONES DE MÁNCORA
Apartotel **$$$**

(☎ 76-2617; www.vivamancora.com/balcones/
index.html; 8-person bungalows S360) This
place easily wins the 'most beautiful
bungalows' plaudit. Set on a cliff overlooking the beach, these three deluxe
bamboo-and-thatch dwellings have
giant overhanging roofs, a full kitchen,
two bedrooms, a living space and lots
of glass frontage for an unimpeded
panorama of the coast. The upstairs
master bedroom is completely open to
the ocean and has its own bathroom.

LAS ARENAS
Bungalows **$$$**

(☎ 25-8240; www.lasarenasdemancora.
com; d S360-420; ❄ ✈) A 5km *mototaxi*
ride from Máncora brings you to this
spruced-up resort with a slick, angular
pool. Enshrined amid a fastidiously
trimmed lawn, the Mediterranean-style
white-and-blue bungalows are scat-
tered along the beachfront and come
with air-con and DVD players. The staff
is professional and there's a playground
to keep the tots entertained. Sea kay-
aks, bicycles and horseback rides are
available.

VICHAYITO
Hotel **$$$**

(☎ 436-4173, in Piura 99-410-4582; www.
vichayito.com; d S243, 6-person bungalows S447;
✈) About 8km south of Máncora, this
is an attractively constructed hotel with
lovely bamboo-and-wood bungalows,
all finished in soothing white tones and
sporting soaring roofs. Isolated and
quiet, the minimalist styling here makes
it a great place to unwind.

 # Eating

Seafood rules the culinary roost in Máncora, with all manner of good and fresh
ceviches, *majariscos* (a mix of seafood
nibbles), *sudados* (seafood soup) and
just plain *pescado* (fish) on offer.

JUGUERÍA MI JANETT
Juice Bar **$**

(Piura 250; juices S1-3; ⏰7am-2:30pm & 5:30-
10pm Mon-Sat, 7:15am-3pm Sun) Hands down,
the best juice place in town.

ANGELA'S PLACE
Bakery Cafe **$**

(☎ 25-8603; Piura 396; breakfasts S4-14, mains
S5-12; ⏰7am-8pm) Angela started selling
her delicious sweet potato, yucca and
wheat breads from her bicycle years
ago. Now you can get them at her cheery
cafe on the main drag, along with creative and substantial vegetarian (and
vegan!) dishes.

HNOS LAMA
Seafood **$**

(☎ 25-8215; Grau 503; meals S10-15; ⏰8am-
8pm) The best of three Lama restaurants,
all owned by different family members,

this one is owned by Orlando and has a reputation for some of the best ceviche (what else?) in town. It's opposite the Eppo terminal.

LAS GEMELITAS   Seafood **$**
(📞 51-6115; Bastidas 154; mains S10-22; 🕐 11am-9pm) Three blocks off the Pan-American Hwy, behind the Cruz del Sur office, this cane-walled restaurant does great seafood and nothing else. Ceviches and *chicharrones* (fried chunks of pork) are the specialty, and the portions are ginormous.

CHAN CHAN   Italian **$$**
(📞 25-8146; Piura 384; meals S15-24; 🕐 6:30-11pm Wed-Mon) Run by Italian chef Udo, this Italian eatery has a cozy atmosphere and lots of bright, white, curving adobe walls. The food here is great, the pizzas look like the real, thin-crust deal and the service is very attentive – it's well worth the splurge. Get here early for a breezy patio seat. To find it, look out for the palm-frond-concealed frontage.

🛈 Information

There is no information office, but the website www.vivamancora.com has tons of useful information. Two ATMs (no bank) accept Visa and MasterCard.

Banco de la Nación (📞 25-8193; Piura 625; 🕐 8:30am-2:30pm Mon-Fri) Change US dollars here.

Costa Norte Lavandería (Piura 212; per kg S5) Hours vary at the laundry; knock even if they look closed.

Emergency 24 Hrs (📞 25-8713; Piura 306; 🕐 24 hr) If you get stung by a ray or break a bone, head to this full-service clinic.

Internet Marlon (📞 25-2437; Piura 520; per hr S2; 🕐 9am-midnight) Attached to the Marlon general store; has the newest computers and the most reliable service.

🛈 Getting There & Away

Air

The nearest airport is in Talara, a 40-minute ride south of Máncora.

Bus

Many bus offices are in the center, with regular minibuses running between Máncora and Punta Sal (30 minutes). The following companies are recommended for long-haul trips:

Cruz del Sur (📞 25-8232; Grau 208)

Oltursa (📞 25-8267; Piura 509)

Ormeño (📞 25-8334; Piura 611)

Tepsa (📞 25-8043; Grau 113)

PUNTA SAL

📞 072 / POP 3300

The long, curvy bay at Punta Sal, 25km north of Máncora, has fine sand and is dotted with rocky bits, but it's still great for a dip in the ocean. The sea here is calm and the lack

Totora reed boats, Punta Sal
PHOTOGRAPHER: PAUL SPRINGETT

of surfer types means that this tranquil oasis of resorts is particularly popular with families.

 ## Sleeping & Eating

Because this area is rather spread out, hotels generally include a meal-plan as part of their rates.

HOTEL CABALLITO DE MAR   Resort **$**
(54-0048, in Lima 01-446-3122; www.hotel caballitodemar.com; r per person incl full board S225-285; @ ≋) Twenty-three ocean-view rooms literally climb up the sea cliff and have pretty bamboo accents and private patios. Hit the restaurant, bar, Jacuzzi, TV room, games room and the gorgeous pool that practically dips its toe into the sea. Activities such as fishing, boating, horseback riding, waterskiing and surfing can be arranged.

PUNTA SAL CLUB HOTEL   Resort **$$**
(54-0088; www.puntasal.com.pe; s/d per person incl full board S252/420; ❄ @ ≋) Off the Pan-American Hwy at Km 1192, this seaside hotel has the full-service deal. Perfect for families, it has minigolf, laundry facilities, banana-boat rides, waterskiing, tennis, volleyball, table tennis, billiards and a wooden-decked pool – and what resort would be complete without a near-life-size replica of a conquistador galleon? It also offers deep-sea fishing trips for US$600 per day in a boat that will take up to six anglers.

Getting There & Away

As with Máncora, the nearest airport is in Talara, to the south. Regular minibuses run to Máncora, a 30-minute drive away.

Iquitos & the Amazon Basin

The Amazon's vastness has long protected it from the outside world. The jungle comprises 50% of the nation, yet only 5% of Peru's population live here. Stretching all the way from the eastern flank of the Andes for thousands of kilometers to the Atlantic Ocean, this wilderness has long been synonymous with the word 'adventure.'

For wildlife enthusiasts, it is a bonanza. More plant types flourish in a single rainforest hectare in the Amazon than in any European country. Exotic birds inhabit its towering canopy and rare mammals patrol its ever-shifting shores. Naturally, this wealth also attracts loggers, energy companies, ranchers and developers. It is, after all, frontier. But with a little bit of daring, you can experience it, too.

Local Yahua people, Río Nanay, Iquitos
PHOTOGRAPHER: PAUL KENNEDY

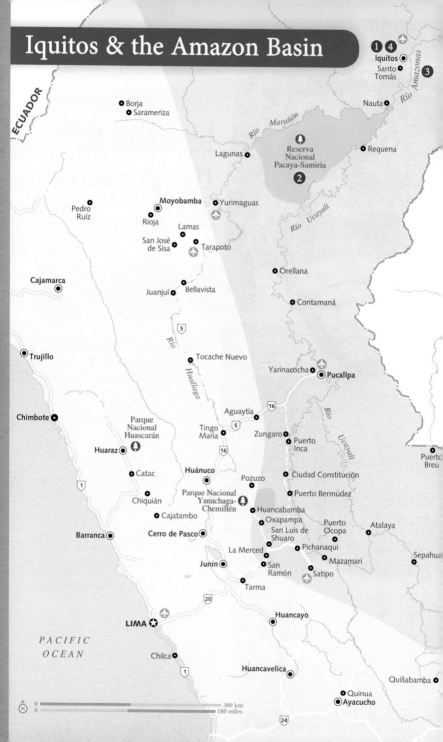

Iquitos & the Amazon Basin

ECUADOR

① ④ ✈
Iquitos ◉
Santo ◉
Tomás
③

Río Amazonas

Borja ◉
◉ Saramériza

Río Marañón

Nauta ◉

Lagunas ◉

Reserva
Nacional
Pacaya-Samiria
②

◉ Requena

Pedro
Ruíz ◉

Moyobamba ◉ ✈ ◉ Yurimaguas
Rioja ◉
Lamas ◉
San José ◉ ✈
de Sisa ◉ Tarapoto

Río Ucayali

Cajamarca
◉

◉ Orellana

Juanjuí ◉ ◉ Bellavista

◉ Contamaná

Río Huallaga
⑤

◉ **Trujillo**

◉ Tocache Nuevo

Yarinacocha ✈ ◉ **Pucallpa**

Chimbote ◉

Parque
Nacional
Huascarán 🌲
Huaraz ◉

Aguaytía ◉
Tingo ◉ ⑤ ⑯
María

Zungaro ◉
◉ Puerto
Inca

Río Ucayali

Puerto
Breu ◉

◉ Catac

⑯
Huánuco ◉

Pozuzo ◉ ◉ Ciudad Constitución

◉ Chiquián

Parque Nacional
Yanachaga-
Chemillén 🌲

◉ Puerto Bermúdez

◉ Cajatambo

①

Huancabamba ◉
Oxapampa ◉
San Luis de ◉
Shuaro

Puerto
Ocopa

◉ Atalaya

Barranca ◉

Cerro de Pasco ◉

La Merced ◉ ◉ Pichanaqui

Sepahua ◉

Junín ◉
San ◉
Ramón
✈
Satipo

◉ Mazamari

⑳
Tarma ◉

PACIFIC
OCEAN

LIMA ✪ ✈

Huancayo
◉

Chilca ◉

①

Huancavelica
◉

Quillabamba ◉

🧭
N
0 _____ 300 km
0 _____ 180 miles

◉ Quinua
◉ **Ayacucho**

㉔

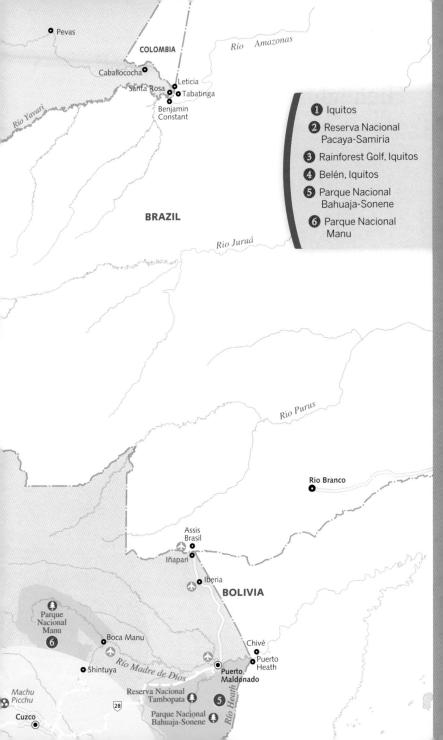

Pevas

COLOMBIA

Río Amazonas

Caballococha
Santa Rosa
Leticia
Tabatinga
Benjamin
Constant

Río Yavarí

BRAZIL

Río Juruá

Río Purus

Río Branco

Assis
Brasil

Iñapari

Iberia

BOLIVIA

Chivé

Parque
Nacional
Manu
6

Boca Manu

Puerto
Heath

Shintuya

Río Madre de Dios

Puerto
Maldonado

Machu
Picchu

28

Reserva Nacional
Tambopata

Cuzco

Parque Nacional
Bahuaja-Sonene

5

Río Heath

1 Iquitos

2 Reserva Nacional
Pacaya-Samiria

3 Rainforest Golf, Iquitos

4 Belén, Iquitos

5 Parque Nacional
Bahuaja-Sonene

6 Parque Nacional
Manu

Iquitos & the Amazon Basin Highlights

1

Iquitos

This sprawling jungle city – that can't be reached by road – is surrounded by some of the most storied rainforest in the world. And, of course, there's also the river, the famed Amazonas, home to 3m-long fish and nurturing trees that are 10 stories tall. Welcome to one of the most remarkable ecosystems the planet has ever known.

Need to Know
WHEN TO GO July and August are driest. **MUST-HAVE TRAVEL ITEM** A good pair of binoculars. **RECOMMENDED BOOK** One River, by Wade Davis. **For more coverage, see p290.**

Iquitos Don't Miss List

BY AURA MURRIETA TORRES,
NATIVE OF IQUITOS AND DIRECTOR OF
EDUCATIONAL INITIATIVES AT THE ACEER
FOUNDATION, AN ENVIRONMENTAL ORGANIZATION

1 TASTE SOME *AGUAJE*

Lots of travelers go to visit the market (p291) in this old part of the city, where the houses float or are built on stilts. While you're there, be sure to try some *aguaje*, a small brown fruit with yellow flesh (it looks like a miniature pineapple). It's very creamy and is often made into ice cream and ice pops and the seed is used from local crafts. In Iquitos, it doesn't get any more local than *aguaje*.

2 GO ON A RIVER CRUISE OF THE AREA

Many travelers go on trips that can last several days. But right next to Iquitos, I recommend visiting the area where the Nanay and Amazonas Rivers converge (p291). The water in each river is a different color, and where they come together, you can literally see a line that divides the water from each river. It's an incredible sight.

3 LOOK FOR PINK DOLPHINS

Seeing these incredible mammals is a 100% unique Amazon experience. Often they'll start playing around your boat, breaching and calling back and forth to each other. It's unforgettable.

4 PILPINTUWASI BUTTERFLY FARM

This butterfly farm and animal rescue center (p296) is definitely worth the visit – especially if you're traveling with children, who will get to see animals that might be more difficult to come across in the wild. It has an orphaned jaguar and some monkeys. It's a lovely spot.

5 BE CONSCIOUS OF THE ENVIRONMENT – TRAVEL BY *PEKI-PEKI*

One of the growing problems we have is noise pollution – emanating from a variety of vehicles, including fast boats. It's bad for the wildlife. I'd advise travelers to travel in small motorboats, such as *peki-pekis*, which don't make as much noise. You're also more likely to encounter wildlife if you get around in quieter forms of transportation.

Watch Manatees Float in the Reserva Nacional Pacaya-Samiria

And not just manatees, but gray dolphins, piranhas, giant river otters and rare river turtles. That doesn't begin to include the reserve's prized birdlife: macaws, tanagers, parrots and, of course, highly charming Amazon kingfishers. The best way to get there: take a meandering river cruise from nearby Iquitos (p290).

Shop at a Floating Market

The floating shantytown of Belén (p291), in Iquitos, is the spot to see one of Latin America's more unusual markets. Set rafts that rise and fall with the current, this storied area attracts a slew of canoes from neighboring communities every morning, all selling fresh jungle produce. It may be controlled chaos, but the comestibles traded here have served as inspiration for plenty of international haute cuisine.

JOHN BORTHWICK

Play Golf...with Piranhas

3 If you were looking for a particularly surreal Amazonian sight, try this one on for size: a nine-hole golf course on the outskirts of the jungle city of Iquitos (p292). In addition to getting the highly unusual experience of playing golf in the middle of the rainforest, hole 4 provides the thrill of teeing onto an island surrounded by piranhas.

5 Venture to the Remote Río Heath

If the lodges in the immediate vicinity of the settlements of Iquitos and Puerto Maldonado feel a mite too urban for you, this meandering river within the confines of the Parque Nacional Bahuaja-Sonene (p308) in the southern Amazon offers extravagant wildlife-watching opportunities: from capybaras to countless avian species, to a faraway clay lick that attracts dense clusters of macaws and parrots.

6 Explore the Ends of the Earth in Manu

A World Heritage Site since 1987, this incredible park (p309) offers everything from mountains to cloud forest to straight up jungle. It isn't always easy to get here, but when you do, it'll be worth it, for the bonanza of kinkajous, pacas, agoutis, ocelots and river turtles – not to mention the towering, undisturbed, rainforest canopy.

Iquitos & the Amazon Basin's Best…

Wildlife-Watching Spots

○ **Parque Nacional Manu** (p309) One of the Amazon's most pristine parks

○ **Reserva Nacional Pacaya-Samiria** (p298) A web of waterways that protects caimans and manatees

○ **Río Madre de Dios** (p304) Excellent bird-watching and fishing

○ **Río Tambopata** (p307) Boasting one of the most spectacular macaw clay licks in the Amazon

Jungle Restaurants

○ **Gran Maloka** (p293) One of the top spots in Iquitos serves up deftly prepared jungle specialties

○ **Burgos's House** (p302) In Puerto Maldonado, tasty local treats, including the banana-leaf tamales known as *juanes*

○ **Taberna del Cauchero** (p294) Where Amazonian cuisine meets global fusion

○ **El Tigre** (p302) Recommended fish dishes at this Puerto Maldonado outpost

Eccentric Experiences

○ **Stay in a hotel inspired by Werner Herzog** (p292) The German film director has a whole inn inspired by his oeuvre

○ **Play golf within sight of piranhas** (p292) Forget Scotland, it's all about Iquitos

○ **Hang out with an anteater named Rosa** (p296) At a butterfly farm in Padre Cocha

○ **Catch sight of a jungle chicken** (p311) On the Río Tambopata

Waterways

○ **Río Amazonas** (p291)
The mack daddy of global waterways

○ **Río Madre de Dios** (p304)
Comfortable lodges nestled into steamy rainforest

○ **Río Heath** (p308) As remote as it gets

○ **Río Tambopata** (p307)
Macaw-central in the southern Amazon

Need to Know

ADVANCE PLANNING

○ **Five Months Before**
Book your multiday Amazon cruise out of Iquitos – these fill up fast!

○ **Three Months Before**
Arrange a stay at a jungle lodge

○ **One Month Before**
Make sure all of your inoculations are up to date

○ **One Week Before** Check that you have necessary gear, such as boots, a hat, repellent and any required medications

RESOURCES

○ *Tropical Nature*, by Adrian Forsyth and Kenneth Miyata. Tropical biology made endlessly fascinating – a must-read book for the Amazon traveler

○ *One River*, by Wade Davis. By the author of *The Serpent and the Rainbow*, ethnobotany in the Amazon has never been this gripping

○ *Tree of Rivers*, by John Hemming. A highly readable history of the world's most storied river

○ Mongabay (www.mongabay.com) A website for all things rainforest

GETTING AROUND

○ **Air** There are daily flights from Lima into Iquitos and Puerto Maldonado; you can also catch flights to Puerto Maldonado from Cuzco

○ **Boat** The way to get around in the Amazon, whether it's a high-end river cruise or in a little *peki-peki*, the small canoes used as water taxis

○ **Taxis** Available in Puerto Maldonado and Iquitos, though far more plentiful are *mototaxis* (rickshaw taxis)

BE FOREWARNED

○ **Illnesses** Malaria and yellow fever still make appearances in the Amazon; make sure you are vaccinated

○ **Insects** They are legion, take repellent with DEET

○ **Robberies** Can be an issue in crowded markets in Puerto Maldonado and Iquitos; watch your wallet

Left: Hummingbird, Río Amazonas;
Above: Bird-watching, Río Tambopata
PHOTOGRAPHERS: (LEFT) PAUL KENNEDY; (ABOVE) ALFREDO MAIQUEZ

Iquitos & the Amazon Basin Itineraries

You could spend weeks exploring the Amazon Basin. Or you could spend just a few days. A couple of well-situated airports and a network of comfortable jungle lodges make visiting the world's most fabled river basin relatively easy.

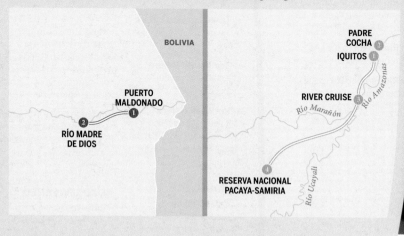

BOLIVIA

PUERTO MALDONADO

RÍO MADRE DE DIOS

PADRE COCHA

IQUITOS

RIVER CRUISE

Río Marañón

Río Amazonas

RESERVA NACIONAL PACAYA-SAMIRIA

Río Ucayali

---

3 DAYS

AROUND PUERTO MALDONADO

Quick Jungle Hop

Start by jetting into the southern jungle town of **(1) Puerto Maldonado**, which can be reached by direct flights from Lima or Cuzco. While you wait for your boat to transport you to your lodge, walk around the colorfully ramshackle town, and climb up the 30m tower known as the Obelisco, which offers terrific views of the area. Something else worth searching out while you're in town: *juanes*, tasty jungle tamales crafted with yucca or rice and seasoned chicken, and steamed in banana leaves.

From there, boat over to one of the nearby lodges on the **(2) Río Madre de Dios**, many of which are less than an hour out of town. From the comfort of your hotel, you can then explore the jungle through hikes and excursions by boat, looking for macaws and parrots and the myriad monkeys that inhabit the Amazon. Likewise, you could also laze around on the deck of your lodge and wait for the wildlife to come to you!

IQUITOS TO THE JUNGLE
Amazon Cruise

The journey starts in **(1) Iquitos**, the largest city in the world that cannot be reached by road. Spend the first day taking in this old rubber boomtown: from the tropical architecture, such as the Casa de Fierro, to the floating shantytown of Belén, where, in the mornings, you'll find a colorful market. Keep your eyes peeled for exotic fruits, such as the pineapple-shaped *aguaje*, which is made into creamy ice pops. If you've got an extra half-day, hop on a *peki-peki* taxi boat over to the village of **(2) Padre Cocha**, where you can pay a visit to Rosa the anteater at the Pilpintuwasi Butterfly Farm.

On the second day, board your **(3) river cruise**. Day trips are available, but if you really want to know what the Amazon is all about, book a three-day expedition along the Río Marañón or the Río Ucayali, which will lead into the waterlogged **(4) Reserva Nacional Pacaya-Samiria**. This sprawling park is home to interesting aquatic jungle animals, including pink and gray river dolphins, caimans and South American river turtles. The further you get away from Iquitos, the more wildlife you are likely to see.

Green parrots, Río Amazonas

Discover Iquitos & the Amazon Basin

At a Glance

o **Iquitos** (p290) A jungle metropolis serves as a gateway to the Amazon River.

o **Reserva Nacional Pacaya-Samiria** (p298) A massive park boasting giant water lilies and rare river turtles.

o **Puerto Maldonado** (p300) A boisterous settlement lies near the wildest areas.

o **Parque Nacional Manu** (p309) Wild and remote, home to caiman and macaws, jungle chickens and jaguars.

Girl in canoe, Río Itaya, Iquitos
PHOTOGRAPHER: PAUL KENNEDY

IQUITOS

🎵 065 / POP 430,000 / ELEV 130M

Linked to the outside world by air and by river, Iquitos is the world's largest city that cannot be reached by road. It's a prosperous, vibrant jungle metropolis. Unadulterated nature encroaches the town in full view of air-conditioned, elegant bars and restaurants that flank the riverside.

You may well arrive in Iquitos for a boat trip down the Amazon or to hole up in a lodge amid extravagant jungle. But whether it's sampling rainforest cuisine, checking out the buzzing nightlife or exploring one of Peru's most fascinating markets in the floating shantytown of Belén, this thriving city may entice you to stay awhile.

 Sights

CASA DE FIERRO
Historic Structure
(southeast cnr Plaza de Armas)
The 'majestic' Casa de Fierro (Iron House), designed by Gustave Eiffel (of Eiffel Tower fame), was imported from Paris around 1890, during the rubber boom. Although three different iron houses were imported at the time, only this one survives. There is now a store on the ground floor and a decent restaurant up top.

While you're wandering around the central part of the city, look for the 19th-century **azulejos** – handmade ceramic tiles from Portugal – that decorate the old mansions that once belonged to the area's rubber barons. You can find these on buildings along Raimondi and the Malecón Tarapacá. Some of the best are the various government buildings along or near the Malecón.

LIBRARY & MUSEUM   Museum
(cnr Malecón Maldonado & Morona; admission for both S3; ☉Mon-Fri) An old building on the corner houses the **Biblioteca Amazónica** (the largest collection of historical documents in the Amazon Basin) and the small **Museo Etnográfico**. The museum includes life-sized fiberglass casts of members of various Amazon tribes.

BELÉN   Floating Shantytown
At the southeast end of town is this **floating shantytown**, consisting of scores of huts, built on rafts, which rise and fall with the river. These rafts sit on the river mud and are dirty, but for most of the year they float on the river – a colorful and exotic sight. Around 7000 people live here, and canoes float from hut to hut selling and trading jungle produce. The best time to visit the shantytown is at 7am, when villagers arrive to sell their produce. To get here, take a cab to 'Los Chinos,' walk to the port and rent a canoe to take you around.

Belén mercado, located within the city blocks in front of Belén (at Hurtado and Jr 9 de Diciembre), is the raucous, crowded affair where all kinds of strange and exotic products are sold. The market makes for exciting shopping and sightseeing, but do remember to watch your wallet.

 **Activities**

River Cruises

Cruising the Amazon is a popular pastime and advance reservations are generally necessary. Cruises focus on the Río Amazonas, both downriver towards the Brazil–Colombia border and upriver to Nauta, where the Ríos Marañon and Ucayali converge. Beyond Nauta, trips continue up these two rivers to the Pacaya-Samiria reserve. Trips can also be arranged on the three rivers surrounding Iquitos: the Itaya, the Amazonas and the Nanay.

Operators quote prices in US dollars and most tours include food, transfers and English speaking guides.

DAWN ON THE AMAZON TOURS & CRUISES   Cruises
(☏ 23-3730, 993-9190, 994-3267; www. dawnontheamazon.com; Malecón Maldonado 185, Iquitos; day trips incl lunch per person US$65, multiday cruises per person per day US$150) The *Amazon I* is a beautiful 33ft wooden craft with modern furnishings, available for either day trips or longer cruises of up to two weeks. You can travel with host Bill Grimes and his experienced crew along the Amazon, or along quieter tributaries. Grimes has exclusive permission to go twice as far into the Pacaya-Samiria reserve as any other tour company. A plus: many cruise operators have fixed itineraries, but Dawn on the Amazon can accommodate individual needs.

AMAZON CRUISES   Cruises
(☏ in the USA 800-747-0567; www.amazoncruise. net; 3-night Marañon & Ucayali cruise per person US$1401, 6-day Marañon & Ucayali cruise per person US$2261) The charming riverboat MV *Amazon Journey (El Arca)* has twice-weekly departures into Pacaya-Samiria. The vessel has 13 cabins with air-con that have upper and lower bunks, and three cabins with three- and four-bed configurations – all with private showers. There is also a restaurant seating 22. Available activities include visiting indigenous communities, hikes, and dolphin-watching. Cruises last three or six days.

GREEN TRACKS AMAZON TOURS & CRUISES   Cruises
(☏ in the USA 970-884-6107, 800-892-1035; www.amazontours.net; 7 days & 6 nights s/d $US2700/5000) With three luxury ships plying the Peruvian Amazon, Green Tracks offers four- to seven-day excursions into Pacaya-Samiria. The *Ayapua* is a 20-passenger, rubber-boom-era boat used for seven-day/six-night voyages, with air-conditioned rooms, a bar and library. *Delfín I* and *Delfín II* are more-modern vessels accommodating 12 and 28 passengers, respectively, and operate four- and five-day cruises to the reserve.

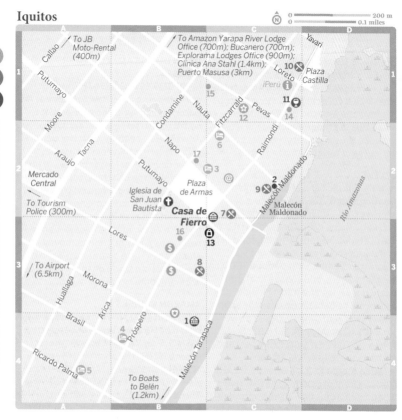

INTERNATIONAL EXPEDITIONS Cruises (in the USA 205-428-1700, 800-633-4734; www.ietravel.com; 10 days & 9 nights per person US$3298) This well-organized company operates three boats: the 15-cabin MV *Amatista,* the 14-cabin MV *Turmalina* and the larger 23-cabin MV *Turquesa.* Its relaxing and pampering nine-day river cruises take in the Ríos Amazon and Ucayali, passing through Requena en route to the Pacaya-Samiria reserve. These are elegant boats with three decks, air-conditioned double cabins with private showers, excellent dining and viewing facilities and experienced guides.

Other Activities

AMAZON GOLF CLUB Golf
(963-1333, 975-4976; Quistacocha; per day S60; ⏰6am-6pm) Practice your swing

at the only golf course in the Amazon. Founded in 2004 by a bunch of nostalgic expats, the 2140m course was built on virgin bushland and it boasts nine greens, and a wooden clubhouse. Hole 4 is a beauty: you tee onto an island surrounded by piranha-infested waters. Just don't fish for lost balls! Club rental is included.

 Sleeping

For a list of jungle lodges outside the Iquitos area, turn to p298.

LA CASA FITZCARRALDO B&B $$
(60-1138/39; www.lacasafitzcarraldo.com, Av La Marina 2153; r incl breakfast S130-200; ❄@🛜🏊) Sequestered within a serene

Iquitos

walled garden a couple of kilometers north of town, this is the most interesting accommodation option. The house takes its title from Werner Herzog's film – Herzog and company stayed here during the filming of *Fitzcarraldo* (see p298). Stay in the mahogany-floored Mick Jagger room, the luxuriant Klaus Kinski suite or five other individually designed rooms. There is a tree house (with wi-fi!) and a swimming pool.

HOTEL EL DORADO PLAZA
Luxury Hotel $$$
(☎ 22-2555; www.grupo-dorado.com; Napo 258; r incl breakfast from S726; ❄ ☀) This modern hotel is the town's best, with 64 well-equipped, spacious rooms (some with plaza views, others overlooking the pool). Jacuzzi, sauna, gym, restaurant, suites, 24-hour room service, two bars and attentive staff make this a five-star hotel.

HOTEL VICTORIA REGIA
Boutique Hotel $$$
(☎ 23-1983; www.victoriaregiahotel.com; Ricardo Palma 252; s/d incl breakfast S210/240, ste S300-450; ❄ @ ☀) A blast of icy, air-conditioned air welcomes guests to this comfortable hostelry. It has excellent

beds and sizeable rooms with minifridges, hairdryers and bathtubs. There is an indoor pool and a restaurant-bar.

MARAÑÓN HOTEL
Hotel $$
(☎ 24-2673; www.hmaranon.k25.net; Nauta 285; s/d incl breakfast S99/130; ❄ ☀) Rooms have good-sized bathrooms as well as the usual amenities, plus the restaurant offers room service. Good value.

HOTEL EUROPA
Hotel $$
(☎ 23-1123; hoteleuropasac@yahoo.es; Próspero 494; s S70-90, d S110-130; ❄) One of the best midrange bargains, the canary-yellow hotel offers air-con, minifridges, a restaurant and laundry service.

Eating

GRAN MALOKA
Amazon Classics $$$
(☎ 23-3126; Lores 170; menú S15, mains S25-40; ◷noon-10pm; ❄) This elegant restaurant features silk tablecloths and wall-length mirrors and serves imaginative regional delicacies such as *chupín de pollo* (chicken, egg and rice soup), Amazon venison with toasted coconut, and the scrumptious Loretan omelet with jungle leaves.

TABERNA DEL CAUCHERO
Amazon Fusion **$$**

(☎ 23-1699; latabernadelcauchero@yahoo.es; Raimondi 449; mains S15-30; ⏰8am-10pm) The only Cordon Bleu chef in Iquitos serves up innovative modern takes on Amazon cuisine in a spacious, stylishly rustic eating area. It even does sushi, and there's a pool.

BUCANERO
Amazon Classics **$$**

(Av Marina 124; mains S20-30; ⏰11am-5pm; ❄) For great river views in civilized air-conditioned environs, this lunch spot has a fish-dominated menu. *Pescado a la plancha* (grilled river fish) with *chicharrones* (fried chunks of pork) goes down remarkably well with an icy Iquiteña (Iquitos beer).

ANTICA
Italian **$$**

(☎ 24-1672; Napo 159; breakfast S7-10, mains S18-30; ⏰7am-midnight) It's the best Italian restaurant in town and has a range of fine imported Italian wines.

LA NOCHE
International **$$**

(☎ 22-2373; Malecón Maldonado 177; sandwiches S8-10; mains S15-25; ⏰7am-late) Friendly service, a cool sophisticated vibe and oodles of tasty food. There's real espresso and a host of gourmet sandwiches for lunch (the vegetarian triple can't be beaten); river fish and crisp salads grace the dinner menu. A chilled-out lounge bar with sofas inhabits the upstairs.

Drinking & Entertainment

Iquitos is a party city and the Malecón is the cornerstone of the lively nightlife scene.

MUSMUQUI
Bar

(Raimondi 382; ⏰to midnight Sun-Thu, to 3am Fri & Sat) A popular bar with an extensive range of aphrodisiac cocktails concocted from wondrous Amazon plants.

Left: Paddling through dense aquatic plantlife, Quebrada Nuevo, Iquitos;
Below: Wildflower, Río Amazonas
PHOTOGRAPHER: (BOTH IMAGES) PAUL KENNEDY

NOA NOA DISCO-PUB
Dance Club
(23-2902; cnr Fitzcarrald & Pevas; admission around S15) A trendy, upscale disco.

Shopping

There are a few shops on the first block of Napo selling jungle crafts, some of high quality and pricey. A good place for crafts is **Mercado de Artesanía San Juan**, on the road to the airport.

You can buy, rent or trade almost anything needed for a jungle expedition at **Mad Mick's Trading Post** (965-75-4976; michaelcollis@hotmail.com; Putumayo 163; 8am-8pm).

Information

Dangers & Annoyances
Street touts and self-styled jungle guides tend to be aggressive, and many are both irritatingly insistent and dishonest. It is best to make your own decisions by contacting hotels, lodges and tour companies directly. Petty thieving is common by opportunistic young children who roam the streets looking for easy prey. Exercise particular caution around Belén, which is very poor.

Emergency
National police (23-3330; Morona 126)
Tourism police (24-2081, 965-93-5932; Lores 834)

Internet Access
Places charge about S3 per hour.
CQC Cyber Coffee (Raimondi 143) Quite fancy.

Medical Services
Clínica Ana Stahl (25-2535; Av La Marina 285; 24 hr) A good private clinic north of town.

295

PAUL KENNEDY

Don't Miss **Pilpintuwasi Butterfly Farm**

A visit to this fascinating butterfly farm is highly recommended. Ostensibly this is a conservatorium and breeding center for Amazonian butterflies. Butterflies aplenty there certainly are, including the striking blue morpho *(Morpho menelaus)* and the fearsome-looking owl butterfly *(Caligo eurilochus)*, which has an owl-like eye on its wing. But it's the farm's exotic animals that steal the show. Raised as orphans and protected within the property are several monkeys, Lolita the tapir and Pedro Bello, a majestic jaguar. You'll also meet capricious Rosa, a giant anteater who wanders around freely, looking for ants.

To get there, take a small boat from Bellavista-Nanay, a tiny port 2km north of Iquitos, to the village of Padre Cocha. The farm is signposted and is a 15-minute walk through the village from the Padre Cocha boat dock. Boats run all day.

NEED TO KNOW

☏ 065-23-2665; www.amazonanimalorphanage.org; Padre Cocha; admission S15; ☺ 9am-4pm Tue-Sun

---

Money

Several banks change traveler's checks and give advances on credit cards, including BCP (cnr Prospero & Putumayo), which has a secure ATM.

Tourist Information

Look for free copies of the monthly *Iquitos Times* (www.iquitostimes.com), which features the latest goings on about town. It is generally distributed at hotels and restaurants.

iPerú Airport (☏ 26-0251; Main Hall, Francisco Secada Vignetta Airport; ☺ 8am-1pm & 4-8pm); City Center (☏ 23-6144; Loreto 201; ☺ 8:30am-7:30pm) English spoken at the airport branch.

Reserva Nacional Pacaya-Samiria Office (☏ 22-3460, Pevas 339; ☺ 8am-4pm Mon-Fri) Entry to the reserve for three days costs S60, payable at Banco de la Nación around the corner.

Getting There & Away

Air

The airport is 7km out of town and receives flights from Lima via LAN (☎ 23-2421; Próspero 232) and Star Perú (☎ 23-6208; Napo 256). There is a domestic departure tax of S14.

A *mototaxi* to the airport costs around S7; a regular taxi, S15.

Boat

Iquitos is Peru's largest, best-organized river port. Puerto Masusa on Av La Marina, about 3km north of the town center, is where the city's numerous riverboats dock.

Getting Around

Taxis are relatively few, but squadrons of busy *mototaxis* can oblige with lifts. Always enter *mototaxis* from the sidewalk side – passing traffic pays scant heed to embarking passengers – and keep your limbs inside at all times. Most rides around Iquitos cost about S2.

Buses and trucks for several nearby destinations, including the airport, leave from near Plaza 28 de Julio. Airport buses are marked Nanay-Belén-Aeropuerto: they'll head south down Arica to the airport.

JB Moto-Rental (☎ 22-2389; Yavari 702) rents motorcycles.

AROUND IQUITOS
Nearby Villages & Lakes

About 16km from town, past the airport, **Santo Tomás** is famous for its pottery and mask making, and has a few bars overlooking Mapacocha, a lake formed by an arm of the Río Nanay. You can rent boats by asking around (a motorboat with driver costs about S30). **Santa Clara** is about 15km away,

on the banks of the Río Nanay. There are white-sand beaches during low water (July to October), and boats are available for rent. Both villages can be reached by *mototaxi* (about S15).

Corrientillo is a lake near the Río Nanay. There are a few bars around the lake, which is locally popular for swimming on weekends. It's about 15km from town; a *mototaxi* will charge about S15.

Laguna Quistacocha

This lake, just 15km south of Iquitos, has a small **zoo** of local fauna and an adjoining **fish hatchery**. The latter helps support 2m-long *paiche* (local river fish), which is now endangered. An attempt to rectify the situation is being made with the breeding program here. A pedestrian walk circles the lake, swimming is possible and paddleboats are available for hire. There are several restaurants and a hiking trail. Admission is S10.

The area is served by minibuses several times an hour from near Plaza

Jaguar, Laguna Quistacocha
PHOTOGRAPHER: PAUL KENNEDY

Herzog's Amazon

Eccentric German director Werner Herzog shot two movies in Peru's jungle, *Aguirre, the Wrath of God* (1972) and *Fitzcarraldo* (1982) – about men facing nature in the Amazon. The movies are cult favorites among cinema fans – but the fact that Herzog even survived the shoots is what's remarkable.

For starters, there was the leading man: Klaus Kinski, a volatile actor prone to fits of rage. During the filming of *Aguirre*, he had altercations with an extra and, later, a cameraman – after which he tried to desert the shoot on a speedboat. (To make him stay, Herzog threatened him with a rifle.) Later, while filming *Fitzcarraldo*, Kinski so antagonized the Matsiguenka tribespeople working as extras, that one of them offered to murder him. Then there was the weather: droughts so dire that the rivers dried, halting shooting, followed by flash floods that wrecked everything.

Herzog once said he saw filming in the Amazon as 'challenging nature itself.' The fact that he completed the films is evidence that in some ways, he did challenge nature – and triumphed.

28 de Julio (cnr Bermudéz with Moore; S2), as well as *mototaxis* (S12).

Reserva Nacional Pacaya-Samiria

Located on the Río Ucayali, west of Iquitos, the 20,800 sq km **Pacaya-Samiria Reserve** (www.pacaya-samiria.com) is one of the largest parks in Peru. An estimated 42,000 people live on and around the reserve, juggling the needs of longtime human inhabitants with the protection of area wildlife.

Pacaya-Samiria is home to aquatic animals such as Amazon manatees, pink and gray river dolphins, two species of caiman, giant South American river turtles and many other bird and animal species. Noteworthy points include **Quebrada Yanayacu**, where the river water is black from dissolved plants; **Lago Pantean**, where you can check out caimans and go medicinal-plant collecting, and **Tipischa de Huana**, where you can see the giant *Victoria regia* waterlilies, big enough for a small child to sleep upon without sinking.

From Iquitos, the best way to get to the reserve is via a multiday river cruise (p291). The nearest lodge is the Pacaya-Samiria Amazon Lodge, listed on p299.

Jungle Lodges & Expeditions

There are numerous lodges both upriver and downriver from Iquitos that offer a mix of relaxation, as well as plenty of wildlife spotting, camping, hiking and fishing (July to September are the best months). Many of these have offices in Iquitos.

 Sleeping

All prices quoted here are approximate; meals, tours and transportation from Iquitos should be included. Lodges will provide containers of purified water for you to fill your own bottle, as well as 24-hour hot water with instant coffee and tea bags, but it is advisable to bring extra water for the journey out.

The following lodges are listed in order of distance from Iquitos.

OTORONGO LODGE　　　　Lodge　$$
(065-22-4192, 965-75-6131; www.otorongoexpeditions.com; Departamento 203, Putumayo 163, Iquitos; 5 days & 4 nights US$590) Travelers

have been giving great feedback about this relatively new, rustic-style lodge, 100km from Iquitos. It's a down-to-earth place, with 12 rooms containing private bathrooms and a relaxing common area, surrounded by walkways to maximize appreciation of the surrounding wildlife. Otorongo is run by a former falconer who can imitate an incredible number of bird sounds. The five-day option can include off-the-beaten-path visits to nearby communities and camping trips deeper in the jungle.

AMAZON YARAPA RIVER LODGE
Luxury Lodge $$$

(☎ 065-993-1172; www.yarapa.com; Av La Marina 124, Iquitos; 4 days & 3 nights s/d US$1020/1840, s/d without bathroom US$940/1680; @) Approximately 130km upriver from Iquitos on the Río Yarapa, this lodge is simply stunning. It has a huge and well-designed tropical biology laboratory, powered by an expansive solar-panel system. Facilities are beautifully maintained and rooms are connected by a series of screened walkways. Eight huge bedrooms with oversized private bathrooms are available and 16 comfortable rooms share a multitude of well-equipped bathrooms. The trip from Iquitos takes three to four hours. Recommended.

TAHUAYO LODGE
Lodge $$

(www.perujungle.com; 8 days per person US$1295); USA (Amazonia Expeditions; ☎ 813-907-8475, 800-262-9669) Iquitos (Av La Marina 100) This lodge, 140km from Iquitos, has exclusive access to the 2500-sq-km Tamshiyacu-Tahuayo reserve, an area of pristine jungle where a record 93 species of mammal have been recorded. The 15 cabins are located 65km up an Amazon tributary, built on high stilts and connected by walkways; half have private bathrooms. There is a laboratory with a library here, too. Wildlife-viewing opportunities are among the best of any lodge listed: it might even include a peek at the pygmy marmosets that nest nearby.

PACAYA-SAMIRIA AMAZON LODGE
Lodge $$$

(☎ 065-23-4128; www.pacayasamiria.com.pe; Raimondi 378, Iquitos; per 1/2 people 3 days & 2 nights US$765/940, per 1/2 people 6 days & 5 nights US$1600/1960) About 190km upriver on the Río Marañón, this excellent lodge

Reserva Nacional Pacaya-Samiria

CYRIL RUOSO/JH EDITORIAL/MINDEN PICTURES

is past Nauta on the outskirts of the Pacaya-Samiria reserve, four hours from Iquitos. It can arrange overnight stays within the reserve. Rooms feature private showers and porches with river views, and the lodge has electricity in the evening. There are special bird-watching programs.

EXPLORAMA LODGES Lodge $$
(☎ 065-25-2530; www.explorama.com; Av La Marina 340, Iquitos) This well-established and recommended company owns and operates various lodges in the area and is an involved supporter of the Amazon Conservatory of Tropical Studies (ACTS). It has a lab at the famed **canopy walkway**, which is suspended above the forest floor to give visitors a bird's-eye view of the rainforest canopy and its wildlife. You could arrange a trip to visit

one or more lodges (each of which is very different) combined with a visit to the walkway. Children under 12 pay half price.

PUERTO MALDONADO

☎ 082 / POP 56,450 / ELEV 250M

Unlike Amazon cities further north, this is a rawer, untidier jungle town with a mercilessly sweltering climate and a fair quantity of mosquitoes. But there's a pay-off: the watery wildernesses in this area offer some of the most unspoiled-yet-accessible jungle locales in the country – as well as excellent accommodation options for travelers who want a dash of luxury with their rainforest. The best part: it's all situated at an easy flight's reach from Cuzco.

Puerto Maldonado

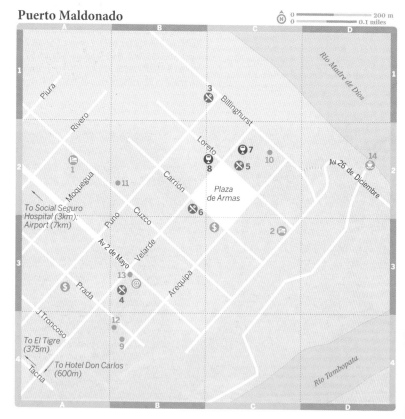

On both the Ríos Tambopata and Madre de Dios, small river ports close to the town center serve the closer jungle lodges; more distant lodges are served by a jetty at Infierno, a 45-minute ride away.

 Sights & Activities

The blue **Obelisco (Fitzcarrald & Madre de Dios; admission S2; ⏱10am-4pm)** was designed as a modern *mirador* (lookout tower); its 30m height offers a distant glimmer of jungle and plenty of corrugated-metal roofs to be admired. Find it situated about 400m northwest of downtown, just off Fitzcarrald.

The **Madre de Dios ferry (per person S1; ⏱dawn-dusk)**, at Puerto Capetania close to the Plaza de Armas, is a cheap way of seeing a little of this major Peruvian jungle river, which is about 500m wide at this point. The river traffic is colorfully ramshackle: *peki-pekis* (motorized canoes) leave from the dock regularly.

 Tours & Guides

Beware of sketchy guides at the airport, who try and take you to a 'recommended' hotel. There are about 30 guides with official licenses granted by the local Ministerio de Industria y Turismo. Many of the best ones work full time for one of the local jungle lodges. Guides charge from S75 to S150 per person per day. The following are recommended:

Hernán Llavé Cortéz
(☏57-3306, 982-61-0065) Speaks some English. If he's not on a tour, you'll find him in the baggage reception area of the airport, waiting for incoming flights.

Gerson Medina Valera
(☏57-4201; gerson_bw@hotmail.com) A birdwatching expert who speaks fluent English. Contact him at Tambopata Hostel (p302).

Victor Yohamona Dumay
(☏982-68-6279; victorguideperu@hotmail.com) A well-known, experienced guide, also reached through Hostal Cabaña Quinta (p302).

 Sleeping

A detailed listing of jungle lodges outside of Puerto Maldonado begins on p305.

ANACONDA LODGE Lodge $$
(☏79-2726; Av Aeropuerto Km 6; www.anacondajunglelodge.com; bungalow s/d/tr S100/160/280, bungalow without bathroom s/d S50/80; ⊛) This cocoon of comfort on the edge of town has eight double-room bungalows with shared bathroom and four luxury bungalows with private facilities; all are mosquito netted. The lodge also has a pool and restaurant-bar serving Thai food and pancake breakfasts.

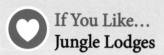

If You Like…
Jungle Lodges

If you like the total jungle-immersion experience, the Peruvian Amazon area has no shortage of lodges. Find your base, then explore the jungle to your heart's delight.

Paseos Amazonicos

(www.paseosamazonicos.com; 3 days & 2 nights per person US$130-180) Iquitos ([☎]065-23-1618; Pevas 246) Lima ([☎]01-241-7576; Office 4, Bajada Balta 131, Miraflores) This company runs three lodges. One of the oldest and best established is Amazonas Sinchicuy Lodge, on a small tributary of the Amazon 30km northeast of Iquitos.

Cumaceba Lodges

([☎]065-22-1456; www.cumaceba.com; Putumayo 184, Iquitos; 3 days & 2 nights US$180-222) This company has been in business since 1995 and operates three budget lodges. Guides speak English, French and even Japanese. The lodges are all aimed at providing travelers with a less costly Amazon experience, and also operate day trips within the Iquitos area for US$65.

Muyuna Amazon Lodge

([☎]office 065-24-2858, 065-993-4424; www.muyuna. com; ground fl, Putumayo 163, Iquitos; 3 days & 2 nights s/d US$385/640) About 140km upriver from Iquitos on the Río Yanayacu, this intimate lodge is surrounded by 10 well-conserved lakes in a remote area less colonized than the jungle downriver, which makes for a great rainforest experience.

Ceiba Tops

(2 days & 1 night per person US$270, 3 days & 2 nights per person US$380; [❄][@][≋]) About 40km northeast of Iquitos on the Amazon, this is Explorama's and the area's most modern lodge and resort. Landscaped grounds surround the pool complex, complete with hydromassage, waterslide and hammock house.

HOSTAL CABAÑA QUINTA   Hotel $$

([☎]57-1045; cabanaquinta_reservas@hotmail. com; Cuzco 535; s/d standard S70/120, s/d superior S120/160; [❄][≋]) Superior rooms boast air-con, minifridges and hot showers. There is a restaurant, room service and a pool.

HOTEL DON CARLOS   Hotel $$

([☎]57-1323, 57-1029; reservasmaldonado@ hoteldoncarlos.com; León Velarde 1271; s/d incl breakfast S150/180) Decent-sized rooms have hot showers, minifridges and TVs. Located about 1km southwest of the center, it is quiet, and the Río Tambopata can be seen from the grounds. There's a restaurant and room service. Airport transfer is included.

TAMBOPATA HOSTEL   Hostel $

([☎]57-4201; www.tambopatahostel.com; Av 26 de Diciembre 234; dm/s/d S20/35/65, s/d without bathroom S25/50; [@]) This relaxing hostel has a mix of dorm and private rooms abutting a garden courtyard with hammocks. Breakfast is included and the owner is one of the town's best guides.

 Eating

Several down-to-earth, excellent-value places serve up regional specialties. Look for *juanes* (banana leaves stuffed with chicken or pork and rice), *chilcano* (a broth of fish chunks flavored with cilantro) and *parrillada de la selva* (a marinated meat grill, often game, in a Brazil-nut sauce).

BURGOS'S HOUSE
Amazon Classics $$

([☎]57-3653; Puno 106; mains S13-22; [◷]10am-10pm) Regional goodies with an emphasis on fish; Burgos's also provides *juanes* and a mixed platter of jungle dishes for S22.

EL TIGRE   Amazon Classics $$

([☎]57-2286; Tacna 456; menú S10-15; [◷]lunch) Ceviche (seafood marinated in lime juice) and other fish dishes are recommended.

LA CASA NOSTRA
Cafe $

(☎ 57-2647; Av 2 de Mayo 287a; snacks S3-8; ⏰7am-1pm & 5-11pm) Serves varied breakfasts, tamales, juices, snacks, desserts and Puerto Maldonado's best coffee.

LOS GUSTITOS DEL CURA
Bakery $

(☎ 57-3107; Loreto 258; snacks S3-8; ⏰11am-10pm) The best ice cream in town can be found at this French-owned patisserie. Sandwiches, cakes and drinks are also dished up, and local *objets d'art* are on sale.

PIZZERÍA EL HORNITO/CHEZ MAGGY
Pizza $$

(☎ 57-2082; Carrión 271; pizzas S15-25; ⏰6pm-late) The best wood-fired pizzas are located here on the plaza.

 **Drinking**

A handful of spots sputter to life late on weekends.

DISCOTECA WITITE
Dance Club

(☎ 57-2419, 57-3861; Velarde 151) The crowd is mixed and on weekends, the partying goes on all night.

TSAICA
Bar

(Loreto 327) Funky indigenous art on the walls make for Puerto's liveliest bar. Recommended.

ℹ Information

Internet Access

Internet is slower here and costs about S2 per hour.

UnAMad (Av 2 de Mayo 287) Best of several places downtown.

Medical Services

Hospital Santa Rosa (☎ 57-1019, 57-1046; Cajamarca 171) A basic hospital.

Social Seguro Hospital (☎ 57-1711) A newer option at Km 3 on the road to Cuzco.

Money

BCP (Carrión 201, on the Plaza de Armas) Changes US dollars or traveler's checks and has a Visa ATM.

Casa de Cambio (Puno at Prada) Money exchange; standard rates for US dollars.

Tambopata Research Center, Reserva Nacional Tambopata (p307)

Tourist Information

Sernanp (57-3278; rn_tambopata@sernanp. gob.pe; Av 28 de Julio, cuadra 8) The national-park office gives information and collects entrance fees; entrance to the Tambopata reserve zone is S30 to S65.

Tourist Booth (airport) Provides limited information on tours and jungle lodges.

Getting There & Away

Most travelers fly here from Lima or Cuzco. The long road and river trips are not recommended unless you have a *lot* of time on your hands.

Air

The airport is 7km out of town. Scheduled flights leave every day to and from Lima via Cuzco with LAN (57-3677; www.lan.com; Velarde 503) and Star Perú (01-705-9000; www.starperu.com; airport).

Light aircraft to any destination can be chartered. Ask at the airport.

Boat

Hire boats at the Río Madre de Dios ferry dock for local excursions.

Bus & Taxi

The 500km road to Cuzco has improved in the last few years, and long sections were already paved when this book was researched. That said, it was dubbed Peru's worst road before improvements began, and while there are now fewer potholes, road works are still causing delays. The journey currently takes 17 to 20 hours, sometimes more in the wet season. When complete, this road will form part of the Interoceanic Hwy to Brazil.

Getting Around

Mototaxis take two or three passengers (and light luggage) to the airport for S5 to S7. Short rides around town cost S2 or less.

AROUND PUERTO MALDONADO
Río Madre de Dios

This important river flows east, past Puerto Maldonado, into Bolivia and Brazil and, eventually, the Amazon proper. The main reason people come here is to stay for a few days in one of several jungle lodges, all of which are to be found between one and two hours upstream from Puerto Maldonado itself.

Here, travelers can partake in fishing and nature trips, and visit beaches and indigenous communities. Lodges often provide rubber boots for the muddy jungle paths.

Madre de Dios and Tambopata lodges quote their prices in US dollars, which include transportation unless stated.

Paddling down the Río Samiria

Transporting fruit down the river, Puerto Maldonado

SEAN CAFFREY

 Sleeping

Most lodge-style accommodations are based along the rivers. These are listed as you travel away from Puerto Maldonado. All of these spots have English-speaking guides available upon request.

CORTO MALTES Lodge **$$**
(☏ 082-57-3831; www.cortomaltes-amazonia. com; s 3 days & 2 nights US$240); Puerto Maldonado (Billinghurst, cuadra 2) The closest lodge to Puerto Maldonado is 5km from town. It offers 15 fully screened, high-ceilinged bungalows with solid mattresses, eye-catching Shipibo indigenous wall art and patios with hammocks. Electricity is available from dusk until 10:30pm, and showers have hot water. The French owners pride themselves on their excellent European-Peruvian fusion cuisine.

INKATERRA RESERVA AMAZONICA
Luxury Lodge **$$$**
(www.inkaterra.com; 3 days & 2 nights s/d US$673/1082, ste per person double occupancy US$739); Cuzco (Map p174; ☏ 084-24-5314;

Plaza Nazarenas 167); Lima (☏ 01-610-0400; Andalucía 174, Miraflores) Further down the Madre de Dios, almost 16km from Puerto Maldonado, this option is exceptionally luxurious. About 40 rustic individual cabins have bathrooms, porches and hammocks. Six suites boast huge bathrooms, writing desks and two queen beds each. Tours include 10km of private hiking trails, and a series of swaying, narrow, canopy walkways above the jungle floor for observation. There's a bar, library and restaurant.

ECOAMAZONIA LODGE Lodge **$$**
(www.ecoamazonia.com.pe; per person 3 days & 2 nights US$210, per person 4 days & 3 nights US$280); Cuzco (Map p174; ☏ 084-23-6159; Garcilaso 210, Office 206); Lima (☏ 01-242-2708; Palacios 292, Miraflores); Puerto Maldonado (☏ 082-57-3491) Roughly 30km from Puerto Maldonado is this rustic spot, with a thatch-roofed restaurant and bar, with fine river views. Forty-seven simple, screened bungalows each have a bathroom and a small sitting area. There are several trails, including a tough 14km hike to a lake. Ayahuasca ceremonies can be arranged by advance request.

305

Around Puerto Maldonado

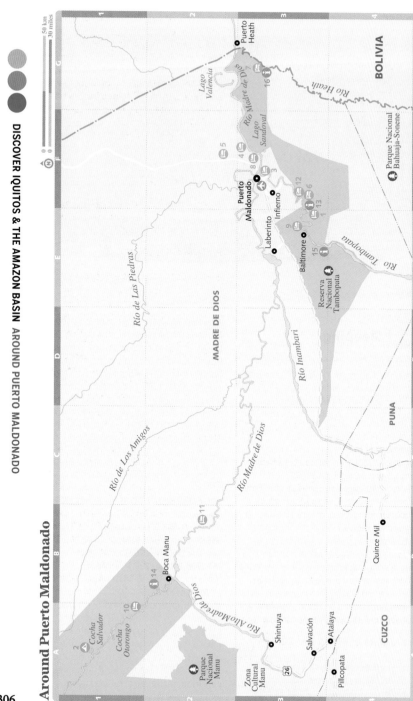

Around Puerto Maldonado

ESTANCIA BELLO HORIZONTE
Lodge **$$**

(☏ 082-57-2748, 982-60-2356; estancia@ estanciabellohorizonte.com; JM Grain 105, Puerto Maldonado; per person 4 days & 3 nights US$320) Away from the rivers, in the jungle itself, is this relaxing Franco-Swiss hideaway. It is situated in a large open clearing on a ridge overlooking the rainforest about 20km from Puerto Maldonado on the east side of the Río Madre de Dios. The bungalows contain smallish, comfortable rooms with bathrooms; each has a hammock and reclining chairs. The main building and dining/bar area offer impressive views of the virgin rainforest. The child-friendly grounds include a football (soccer) pitch, a volleyball court, a swimming pool and signposted jungle walks.

Río Tambopata

The Río Tambopata is a major tributary of the Río Madre de Dios, joining it at Puerto Maldonado. Boats go up the river, past several lodges, and into the **Reserva Nacional Tambopata** (admission S30), an important protected area divided into the reserve itself and the **zona de amortiguamiento** (buffer zone). One of the reserve's highlights is the Colpa de Guacamayos (Macaw Clay Lick), one of the largest natural clay licks in the country. It attracts hundreds of birds and is a spectacular sight.

Travelers heading up the Río Tambopata must register their passport numbers at the Puesto Control (Guard Post) and show their national-park entrance permits obtained in Puerto Maldonado at the Sernanp office (p304). If you are on a guided tour, this will be arranged for you.

 ## Sleeping

Lodges are listed in the order in which you would arrive at them if traveling from Puerto Maldonado.

POSADA AMAZONAS
Luxury Lodge **$$$**

(s/d 3 days & 2 nights US$385/590) About two hours from Puerto Maldonado, along the Río Tambopata, and followed by a 10-minute uphill walk, is this 30-room lodge with large double rooms with private showers and open windows that overlook the rainforest. There are excellent chances of seeing macaws and parrots, and giant river otters are often found swimming in lakes close by. Your assigned English-speaking guide stays with you throughout the duration of your stay. There is a medicinal-plant trail and, a short hike from the lodge, a 30m-high observation platform giving superb views of the rainforest canopy. Mosquito nets are provided and electricity is available at lunchtime and from 5:30pm to 9pm. Book with **Rainforest Expeditions** (www .perunature.com) Cuzco (Map p174; ☏ 084-24-6243; cusco@rainforest.com.pe; Portal de Carnes 236); Lima (☏ 01-421-8347; postmaster@rainfor est.com.pe; Aramburu 166, Miraflores); Puerto Maldonado ☏ 082-57-2575; pem@rainforest.com. pe; Av Aeropuerto Km 6, CPM La Joya).

EXPLORER'S INN
Lodge **$$**

(www.explorersinn.com; s/d 3 days & 2 nights US$238/396) Cuzco (☏ 084-23-5342; Plateros 365); Lima (☏ 01-447-8888, 01-447-4761; sales@ explorersinn.com; Alcanfores 459, Miraflores) Puerto Maldonado (☏ 082-57-2078) About 58km from Puerto Maldonado, Explorer's

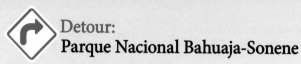

Detour:
Parque Nacional Bahuaja-Sonene

About two hours south of the Río Madre de Dios and along the Río Heath, the **Parque Nacional Bahuaja-Sonene** (admission S30) has some of the best wildlife in Peru's Amazon region. Infrastructure in the park, one of the nation's largest, is limited, and wildlife-watching trips are in their infancy here – making this a spot for dedicated adventurers.

The best (read: only) place to stay in the area is the **Heath River Wildlife Center** (s/d 5 days & 4 nights US$915/1430), a 10-room lodge owned by the Ese'eja indigenous people of Sonene, located five hours by boat from Puerto Maldonado. Units in the simple thatched lodge come equipped with hot water, and guiding and cultural services are available. Travelers can also take advantage of trails that lead right into the Bahuaja-Sonene. Capybaras are frequently seen, and guided tours to a nearby *colpa* (clay lick), to see macaws and parrots, can be arranged.

Park entrance fees are included. The first and last nights of tours are spent at a lodge on Lake Sandoval. To arrange a stay, contact **InkaNatura** (www.inkanatura. com) Cuzco (Map p174; ☎ 084-23-1138; Ricardo Palma J1 Urb Santa Mónica & Plateros 361); Lima (☎ 01-440-2022; Manuel Bañón 461, San Isidro).

has 15 rustic double and 15 triple rooms, all with bathrooms and screened windows. The central lodge has a restaurant, a bar and a small museum. The lodge is located in the former 55-sq-km Zona Preservada Tambopata. More than 600 species of bird have been recorded here. The 38km of trails around here can be explored independently or with guides. Rates include meals and tours. Four-night stays include a visit to the clay lick to see macaws (single/double US$530/900).

CAYMAN LODGE AMAZONIE
Lodge **$$$**

(☎ 082-57-1970; www.cayman-lodge-amazonie .com; s/d 2 days & 3 nights US$400/560); Puerto Maldonado (Arequipa 655) Some 70km from Puerto Maldonado, Cayman is run by an effervescent Frenchwoman Anny and her English-speaking Peruvian partner, Daniel. The lodge boasts an open, relaxing environment with banana, *cocona* (peach tomato) and mango trees in a lush tropical garden. There is also a five- to seven-day shamanism program, where you can learn about tropical medicine. There is a

large bar and restaurant. The rooms are small, but comfortable; windows have mosquito meshes. One of its more arresting features is the hammock house, from where you can watch the sun set over the Río Tambopata.

LIBERTADOR TAMBOPATA LODGE
Luxury Lodge **$$**

(☎ 082-57-1726, 082-968-0022; www .tambopatalodge.com; s/d 3 days & 2 nights US$379/614); Puerto Maldonado (Prada 269) This considerably more luxurious lodge is still within the Reserva Tambopata. A short boat ride from here will get you into primary forest. Tours to nearby lakes and to the salt lick are included on tours of four days or longer (single/ double from US$688/1160). There are 12km of well-marked trails. The lodge consists of a series of spacious individual bungalows, some of which have solar-generated hot water. Each enjoys a tiled patio with a table and chairs, and all look out onto a lush tropical garden. There is a restaurant and a bar complex: the overall effect is like a set from the TV series *Lost*.

MANU AREA

The Manu area encompasses the Parque Nacional Manu and much of the surrounding area. Covering almost 20,000 sq km, the park is divided into three zones: the largest sector is the *zona natural,* comprising 80% of the total park area and closed to unauthorized visitors. The second sector, still within the park proper, is the *zona reservada,* where controlled research and tourism activities are permitted. The third sector, covering the southeastern area, is the *zona cultural,* where most other visitor activity is concentrated.

Parque Nacional Manu

This national park starts in the eastern slopes of the Andes and plunges down into the lowlands, playing host to a great diversity of wildlife over a wide range of cloud forest and rainforest habitats. Unesco declared it a World Natural Heritage Site in 1987.

One reason the park is so successful in preserving such a large tract of virgin jungle and its wildlife is that it is remote. During a one-week trip you can reasonably expect to see scores of different bird species, several monkey species and possibly a few other mammals, including jaguars, tapirs, giant anteaters, tamanduas, capybaras, peccaries and giant river otters. Smaller mammals that inhabit the area include kinkajous, pacas, agoutis, squirrels, brocket deer, ocelots and armadillos. Other wildlife includes river turtles and caiman, snakes and a variety of other reptiles and amphibians. Colorful butterflies and less pleasing insects also abound.

The best time to go is during the dry season (June to November); Manu may be inaccessible or closed during the rainy months (January to April), except to visitors staying at the two lodges within the park boundaries.

It is illegal to enter the park without a guide. It is also worth noting that travelers often report delays upon returning from Manu (of up to several days), so don't plan an international airline connection for the day after your trip.

 ## Tours

The number of permits to operate tours into Parque Nacional Manu is limited; only about 3000 visitors are allowed in annually. Visitors must book well in advance. All of the tours listed here are licensed to operate in the park and maintain low-impact practices. These companies provide transportation, food, purified drinking water, guides, permits

Parque Nacional Manu
PHOTOGRAPHER: DAVID TIPLING

and camping equipment or screens in lodge rooms. Personal items such as sleeping bags (if camping), insect repellent, sunblock, flashlights, suitable clothing and bottled drinks are the traveler's responsibility. Binoculars and a camera with a zoom lens are highly recommended. English-speaking guides are available.

MANU EXPEDITIONS
(off Map p174; ☎ 084-22-5990, 084-22-4235; www.manuexpeditions.com; Clorinda Matto de Turner 330, Urb Magisterial, Cuzco) Owners of the only tented camp within the national park, and co-owners of the Manu Wildlife Center, this outfit comes highly recommended. Its guides are excellent and highly knowledgeable. The most-popular trip leaves from Cuzco and lasts nine days, including overland transportation to Manu with two nights of camping at the company's Cocha Salvador Safari Camp, three nights at the Manu Wildlife Center, three nights at other lodges and a flight back to Cuzco. This costs US$1895.

MANU NATURE TOURS
(off Map p174; ☎ 084-25-2721; www.manuperu.com; Pardo 1046, Cuzco) This place operates the respected Manu Lodge, the only fully appointed lodge within the reserve and open year-round. The lodge has 12 double rooms plus a bar-cum-dining room next to a lake that's home to a breeding family of giant otters. A five-day tour, flying in or out, is US$1628 per person, double occupancy. Three-day tours are from US$1109/1618 for one/two people. All meals are provided.

✒ PANTIACOLLA TOURS
(☎ 084-23-8323; www.pantiacolla.com; Saphi 554, Cuzco) This outfit owns three lodges in the Manu region and is frequently recommended by a variety of travelers for its knowledgeable and responsibly executed tours. It also works with local indigenous groups on a variety of conservation and sustainability projects.

Hoatzin, Parque Nacional Manu (see boxed text, opposite)

DAVID TIPLING

Punk Chickens

Listen carefully as your boat passes the banks of the Río Tambopata. If you hear lots of hissing, grunting and sounds of breaking vegetation, it is likely that you have stumbled upon the elaborate mating ritual of one of the Amazon's weirdest birds, the hoatzin. This is an oversized wild chicken with a blue face and a large crest on its head (hence the nickname 'punk chicken').

Scientists have been unable to classify this bird as a member of any other avian family, mainly due to the two claws the young have on each wing. To evade predators, hoatzin chicks will fall out of the nest to the river and use their claws to help them scramble back up the muddy banks. The clawed wing is a feature no other airborne creature since the pterodactyl has possessed. The hoatzin's appearance is outdone by its terrible smell, which may well be the first indication they are nearby. They also taste bad, so are rarely hunted. In this age of rainforest depletion, they are one of the few native birds with a flourishing population.

INKANATURA

(www.inkanatura.com) Cuzco (Map p174; ☏ 084-25-5255; Ricardo Palma J1 Urb Santa Mónica & Plateros 361) Lima (☏ 01-440-2022; Manuel Bañón 461, San Isidro) USA (Tropical Nature Travel; ☏ 1-877-888-1770, 1-352-376-3377; POB 5276, Gainesville FL 32627-5276) A highly respected international agency and co-owner of the Manu Wildlife Center. The operators can combine a visit here with trips to other parts of the southern Peruvian rainforest, including Pampas del Heath near Puerto Maldonado, where they also have a lodge.

Peru
In Focus

The streets of Cuzco bathed in early morning light
PHOTOGRAPHER: RALPH HOPKINS

Peru Today

LarcoMar shopping mall (p82), Miraflores, Lima

" *Gastronomic festivals, such as La Mistura, draw upwards of 250,000 visitors* "

belief systems
(% of population)

81
Roman Catholic

13
Evangelical

6
Other

if Peru were 100 people

45 would be of Indigenous origin

37 would be of Mestizo origin

15 would be of European origin

3 would be of Other origin

population per sq km

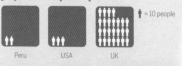

≈ 10 people

Peru   USA   UK

A Cultural Renaissance

For a country born of a tumultuous history, Peru has its moments of incredible grace. There is the Nobel Prize-winning literature, the baroque architecture and, of course, the food – a sublime combination of regional specialties that have spent the last 500 years on a slow simmer and are now ready to be served. Peru, in case you haven't heard, is in the midst of a buzzing culinary renaissance.

Led by a charismatic celebrity chef named Gastón Acurio, the country's native cuisine is the subject of write-ups in international food magazines and foodie blogs. Once regarded as a charmless capital city, Lima is now a bastion of fine dining. Gastronomic festivals, such as La Mistura, draw upwards of 250,000 visitors. The foodie pride has had a ripple effect on other aspects of the culture: fashion designers produce avant-garde outfits with alpaca knits while cutting-edge musical groups fuse elements of folk and electronica.

PAUL KENNEDY

accept a suitcase full of money. Fujimori himself was later convicted on an array of charges, including embezzling and ordering extrajudicial killings. Though he's currently serving time in prison, this might not be the last we hear of him. His daughter Keiko is running for presidency in 2011. She has hinted that if she wins, she will pardon her father.

The Road Ahead

The country still faces significant challenges. President Alan García has seen his approval rating steadily sink since he took office in 2006. In 2008 his entire cabinet was forced to resign due to allegations of corruption. On the environmental front, the opening of the Interoceanic Hwy, connecting Peru to Brazil and running right through the Amazon, could have a negative impact on rainforest ecosystems. There is also the poverty to contend with: one in five Peruvians still lives on less than US$2 a day.

To some, these problems might seem insurmountable, but being Peruvian has always required a little bit of defiance. In the 1950s, journalist Jorge Donayre Belaúnde penned a poem to his homeland called '*Viva el Perú...¡Carajo!*' (Long Live Peru...Damn It!). The verse is an epic, warts-and-all tribute to Peru, depicting life in Andean villages as well as sprawling urban shantytowns. Peruvians, wrote Donayre, aren't scared off by difficult circumstances – be it cataclysmic earthquakes or the bad habits of their politicians. In the face of adversity, there is an intractable optimism. In the five decades since Donayre first wrote those words, that hasn't changed one bit.

Viva el Perú...¡Carajo!

A Time of Renewal

The country's cultural boom comes at a time of unparalleled economic expansion, linked to significant growth in mining and agriculture. Since 2004, Peru's gross domestic product has grown steadily every year – even in 2010, when most world economies were painfully shrinking. The influx of wealth has allowed the country to greatly improve its infrastructure and alleviate the most extreme cases of poverty. It's a remarkable turnaround for a nation that was torn apart by a period of protracted guerrilla war in the 1980s and '90s.

This is not to say that Peru is without political drama. The country has been riveted by the legal trials of former President Alberto Fujimori. Elected in 1990, Fujimori cracked down on guerrilla groups, but also ruled with an iron fist. His presidency ended in 2001, when his security chief was caught bribing just about anyone willing to

History

Moche-era ceramics

When the Spanish arrived in the 16th century, the Andes had already seen epic clashes among civilizations. There had been the deity-obsessed Chavín, the militaristic Wari and the artistic Moche. But the encounter that remains most embedded in the Peruvian psyche is the seismic encounter between the Incas and Spaniards. It's a tragic history, yet one that has produced a new culture, a new race and a fascinating new civilization.

Civilization's Early Roots

Though human presence in the Andes dates back roughly 16,000 years, it wasn't until about 3000 BC that settlements began to flourish. These early cultures built many structures for ceremonial purposes, primarily along the coast. Some of the oldest have been discovered at Caral (p87), 200km north of Lima. Almost five thousand years old, this 626-hectare site is evidence of what is thought to be the oldest civilization in

c 3000 BC
Some of the first structures are built at the coastal ceremonial center of Caral.

the Americas – existing at roughly the same time as the ancient cultures of Egypt, India and China. It contains irrigation systems, sunken circular courts and pyramidal structures. In June of 2009 Caral was declared a Unesco World Heritage Site.

The Chavín Horizon

Fast forward a couple of thousand years and you'll end up in the era known as the Chavín Horizon – named after the site of Chavín de Huántar (p251), east of Huaraz. This was a rich period of development for Andean culture – when greater urbanization occurred and artistic and religious phenomena appeared over the central and northern highlands, as well as the coast. Lasting roughly from 1000 BC to 300 BC, the salient feature of the Chavín influence is the repeated representation of a stylized feline (jaguar or puma).

The Birth of Local Cultures

After Chavín, numerous regional cultures became important in scattered areas of the country. South of Lima, near the Península de Paracas, was a coastal community whose most significant phase is referred to as Paracas Necropolis (AD 1–400), after a large burial site. Some of the finest pre-Columbian textiles have been unearthed here: intricate fabrics that depict oceanic creatures, feline warriors and stylized anthropomorphic figures. Nearby, the Nazca culture (200 BC–AD 600) carved giant, enigmatic designs into the desert. Known as the Nazca Lines (p108), these were mapped early in the 20th century, though their ultimate purpose remains unknown.

On the north coast, it was the Moche who were influential. They settled the area around Trujillo from about AD 100 to 800 and are known for their astonishing, highly individualistic ceramic heads, no two of which are exactly alike. They also left behind temple mounds, such as the Huacas del Sol y de la Luna (Temples of the Sun and Moon; p262), near Trujillo, and the impressive burial site of Sipán (p272), north of Chiclayo.

Wari Expansion

The Wari – an ethnic group from the Ayacucho Basin – emerged as a force to be reckoned with for 500 years beginning in AD 600. They were vigorous military conquerors that built important outposts throughout a vast territory from Chiclayo to Cuzco. As with many conquerors, the Wari attempted to subdue others by emphasizing their own traditions over local belief. Thus from about AD 700 to 1100, Wari influence is noted in the art, technology and architecture of cultures around

200 BC
The Nazca culture builds giant glyphs that adorn the southern desert to this day.

AD 500
The Moche construct the Huacas del Sol y de la Luna, adobe temples near present-day Trujillo.

c 800
The fiercely independent Chachapoyas build Kuélap, a citadel in the northern highlands.

The Best Ruins

Peru. These include finely woven textiles featuring stylized designs of figures, some of which contain record-breaking thread counts. The Wari are most significant, however, for creating an extensive network of roadways and for expanding the terrace agriculture system, an infrastructure that the Incas would employ to their advantage centuries later.

Regional Kingdoms

The Wari were replaced by a number of small nation-states that thrived from about AD 1000 to the early 1400s, when the Incas started to consolidate their conquest. One of the biggest of these were the Chimú, of the Trujillo area, whose capital was the famed Chan Chan (p260), the largest adobe city in the world. Nearby were the Sicán, from the Lambayeque area, renowned metallurgists who produced the *tumi* – a ceremonial knife with a rounded blade used in sacrifices. (It has since become a national symbol.)

Other coastal cultures emerged at this point, including the Ica, the Chincha and the Chancay. The latter were known for their geometrically patterned lace and their crude-if-humorous pottery.

In the northern Andes, the cloud-forest-dwelling Chachapoyas culture erected the expansive mountain settlement of Kuélap in a remote patch of the Utcubamba Valley.

Enter the Incas

The Inca presence dates back to the 12th century, in the area around Cuzco. For several hundred years, they remained a small regional state, until 1438, when their ninth king, Inca Yupanqui, defended Cuzco from the invading Chanka people to the north. Emboldened by his victory, he took the name Pachacutec, which means 'Transformer of the Earth' and proceeded to bag much of the Andes. Under his reign, he grew his territory from a regional fiefdom in the Cuzco Valley into an empire of 10 million people, covering most of Peru, in addition to parts of Ecuador, Bolivia and Chile.

Pachacutec's grandson, Huayna Cápac, continued this expansion. By the early 16th century, the Inca empire extended well into present-day Colombia. Unfortunately, Huayna Cápac wouldn't be around to savor his victories. He died unexpectedly in 1525. Without a clear plan for succession, two of the king's children

c 1000
The Chimú begin development of Chan Chan, a sprawling adobe city outside Trujillo.

TOM COCKREM

1100–1200
The Incas emerge as a presence in the Cuzco Valley.

fought for control: the Quito-born Atahualpa, who commanded the Inca armies of the north, and Huáscar, who was based in Cuzco. The ensuing struggle plunged the empire into a bloody civil war, with Atahualpa emerging the victor in April of 1532. The vicious nature of the conflict left the Incas with enemies throughout the Andes, which contributed to the willingness of some tribes to cooperate with the Spanish when they arrived just five months later.

The Spanish Invade

Francisco Pizarro landed in Tumbes, on the north coast of present-day Peru in September of 1532 with a shipload of arms, horses and slaves – and a battalion of 168 men. Atahualpa, at this time, was in the northern highland city of Cajamarca, on his way to Cuzco to claim his throne. The Spaniard quickly deduced that the empire was in a fractious state. Pizarro went to Cajamarca and approached Atahualpa with promises of brotherhood, but soon enough, he and his men had launched a surprise attack that left thousands dead and Atahualpa a prisoner of war. And thus began one of the most famous ransoms in history: in order to regain their leader's freedom, the Incas filled an entire room with silver and gold. But it wasn't enough. The Spanish eventually sentenced Atahualpa to death by strangulation.

The invasion would bring on a cataclysmic collapse of indigenous society. One scholar estimates that the native population – around 10 million when Pizarro arrived – was reduced to 600,000 within a century.

The Tumultuous Colony

The Spanish established their administrative capital of Lima, on the central desert coast, on January 6, 1535. The unrest began almost immediately, with conquistadors fighting among themselves over the spoils of the new viceroyalty. Many of them met violent deaths, including Francisco Pizarro, who was stabbed to death in Lima by a rival faction in 1541. Things grew relatively more stable after the arrival of Francisco de Toledo as viceroy in 1569, an able Spanish administrator who brought some order to the emerging colony.

In the new colonial society, Spaniards held the leadership positions, while *criollos* (Spaniards born in Peru) were confined to middle management. *Mestizos*, people

IN FOCUS   HISTORY

The Best Historic Churches

1 Iglesia de Santa Domingo, Lima (p68)

2 Iglesia de La Compañía de Jesús, Cuzco (p177)

3 Catedral de Puno (p144)

4 Monasterio de Santa Catalina, Arequipa (p115)

5 Catedral de Trujillo (p254)

1438–71
Machu Picchu is built during the reign of Inca Yupanqui.

1532
Atahualpa wins control over Inca territories; the Spanish land in Peru and execute him months later.

1671
Santa Rosa de Lima, the first saint of the Americas, is canonized.

The Best Peruvian Writers

1 El Inca Garcilaso de la Vega, chronicler

2 Ricardo Palma, writer

3 Abraham Valdelomar, essayist

4 César Vallejo, poet

5 José Carlos Mariategui, political theorist

6 Mario Vargas Llosa, novelist

who were of mixed blood, were further down the social scale. Full-blooded *indígenas* resided at the bottom, exploited as *peones* (expendable laborers).

Tensions between *indígenas* and Spaniards reached a boiling point in the late 18th century, when the crown levied a series of new taxes that hit the indigenous poor the hardest. In 1780 José Gabriel Condorcanqui, a descendant of Inca king Túpac Amaru, executed a Spanish administrator on charges of cruelty. His act unleashed an indigenous rebellion that spread throughout the Andes. The Spanish reprisal was swift – and brutal. In 1781 Condorcanqui watched his followers, his wife and his sons killed in the main plaza in Cuzco, before being drawn and quartered himself.

Independence

For Peru, the struggle for nationhood happened on two fronts. Argentine revolutionary José de San Martín led independence campaigns in Argentina and Chile, before entering Peru at the port of Pisco in 1820. With San Martín's arrival, royalist forces retreated into the highlands, and, on July 28, 1821, independence was declared. But real independence wouldn't materialize for another three years: with Spanish forces still at large in the interior, San Martín needed more men to fully vanquish the Spanish.

Enter Simón Bolívar, the venerated Venezuelan revolutionary, who had led independence fights in Venezuela, Colombia and Ecuador. San Martín met with Bolívar privately in 1822 to seek help on the Peruvian campaign. Bolívar, however, was not interested in sharing command, so San Martín withdrew. Within a year, Bolívar had defeated the Spanish. In early 1826 the last detachment of royal soldiers left Peru.

The New Republic & The War of the Pacific

Through much of the 19th century, there was a revolving door of regime changes as regional *caudillos* (chieftains) scrambled for power. In 1845 the country would find some measure of stability under the governance of Ramón Castilla, who abolished slavery, paid off some of Peru's debt and established a public school system. But with his passing, in 1867, the country once again descended into chaos and fiscal mismanagement.

1821
Independence from Spain is declared on July 28, but battles continue for several years.

1879–83
Chile wages war against Peru over nitrate-rich lands in the Atacama Desert. Peru loses.

1911
US historian Hiram Bingham arrives at Machu Picchu.

By 1874 Peru was bankrupt and in a weak position to deal with the expanding clash between Chile and Bolivia over nitrate-rich lands in the Atacama Desert. The war was a disaster for Peru (and Bolivia). The Chileans, who had the support of the British, led a land campaign deep into the country, ransacking Lima and making off with the contents of the National Library in the process. By the time it was all over, in 1884, Peru had permanently lost its southernmost region of Tarapacá and the Bolivians had lost their coast.

Intellectuals, Dictatorships & Revolutionaries

Much of the country's 20th-century history is a blur of dictatorships punctuated by periods of democracy. But socially, Peru was moving in a new direction. As one century gave way to the next, intellectual circles saw the rise of *indigenismo*, a continent-wide movement that advocated for a dominant role for indigenous people. Writers, poets and thinkers all advanced the cause. In 1924 the APRA party (American Popular Revolutionary Alliance) was founded, which espoused populist

Many of Peru's cities have well-preserved examples of colonial architecture
PHOTOGRAPHER: ANNELIES MERTENS

1970
A 7.7-magnitude earthquake in the north kills almost 80,000 people, and leaves 140,000 injured.

1980
Sendero Luminoso organizes its first guerrilla actions in the Andes – the beginning of the Internal Conflict.

1985
Alan García is elected, the first APRA candidate to reach the presidency.

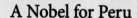

A Nobel for Peru

Mario Vargas Llosa (b 1936), Peru's most famous writer, was awarded the Nobel Prize in Literature in 2010 for stories that explore the vagaries of corruption and power. The honorific caps an extraordinary life: as a young man, Vargas Llosa had an affair with an aunt, whom he later married (an incident he fictionalized in *Aunt Julia and the Scriptwriter*). In the '70s, he came to blows with Colombian Nobel Laureate Gabriel García Márquez. The following decade, he ran for the presidency – and lost. Upon winning the Nobel, he told a reporter: 'Death will find me with my pen in hand.'

values and celebrated 'Indo-America.' (It was declared illegal for long periods of the 20th century.)

Indigenismo even saw traction among unlikely figures. One of Peru's most fascinating military dictators was Juan Velasco Alvarado, a former army commander who took control of Peru starting in 1968. In his rhetoric, Velasco celebrated the indigenous peasantry, championed agrarian reform and even made Quechua an official language. Ultimately, however, his economic policies were failures, and he was pushed out of office by conservative military commanders in 1975.

The Internal Conflict

The country returned to civilian rule in 1980, but with the economy stalled, the inequities facing *campesinos* fell off the radar. It was at this time that a radical Mao-ist guerrilla group from Ayacucho began its unprecedented rise. Sendero Luminoso (Shining Path) wanted nothing less than a complete overthrow of the social order through armed struggle. This resulted in two decades of escalating violence, with Sendero (as well as other, smaller guerrilla groups) assassinating political and community leaders and carrying out bomb attacks.

In response, the government sent in the military – a heavy-handed outfit that knew little about how to handle an insurgency. Caught in the middle were tens of thousands of *campesinos* who bore the brunt of the casualties. The conflict ultimately left an estimated 70,000 dead.

Aggravating the situation was the wheezing economy. In the late 1980s, President Alan García suspended foreign debt payments and nationalized the banks – actions that eventually led to a hyperinflation rate of 7500%, among other problems. There were food shortages and riots, and the government declared a state of emergency.

1987
A Moche leader's tomb is discovered near Lambayeque. He is dubbed *El Señor de Sipán*.

1990
Alberto Fujimori, an agronomist of Japanese descent, is elected president.

OTHER IMAGES

Soon after his term was over, García fled the country after being accused of embezzling millions of dollars. (He returned in 2001, when the statute of limitations on his case ran out.)

This period represents one of Peru's darkest hours.

Fujishock

In 1990 Alberto Fujimori, an agronomist of Japanese descent, was elected president and implemented an austerity plan now known as 'Fujishock.' It ultimately succeeded in reducing inflation and stabilizing the economy, but not without costing the average Peruvian dearly. Fujimori followed this, in 1992, with an *autogolpe* (coup from within), a move that stocked the legislature with his allies. Peruvians tolerated the move: the economy was growing and Sendero Luminoso's leadership had been apprehended. As the country faced the new millennium, the violence began to wind down.

By the end of Fujimori's second term, however, he was being plagued by allegations of corruption. After running for a third term (technically unconstitutional), it was revealed that his security chief had been embezzling government funds and bribing officials. Fujimori was ultimately declared 'morally unfit' to govern by the legislature and was voted out of office. He was later convicted of ordering extrajudicial killings and misappropriating government funds, and is now serving three decades in prison.

A Period of Renewal

Since then, the country has enjoyed a rare period of reconciliation. In 2001 shoe-shine-boy-turned-Stanford-economist Alejandro Toledo became the first person of Quechua ethnicity to ever be elected President – an important step in correcting some of the inequalities faced by indigenous Peruvians. Toledo's term was followed, in 2006, by the re-election of Alan García to the presidency. Unlike his first go in office, his second term has been relatively stable. (Though it hasn't been without moments of drama: in 2008, his entire cabinet was forced to resign after allegations of bribery and corruption surfaced.) But, overall, the economy has performed well and strong local governance in Lima has left the capital renewed. For Peruvians, it is a rare moment of prosperity and hope.

2001
Alejandro Toledo becomes the first Quechua president of Peru.

2003
An independent commission releases a report on the Internal Conflict: death toll estimates reach 70,000.

2010
Peruvian writer Mario Vargas Llosa wins the Nobel Prize in Literature.

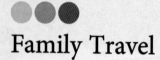

Family Travel

Girl with lamb, Plaza de Armas, Cuzco

MICHAEL TAYL

In a country that holds the family dear, children are welcome just about everywhere – so expect them to be patted on the head...a lot. Peru's vast array of archaeological sites should inspire plenty of young action heroes. If not, a few tales about pre-Columbian human sacrifice should do the trick. Though be prepared: few spots have dedicated facilities for little ones.

The Basics

Given the somewhat complicated nature of travel around Peru, don't try to overdo things, especially if you're traveling with small children who aren't used to being at higher elevations. Altitude sickness – a problem for adults in the Andes – becomes immeasurably more complicated in children (especially toddlers) who can't always effectively communicate their symptoms. If you're going to be well above sea level, be on the lookout for signs of headache, nausea, dizziness or weakness. If you suspect that your child has altitude sickness, seek medical attention.

Unfortunately, little research has been done in this area, but some pediatricians advise waiting until a child is eight or nine years old before traveling to elevations over 3000m. Beyond that age, consult the altitude acclimatization advice on p350.

Dining

'Kids' meals' (small portions at small prices) are not normally offered, but most establishments will obligingly produce simple foods on request, including grilled steak (*bistec a la plancha*) or grilled chicken (*pollo a la plancha*). Other basic items include cheese sandwiches (*sándwich de queso*), hamburgers (*hamburguesas*) and pasta. If traveling with an infant, stock up on formula and baby food before heading into rural areas.

Young children should avoid water and ice as they're more susceptible to stomach illnesses.

Transportation

Children under the age of 12 receive discounts of 25% to 50% for airline travel, while infants under two pay only 10% of the fare provided they sit on their parent's lap. On buses, children pay full fare if they occupy a seat, but aren't normally charged if they sit on their parent's lap. Often, someone will give up a seat for a parent traveling with a small child, or they'll offer to put your child on their lap (don't be put off by this – it's normal).

Other Practicalities

Cribs and high chairs are not normally available – except at established family hotels and restaurants, respectively. It's best to call ahead.

Breastfeeding in public is not uncommon, but most women discreetly cover themselves. Poorly maintained public bathrooms may be a concern for parents. Always carry toilet paper and wet wipes.

For more advice, see Lonely Planet's *Travel with Children* or log on to www.travelwithyourkids.com and www.familytravelnetwork.com.

Need to Know

- **Changing facilities** Rare beyond airports, malls and some chain restaurants
- **Cribs** Request ahead; these may be difficult to find in remote or rural areas
- **Highchairs** Call ahead; not always available
- **Kids' menus** Rare
- **Nappies (diapers)** Available at supermarkets and large pharmacies in bigger cities
- **Strollers** Bring your own
- **Transportation** Reserve seats where possible to avoid standing

Ancient Peru

Excavations of the ruins at Caral (p87)

GEORGE STEINMETZ/COR

Despite the best efforts of the Spanish – who ransacked temples and melted down sacred gold objects – Peru's archaeological legacy is rich. The area has been home to civilizations large and small. As a result, travelers can see sumptuous textiles, striking ceramics and monumental structures so well engineered that they have not only survived conquest, but calamitous earthquakes as well. For the Indiana Jones set, the adventure begins here.

Caral

Just a couple of hundred kilometers north of Lima on the Pacific coast lies one of the most exciting archaeological sites in Peru. It may not look like much – half a dozen temple mounds, a few sunken amphitheaters and remnants of structures crafted from adobe and stone – but it is. This 626-hectare spot is the oldest known city in the Americas: Caral.

Situated in the Supe Valley, this Preceramic civilization developed almost simultaneously with the ancient cultures of Mesopotamia and Egypt about 5000 years ago, and it predates the earliest civilizations in Mexico by about 1500 years. Caral was not a militaristic settlement, but a religious one that venerated its holy men and paid tribute to unknown agricultural deities (at times, with human sacrifice). They cultivated crops such as cotton, squash and beans and were knowledgeable fishers. Archaeological finds at the site include textiles, necklaces, ceremonial burials and crude, unbaked clay figurines depicting female forms.

Much of the complex has yet to be excavated – expect further discoveries.

Chavín

If Caral is evidence of the earliest sign of functional urban settlement, then Chavín de Huántar (p251), near Huaraz, represents the spread of a unified religious and artistic iconography. In a broad swath of the northern Andes, from roughly 1000 BC to 300 BC, a common culture arose around a feline deity that appears on carvings, friezes, pottery and textiles from the era. There is only patchy information available on Chavín and the structure of its society, but its importance is without question: in Peru, this represents the birth of art.

It is still debated whether the temple at Chavín de Huántar was this culture's capital or merely an important ceremonial site, but what is without doubt is that the setting is extraordinary. With the stunning Cordillera Blanca as a backdrop, the remnants of this elaborate ceremonial complex – built over hundreds of years – include a number of temple structures, as well as a sunken court with stone friezes of jaguars. Here, archaeologists have found pottery from all over the region filled with *ofrendas* (offerings), including shells from as far away as the Ecuadorian coast, and carved bones (some human) featuring supernatural motifs.

Paracas & Nazca

As the influence of Chavín culture waned, a number of smaller, regional ethnicities rose in its stead. Along the country's south coast, from about 700 BC to AD 400, the culture known as Paracas – situated around modern-day Ica – produced some of the most renowned textiles created in the Andes. The most impressive of these were woven during the period known as the Paracas Necropolis (AD 1 to 400), so named for a massive gravesite on the Península de Paracas uncovered in 1927 by famed Peruvian archaeologist Julio Tello.

The magnificent textiles recovered from the graves – layer upon layer of finely woven fabrics wrapped around mummy bundles – provide important clues about day-to-day life and beliefs. Featured on these intricate cloths are depictions of flowers, fish, birds, knives and cats, with some animals represented as two-headed creatures. Also significant are the human figures, such as warriors carrying

Human Sacrifice in the Andes

Numerous pre-Columbian cultures in the area of Peru engaged in human sacrifice – including the Inca and the Moche (the latter of whom depicted the act on their ceramics). Often, this was a way of paying tribute to natural forces in the universe that allowed their respective civilizations to survive. Though details on how exactly the practice was regulated and who was chosen for sacrifice remain sketchy (none of the pre-Columbian cultures in the Andes left behind a written language), recent archaeological work is beginning to shed some light on the practice.

The Best
ARCHAEOLOGICAL MUSEUMS

shrunken trophy heads, and supernatural anthropomorphic creatures equipped with snake tongues and *lots* of claws.

During roughly the same period, the Nazca culture (200 BC to AD 600), to the south, was producing an array of painted pottery, as well as incredible weavings that featured both geometric and ornate images. These works showcased everyday objects (beans, birds and fish), as well as supernatural cat- and falcon-men in an array of explosive colors. The Nazca were skilled embroiderers: some weavings feature tiny dangling figurines that must have induced blindness in their creators. The culture is best known, however, for the Nazca Lines (p108), a series of mysterious geoglyphs carved into a 500-sq-km area in the desert.

The Moche

Inhabiting the Peruvian north coast from about AD 100 to 800, the Moche were accomplished in many areas. Though not inherently urban, they built sophisticated ceremonial centers, such as the frieze-laden Huacas del Sol y de la Luna (p262), outside of modern-day Trujillo. They also created elaborate burial sites for their leaders, such as that at Sipán (p270), near Chiclayo. They had a well-maintained network of roads and a system of relay runners that carried messages, probably in the form of symbols carved onto beans.

But it's their pottery that makes them a standout: lifelike depictions of individuals (scars and all) that are so skillfully rendered, some of them seem as if they are about to talk. In some cases, artists created many portraits of a single person over the course of their lifetime; one scholar recorded 45 different pieces depicting the same model. Many ceramics are dedicated to showcasing macho activities (hunting and human sacrifice). This doesn't mean that they didn't know a thing or two about love. The pottery artifacts of the Moche are renowned for their encyclopedic depictions of human sex.

The Wari

From about AD 600 to 1100, the Andes saw the rise of the first truly expansive kingdom. The Wari were avid empire builders, expanding from their base around Ayacucho to a territory that occupied an area from Chiclayo to Cuzco. Expert agriculturalists, they improved production by developing the terrace system and creating a network of canals for irrigation.

In the area of weaving, the culture was highly skilled, producing elegant fabrics with elaborate stylized designs. The Wari were masters of color, using as many as 150 distinct shades, which they incorporated into woven and tie-dyed patterns. Many of these textiles feature abstract, geometric designs, as well as supernatural figures – most common is a winged deity holding a staff.

Incas versus Romans

It's not just the classical European civilizations that were expansive. At its acme, the Inca empire was larger than imperial Rome and boasted more than 40,000km of roadways. For a page-turning read about this incredible society, pick up Kim MacQuarrie's gripping 2007 book, *The Last Days of the Incas*.

Chimú & Chachapoyas

Following the demise of the Wari, a number of small nation-states emerged in different corners of the country. They are too numerous to detail here, but there are two that merit discussion because of the art and architecture they left behind. The first of these is the Chimú, which were based around present-day Trujillo.

Between about AD 1000 and 1400, this incredible north-coast civilization built the largest known adobe city in the Americas. Chan Chan (p260) is a sprawling, 36-sq-km complex, which once housed an estimated 60,000 people. Within the society, there was an accomplished artisan class, which produced, among other things, some outrageous-looking textiles, some of which were covered top-to-bottom in tassels.

To the interior in the northern highlands is the abandoned cloud-forest citadel of Kuélap, built by the Chachapoyas culture in the remote Utcubamba Valley beginning around AD 800. It is an incredible series of structures, composed of more than 400 circular dwellings, in addition to some unusual, gravity-defying pieces, such as an inverted cone known as El Tintero (The Inkpot). Unfortunately, almost nothing is known about the people who built it, who are largely remembered for having fiercely resisted the Inca conquest.

The Incas

Peru's greatest engineers were also its greatest empire builders. Because the Incas made direct contact with the Spanish, they also happen to be the pre-Columbian Andean culture that is best documented – not only through Spanish chronicle, but also through narratives produced by some of the descendants of the Incas themselves. (The most famous of these chroniclers is El Inca Garcilaso de la Vega.)

The Incas were a Quechua ethnicity which, from AD 1100 until the arrival of the Spanish in 1532, steadfastly grew a small territory around Cuzco into a highly organized empire that extended over more than 37° latitude from Colombia to Chile. It was an absolutist state with a strong army, where ultimate power resided with the *inca* (king). Its history is ridden with a succession of colorful royals who would make for an excellent TV movie – complete with fratricide, great battles and plenty of beautiful maidens.

The society was bound by a rigid caste system: there were nobles, an artisan and merchant class, and peasants. The latter supplied the manual labor for the Incas' many public-works projects. Citizens were expected to pay tribute to the crown in the form of labor – typically three months out of the year – enabling them to develop and maintain an extensive network of roadways and canals. The Incas also kept a highly efficient communications system: a body of *chasquis* (relay runners), who could make the 1600km trip between Quito and Cuzco in just seven days. Also notable was their social-welfare system: the Incas warehoused surplus food for distribution to areas and people in need.

On the cultural front, the Incas had a strong tradition of music, oral literature and weaving. But they are best known for their monumental architecture. The Inca capital of Cuzco (p172), along with the constructions at Sacsaywamán (p199), Pisac (p202), Ollantaytambo (p206) and the fabled Machu Picchu (p214), are all incredible examples of the imperial style of building. Carved pieces of rock, without mortar, are fitted together so tightly that it is impossible to fit a knife between the stones. Most interestingly, walls are built at an angle and windows in a trapezoidal form, so as to resist seismic activity.

Nestled into spectacular natural locales, these structures, even in a ruined state, are unforgettable. Their majesty was something the Spanish acknowledged, even as they pried them apart. 'Now that the Inca rulers have lost their power,' wrote Spanish chronicler Pedro Cieza de León in the 16th century, 'all these palaces and gardens, together with their other great works, have fallen, so that only the remains survive. Since they were built of good stone and the masonry is excellent, they will stand as memorials for centuries to come.'

León was right. The Inca civilization did not survive the Spanish, but their architecture did – a reminder of the many grand societies we are just beginning to understand.

Inca ruins, Ollantaytambo (p206)
PHOTOGRAPHER: WES WALKER

Outdoor Activities

Nevado Quitaraju, Cordillera Blanca (p249)

GRANT DIXON

Hike ancient Inca roadways studded with ancient ruins. Raft one of the world's deepest canyons. Sandboard down oversized dunes. In Peru, this is just the beginning of a long menu of activities that can be devoured by devoted adrenaline junkies. There's also surfing, trekking, biking and paragliding. Gear up – and take the Band-Aids. You're in for one heck of a wild ride.

Trekking & Hiking

The variety of trails in Peru is downright staggering. The main trekking centers are Cuzco and Arequipa in the southern Andes, and Huaraz in the north. The country's most famous trek is the Inca Trail to Machu Picchu (p220), but there are plenty of other less-crowded, equally magnificent routes, too.

In Arequipa, you can trek through two world famous canyons: the Cañón del Colca (p124) and the Cañón del Cotahuasi (p130). The scenery is guaranteed to knock you off your feet – and, during the wet season, when some Andean trekking routes are impassable, Colca is invitingly lush and green.

Outside Huaraz, the Cordillera Blanca (p249) can't be beat for vistas of rocky, snowcapped mountaintops. The classic and favorite trekking route is the five-day journey from Llanganuco to Santa Cruz (p248), otherwise known as the Santa Cruz trek. Shorter overnight trips in the area go to mountain base camps, alpine lakes and even along an old Inca road.

Local outfitters can generally provide equipment, guides, porters and *arrieros* (mule drivers). If you prefer to trek ultralight, bring your own gear, as rental items tend to be heavy. Certain areas of Peru, such as the Inca Trail, require guides; in other places, such as in the Cordillera Huayhuash, there have been muggings, so it's best to trek with a local.

Whatever adventure you choose, be prepared to spend a few days acclimatizing to the dizzying altitudes – or face a heavy-duty bout of altitude sickness.

Trekking is most rewarding during the dry season (May to September) in the Andes.

Mountain, Rock & Ice Climbing

Peru has the highest tropical mountains in the world, offering some absolutely inspired climbs. The Cordillera Blanca, with its dozens of snowy peaks exceeding 5000m, is one of the top destinations for this in South America. Huaraz (p241) has tour agencies, outfitters, guides, information and climbing equipment for hire (though it's best to bring your own gear for serious ascents). Nearby, Ishinca (5530m) and Pisco (5752m) provide two ascents easy enough for relatively inexperienced climbers. Rock and ice climbing are also taking off in the area, and some outfitters can organize group trips.

In southern Peru, Arequipa (p117) is surrounded by snowy volcanic peaks, some of which can be scaled by beginners (as long as you've got lots of determination and some wilderness experience). The most popular climb is to El Misti (5822m), which, despite its height, does not involve technical climbing. You'll find other tempting climbs in the peaks that tower above the Cañón del Colca (p124).

For beginners looking to bag their first serious mountain, Peru may not be the best place to start since the sport is relatively new and many guides are inexperienced. As always, check all rental gear before setting out.

High-elevation climbing is best done during the dry season (mid-June to mid-July). Acclimatization to altitude is essential.

River Running

Also known as white-water rafting, river running is growing in popularity around Peru and trips can range from a few hours to more than two weeks.

Cuzco (p182) is undoubtedly the main town for the greatest variety of river-running options. The choices range from a few hours of mild rafting on the

The Deepest Canyon

Not far outside of Arequipa, in southern Peru, the Cañón del Colca (p124), at 3191m deep, was long thought to be the deepest canyon in the western hemisphere. That honor has since been taken by the Cañón del Cotahuasi (p130), beyond Nevado Coropuna to the west, which has a floor that lies 3345m below its adjacent snowy peaks. Both of these canyons are more than twice as deep as Arizona's Grand Canyon – which has a depth of about 1500m.

Urubamba to adrenaline-pumping rides on the Santa Teresa to several days on more remote waterways.

Arequipa (p117) is another rafting center. Here, the Río Chili is most frequently run, with a half-day beginners' trip leaving daily between March and November.

Note that rafting is not regulated in Peru. Deaths are reported every year and rescues in remote areas can take days. Book excursions only with reputable, well-recommended agencies and avoid cut-rate trips. A good operator will have insurance and highly experienced guides with certified first-aid training. Choose one that provides top-notch equipment, including self-bailing rafts, US Coast Guard-approved life jackets, first-class helmets and spare paddles.

For more on river running in Peru, visit www.peruwhitewater.com.

Surfing

With consistent, uncrowded waves and plenty of remote breaks to explore, Peru attracts dedicated locals and international diehards alike.

Waves can be found the moment you land. Along the southern part of Lima, you'll see surfers riding out popular breaks at Miraflores (known as Waikiki), Barranquito and La Herradura. (This latter spot has an outstanding left point break, but it gets crowded when there is a strong swell.) In-the-know surfers prefer the breaks with smaller crowds further south, near the village of Punta Hermosa. Nearby, you'll find Punta Rocas, where annual international and national championships are held, as well as Pico Alto, a 'kamikaze' reef break that boasts one of the largest waves in Peru (seriously, experts only).

Peru's north coast has a string of excellent breaks up and down the shoreline, including at Huanchaco (p263) and Máncora (p273). The most famous of these is at Puerto Chicama, where rides of more than 2km are possible on a wave considered to be the longest left hand in the world.

The water is cold from April to mid-December (as low as 15°C/60°F), when wet suits are generally needed. Indeed, many surfers wear wet suits year-round, even though the water is a little warmer (around 20°C, or 68°F, in the Lima area) from January to March. The far north coast (north of Talara) stays above 21°C (70°F) most of the year.

Note that facilities are limited and equipment rental is expensive. The scene on the north coast is the most organized, with surf shops and hostels that offer advice, rent boards and organize surfing day trips. If you're serious about surfing, however, bring your own board.

For more information check out surfing websites such as www.peruazul. com, www.vivamancora.com and www.wannasurf.com; the latter provides a comprehensive, highly detailed list of just about every break in Peru.

Sandboarding

For something completely different, hit waves...of sand. Sandboarding down the giant desert dunes is growing in popularity at spots such as Huacachina (p106) on Peru's south coast. Nazca's Cerro Blanco (2078m) is the highest known sand dune in the world. Some hotels and travel agencies offer tours in *areneros* (dune buggies), where you are hauled to the top of the dunes, then get picked up at the bottom. (Choose your driver carefully; some are notoriously reckless.)

For more information on sandboarding worldwide, check out *Sandboard Magazine* at www.sandboard.com.

The Best
WILDLIFE-WATCHING SPOTS

1 Parque Nacional Manu (p309)

2 Cañón del Colca (p124)

3 Islas Ballestas (p103)

4 Parque Nacional Huascarán (p249)

Mountain Biking & Cycling

In Peru mountain biking is still a fledgling sport. That said, both easy and demanding single-track trails await mountain bikers outside of Huaraz (p241) and Arequipa (p118). If you're experienced, there are incredible mountain-biking possibilities around the Sacred Valley, all accessible from Cuzco (p183).

In Lima, it is also possible to book bicycle day tours (p69) around the city.

Mountain-bike rental in Peru tends to be basic, so if you are planning on serious biking it's best to bring your own. (Airline transport policies vary, so shop around.) You'll also need a repair kit and extra parts.

Swimming

Swimming is popular along the Peruvian coast from January to March, when the waters of the Pacific Ocean are warmest. It ain't Ibiza, though. The shoreline is, by and large, composed of desert and not much else. But when the sky is blue and the waves are crashing, it nonetheless becomes quite the scene. The most attractive beaches lie to the north, at laid-back Huanchaco (p263) and the perennially busy jet-set resorts at Máncora (p273).

Watch for dangerous currents and note that beaches near major coastal cities are often polluted.

Horseback Riding

Horse rentals can be arranged in many tourist destinations, but the rental stock is not always treated well, so check your horse carefully before you saddle up. For a real splurge, take a ride on a graceful Peruvian *paso* horse. Supposedly the descendants of horses with royal Spanish and Moorish lineage ridden by the conquistadors, they are reputed to have the world's smoothest gait. Stables around Peru advertise rides for half a day or longer.

Paragliding

Popular paragliding sites include the coastal clifftops of Miraflores in Lima (p69) and various points along the south coast. Because there are few paragliding operators in Peru, book ahead through the agencies in Lima.

Traditional Music

Musicians performing on Plaza Regocijo, Cuzco (p172)

BRUCE BI

Like its food, Peru's traditional music is an intercontinental fusion of elements. Pre-Columbian cultures contributed bamboo flutes, Spaniards brought stringed instruments and Africans gave it a backbone of fluid, percussive rhythm. Music here tends to be a regional affair: African-influenced landós are predominant on the coast, indigenous huaynos are heard in the Andes and criollo (creole) waltzes are danced to in major urban centers.

Highland Rhythms

In the Andes, *huayno* is the purest expression of pre-Columbian music. Stylistically, it's heavy on bamboo instruments such as *quenas* (flutes) and *zampoñas* (panpipes). But string instruments are incorporated into these compositions, too. These include *charango* (a small, 10-string instrument sometimes crafted out of an armadillo shell) as well as mandolins (which can have between eight and 10 strings). Also seen are *ocarinas*, small, clay instruments with up to 12 holes. For percussion, drums are typically made from a hollowed tree trunk covered with a stretched goatskin.

The most famous *huayno* is 'El Cóndor Pasa,' which was made over as a pop standard in the 1970s by Simon and Garfunkel.

The Best
PERUVIAN SONGS

1 *Cada Domingo a las 12 después de la misa*, by Arturo 'Zambo' Cavero

2 *La flor de la canela*, by Chabuca Granda

3 *Azucar de caña*, by Eva Ayllón

4 *El huerto de mi amada*, by Los Morochucos

5 *Propiedad privada*, by Lucha Reyes

6 *La danza de los Mirlos*, by Los Mirlos

Creole on the Coast

On the coast, *música criolla* (creole music) has its roots in both Spain and Africa. The main instrumentation consists of guitars and a *cajón*, a wooden box used as a drum. The most famous of all *criollo* styles is the *vals peruano* (Peruvian waltz), a fast-moving 3/4-time waltz full of complex guitar melodies.

The most legendary *criolla* singer is Chabuca Granda (1920–83), whose breathy vocals and expressive lyrics are full of longing and nostalgia. Other renowned crooners include the flamboyant Lucha Reyes (1936–73) and the gravel-voiced Arturo 'Zambo' Cavero (1940–2009).

Leaning more towards African rhythms is *landó*, which includes elements of call-and-response and heavy percussion. Standout performers in this genre include contemporary singers Susana Baca (b 1944) and Eva Ayllón (b 1956).

Amazon Fusion

One of the most curious musical styles to emerge from Peru in recent years is *chicha*, which got its start in the area of the Amazon and features a highly danceable blend of surf guitars, *huaynos* and Colombian *cumbias*. Well-known *chicha* bands include Los Shapis, Los Mirlos and Grupo Belen de Tarma. A very worthwhile compilation in this area is *The Roots of Chicha*, produced by Barbès Records, a groovy album of the genre's best.

Time to Dance

Naturally, all that music means there's plenty of dancing. The national dance is the *marinera*, which has its roots in Peruvian colonial history. Performed to *música criolla*, it is a flirtation between a man and a woman, who circle each other in a rhythmic courtship. Other dances include the *zamacueca*, which is closely related to the *marinera*, and the omnipresent *vals peruano*, both of which are danced by couples. *Zapateo* (literally 'foot-stomping') is a popular Afro-Peruvian dance.

Food & Drink

Ceviche broth with seafood, La Mar (p78), Lima

CAROLINA MIRANDA

Peru has long been a place where the concept of 'fusion' was part of everyday cooking. Here, nutty Andean stews mingle with Asian stir-fry techniques and Spanish dishes absorb the flavors of the Amazon. Food is a religion in Peru – a place where humble street vendors are hyperattentive to preparation and high-end restaurants spotlight local flavors, serving up deft interpretations of Andean favorites. Serious foodies: consider this your paradise, found.

Staples

Peruvians typically begin their day with corn tamales or a sandwich (on the coast) or soup (in the highlands), although American-style breakfasts are also popular. Lunch is the main meal of the day and generally includes three courses: an appetizer, main dish and dessert. Dinner tends to be lighter.

Much of the country's cooking begins and ends with the humble potato. The tuber is from Peru, where hundreds of local varieties are transformed into a mind-boggling number of incredible dishes. Standouts include *papa a la huancaína* (potato bathed in a creamy cheese sauce) and *causa* (an architectural potato terrine layered with seafood, vegetables or chicken). Potatoes are also found in *lomo saltado*, the simple beef stir-fry dish that headlines every Peruvian menu.

The Best
PERUVIAN DISHES

1 *Ají de gallina* – shredded chicken in a spicy walnut sauce

2 *Chicha morada* – a refreshing beverage made from purple corn

3 *Papa rellena* – potato stuffed with ground beef and deep-fried

4 *Chupe de camarones* – buttery shrimp bisque

5 *Tacu tacu* – pan-fried rice and beans

6 *Chicharrones* – deep-fried chunks of pork

Regional Flavors

The Coast

Along the coast, ceviche plays a starring role. A chilled concoction of fish, shrimp or other seafood marinated in lime juice, onions, cilantro and chili peppers, it is typically served with a wedge of boiled corn and sweet potato. *Tiradito* is a Japanese-influenced version: sashimi-style fish served without onions, and often bathed in a creamy pepper sauce.

Seafood, in general, is a major facet of coastal cooking. Fish is prepared dozens of ways: *al ajo* (bathed in garlic), *frito* (fried) or *a la chorrillana* (cooked in white wine, tomatoes and onions). Shellfish appears regularly in soups, stews and omelets. *Choros a la chalaca* (chilled mussels with fresh corn salsa), *conchitas a la parmesana* (oven-roasted scallops with cheese) and *pulpo al olivo* (octopus in a smashed olive sauce) are favorites.

On the north coast, where the regional cuisine is particularly renowned, other popular dishes include *seco de cabrito* (goat stewed in cilantro) and *arroz con pato a la chiclayana* (duck and rice simmered in cilantro and beer).

The Highlands

Soups are a gut-warming experience in Peru – especially in the chilly highlands. *Chupe de camarones* (shrimp bisque) is a mainstay, along with *sopa a la criolla* (a lightly creamy soup of beef, noodles and vegetables) and *caldo de gallina* (a fragrant chicken soup with vegetables). Throughout the highlands, you'll also find *cuy* (guinea pig), prepared myriad ways. Often, it is roasted or served *chactado* (seared under rocks).

Practical Information

Throughout this guidebook, the order of restaurant listings follows the author's preference, and each place to eat is accompanied by one of the following pricing symbols.

- $ <S24 per meal per person
- $$ S24 to S45 per meal per person
- $$$ > S45 per meal per person

We define a meal as three courses (including dessert) and a drink. Prices in Lima and major tourist centers will generally be more expensive. Restaurant hours in Peru are generally 10am to 10pm, though some close between 3pm and 6pm.

A Peruvian Pisco Primer

Pisco (grape brandy) production dates back to the early days of the Spanish colony, when it was distilled on private haciendas near Ica and then sold to sailors making their way through the port of Pisco. By the early 20th century, the pisco sour (a cocktail of grape brandy with lime juice and sugar) had become popular at high-end Lima hotels.

The three principal types of pisco are *Quebranta, Italia* and *acholado*. *Quebranta* (a pure-smelling pisco) and *Italia* (slightly aromatic) are each named for the varieties of grape from which they are crafted. *Acholado* is a blend, with harsher, alcohol top-notes (best for mixed drinks). There are many small-batch specialty piscos made from grape must (pressed juice with skins), known as *mosto verde*. These are deliciously fragrant and are best sipped straight.

Among the finest brands are Viñas de Oro, LaBlanco, Don Santiago and Gran Cruz. Any pisco purchased in a bottle that resembles the head of an Inca will make for an unusual piece of home decor – and a guaranteed hangover.

The area around Arequipa is renowned for its *picantes* (spicy, bubbling stews served with chunks of white cheese) and *rocoto relleno* (stuffed hot peppers).

The Amazon

The Amazon region adds tropical notes to Peruvian menus. (Look for pisco cocktails made with *aguaymanto*, a regional gooseberry.) In addition, you'll find tropical varieties of tamales known as *juanes* – tender mashed yucca stuffed with seasoned chicken and steamed in banana leaves. Also popular is *patarashca* (platters of fresh-grilled Amazon fish and shrimp doused in garlic and cilantro).

Sweets

Desserts tend to be diabetes-inducing concoctions. *Suspiro a la limeña* is the most famous, consisting of caramel topped with sweet meringue. Also popular are *alfajores* (caramel cookie sandwiches) and *crema volteada* (flan). Lighter and fruitier is *mazamorra morada,* a purple-corn pudding studded with chunks of pineapple.

Specialty Drinks

Herbal tea is very popular, with the most notable being *mate de coca*, coca-leaf tea. It won't get you high, but can soothe stomach ailments and help with acclimatizing to the high altitude.

In the Andes, homemade *chicha* (corn beer) is very popular. It tastes slightly bitter and is typically sold in traditional markets. On the coast, nonalcoholic *chicha morada*, a sweet purple-corn drink is also common.

Arts & Crafts

Traditional weaver at work, Pisac (p201)

GRANT DIXO

With a history that dates back thousands of years, it comes as no surprise that Peru also has a rich arts and crafts tradition. From brightly colored textiles and bold ceramics to ornate pieces of silver and baroque-style painting, expect to find work that is as varied as it is sublime. The hard part will be deciding what to take home.

Andean Textiles

Of all of its traditions, Peru is perhaps best known for its extraordinarily rendered textiles. Both Andean and coastal indigenous cultures have long woven rugs, ponchos and blankets decorated with elaborate geometric and anthropomorphic designs.

In fact, the type of weaving a person wore within pre-Columbian society denoted their social status. The working classes donned coarser grades of textiles with simple graphic designs, while finer fabrics – incorporating feathers and even bat hair – were reserved for the nobility. On the coast, Paracas is historically famous for its weaving, producing stellar textiles that depicted images of felines, serpents and birds.

Today, travelers can find textiles inspired by and incorporating some of these indigenous designs at crafts markets around the country. Cuzco (p172) is a particularly good spot to find finely woven pieces.

Ceramics

Pottery in Peru is also exceptional. The most stunning designs are those made in the tradition of the Moche people of the northern coast, who thrived for six centuries from AD 100. Vases and other vessels are made to depict humans in a realist style. The most famous of these – the *huacos eróticos* – depict a variety of sexual acts.

Also popular is pottery made in the Chancay style. Known as *cuchimilcos*, these are humorous, cartoonish figures crafted with sand-colored clay and painted with brown ink. In the north, a more contemporary style from the village of Chulucanas is also prevalent. These feature graphic black-and-white designs, as well as pieces that depict human figures in a rounded shape.

Pottery in all of these styles can be found at the sprawling crafts markets in Lima (p82).

Religious Crafts

Religious crafts are bountiful in most regions, with *retablos* (three-dimensional dioramas) from the Ayacucho region being particularly renowned. These elaborate and colorful box displays generally feature scenes from Christian life, such as the lives of the saints, the nativity or local religious processions. Elements of indigenous culture are also prominent, depicting Quechua rituals and native articles such as coca leaves.

Arbolitos de la vida (trees of life) are another common religious item: elaborate, painted ceramic trees that depict a variety of religious and domestic scenes. Look for these at souvenir markets around the country.

Andean Baroque

Beginning in the 16th century, the fusion of Spanish and indigenous cultures resulted in a remarkable school of art whose visual influences can be felt to this day. The *escuela cuzqueña* (Cuzco School) was a movement in which native and mestizo artists (almost always unattributed) created works of painting inspired by mannerist and late Gothic art, but infused with an indigenous palette and iconography. The pieces generally feature holy figures in earthy Andean colors (think:

Tips for Buying Textiles

o **Buy locally** The market has been flooded with knockoffs from Asia, so buy directly from weavers, or shops that deal directly with weavers.

o **Ask questions** Ask who made it, where it's from and what the designs represent. A good dealer will know.

o **Inspect the work** Check to see if the fibers are spun tightly and be on the lookout for synthetic materials. The best textiles are made only from alpaca or sheep's wool.

o **Be realistic** Quality textiles are expensive to produce. If the price is too good to be true, it probably isn't the real deal.

The Best Souvenirs

1 A *cuchimulco* – the humorous figurative pottery created in the Chancay style

2 Baroque frames – they'll make your vacation photos look amazing

3 *Huayruros* – red and black seeds that bring all kinds of good luck

4 Andean textile placemats – gorgeous and functional

5 Inca Kola T-shirts – because why not?

brown, terra-cotta, ochre and yellow) decorated with an elaborate lace of gold paint.

Today, the countless works produced by this school hang in museums and churches throughout Peru – and reproductions of all sizes are sold in many crafts markets. In recent years, artists have begun incorporating additional indigenous elements into these works, portraying figures decked out in traditional highland dress and the earflap hats known as *chullos*.

Also popular at markets are ornate baroque-style frames and other items carved out of wood. You can find these in a variety of stains or embellished with gold leaf (or more likely, gold paint).

Other Crafts

Other popular items are hand-tooled leather furnishings, including folding chairs, poufs and coffee tables, as well as fine filigree jewelry crafted from silver and gold, hand-woven baskets, llama skin rugs and all sorts of religious icons. If you're looking for unique gifts to take home, ask around for *huayruros* (black and red seeds), as well as *seguros* (religious charms), both of which Peruvians regard as powerful sources of good luck.

As with crafts buying the world over: shop around. Price and quality vary greatly.

Survival Guide

Drinks seller, Huaraz
PHOTOGRAPHER: AARON MCCOY

Directory

Accommodations

Accommodations in Peru range from basic crash pads to cozy Spanish-style B&Bs to luxury lodges that offer bath butlers and turndown service. In touristy areas, you'll find plenty of accommodations, and in every imaginable guise. Choices in small villages, however, may be limited. In well-trod destinations, hotel staff will generally speak some English (in addition to other languages), but in rural areas, you might need a grasp of basic Spanish.

Many places will store your luggage for free if you have a late bus or flight to catch after checkout; some spots may charge a fee for this. When storing bags, it is always a good idea to lock them and get a receipt.

CATEGORIES

Hotels are the most standard type of accommodations and will normally include private hot showers, telephone, TV and other facilities, such as a cafe or restaurant. Smaller than a hotel, an *hostal* is like a guesthouse, offering private rooms with bathrooms and

fairly reliable hot water. In some cases, these will include a very simple continental breakfast. Better *hostales* offer hot breakfasts and many of the same services as small hotels, while cheaper ones may have shared bathrooms. *Hospedajes* and *albergues* are generally small, family-owned inns. Expect basic rooms, including dormitory-style accommodations, and, in some cases, a shared kitchen. In remote settings, don't count on *hospedajes* and *albergues* to have hot showers, private bathrooms or many other amenities.

Street noise can be an issue in hotels at all budget levels, so choose your room accordingly. Within most types of accommodations, *habitación simple* refers to a single room, *habitación doble* to a double room with two single beds, and *habitación matrimonial* to a double room with a double or queen-sized bed. If you're traveling as a couple, be sure to ask for the latter, or you'll find yourself sleeping in separate beds.

COSTS

Accommodation costs vary greatly in Peru, depending on the season and the region. Rates in this book are generally for the high season, but note that prices often fluctuate

from season to season and year to year.

Cities that are pricier than average include Lima, Cuzco, Iquitos, Huaraz and Trujillo. In other cities, at off-peak times, you can get good deals with a little bit of negotiation. Walk-in guests should ask for the 'best price' *(mejor precio)*. Paying cash always helps; and be sure to ask for discounts if you're staying somewhere for more than five nights.

In the jungle lodges of the Amazon and in popular beach destinations such as Máncora, all-inclusive resort-style pricing may be the norm. At these places, discounts are rarely offered.

PRICE INDICATORS

The price indicators in this book – $ (budget), $$ (mid-range), $$$ (top end) – refer to the cost of a double room, including bathroom (any combination of toilet, bathtub and shower) and excluding breakfast unless otherwise noted.

CATEGORY	COST
$	up to S75 (up to US$27)
$$	from S75 to S240 (from US$27 to US$86)
$$$	S240 and over (US$86 and over)

Book Your Stay Online

For more accommodations reviews by Lonely Planet authors, check out hotels.lonelyplanet.com/Peru. You'll find independent reviews, as well as recommendations on the best places to stay. Best of all, you can book online.

RESERVATIONS

If you are flying into Lima, a reservation for your first night is a good idea since a lot of places can arrange airport pickup. Also, because many flights arrive late at night or very early in the morning, this is an inadvisable time to begin searching for a place to sleep. In Cuzco, during the blockbuster tourist months of July and August, be sure to reserve a hotel room well in advance. Likewise, in the Amazon, advance reservations are generally required at remote jungle lodges – which aren't usually equipped to handle drop-in clientele.

TYPES OF ACCOMMODATIONS

APARTMENTS

Midrange and high-end travelers can find a limited number of furnished homes and apartments available for short-term rentals (primarily in Lima, and to a lesser extent, Cuzco). Check www.vrbo.com and www.cyberrentals.com for listings.

HOTELS

Budget

All budget spots listed in this book have rates of less than S75 per night. Basic one- and two-star hotels are among Peru's cheapest accommodations and are generally very basic, simply furnished spots. In this price range, expect to find small rooms, with decent beds and a shared or private bathroom. In the major cities, these options usually include hot showers; in rural and remote areas, they might not.

Practicalities

o **Electricity** Electrical current is 220V/60Hz AC. Standard outlets accept round prongs, but many places will have dual-voltage outlets that take flat prongs. Even so, you may need an adapter with a built-in surge protector.

o **Magazines** The most well known political and cultural weekly is *Caretas* (www.caretas.com.pe), while *Etiqueta Negra* (etiquetanegra.com.pe) focuses exclusively on culture. For alternative travel journalism in Spanish and English, pick up the monthly *Rumbos* (www.rumbosdelperu.com).

o **Newspapers** The government-leaning *El Comercio* (www.elcomercioperu.com.pe) is the leading daily. For opposing viewpoints, see the slightly left-of-center *La República* (www.larepublica.com.pe). In English, look for the *Peruvian Times* (www.peruviantimes.com).

o **TV** Cable and satellite TV are widely available. Local stations have a mix of news, variety shows, talk shows and *telenovelas*, Spanish-language soap operas.

o **Video** Buy or watch videos on the NTSC system (compatible with North America).

o **Websites** Three helpful and informative online resources in English are www.expatperu.com, www.enperublog.com and www.theperuguide.com.

o **Weights & Measures** Peruvians use the metric system except for gas (petrol), which is measured in US gallons.

Midrange

Mid-priced hotels range from S75 to S240 for a double room. Again, these accommodations can include everything from small, no-frills business hotels to cozy B&Bs with trickling fountains and Peruvian art. Many midrange places will accept credit cards, sometimes for an additional fee.

At this level, rooms generally have private bathrooms with hot-water showers, and small portable heaters or fans may be provided for climate control. Some newer spots are also equipped with air-conditioning and, in some cases, wi-fi.

Top End

Hotels in this category cost upwards of S240. Like top-end hotels everywhere, these run the gamut from design-conscious boutique spaces to international chains to atmospheric spots bearing all manner of baroque detailing.

Top-end hotel rates frequently include a 19% tax in the room rate. Many high-end places also tack on a nonrefundable 'service charge' of 10%.

Peru's top hotels are generally equipped with en-suite bathrooms with bathtubs, international direct dial phones, internet access (either through high speed cable or wi-fi), dual-voltage outlets, central heating or air-conditioning, hair dryers, in-room safes and cable TV; some may come with minifridges, microwaves or coffee makers.

Business Hours

Posted hours are a guideline and services can be slow. Be patient, and forget about getting anything done on a Sunday, when most businesses (other than restaurants) are closed.

Lima has pharmacies, bookstores and electronics supply shops that are open every day. In other major cities, taxi drivers often know where the late-night stores and pharmacies are located. Most cities are equipped with 24-hour ATMs.

In smaller cities and towns, many shops and offices close for lunch (usually from 1pm until around 3pm), but some banks and post offices stay open. In addition, many restaurants open only for lunch, or breakfast and lunch, especially in small towns.

Typically, opening hours are as follows:

Banks 9am-6pm Mon-Fri, some 9am-1pm Sat

Bars and clubs 5:30pm-midnight, though some go all night

Restaurants 10am-10pm, some closed 3-6pm

Shops 9am-6pm Mon-Fri, some 9am-6pm Sat

Climate

Peru has three main climatic zones: the tropical Amazon jungle to the east; the arid coastal desert to the west; and the Andean mountains and highlands in between. In the Andes, which have altitudes of more than 3500m, average daily temperatures fall below 10°C (50°F) and overnight temperatures can dip well below freezing. Travelers flying straight to Cuzco (3326m), or other high-altitude cities, should allow several days to acclimatize since *soroche* (altitude

sickness), can be a problem (see p349).

June to August is the dry season in the mountains and altiplano (Andean plateau); the wettest months are from December to March. It rains all the time in the hot and humid rainforest, but the driest months there are from June to September; however, even during the wettest months, from December to May, it rarely rains for more than a few hours at a time. Along the arid coastal strip, the hot summer months are from December through March. Some parts of the coastal strip rarely receive rain, if at all. From April to

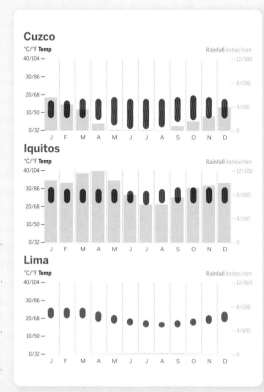

November, Lima and other areas by the Pacific Ocean are enclosed in *garúa* (coastal fog, mist or drizzle) as warmer air masses off the desert and drifts over the ocean where the cold Humboldt Current hits.

The El Niño effect, which occurs on average every seven years, is when large-scale changes in ocean currents and rising sea-surface water temperatures bring heavy rains and floods to coastal areas, plunging tropical areas into drought and disrupting weather patterns worldwide. The name El Niño (literally 'the Child') refers to the fact that this periodic weather pattern is usually noticed around Christmas. El Niño is usually followed the next year by La Niña, when ocean currents that cool abnormally create even more havoc and destruction.

Customs Regulations

Peru allows duty-free importation of 3L of alcohol and 20 packs of cigarettes, 50 cigars or 250g of tobacco. You can import US$300 of gifts.

It is illegal to take pre-Columbian or colonial artifacts out of Peru, and it is illegal to bring them into most countries. If purchasing reproductions, buy only from a reputable dealer and ask for a detailed receipt. Purchasing animal products made from endangered species or even just transporting them around Peru is also illegal.

Coca leaves are legal in Peru, but not in most other countries, even in the form of tea bags. People subject to random drug testing should be aware that coca, even in the form of tea, may leave trace amounts in their urine.

Electricity

220V/60Hz

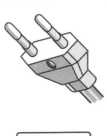

220V/60Hz

Gay & Lesbian Travelers

Peru is a strongly conservative, Catholic country. While many Peruvians will tolerate homosexuality on a 'Don't ask; don't tell' level when dealing with foreign travelers, gay rights in a political or legal context does not exist as an issue. When it does arise in public, hostility is most often the response. As a result, many gays in Peru don't publicly identify themselves as such, and some men, in keeping with the macho nature of Peruvian culture, will identify as straight, even if they are gay.

Public displays of affection among gay couples are rarely seen. Outside gay clubs, it is advisable to keep a low profile. HIV/AIDS transmission, both homosexual and heterosexual, is a growing problem in Peru, so use condoms. Lima is the city most accepting of gay people, but this is on a relative scale. Beyond that, the tourist towns of Cuzco, Arequipa and Trujillo tend to be more tolerant than the norm.

FYI: the checkered rainbow flag seen around Cuzco and in the Andes is *not* a gay pride flag – it's the flag of the Quechua people.

There are several organizations that provide resources for gay and lesbian travelers:

Gay Lima (lima.queercity.info) A handy guide to the latest gay and gay-friendly spots in the capital.

347

Gayperu.com (www
.gayperu.com) A Spanish-
language online guide that
lists everything from bars
to bathhouses; also runs a
multilingual travel agency
(www.gayperutravel.com).

Lima Tours (Map p64; 🕿 01-
619-6901; www.limatours
.com.pe; Jirón Belén 1040,
Central Lima) A travel agency
that is not exclusively gay, but
that organizes gay-friendly
group trips around the
country.

Rainbow Peruvian Tours
(Map p70; 🕿 01-215-6000;
www.perurainbow.com; Río de
Janeiro 216, San Isidro, Lima)
Gay-owned tour agency
based in Lima that organizes
package excursions around
Peru.

Health

BEFORE YOU GO

Prevention is the key to
staying healthy while abroad.
Travelers who receive the
recommended vaccines and
follow common-sense precau-
tions usually come down with
nothing more than a little
diarrhea. Since most vaccines
don't provide immunity
until at least two weeks after
they're given, visit a doctor
four to eight weeks before
departure.

Bring medications in
their original, clearly labeled
containers. If carrying
syringes or needles, be sure
to have a physician's letter
documenting their medical
necessity.

INSURANCE

If your health insurance
doesn't cover you for medical
expenses abroad, get extra
travel insurance – check
p350 for more information.
Find out in advance if your
travel insurance will make
payments directly to providers or reimburse you later for
overseas health expendi-
tures. Many doctors in Peru
expect immediate payment,
generally in cash, though
more upscale clinics in bigger
cities and towns will accept
credit cards.

RECOMMENDED VACCINATIONS

The only required vaccine
for Peru is yellow fever, and
that's only if you are arriving
from a country in Africa or the
Americas where yellow fever
occurs. However, it is strongly
recommended that all travelers should also be covered
and vaccinated for chicken
pox, hepatitis A, hepatitis B,
measles, rabies, tetanus and
typhoid. Consult with your
doctor and make sure children
are up to date with routine
vaccinations as well.

For further information,
see *Healthy Travel Central
& South America*, also from
Lonely Planet. If you're
traveling with children,
Lonely Planet's *Travel with
Children* may be useful. For
further information, the
Lonely Planet website (www
.lonelyplanet.com) is a good
place to start.

IN PERU

AVAILABILITY OF HEALTH CARE

There are numerous high-
quality medical clinics and
hospitals in Lima that are
open 24 hours for all manner
of emergencies (for details
see p83). These also offer
myriad subspecialty consultations – from dentistry
to gynecology. For a list of
recommended doctors and
clinics in Lima, check out the
website for the **US embassy**
(lima.usembassy.gov/acs_peru
.html).

In general, regional capitals
and popular tourist areas
such as Cuzco will have
at least one good clinic or
hospital that can ably handle
emergency care and other
medical problems. However,
access to care becomes
more problematic in remote
areas. For important or life-
threatening procedures, it is
best to seek care in Lima.

If you are traveling
around Peru and develop
a life-threatening medical
problem, you may want to
be evacuated to Lima or to
another country with state-
of-the-art medical care.
Since this may cost tens
of thousands of dollars, be
sure your insurance covers
this before you depart. You
can find a list of medical
evacuation and travel
insurance companies on
the website of the **US State
Department** (travel.state
.gov/travel/tips/brochures/
brochures_1215.html).

Note that most doctors and
hospitals expect payment in
cash, regardless of whether
you have insurance.

Pharmacies in Peru
are known as *farmacias* or
boticas, and are identified by
a green or red cross in the
window. They're generally
reliable and the ones in
larger cities and towns

usually offer most of the medications available in other countries.

ENVIRONMENTAL HAZARDS

Altitude Sickness

Those who ascend rapidly to altitudes greater than 2500m (8100ft) may develop altitude sickness. In Peru, this includes Cuzco (3326m) and Lake Titicaca (3820m). Being physically fit offers no protection. Those who have experienced altitude sickness in the past are prone to future episodes. The risk increases with faster ascents, higher altitudes and greater exertion. Symptoms may include headaches, nausea, vomiting, dizziness, malaise, insomnia and loss of appetite. Severe cases may be complicated by fluid in the lungs (high-altitude pulmonary edema) or swelling of the brain (high-altitude cerebral edema). If symptoms are more than mild or persist for more than 24 hours (less at high altitudes), descend immediately by at least 500m and see a doctor. To help prevent altitude sickness, the best measure is to spend two nights or more at each rise of 1000m.

When traveling to high elevations, it's also important to avoid overexertion, eat light meals and abstain from alcohol. Altitude sickness should be taken seriously; it can be life threatening when severe.

Food & Water

Salads, vegetables and fruit should be disinfected by washing with purified water or peeled whenever possible. When consuming seafood, look for restaurants that are clean and busy. Steaming does not make bad shellfish safe for eating. This is rarely a problem on the coast, as long as it is served fresh in a reputable restaurant.

Tap water in Peru is not safe to drink. Vigorous boiling of water for one minute is the most effective means of water purification. At altitudes greater than 2000m (6500ft), boil for three minutes. Another option is to disinfect water with iodine or water-purification pills. Follow the instructions carefully.

Mosquito Bites

To prevent mosquito bites, wear long sleeves, long pants, a hat and shoes (rather than sandals). Bring along a good insect repellent, preferably one containing DEET, which should be applied to exposed skin and clothing, but not to eyes, mouth, cuts, wounds or irritated skin. In general, adults and children aged over 12 should use preparations containing 25% to 35% DEET, which usually lasts about six hours.

Children aged between two and 12 should use preparations containing no more than 10% DEET, applied sparingly, which will usually last about three hours. Compounds containing DEET should not be used on children under the age of two.

Sunburn & Heat Exhaustion

Stay out of the midday sun, wear sunglasses and a wide-brimmed sun hat, and apply sunblock with SPF 15 or higher and UVA and UVB protection, before exposure to the sun. Be aware that the sun is more intense at higher altitudes, even though you may feel cooler.

INFECTIOUS DISEASES

Cholera is an intestinal infection acquired through ingestion of contaminated food or water. The main symptom is profuse, watery diarrhea, which may cause life-threatening dehydration. The key treatment is drinking oral rehydration solution. Cholera occurs regularly in Peru, but it's rare among travelers.

Dengue fever is a viral infection transmitted by aedes mosquitoes, which usually bite during the daytime and are often found close to human habitations. They breed primarily in artificial water containers, such as cans, plastic containers and discarded tires. As a result, dengue is especially common in densely populated, urban environments, including Lima and Cuzco. Dengue usually causes flu-like symptoms, including fever, muscle aches, joint pains, headaches, nausea and vomiting, often followed by a rash. The body aches may be quite uncomfortable, but most cases resolve uneventfully in a few days.

Hepatitis A is a viral infection of the liver and is usually acquired by ingestion of contaminated water, food or ice, though it may also be acquired by direct contact with infected persons.

Hepatitis A is the second most common travel-related infection (after travelers' diarrhea) in Peru – and is most common at lowland elevations in the Amazon. Most cases are resolved without complications, though hepatitis A occasionally causes severe liver damage. There is no treatment; to aid recovery, avoid alcohol and eat simple, nonfatty foods. The vaccine is highly effective, though its safety has not been established for pregnant women or children under the age of two. (Instead, opt for a gamma globulin injection.)

Like hepatitis A, **hepatitis B** is a liver infection that occurs worldwide but is more common in developing nations. Unlike hepatitis A, the disease is usually acquired by sexual contact or by exposure to infected blood, generally through blood transfusions or contaminated needles.

HIV/AIDS has been reported in all South American countries. Exposure to blood or blood products and bodily fluids may put an individual at risk. Be sure to use condoms for all sexual encounters.

Malaria is transmitted by mosquito bites, usually between dusk and dawn. The main symptom is high spiking fevers, which may be accompanied by chills, sweats, headache, body aches, weakness, vomiting or diarrhea. It is strongly recommended that travelers visiting any of the Amazon areas in Peru take malaria pills.

Rabies is still found in Peru and most cases are related to bites from dogs or vampire bats. All animal bites and scratches should be thoroughly cleansed immediately with large amounts of soap and water, and local health authorities should be contacted to determine whether further treatment is necessary.

Tetanus occurs when a wound becomes infected by a germ that lives in feces. Clean all cuts, punctures or animal bites. It is preventable with immunization.

Typhoid fever is caused by ingestion of food or water contaminated by a species of salmonella known as *Salmonella typhi*.

Yellow fever is a life-threatening viral infection that begins with flu-like symptoms and may include fever, chills, headache, muscle aches, backaches, loss of appetite, nausea and vomiting. A vaccine is strongly recommended for all those who visit any jungle areas of Peru at altitudes less than 2300m (7546ft).

TRAVELERS' DIARRHEA

You get diarrhea from ingesting contaminated food or water. If you develop diarrhea, drink plenty of fluids, preferably an oral rehydration solution containing salt and sugar. A few loose stools don't require treatment but if you start having more than four or five stools a day, you should start taking an antibiotic and an antidiarrheal agent. If diarrhea is bloody, persists for more than 72 hours or is accompanied by fever, shaking chills or severe abdominal pain, seek medical attention. See p350 for tips on reducing your risk.

Insurance

Having a travel-insurance policy to cover theft, loss, accidents and illness is highly recommended. Many policies include a card with toll-free or collect-call hot-lines for 24-hour assistance. Check if the policy coverage includes worst-case scenarios, such as evacuations and flights home. A variety of travel-insurance policies are available. Those handled by **STA Travel** (www.statravel .com) and other budget travel organizations are usually good value.

If your bags are lost or stolen, the insurance company may demand a receipt as proof that you bought the goods in the first place. You must usually report any loss or theft to local police (or airport authorities) within 24 hours. Make sure you keep all documentation to make any claim.

Internet Access

Accessing the internet is a snap in Peru. Wi-fi is becoming increasingly common in big cities and larger towns, where internet cafes are also plentiful. Even tiny towns will usually have at least one internet cafe. Some fast-food outlets in big cities offer free wi-fi.

Rates for high-speed connections at internet cafes average less than S2 per hour, and it's only in remote places that you will pay more for slower connection speeds. Hotel business centers can charge up to US$6 per hour. Many midrange and top-end establishments now offer wi-fi in lounge areas and guest rooms.

Before plugging in your laptop, ensure that your power source adheres to Peru's 220V/60Hz AC electricity supply. You may need a portable converter with a built-in surge protector.

Legal Matters

Your own embassy is of limited help if you get into trouble with the law in Peru, where you are presumed guilty until proven innocent. If you are the victim, the *policía de turismo* (tourist police; Poltur) can help, and usually have someone on hand who speaks a little English. There are Poltur stations in more than a dozen cities, with the main headquarters situated in Lima (p83).

Avoid any conversation with people who offer you drugs. Peru has draconian penalties for possessing even a small amount of drugs; minimum sentences are several years in jail. Should you be stopped by a plainclothes police officer, don't hand over any documents or money. Never get into a vehicle with someone claiming to be a police officer. Insist on meeting them at a bona fide police station instead.

If you are imprisoned for any reason, make sure that someone else knows about it as soon as possible. (If you are a member of the South American Explorers Club, they can be helpful in this regard. See boxed text, p71.) Being detained in prison for extended periods of time before a trial begins is not uncommon.

Money

Peru uses the *nuevo sol* (S), which comes in bills of S10, S20, S50, S100 and (rarely) S200. The *nuevo sol* (new sun) is divided into 100 *céntimos*, with copper- and silver-colored coins of S0.05, S0.10 and S0.20, and S0.50. There are also S1, S2 and S5 coins – the latter two of which come in a combination of silver and copper.

ATMS

Cajeros automáticos (ATMs) are found almost everywhere. ATMs are linked to the international Plus (Visa), Cirrus (Maestro/MasterCard) systems, American Express and other networks. They accept most bank cards on prominent international networks.

Both US dollars and *nuevos soles* are readily available from many ATMs (especially in Lima). For safety reasons, use ATMs inside banks, preferably during daylight hours.

CASH

US dollars are accepted by many tourist-oriented businesses, including hotels and tour agencies. However, you'll need nuevos soles to pay for local transportation, meals and other incidentals. When receiving local currency, always ask for *billetes pequeños* (small bills), as S100 bills are hard to change for small purchases. Carry as much spare change as possible, especially in small towns. Public bathrooms often charge a small fee for use and getting change for paper money can be difficult.

Do not accept torn or vandalized money as it will likely not be accepted. It is best not to change money on the street as counterfeits can be a problem. Authentic bills contain watermarks, embossed printing and a metal strip running through the bill that reads 'Peru' in clear, tiny letters. In addition, tiny pieces of colored thread and holographic dots scattered on the bill should be embedded in the paper, not glued on.

CHANGING MONEY

The best currency for exchange is the US dollar, although the euro is increasingly accepted. All foreign currencies must be in flawless condition.

Cambistas (money-changers) hang out on street corners near banks and *casas de cambio* (foreign-exchange bureaus) and give competitive rates. Officially, they should wear a vest and badge identifying themselves as legal.

CREDIT CARDS

Many top-end hotels and shops accept *tarjetas de crédito* (credit cards) but usually charge you a 7% (or greater) fee. The most widely accepted cards are Visa and MasterCard, although American Express and a few others are valid, as well as for cash advances at ATMs. Before you leave home, notify your bank that you'll be using your credit card abroad to avoid problems.

TAXES & TIPPING

International departure taxes are payable in US dollars or *nuevos soles* (cash only). Expensive hotels will add a 19% sales tax and 10% service charge; the latter is generally not included in quoted rates. High-end restaurants also charge combined taxes of more than 19%, plus a service charge (*servicio* or *propina*) of 10%. At restaurants that don't do this, you may tip 10% for good service. Taxi drivers do not generally expect tips (unless they've assisted with heavy luggage), but porters and tour guides do.

TRAVELER'S CHECKS & CARDS

Cheques de viajero (traveler's checks) can be refunded if lost or stolen but exchange rates are quite a bit lower than for US dollars. Traveler's checks may also be impossible to change in small towns. Almost all businesses and some *casas de cambio* refuse to deal with them, so you will need to queue at a bank to change them. American Express checks are the most widely accepted.

Reloadable traveler's check cards are a better option: these work just like ATM cards, but are not linked to your home bank account.

These cards enjoy some of the same protections as traveler's checks, and can be replaced more easily than ATM cards. During your trip, you can add more funds to a traveler's check card either online or via telephone. **American Express** (www .americanexpress.com) offers traveler's check cards, as do many **Visa providers** (www .cashpassportcard.com).

Public Holidays

On major holidays, banks, offices and other services are closed, hotel rates can triple and transportation is very crowded, so book ahead. Major holidays may be celebrated for days around the official date.

Major national, regional and religious holidays include the following:

Año Nuevo (New Year's Day) January 1

Good Friday March/April

Labor Day May 1

Inti Raymi June 24

San Pedro y San Pablo (Feasts of Sts Peter & Paul) June 29

Fiestas Patrias (National Independence Days) July 28-29

Feast of Santa Rosa de Lima August 30

Battle of Angamos Day October 8

Todos Santos (All Saints' Day) November 1

Fiesta de la Purísima Concepción (Feast of the Immaculate Conception) December 8

Christmas December 25

Safe Travel

Peru's grinding poverty – more than half of the country lives under the poverty line, with a fifth of the population surviving on less than US$2 a day – means that petty crime is common. The biggest annoyance most travelers will experience, however, is a case of the runs, so don't let paranoia ruin your holiday.

CORRUPTION & SCAMS

The military and police (even sometimes the tourist police) have a reputation for being corrupt. While a foreigner may experience petty harassment (usually to procure payment of a bribe), most police officers are quite courteous to tourists.

Perhaps the most pernicious thing travelers face are the persistent touts that gather at bus stations, train stations, airports and other tourist spots to offer everything from discounted hotel rooms to local tours. Many touts – including taxi drivers – will say just about anything to steer you to places they represent. They will tell you the establishment you've chosen is a notorious drug den, it's closed or is overbooked. Do not believe everything you hear. If you have doubts about a place you've decided to stay at, ask to see a room before paying up.

It is not advisable to book hotels, travel arrangements or transportation through these independent agents. Often, they will demand cash up-front for services that never materialize. Stick to reputable, well-recommended agencies and you'll be assured a good time.

ENVIRONMENTAL HAZARDS

Some of the natural hazards you might encounter in Peru include earthquakes and avalanches. Rescues in remote regions are often done on foot because of the inability of helicopters to reach some of the country's more challenging topography.

THEFTS, MUGGINGS & OTHER CRIME

Peru's widespread poverty means that street crimes such as pickpocketing, bag-snatching and muggings are all too common. Sneak theft is the most widespread type of crime, while muggings and other attacks happen with less regularity. As with every other place on earth, a little common sense goes a very long way.

The *policía de turismo* can be found in major cities and tourist areas and can be helpful with criminal matters. If you are unsure how to locate them, contact the main office in Lima (p83). If you are the victim of a crime, file a report with the tourist police immediately.

If you have taken out travel insurance and need to make a claim, Poltur will provide you with a police report. Stolen passports can be reissued at your embassy. After receiving your new passport, go to the

nearest Peruvian immigration office (p355) to get a new tourist card. For more on legal issues, see p351.

For issues affecting female travelers, turn to p355.

TRANSPORTATION ISSUES

When taking buses, choose operators carefully. The cheapest companies will be the most likely to employ reckless drivers and have roadside breakdowns. Overnight travel by bus can get brutally cold in the highlands (take a blanket or sweater). For more on overland transportation in Peru, see p357.

Telephone

Public pay phones operated by **Telefónica-Perú** (www.telefonica.com.pe) are found almost everywhere. These can be easily operated with phone cards available at supermarkets, pharmacies and corner newsstands. Some internet cafes have private phone booths with 'net-to-phone' and 'net-to-net' capabilities, where you can talk cheaply.

When calling Peru from abroad, dial the international access code for the country you're in, then Peru's country code (51), then the area code *without the 0* and finally, the local number. When making international calls from Peru, dial the international access code (00), then the country code of where you're calling to, then the area code and finally, the local phone number.

In Peru, any telephone number beginning with a 99

or 98 is a cell-phone number. Numbers beginning with 0800 are often toll-free only when dialed from private phones, not from public pay phones. See the inside front cover of this book for useful dialing codes.

There's an online telephone directory at www.paginasamarillas.com.pe.

CELL PHONES

It's possible to use a tri-band GSM world phone in Peru (GSM 1900). Other systems in use are CDMA and TDMA. This is a fast-changing field, so check the current situation before you travel.

Cell-phone rentals are often available in major cities and tourist centers. These are generally cheap and offer pay-as-you go plans that can be easily refilled with the purchase of a phonecard. The easiest place to rent cell phones is in the baggage claim section at the international airport in Lima.

PHONECARDS

Called *tarjetas telefónicas,* these cards are widely available. The most common are Telefónica-Perú's 147 cards: you dial 147, then enter your personal code (which is on the back of the card), listen to a message telling you how much money you have left on the card, dial the number, and listen to a message telling you how much time you have left for this call. The drawback is it's in Spanish. The 147 card is best used for long-distance calls. For local calls, the Holá Peru card is cheaper, and works the same way except that you begin by dialing 0800.

353

Time

Peru is five hours behind Greenwich Mean Time (GMT). It's the same as Eastern Standard Time (EST) in North America.

Daylight Saving Time (DST) isn't used in Peru, so add an hour to all of these times between the first Sunday in April and the last Sunday in October.

Toilets

You should always avoid putting anything other than human waste into the toilet. Even a small amount of toilet paper can muck up the entire system – that's why a small, plastic bin is routinely provided for disposing of the paper. A well-run hotel or restaurant, even a cheap one, will empty the bin and clean the toilet every day.

Public toilets are rare outside of transportation terminals, restaurants and museums, but restaurants will generally let travelers use a restroom (sometimes for a charge). Those in terminals usually have an attendant who will charge you about S0.50 to enter and provide you with toilet paper. Public restrooms frequently run out of toilet paper, so always carry some with you.

Tourist Information

The government's official tourist agency, **PromPerú**

(www.peru.info), doesn't have any international offices, but its website – in Spanish, English and other languages – is an easy way to obtain information before you depart. In the USA and Canada, you can call its toll-free **hotline** (☎ 866-661-7378).

PromPerú runs helpful tourist information offices, called iPerú, in the following cities:

Arequipa Airport (☎ 054-44-4564; 1st fl, Main Hall, Rodríguez Ballón Airport; ⏰10am-7:30pm); Plaza de Armas (☎ 054-22-3265; Portal de la Municipalidad 110; ⏰8:30am-7:30pm)

Cuzco Airport (☎ 084-23-7364; Main Hall, Velasco Astete Airport; ⏰6am-4pm); City Center (☎ 084-23-4498; Office 102, Galerías Turísticas, Av Sol 103; ⏰8:30am-7:30pm); Machu Picchu (☎ 084-21-1104; Edificio del Instituto Nacional de Cultura, Pachacútec, cuadra 1; ⏰9am-1pm & 2-8pm)

Huaraz (☎ 043-42-8812; Oficina 1, Pasaje Atusparia, Plaza de Armas; ⏰9am-6pm Mon-Sat, to 2pm Sun)

Iquitos Airport (☎ 065-26-0251; Main Hall, Francisco Secada Vignetta Airport; ⏰8am-1pm & 4-8pm); City Center (☎ 065-23-6144; Loreto 201; ⏰8:30am-7:30pm)

Lima Airport (☎ 01-574-8000; Main Hall, Jorge Chávez International Airport; ⏰24hr); Miraflores (☎ 01-445-9400; Module 14, by movie theater box office, LarcoMar Center; ⏰noon-8pm); San Isidro (Map

p70; ☎ 01-421-1627; Jorge Basadre 610; ⏰9am-6pm Mon-Fri)

Puno (☎ 051-36-5088; Plaza de Armas, cnr Lima & Destua; ⏰8:30am-7:30pm)

Trujillo (☎ 044-29-4561; mezzanine level, Municipalidad de Trujillo, Plaza Mayor, Jirón Pizarro 412; ⏰8am-7pm Mon-Sat, to 2pm Sun)

There is a 24-hour **iPerú hotline** (☎ 01-574-8000), which can provide general information and nonemergency assistance.

Travelers with Disabilities

Peru offers few conveniences for travelers with disabilities. Signs in Braille or phones for the hearing-impaired are virtually nonexistent, while wheelchair ramps and lifts are few and far between. Most hotels do not have wheelchair-accessible rooms, at least not rooms specially designated as such. Bathrooms are often barely large enough for an able-bodied person to walk into, so few are accessible to wheelchairs. Toilets in rural areas may be of the squat variety.

Nevertheless, there are Peruvians with disabilities that get around, mainly with the help of others. It is not particularly unusual to see mobility-impaired people being carried bodily to a seat on a bus, for example. Speaking Spanish can be the key in securing assistance. If possible, bring along an able-bodied traveling companion.

Organizations that provide information for travelers with disabilities:

Access-Able Travel Source (www.access-able.com) Listings of accessible transportation and tours, accommodations, attractions and restaurants.

Apumayo Expediciones (☎/fax 084-24-6018; www.apumayo.com; Interior 3, Calle Garcilaso 265, Cuzco) An adventure-tour company that takes disabled travelers to Cuzco, Machu Picchu and the Sacred Valley.

Conadis (☎ 01-332-0808; www.conadisperu.gob.pe; Av Arequipa 375, Santa Beatriz) Governmental agency that provides Spanish-language information and advocacy for people with disabilities.

Visas

With a few exceptions (such as some Asian, African and communist countries), visas are not required for travelers entering Peru. Tourists are permitted a 30- to 90-day stay, which is stamped into their passports and onto a tourist card, called a Tarjeta Andina de Migración (Andean Immigration Card), which you must return upon leaving the country. The actual length of stay is determined by the immigration officer at the point of entry. Be careful not to lose your tourist card, or you will have to queue up at an *oficina de migraciónes* (immigration office), also simply known as *migraciónes,* for a replacement card. It's a good idea to carry your passport and tourist card on your person

at all times, especially when traveling in remote areas (it's required by law on the Inca Trail). For security, make a photocopy of both documents and keep them in a separate place from the originals.

Women Travelers

Most female travelers to Peru will experience little more than shouts of *mi amor* (my love) or an appreciative hiss. If you are fair-skinned with blond hair, however, be prepared to be the center of attention. Peruvian men consider foreign women to have looser morals than locals and will often make flirtatious comments to single women.

Whistling and catcalls in the streets are run-of-the-mill – and should be treated as such. Ignoring all provocation and staring ahead is generally the best response. If someone is particularly persistent, roll your eyes or try a potentially ardor-smothering phrase such as *soy casada* (I'm married). Behavior such as this should be the exception: most Peruvians tend to be protective of lone women.

In tourist towns such as Cuzco, it's not uncommon for fast-talking charmers to attach themselves to gringas. Many of these young Casanovas (known as *bricheros*) are looking for a meal ticket, so approach any professions of undying love with extreme skepticism.

Likewise, use common sense when meeting men in public places. In Peru,

outside of a few big cities, it is rare for a woman to belly up to a bar for a beer, and the ones that do tend to be prostitutes. If you feel the need for an evening cocktail, opt for a restaurant instead. When meeting someone, make it very clear if only friendship is intended. As in any part of the world, use your big city smarts: be aware of your surroundings, seek reputable tour operators and taxi companies and, if traveling alone, opt for better hotels in good neighborhoods.

In highland towns, dress is generally fairly conservative and women rarely wear shorts, opting instead for long skirts. Slacks are fine, but note that shorts, miniskirts and revealing blouses may draw unwanted attention.

On a more mundane note: tampons can be difficult to find in small villages, so stock up in bigger cities and towns.

Transport

Getting There & Away

Shop around for the best-priced airfares to Peru. Also, flights, tours and tickets can

Climate Change & Travel

Every form of transport that relies on carbon-based fuel generates CO_2, the main cause of human-induced climate change. Modern travel is dependent on aeroplanes, which might use less fuel per kilometer per person than most cars but travel much greater distances. The altitude at which aircraft emit gases (including CO_2) and particles also contributes to their climate change impact. Many websites offer 'carbon calculators' that allow people to estimate the carbon emissions generated by their journey and, for those who wish to do so, to offset the impact of the greenhouse gases emitted with contributions to portfolios of climate-friendly initiatives throughout the world. Lonely Planet offsets the carbon footprint of all staff and author travel.

be booked online through Lonely Planet (www.lonelyplanet.com/travel_services).

ENTERING THE COUNTRY

Arriving in Peru is typically straightforward, as long as your passport is valid for at least six months beyond your departure date. When arriving by air, US citizens must show a return ticket or open-jaw onward ticket. For information on Peruvian visas, see p355.

 AIR

There are direct flights to Peru (mainly to Lima) from cities all over the Americas and continental Europe.

Note: if you're headed to Cuzco, but are flying into Peru from another continent, your flight will likely land in Lima late at night. This will require an overnight stay since domestic flights to Cuzco generally depart in the morning.

There is a departure tax of US$31 (payable in nuevos soles) for all international flights, to be paid in cash.

AIRPORTS & AIRLINES

Located in the port city of Callao, Lima's **Aeropuerto Internacional Jorge Chávez** (01-517-3100; www.lap.com.pe; Callao) is serviced by flights from North, Central and South America, and two regular direct flights from Europe (Madrid and Amsterdam). Check the airport website or call 01-511-6055 for updated departure and arrival schedules for domestic and international flights. Cuzco (p196) has the only other airport with international service – to La Paz, Bolivia.

TICKETS

The high season for air travel to and within Peru is late May to early September, as well as around major holidays (p352). Lower fares may sometimes be offered outside peak periods.

It is essential that you reconfirm all flights 24 to 72 hours in advance, either on the telephone or online, or you may get bumped off the flight.

There are direct (nonstop) flights to Lima from Atlanta, Dallas-Fort Worth, Houston, Los Angeles, Miami and New York. In other cases, flights will connect either in the US or in Latin American gateway cities such as Mexico City and Bogota.

Getting Around

 AIR

Domestic-flight schedules and prices change frequently. Most big cities are served by modern jets, while smaller towns are served by propeller aircraft.

Note: the departure tax for all domestic flights is approximately US$6 (cash).

AIRLINES IN PERU

Most airlines fly from Lima to regional capitals, but service between provincial cities is limited. The following domestic airlines are the most reliable:

LAN (01-213-8200; www.lan.com)

LC Busre (01-619-1313; www.lcbusre.com.pe)

Peruvian Airlines (01-717-2222; www.peruvianairlines.pe)

Star Perú (01-705-9000; www.starperu.com)

TACA (01-511-8222; www.taca.com)

Be at the airport at least 60 minutes before your flight departs (at least 90 minutes early in Cuzco, and two hours in Lima). This is a precaution as your flight may be overbooked,

Peru Air Routes

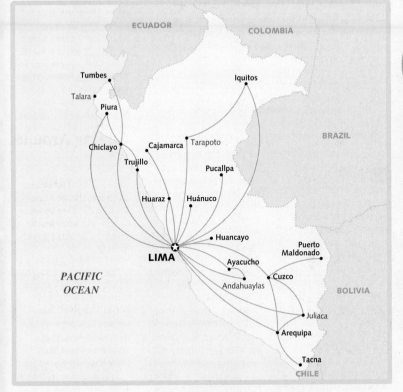

baggage handling and check-in procedures can be chaotic, and it's not unknown for flights to leave *before* their official departure time because of predicted bad weather.

TICKETS

Two one-way tickets typically cost the same as a round-trip ticket. The peak season for air travel within Peru is late May to early September, as well as around major holidays.

You can buy tickets online or via a recommended travel agent. It's almost impossible to buy tickets just before major holidays (p352).

Ensure all flight reservations are *confirmed* and *reconfirmed* 24 and 72 hours in advance; airlines are notorious for overbooking and flights are changed or canceled with surprising frequency. Many midrange and top-end hotels will do this free of charge if you ask. Confirmation is essential during the peak travel season, particularly during the busy months of June, July and August.

BICYCLE

The major drawback of cycling in Peru is the country's bounty of kamikaze motorists. On narrow, two-lane highways, drivers can be a serious hazard to cyclists. Cycling is more enjoyable and safer, though very challenging, off paved roads. Mountain bikes are recommended, as road bikes won't stand up to the conditions.

Reasonably priced rentals (mostly mountain bikes) are available in popular tourist destinations, including Cuzco (p183), Arequipa (p118) and Huaraz (p241). These bikes are rented for local excursions, not to make trips all over the country.

For long-distance touring, bring your own bike from home. Airline policies on carrying bicycles vary, so shop around.

A Note About Prices

Prices in this guidebook are generally listed in Peruvian nuevos soles. However, many higher-end hotels will only quote prices in US dollars; likewise for many travel agencies and tour operators. Therefore, prices in this book are generally listed in soles, except in cases where a business quotes its costs in dollars.

Both currencies have experienced fluctuations in recent years, so expect many figures to be different from what may be printed in the book.

BOAT

There are no passenger services along the Peruvian coast. In the Andean highlands, there are boat services on Lake Titicaca. Small, motorized vessels take passengers from the port in Puno to visit various islands on the lake (p154), while catamarans zip over to Bolivia.

In Peru's Amazon Basin, boat travel is of major importance. Larger vessels ply the wider rivers. Dugout canoes powered by outboard engines – known as *peki-pekis* – act as water taxis on smaller waterways.

BUS

Buses are the usual form of transportation for most Peruvians and many travelers. Fares are cheap and services are frequent on the major long-distance routes, but buses are of varying quality. Less-traveled and remote rural routes are often served by older, more uncomfortable vehicles, many with inadequate legroom for taller travelers.

Scores of competing Peruvian bus companies have their own offices, and no single company covers the entire country. In some towns, the companies have their offices in one main bus terminal. In many cities, bus companies are clustered around a few city blocks, while elsewhere the terminals may be scattered all over town. For a rundown of recommended companies with offices in Lima, see p84.

Buses can be significantly delayed during the rainy season, from January through April, because of landslides and other conditions.

CLASSES & RESERVATIONS

The bigger companies often have luxury buses (called Imperial, Royal, Business, Executive or something similar), for which they charge more than *económico* buses. The former are express services with toilets, snacks, videos and air-conditioning. Some companies offer *bus-camas* (bed buses), on which the seats recline halfway or almost fully – you can sleep quite well on them.

Reservations for short journeys aren't usually necessary. Just go to the terminal and buy a ticket for the next bus to your destination. For long-distance or overnight journeys, or if you're headed to popular destinations such as Cuzco, buy your tickets well in advance.

LUGGAGE

When waiting in bus terminals, be sure to watch your luggage carefully. Some terminals have left-luggage facilities. If you use this service, don't leave any valuables in your bag.

During the journey, your luggage will travel in the luggage compartment unless it is small enough to carry on board. You are given a baggage tag in exchange for your bag, which should be securely closed or locked.

Never leave hand luggage with important valuables (such as passports and money) in the overhead racks of a bus since theft is common. Keep your valuables on your lap or between your legs.

CAR & MOTORCYCLE

It's a long ride from Lima to most destinations, so it's best to fly to most cities around the country and then rent a car from there. But given all the headaches and potential hazards of driving yourself around, consider hiring a taxi instead (p358), which is often cheaper and easier.

If you are driving and are involved in an accident that results in injury, know that drivers are routinely imprisoned for several days or weeks until innocence has been established. For more advice on legal matters, see p351.

DRIVER'S LICENSE & RENTAL

A driver's license from your own home country is sufficient for renting a car. Major rental companies have offices in Lima (p84) and a few other large cities. Renting a motorcycle is an option mainly in jungle towns, where you can go for short runs around town on dirt bikes, but not much further.

Economy car rental starts at US$50 per day. But that doesn't include sales tax of 19%, 'super' collision-damage waiver, personal accident insurance and so on, which together can climb to more than US$100 per day – not including excess mileage. Vehicles with 4WD are more expensive. Make sure you completely understand the rental agreement before you sign. A credit card is required, and renters normally need to be more than 25 years of age.

ROAD RULES & HAZARDS

Bear in mind that the condition of rental cars is often poor, roads are potholed (even the paved Pan-American Hwy), gas is expensive, and drivers are aggressive, regarding speed limits, road signs and traffic signals as mere guides, not the law.

Moreover, road signs are often small and unclear.

Driving is on the right-hand side of the road. Driving at night is not recommended because of poor conditions, speeding buses and slow-moving, poorly lit trucks. At night, bandits can be a problem on roadways in remote regions.

Theft is all too common, so you should not leave your vehicle parked on the street. When stopping overnight, park the car in a guarded lot (the better hotels have them).

Gasoline or petrol stations (called *grifos*) are few and far between. At the time of research, the average cost of *gasolina* in Peru was about S16 to S17 (more than US$5 to US$6) per US gallon.

LOCAL TRANSPORTATION

In most towns and cities, it's easy to walk everywhere or take a taxi. Using local buses, *micros* and *combis* can be tricky, but is very inexpensive.

TAXI

Taxis are plentiful. Private cars that have a small taxi sticker in the windshield aren't necessarily regulated. Safer, regulated taxis usually have a lit company number on the roof and are called for by telephone. These are more expensive than taxis flagged down on the street, but are more reliable.

Always ask the fare in advance, as there are no meters. It's acceptable to haggle; try to find out what the going rate is before taking a cab, especially for long trips. The standard fare for short runs in most cities is around S5. Tipping is not the norm, unless you have hired a driver for a long period or he has helped you with luggage or other lifting.

Hiring a private taxi for long-distance trips costs less than renting a car and takes care of many of the problems outlined earlier (see p358). Not all taxi drivers will agree to drive long distances, but if one does, you should carefully check the driver's credentials and vehicle before hiring.

TRAIN

Few areas of Peru are serviced by rail. However, in the area of Cuzco, the privatized rail system, **PeruRail** (☏ 084-58-1414; www.perurail.com), has daily services between Cuzco and Aguas Calientes (for Machu Picchu), and services between Cuzco and Puno on the shores of Lake Titicaca. Check the website for details.

A-Z

Language

Spanish pronunciation is not difficult as most of its sounds are also found in English. You can read our pronunciation guides below as if they were English and you'll be understood just fine.

Peruvian Spanish is considered one of the easiest varieties of Spanish, with less slang in use than in many other Latin American countries, and relatively clear enunciation.

To enhance your trip with a phrasebook, visit **lonelyplanet.com**. Lonely Planet iPhone phrasebooks are available through the Apple App store.

BASICS

Hello.
Hola. .... *o·*la

How are you?
¿Qué tal? .... ke tal

I'm fine, thanks.
Bien, gracias. .... byen *gra·*syas

Excuse me. (to get attention)
Disculpe. .... dees·*kool·*pe

Yes./No.
Sí./No. .... see/no

Thank you.
Gracias. .... *gra·*syas

You're welcome./That's fine.
De nada. .... de *na·*da

Goodbye. /See you later.
Adiós./Hasta luego. .... a·*dyos/as·*ta *lwe·*go

Do you speak English?
¿Habla inglés? .... a·bla een·*gles*

I don't understand.
No entiendo. .... no en·*tyen·*do

How much is this?
¿Cuánto cuesta? .... *kwan·*to *kwes·*ta

Can you reduce the price a little?
¿Podría bajar un poco el precio? .... po·*dree·*a ba·*khar* oon *po·*ko el *pre·*syo

ACCOMMODATIONS

I'd like to make a booking.
Quisiera reservar una habitación. .... kee·*sye·*ra re·ser·*var* *oo·*na a·bee·ta·*syon*

How much is it per night?
¿Cuánto cuesta por noche? .... *kwan·*to *kwes·*ta por *no·*che

EATING & DRINKING

I'd like ..., please.
Quisiera ..., por favor. .... kee·*sye·*ra ... por fa·*vor*

That was delicious!
¡Estaba buenísimo! .... es·*ta·*ba bwe·*nee·*see·mo

Bring the bill/check, please.
La cuenta, por favor. .... la *kwen·*ta por fa·*vor*

I'm allergic to ...
Soy alérgico/a al ... (m/f) .... soy a·*ler·*khee·ko/a al ...

I don't eat ...
No como ... . no *ko·*mo ...

chicken	*pollo*	*po·*yo
fish	*pescado*	pes·*ka·*do
meat	*carne*	*kar·*ne

EMERGENCIES

I'm ill.
Estoy enfermo/a. (m/f) .... es·*toy* en·*fer·*mo/a

Help!
¡Socorro! .... so·*ko·*ro

Call a doctor!
¡Llame a un médico! .... *ya·*me a oon *me·*dee·ko

Call the police!
¡Llame a la policía! .... *ya·*me a la po·lee·*see·*a

DIRECTIONS

I'm looking for (a/an/the) ...
Estoy buscando ... . es·*toy* boos·*kan·*do ...

ATM
un cajero automático .... oon ka·*khe·*ro ow·to·*ma·*tee·ko

bank
el banco .... el *ban·*ko

... embassy
la embajada de ... . la em·ba·*kha·*da de ...

market
el mercado .... el mer·*ka·*do

museum
el museo .... el moo·*se·*o

restaurant
un restaurante .... oon res·tow·*ran·*te

toilet
los servicios .... los ser·*vee·*syos

tourist office
la oficina de turismo .... la o·fee·*see·*na de too·*rees·*mo

Behind the Scenes

Author Thanks
CAROLINA A MIRANDA

To the readers who submitted tips on divine ceviche, to the friends who shared their secret eats, to the pisco sours at the Haiti in Miraflores, to the Lonely Planet team – the awesome Kathleen Munnelly, Martine Power and Mark Griffiths! – you kick ass. Special *gracias* to all of the folks in Peru who gave of their time to help out with interviews and fact-checking; to Rosa Lowinger, for being Rosa; and the Miranda Silvas, for being great cooks. Bear hugs to Ed Tahaney, who wholeheartedly supports my wandering. For Felipe, who woulda been proud of this book.

Acknowledgments

Climate map data adapted from Peel MC, Finlayson BL & McMahon TA (2007) 'Updated World Map of the Köppen-Geiger Climate Classification', *Hydrology and Earth System Sciences*, 11, 163344.

Cover photographs: Front: Machu Picchu, Jacob Halaska, Getty Images; Back: Llamas in ceremonial garb on the altiplano (Andean plateau), Puno, Wes Walker, Lonely Planet Images.

Many of the images in this guide are available for licensing from Lonely Planet Images: www.lonelyplanetimages.com.

This Book

This first edition of Lonely Planet's Discover Peru guidebook was researched and written by Carolina A Miranda (coordinating author), Aimée Dowl, Katy Shorthouse, Luke Waterson and Beth Williams. This guidebook was commissioned in Lonely Planet's Oakland office, and produced by the following:

Commissioning Editors Heather Dickson, Kathleen Munnelly
Coordinating Editor Martine Power
Coordinating Cartographer Mark Griffiths
Coordinating Layout Designer Lauren Egan
Managing Editors Bruce Evans, Annelies Mertens
Managing Cartographer Alison Lyall
Managing Layout Designer Celia Wood
Assisting Editors Justin Flynn, Sophie Splatt
Assisting Cartographer Brendan Streager
Assisting Layout Designers Mazzy Prinsep, Kerrianne Southway
Cover Research Naomi Parker
Internal Image Research Sabrina Dalbesio
Language Content Branislava Vladisavljevic
Thanks to
Shahara Ahmed, Judith Bamber, Melanie Dankel, Janine Eberle, Ryan Evans, Chris Girdler, Laura Jane, Indra Kilfoyle, Yvonne Kirk, Nic Lehman, John Mazzocchi, Wayne Murphy, Piers Pickard, Malisa Plesa, Averil Robertson, Lachlan Ross, Mik Ruff, Laura Stansfeld, John Taufa, Juan Winata

NOTES

NOTES

Index

C

I

000 Map pages

How to Use This Book

These symbols will help you find the listings you want:

- ⊙ Sights
- ⊕ Activities
- ⊖ Courses
- ⊕ Tours
- ⊗ Festivals & Events
- ⊟ Sleeping
- ⊗ Eating
- ⊙ Drinking
- ⊗ Entertainment
- ⊕ Shopping
- ⊕ Information/Transport

These symbols give you the vital information for each listing:

- ☏ Telephone Numbers
- ⊙ Opening Hours
- Ⓟ Parking
- ⊖ Nonsmoking
- ❄ Air-Conditioning
- @ Internet Access
- ⊚ Wi-Fi Access
- ⊠ Swimming Pool
- ⊘ Vegetarian Selection
- ⊡ English-Language Menu
- ⊞ Family-Friendly
- ⊠ Pet-Friendly
- ⊡ Bus
- ⊠ Ferry
- Ⓜ Metro
- Ⓢ Subway
- ⊖ London Tube
- ⊡ Tram
- ⊡ Train

Reviews are organised by author preference.

Look out for these icons:

- **FREE** No payment required
- ◢ A green or sustainable option

Our authors have nominated these places as demonstrating a strong commitment to sustainability – for example by supporting local communities and producers, operating in an environmentally friendly way, or supporting conservation projects.

Map Legend

Sights
- ⊙ Beach
- ⊙ Buddhist
- ⊙ Castle
- ⊙ Christian
- ⊙ Hindu
- ⊙ Islamic
- ⊙ Jewish
- ⊙ Monument
- ⊙ Museum/Gallery
- ⊙ Ruin
- ⊙ Winery/Vineyard
- ⊙ Zoo
- ⊙ Other Sight

Activities, Courses & Tours
- ⊖ Diving/Snorkelling
- ⊕ Canoeing/Kayaking
- ⊕ Skiing
- ⊕ Surfing
- ⊕ Swimming/Pool
- ⊕ Walking
- ⊕ Windsurfing
- • Other Activity/Course/Tour

Sleeping
- ⊟ Sleeping
- ⊖ Camping

Eating
- ⊗ Eating

Drinking
- ⊙ Drinking
- ⊖ Cafe

Entertainment
- ⊕ Entertainment

Shopping
- ⊕ Shopping

Information
- ⊖ Bank
- ⊖ Embassy/Consulate
- ⊕ Hospital/Medical
- ⊚ Internet
- ⊚ Police
- ⊕ Post Office
- ⊚ Telephone
- ⊙ Toilet
- ⊖ Tourist Information
- • Other Information

Transport
- ⊕ Airport
- ⊗ Border Crossing
- ⊕ Bus
- ⊕ Cable Car/Funicular
- ⊖ Cycling
- ⊖ Ferry
- Ⓜ Metro
- ⊕ Monorail
- Ⓟ Parking
- ⊙ Petrol Station
- ⊙ Taxi
- ⊕ Train/Railway
- ⊕ Tram
- • Other Transport

Routes
- Tollway
- Freeway
- Primary
- Secondary
- Tertiary
- Lane
- Unsealed Road
- Plaza/Mall
- Steps
-)(Tunnel
- Pedestrian Overpass
- Walking Tour
- Walking Tour Detour
- Path

Geographic
- ⊕ Hut/Shelter
- ⊕ Lighthouse
- ⊕ Lookout
- ▲ Mountain/Volcano
- ⊖ Oasis
- ⊙ Park
-)(Pass
- ⊕ Picnic Area
- ⊕ Waterfall

Population
- ⊙ Capital (National)
- ◉ Capital (State/Province)
- ● City/Large Town
- ○ Town/Village

Boundaries
- – – – International
- ----- State/Province
- — — Disputed
- ⋯ Regional/Suburb
- Marine Park
- ⌐ Cliff
- ⌐ Wall

Hydrography
- River/Creek
- Intermittent River
- Swamp/Mangrove
- Reef
- Canal
- Water
- Dry/Salt/Intermittent Lake
- Glacier

Areas
- Beach/Desert
- Cemetery (Christian)
- Cemetery (Other)
- Park/Forest
- Sportsground
- Sight (Building)
- Top Sight (Building)

BETH WILLIAMS

Nazca, Arequipa & the South While earning a degree in Latin American Studies, Beth spent summers traveling and serving pisco sours at a Peruvian restaurant in her hometown of Portland, Oregon, in the USA. She then followed an interest in women's health to a village nestled at 3000m in the Peruvian Andes. There she spent a year building 'vertical' birthing facilities for Quechua women to give birth in the traditional fashion – standing up. Beth then re-treated to sea level to work for a Peruvian nonprofit in Lima, during which time she added four stamps to her passport and traveled the Peruvian Pan-American Hwy at least five times. What's next? A master's at New York's Columbia University.

Our Story

A beat-up old car, a few dollars in the pocket and a sense of adventure. In 1972 that's all Tony and Maureen Wheeler needed for the trip of a lifetime – across Europe and Asia overland to Australia. It took several months, and at the end – broke but inspired – they sat at their kitchen table writing and stapling together their first travel guide, *Across Asia on the Cheap*. Within a week they'd sold 1500 copies. Lonely Planet was born.

Today, Lonely Planet has offices in Melbourne, London and Oakland, with more than 600 staff and writers. We share Tony's belief that 'a great guidebook should do three things: inform, educate and amuse'.

Our Writers

CAROLINA A MIRANDA

Coordinating author, Lima Born of a Peruvian father from the Chiclayo area, Carolina has spent her life making regular sojourns to Peru to wander around the Andes and eat as much ceviche as is humanly possible. When not experimenting with pisco sour ratios (three parts pisco, one part lime juice, simple syrup to taste), she makes her living as a writer in New York City. She has written articles for *Time*, *Budget Travel* and *Travel + Leisure*, and is a regular contributor to WNYC, New York Public Radio. She blogs about culture at C-Monster.net and can also be found on Twitter (@cmonstah).

Read more about Carolina at:
lonelyplanet.com/members/carolinamiranda

AIMÉE DOWL

Huaraz, Trujillo & the North Whether spotting condors in the *páramo* or chasing hummingbirds in the cloud forest, prancing around glaciers or trekking up jungle volcanoes, Aimée feels right at home in the high altitudes and ancient cultures of the Andes. Holding no hard feelings toward destinations at sea level, however, she also finds that the Peruvian Amazon is one her favorite places on earth. Aimée lives at a cool 2850m in Quito, Ecuador, where she is a freelance travel and culture writer and has worked as a secondary educator. Her work has appeared in *The New York Times*, *Viajes*, *Ms. Magazine*, *BBC History* and four Lonely Planet books.

Read more about Aimée at:
lonelyplanet.com/members/aimeedowl

KATY SHORTHOUSE

Puno & Lake Titicaca; Cuzco, Machu Picchu & Around Katy's career highlights include walking the Inca Trail 13 times and Australia's Overland Track seven times, guiding multisport tours in Ecuador and Patagonia, and running an adventure business in New Zealand. Lowlights include writing junk mail, telemarketing and cleaning toilets. Katy aspires to travel but she keeps stopping and putting down roots, with the result that she now divides her time between Peru, New Zealand and Australia (and lives in dread of finding somewhere else she likes).

Read more about Katy at:
lonelyplanet.com/members/katyshorthouse

LUKE WATERSON

Iquitos & the Amazon Basin Raised in the remote Somerset countryside in southwest England, Luke quickly became addicted to exploring out-of-the-way places. Having completed a Creative Writing degree at the University of East Anglia in Norwich, he shouldered his backpack and vowed to see as much of the world as was humanly possible. He has spent almost two years backpacking South America and writes for various travel publications and the *Guardian*. When not wolfing down a plate of *lomo saltado* or hiking through the Andes, he can be found living on a rather smaller hill outside London, hatching further travel plans.

Read more about Luke at:
lonelyplanet.com/members/lukewaterson

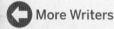 More Writers ....

Published by Lonely Planet Publications Pty Ltd
ABN 36 005 607 983
1st edition – June 2011
ISBN 978 1 74220 002 6
© Lonely Planet 2011   Photographs © as indicated 2011
10 9 8 7 6 5 4 3 2 1
Printed in Singapore